THE COMPLETE ARTIST

The Complete Artist

A Manual of Instruction

Edward Jones

Dryad Press Ltd, London

© Edward Jones 1988
First published in 1988

ISBN 0 8521 9717 9

British Library Cataloguing in Publication Data
Jones, Edward
   The complete artist : a manual of instruction.
   1. Drawings – Manuals
   I. Title
   741.2

Typeset by Tek-Art Ltd, Kent
Origination by Spectrum Reproductions, Essex
Printed by Colorcraft Ltd, Hong Kong
for the Publishers
Dryad Press Ltd.
8 Cavendish Square
London W1M 0AJ

PREFACE

In 1983 the first structured courses in Fine Art were commenced at Urchfont Manor Adult Residential College, near Devizes in Wiltshire. They are designed for mature students, and encompass criteria for GCE Advanced Level Art. They also embrace the normal syllabus for art college foundation studies.

The first part of the course lasts two years and deals entirely with drawing. Each year's teaching consists of five two-day concentrated tutorial sessions plus one complete week. At each tutorial a particular aspect of drawing is dealt with, and projects relating to that tutorial are then set as homework. At the end of the two-year period the completed projects, together with other course work, are submitted to an independent examiner for assessment.

The drawing course is followed by a similarly-structured course on painting in all media, and the appreciation of colour theory. This course lasts one year, and is taught in five two-day and one complete week's tutorial sessions. Again the projects and the course work are submitted to an independent examiner for assessment.

Following the success of these courses it was felt that for future students, it would be of immense assistance to have the courses available in book form. At the same time, this would prove a boon for those people wishing to gain an understanding of the practicalities of drawing and painting, but who do not find it possible to attend. I am sure that this book will also prove to be of value to full-time art students and practising artists.

CONTENTS

INTRODUCTION

Having decided to write a book of instruction entitled *The Complete Artist*, I felt that, in order to present the information in a logical order, it was necessary to begin with drawing in all media, encompassing a broad spectrum of subject matter from still life, landscape, flowers, marine, industrial, townscapes, figure and portrait drawing. I have followed this by a section on colour theory, then by the technique of painting in all the principal media; covering the same range of subjects dealt with in the section on drawing. The final part is given over to themes and specific subject matter, including avant-garde painting, presentation of work and conclusions regarding the forward progression of the visual arts.

I have tried to communicate my ideas and methods without resorting to the use of artists' jargon. As far as is possible, I have stressed the importance of accurate observation coupled with sound drawing, and at the same time emphasised the importance of understanding the construction and underlying anatomy of everything we wish to draw and paint. By adopting the observation approach I hope to encourage the beginner to explore the fascination of painting, whilst at the same time perhaps suggesting a different approach for the more experienced artist. You, the reader, will now be the judge of whether or not I have succeeded in all I have tried to do.

I have tried wherever possible to show the development of current techniques, and in order to do this have referred to the history of painting and drawing. As a consequence, the techniques described will give sound guidelines for the expression of any subject.

If there seems to be an emphasis on drawing, this is because I firmly believe that sound drawing is the basis of great painting. To this end, as in previous writings, I have attempted to redress the imbalance that has existed for so long in this area of art education. This does not imply that individual expression and interpretation should or need be inhibited, or even controlled. On the contrary, I hope this book will give every encouragement to both interpretation and expression, built on a sound foundation of knowledge and skill acquired from the understanding of the craft skills of drawing and painting.

This introduction would not be complete without my sincere thanks to Dryad Press Limited, in particular to William Waller, Managing Director, and Sandra Winfield, Editorial Assistant, for all their help and patience in the production of the book.

My most sincere thanks must be extended to the Daler Rowney Company Limited, artists materials manufacturers, who have sponsored me for many years and who have kindly supplied the materials and photographs for the illustrations and the technical information regarding products. Very special thanks must be given to the many owners of my work who have placed their pictures at my disposal for reproduction in the book.

It would be impossible to mention by name everybody who has helped me towards the writing of this book, but to all my friends, colleagues and students, particularly my students from Urchfont Manor College, I can only say a heartfelt thank you for all their help, understanding and encouragement.

In conclusion, I hope this book will enable you to share with me my joy in painting, a joy that is endless, that overcomes loneliness and depression, that can be communicated to others and that will continue to live for others long after we are gone.

Edward Jones
Poole, Dorset
1988

PART ONE

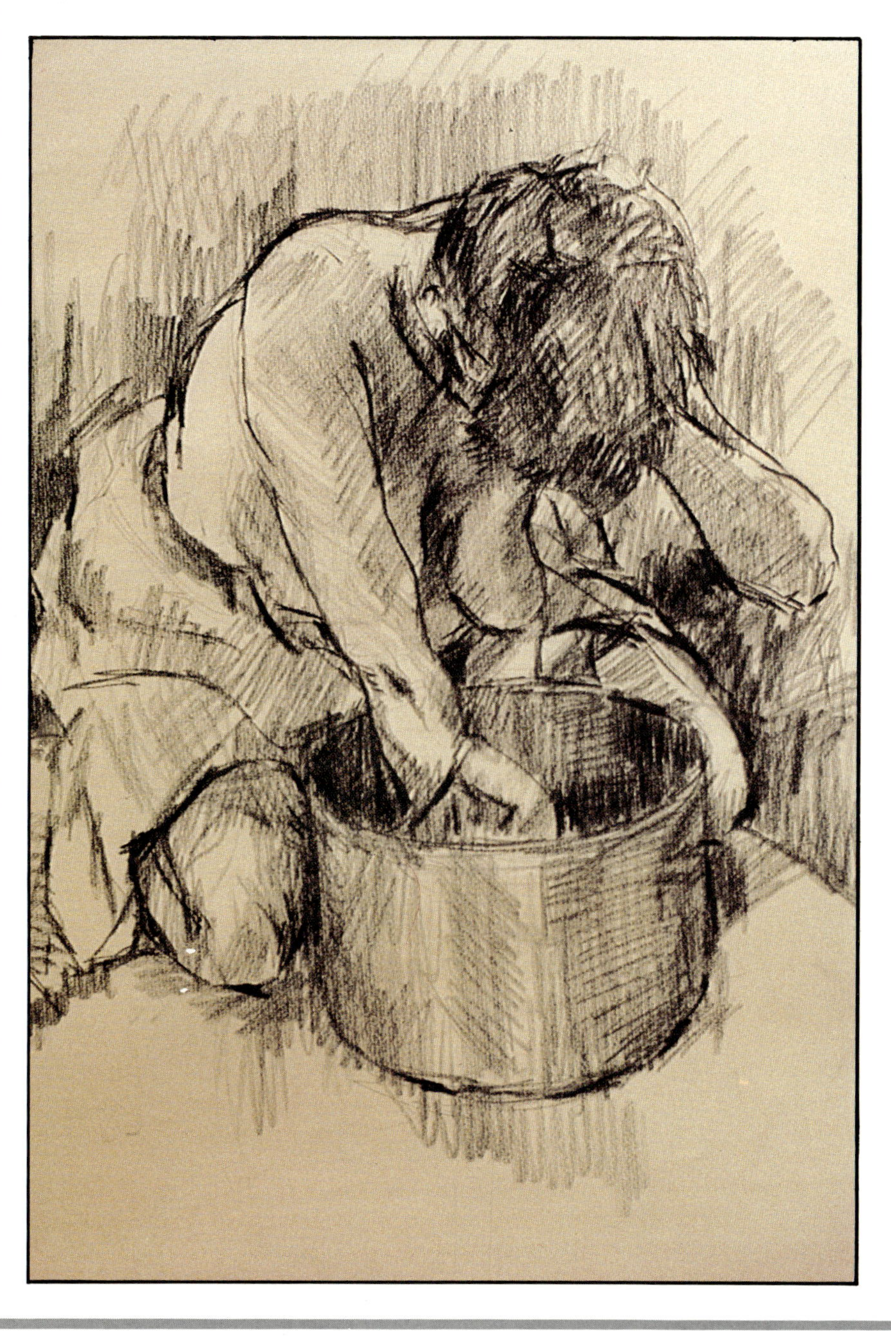

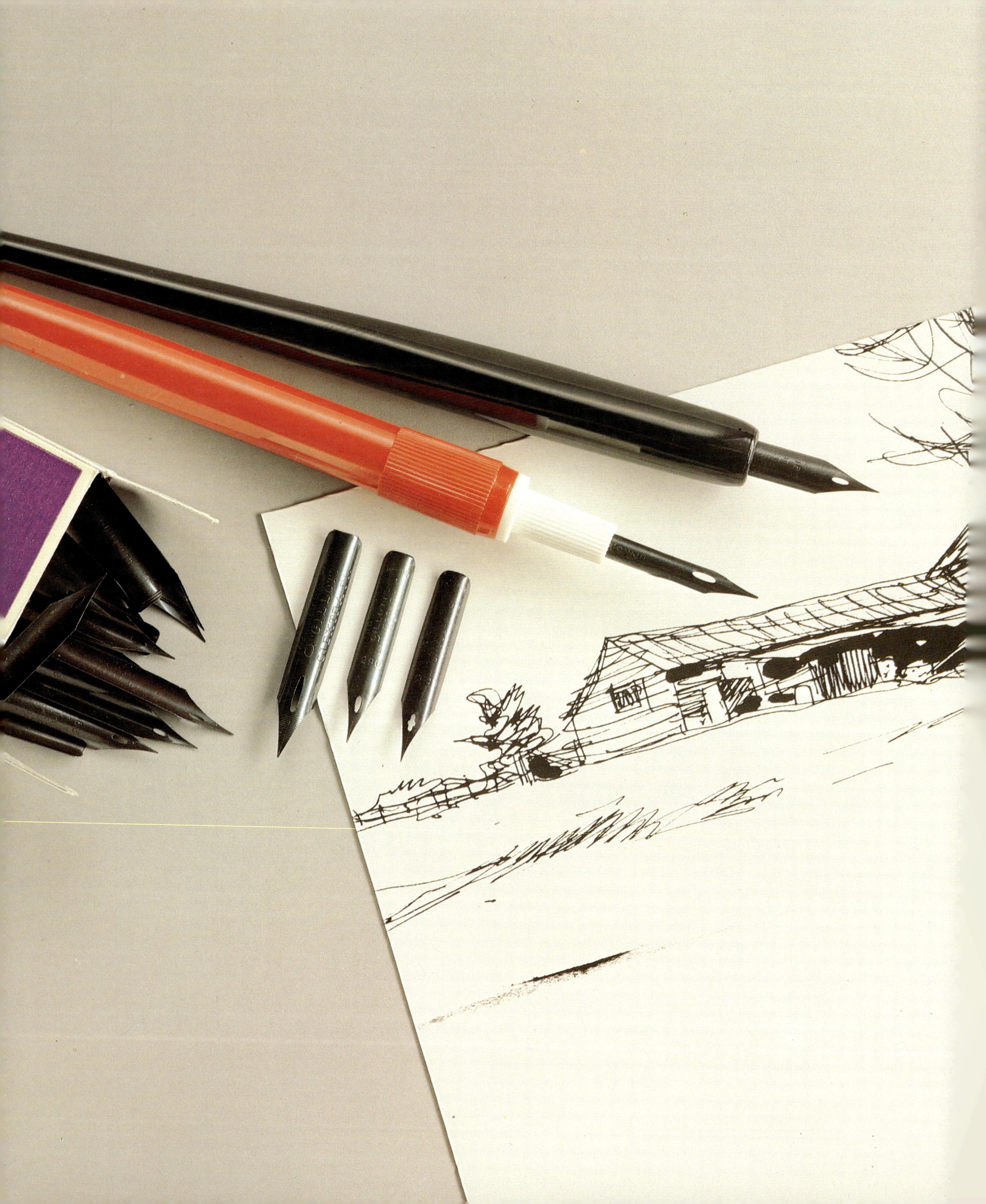

1. MATERIALS AND LANGUAGE OF DRAWING

It is not known when man first began to draw, as the act of drawing in an interpretive way is, without doubt, one of the earliest means of communication. It is a common language which knows no national boundaries. The earliest forms of drawing that survive today are in Scandinavia. These are marks etched into a rock face with a sharp implement, such as a bone or antler. These drawings preceded the cave paintings at Lascaux and Altimira which, according to various historians, are between 15,000 and 20,000 years old.

Such statements do, however, pose the question, what is drawing, as opposed to painting? Can these two be separated – indeed, should they be separate? No clear division is possible, nor is it necessary, as any form of categorisation is merely for our own purposes and not because of any demand made by the subject.

Materials have, of course, changed with the passage of time. Early drawings were made with a form of charcoal or ink, usually as a guide for later painting. The media for this form of drawing were either wood or papyrus. As time passed, more reliable materials such as vellum, and finally paper, became available. With these developments the number of drawing media increased. In addition to charcoal and inks, the use of silver, gold and platinum became popular. In early times, inks were applied with reeds, but the Romans used pens with bronze nibs.

Whilst many of these tools still exist and are in use today, in the eighteenth century the graphite pencil was developed, giving the artist a fluid, fine line-drawing implement which revolutionised drawing for all time. Today we have the advantage of a further range of drawing media, such as felt-tip, ballpoint and brush pens. Of course our drawing equipment is not limited to those media mentioned so far. It is also possible for us to draw with the brush, using inks, as Oriental artists do.

For many centuries, drawing was used merely as an aid to painting. The affluence that occurred as a result of the Renaissance increased the desire of the new rich to indulge their love of the arts. As they were not as wealthy as the aristocracy, they were often unable to afford the more expensive paintings. Any drawings that were produced were, however, often destroyed on completion of the final work. Late in the fifteenth century artists, in response to the new demand, began to consider their drawings as finished works of art.

Pens and nibs

The advent of the graphite pencil in the eighteenth century coincided with a general increase in travel. It became part of their education for ladies and gentlemen to take pencils and sketchbooks on the Grand Tour in much the same way that tourists will take a camera today.

Reproduction techniques improved substantially during the nineteenth century. These relied very largely on line, and encouraged further interest in artists' original drawings. These factors, coupled with the interest that had been generated in Japanese wood-cuts with their colour and use of inks, increased the number of ways in which drawing could be extended. This resulted in new techniques being sought, in conjunction with a combining together of many of the media such as pen, ink and wash, pencil, inks, charcoal, chalks and crayon. Because of these various influences there has been a great revival in traditional drawing of a vast range of subject matter. It is not surprising that for great artists of any period, drawing has been the foundation for great painting. It is therefore important that before we begin our exploration into the practice of drawing and painting, we familiarise ourselves with the materials we shall be using. As drawing is our main consideration to begin with, the only reference to colour at this stage will be made in connection with drawing. Initially, a pencil, a sheet of paper and a drawing board are all that is needed to make a good start.

Pencils

Pencils are made in a number of grades, ranging from hard to soft. Hard grades are suffixed with the letter H and the soft grades by the letter B. My preference is for HB, B, 2B and 4B, although there are many softer grades.

Drawing board

The drawing board needs to be large enough to accommodate an imperial or A2 sheet of paper, stiff enough not to bend or warp and yet light enough to take out of doors for landscape work.

Inks

A large variety of inks is available to us for both writing and drawing. Pure drawing inks come in a variety of colours, but for our purposes black will suffice. Black, or Indian ink, as it is often called, is available in both waterproof and non-waterproof varieties. The waterproof type is used to make drawings that can have a colour wash or tone wash laid over the drawing without fear of the drawing running. Non-waterproof inks are best used when you wish to dilute the ink with water (preferably distilled) to produce a paler line or tone.

Pastels, chalks and crayons

All pastels, chalks and crayons are made from powered pigments. In pastels the pigments are mixed with a binder, such as gum or resin, and added to China clay. This is then formed into sticks ready for use. With chalks or crayons the process is similar, except that the pigments are mixed with oil or wax before being formed.

Conté-crayon is named after its inventor and is a mixture of clay, graphite, water and extender. This is made into square sticks and pencils. Whilst the variety of colours within the conté range is extensive, for our purpose the normal collection of black, bistre, sanguine and white will suffice. Oil pastels are different from those mentioned earlier, as their pigments are bound in oil, making them a most suitable medium for preparatory work for oil painting. Used in conjunction with a brush dipped in turpentine, the colours can be brushed out in thin washes, giving the opportunity to see a colour and tone plan.

Miscellaneous extras

All artists accumulate a number of assorted items which they find are of use in their drawing tool-kit. Here are just a few of mine. A water-pot is a must, as are an enamel plate for diluting inks, a putty rubber, masking tape, a scalpel, an aerosol can of fixative, some thin, medium and scene-painter's charcoal and, finally, some bulldog clips and a fabric-type powder-puff. There is, however, one further item of equipment that we should consider: an easel. Easels, although not essential, are in terms of convenience, very desirable. The type I favour is known as a box easel. Not only is it rigid (an essential qualification

Easels

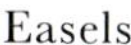

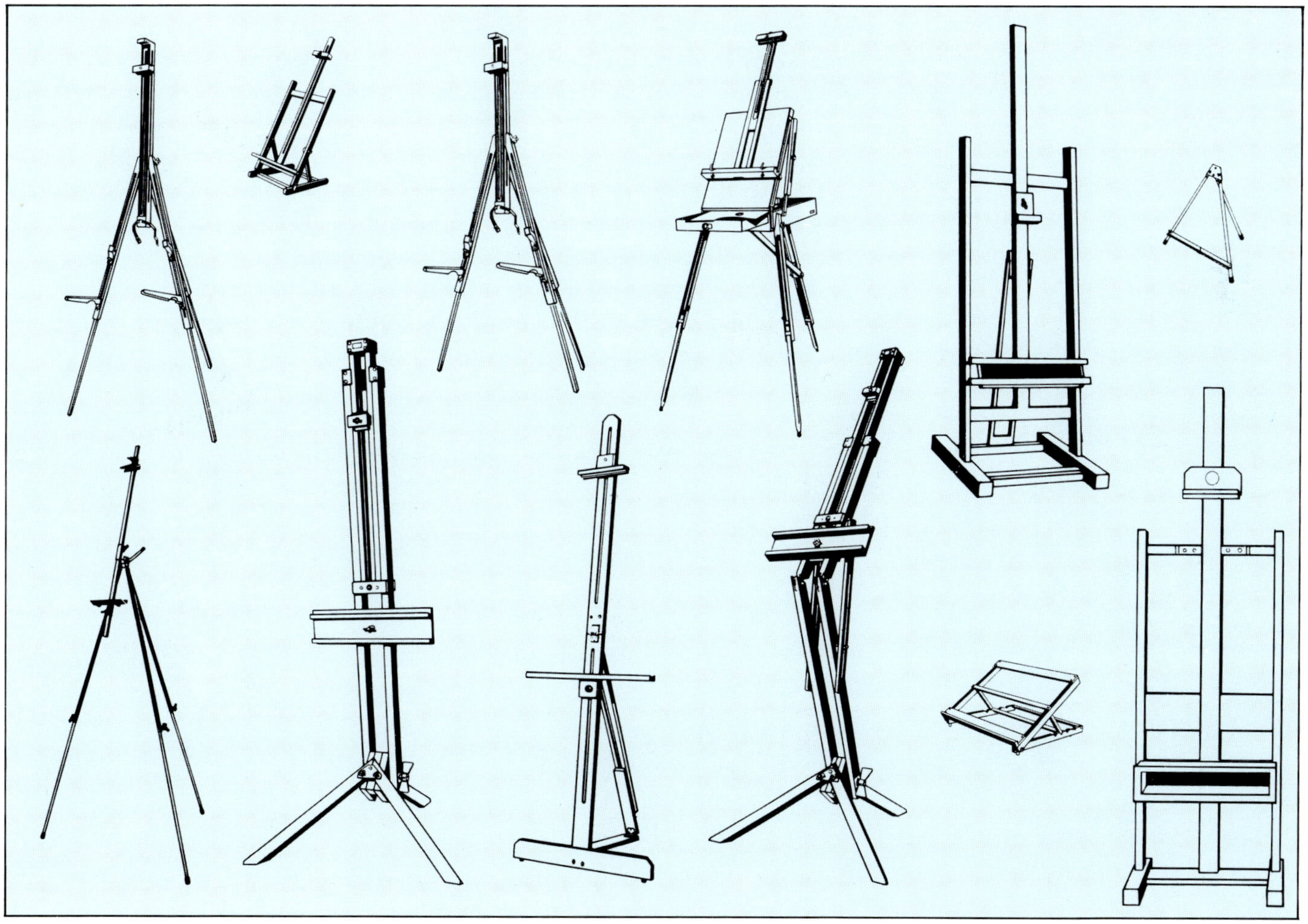

for any easel), but all necessary drawing and painting equipment can be carried in the box area. This easel is portable and suitable for all conditions. There are less expensive forms of easel available, from the lightweight sketching variety to the large studio easel. If space is at a premium, you may prefer a radial easel, which is rigid and takes up very little space. An ideal arrangement is to have a radial easel for working in the studio and a sketching easel for outdoor work.

It is essential first to find out what you can do, what sort of marks your drawing media can make, and how these marks will appear differently on different papers. For this exercise I suggest that you use sheets of the following papers: cartridge, sugar, Ingres pastel (any colour will do, provided it is not too dark), newsprint and water-colour. With any of the already mentioned media, make a few scribbles and see how the texture of the mark varies according to the surface to which it is applied.

In this first chapter, the most important step is to come to terms with the language of drawing. For this you need a simple alphabet of shapes which can be applied to, and take into account the structure of, all natural forms. Since ancient times, the only shapes that have fulfilled this requirement are geometric: they are, the square or cube, the circle or sphere, the cylinder and the triangle or cone. Fig 1 illustrates these shapes. As you progress through the following chapters and their related projects and exercises, you will notice how geometric shapes play an important part in an understanding of every form of subject you wish to draw or paint.

Apply these shapes to a simple subject. Set up a very simple still life of fruit and books as shown in Fig 2. You will immediately see that the apples are spheres and the books are cubes. This simple exercise using the geometric language enables you to understand the structure of form, and gives the means to establish the relationship between objects and their proportions. From such a simple arrangement drawn in this manner, it is a simple step to observe and explore perspective, light, shade and tone.

FIG 1 Geometric shapes (Pencil)

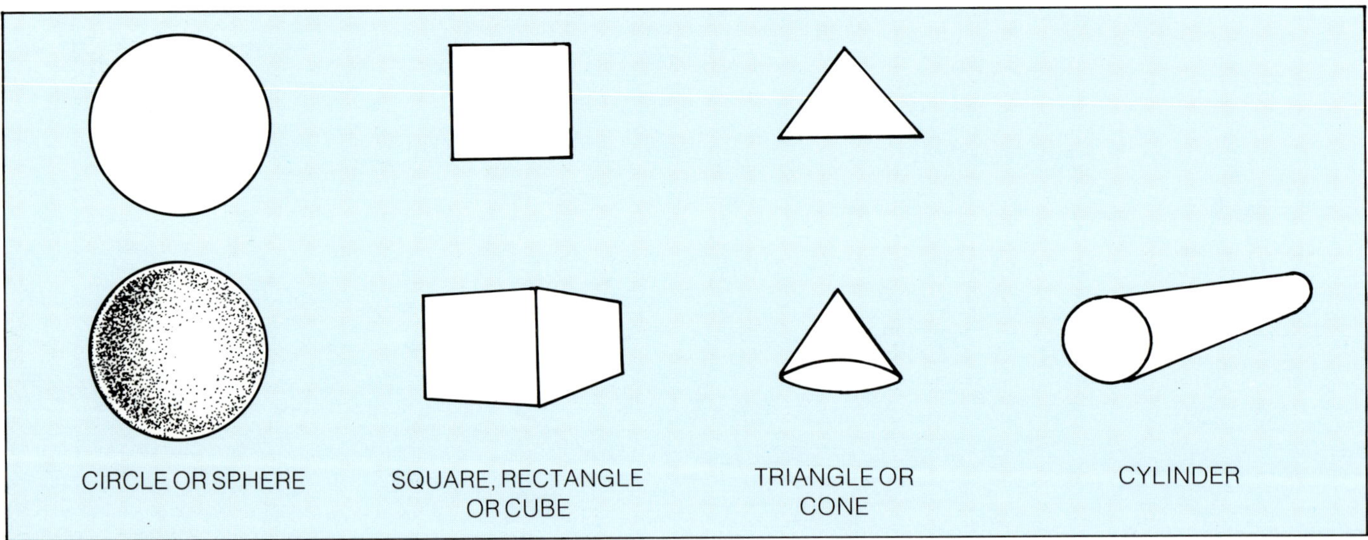

FIG 2 Still life fruit and books (Pencil)

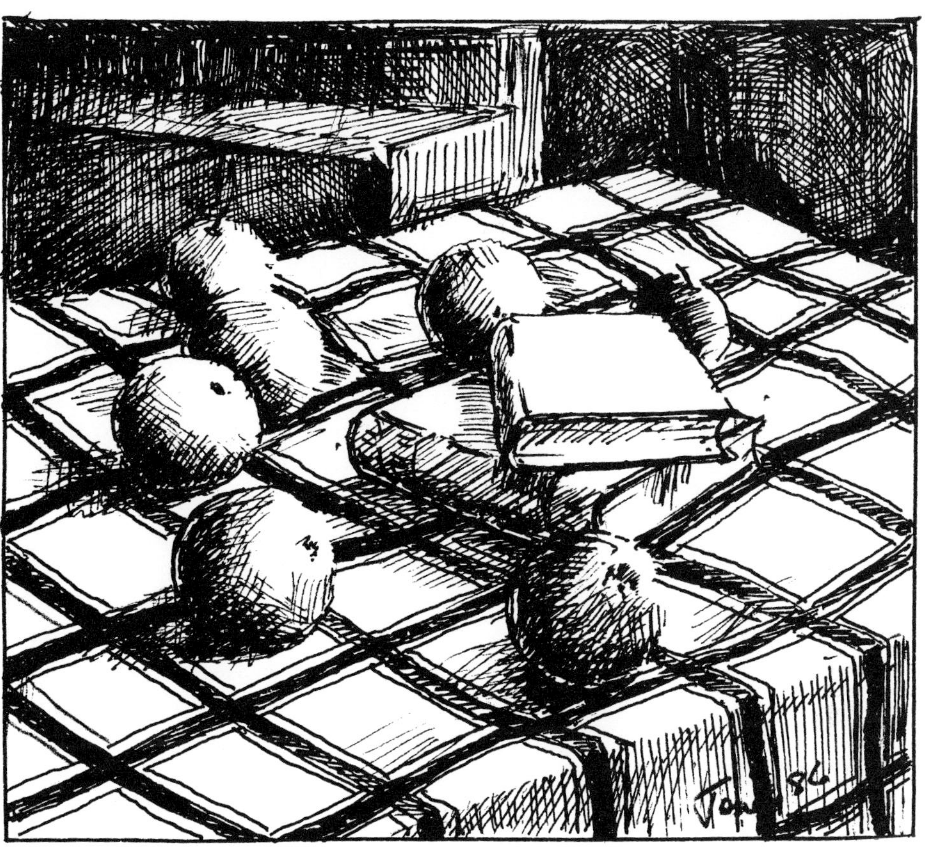

FIG 3 Doodle and construction drawing of Fig 2 (Pencil)

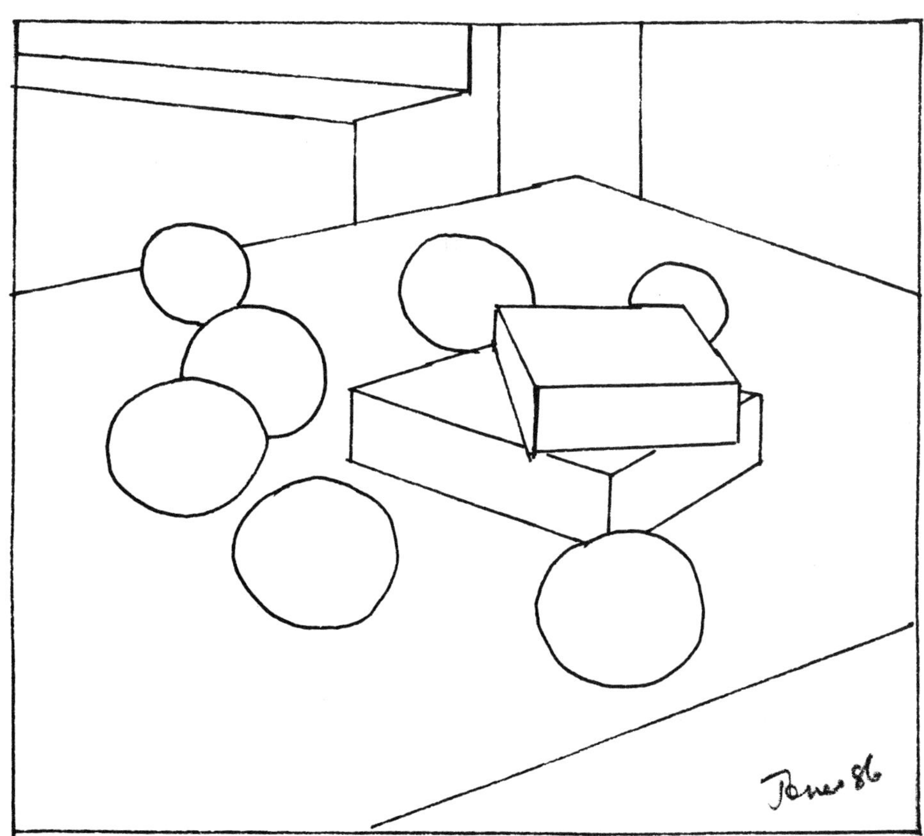

Having seen the application of these shapes to a specific subject, I feel that unless you can produce a drawing tht is pleasing to look at, all your understanding will be to no avail. The positioning of the subject on the sheet of paper and the scale of your drawing both play an important part in communicating your reaction to the subject to the spectator. I have therefore recommended for some years that for a newcomer to the art of drawing it is a good habit first to doodle the subject on a separate sheet of paper in such a way as to explore the paper's space. This is shown by my still life doodle of apples and books. The doodle is not meant to be accurate; it is done simply to help you decide on the scale and arrangement and, most valuably, to familiarise you with the subject. It is only by drawing that you can learn about your subject. Fig 3 is an example of a doodle of this arrangement, using a 2B pencil. Armed with the knowledge gained from your doodle, you can now begin your drawing. Using a series of faint straight lines, position the subject in accordance with the doodle. At this stage the drawing is called a *schematic*, and when this is complete you can apply the language of shapes to achieve a structure (see Fig 2). In this simple introduction to the language of drawing you have made the first step along the road towards becoming an artist. Progressively, it will become apparent that you cannot copy Nature (indeed any work that approaches the copying of Nature is illusory), but you can, within your range of skills, imitate Nature's offerings. This too is illusory, however. If you are at all perceptive, with a degree of sensitivity, it is certain that you will wish to express your reaction, emotional or otherwise, to a visual experience. This statement implies a certain selectivity within the subject content. It also infers that to depart from realism, within certain bounds, is acceptable. All these aspects are under our control and each of us will react differently to the subject. It is these differences that make drawing and painting such a fascinating pursuit. I would recommend that you examine the drawings of the masters; you will see they have used the same language as we have. I would certainly advise an in-depth study of the drawings of Mantegna, Leonardo, Michelangelo, Titian, Rembrandt, Velasquez, Rubens, Ingres, Delacroix, Degas and Picasso. Drawing is like writing: if you can write, you can draw. With this mental attitude and the will to practise in order to attain the necessary co-ordination of hand and eye, coupled with an ability to look and understand in terms of drawing the chosen subject, drawing becomes exactly like writing. In other words it becomes a reflex action.

I have found doodling and mentally drawing the subject to be of tremendous help. It clarifies one's thinking and gives an opportunity to make decisions. Finally, it enables you to start your work with a finished picture in mind. This discipline will allow the subject to become the catalyst for your creative instincts. It will encourage you to experiment and innovate, with the result that the work will be original and totally yours. With the previous exercise in mind, arrange a more complex still life, using your original subject as a starting point. To this we will add a wine bottle, a basket for the fruit and a drape, arranged

FIG 4 *Still life*. Wine bottle, basket, fruit and drape (Pencil)

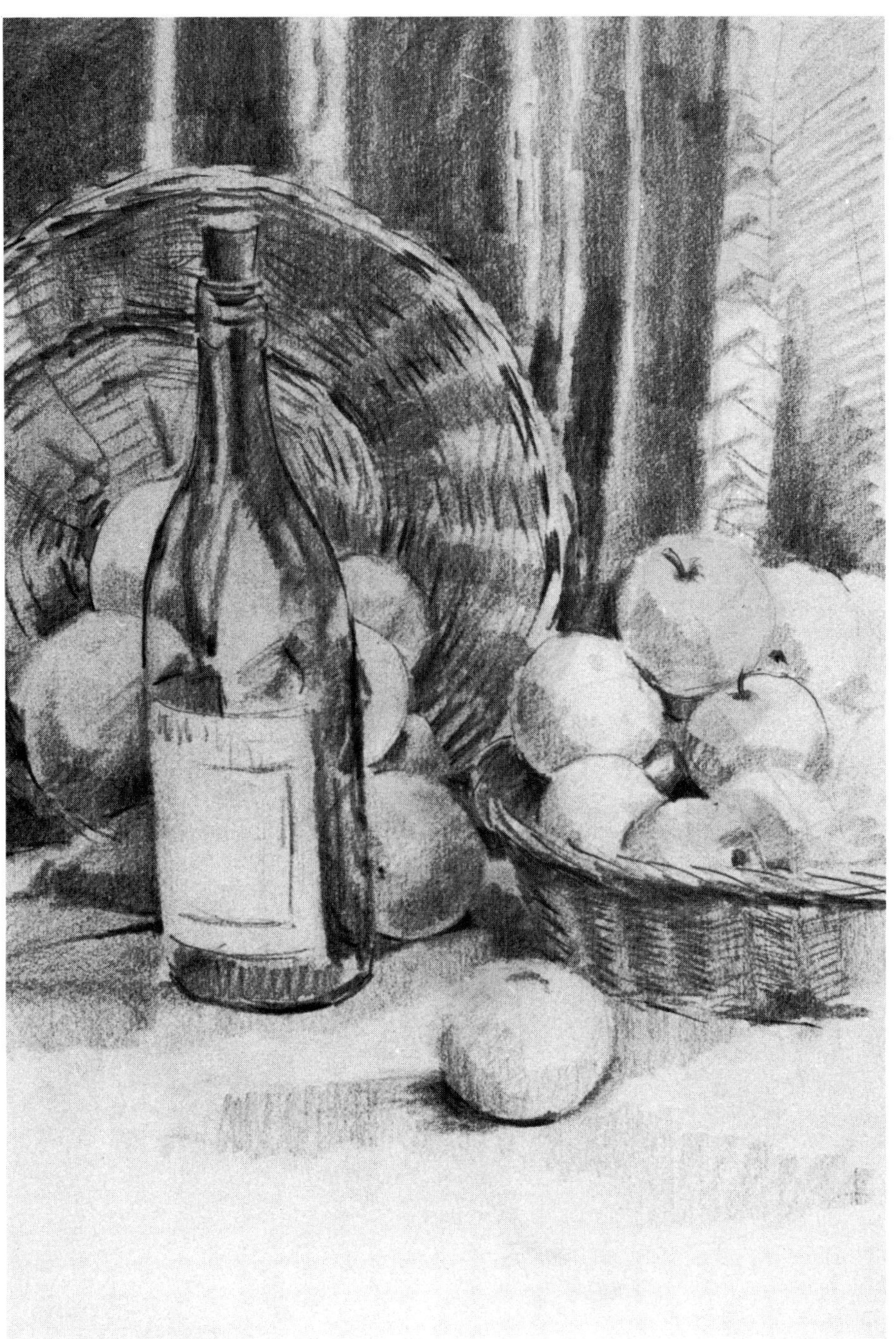

as illustrated in Fig 4.

   With your drawing board ready prepared with a A3 sheet of paper (have several sheets on the board, as this will ensure that the board's texture will not show in the drawing) and a 2B pencil, you are ready to see what you can do. When you have gone as far as you can, try another in charcoal – in fact, do several, using a different medium each time (this will help to build confidence). When you feel ready, take a new sheet of paper of the same size and produce the schematic, using the doodle drawings as a reference. You will notice that at no stage have I

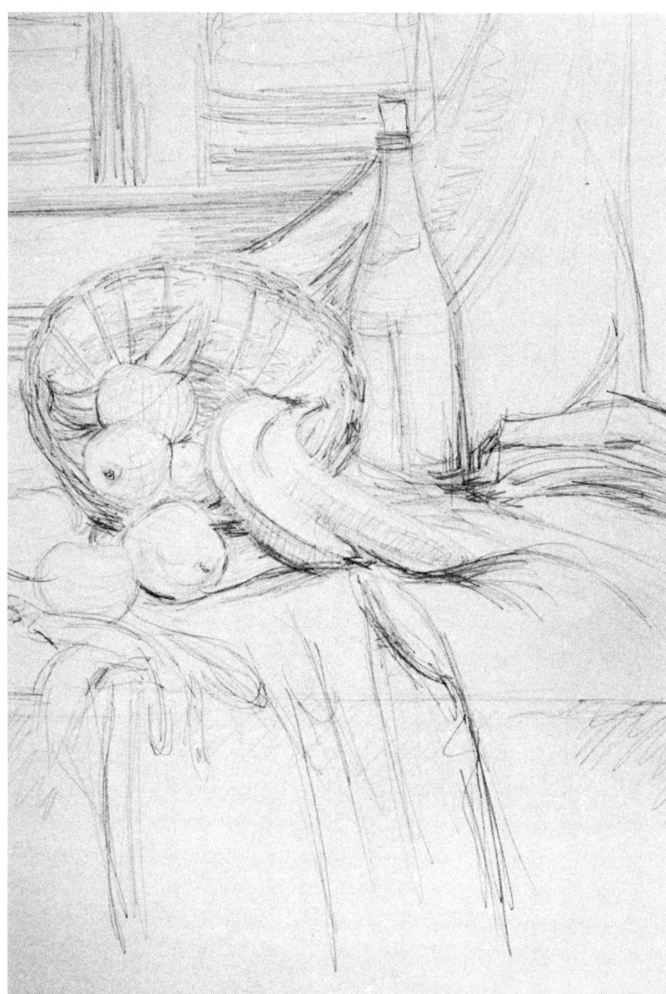

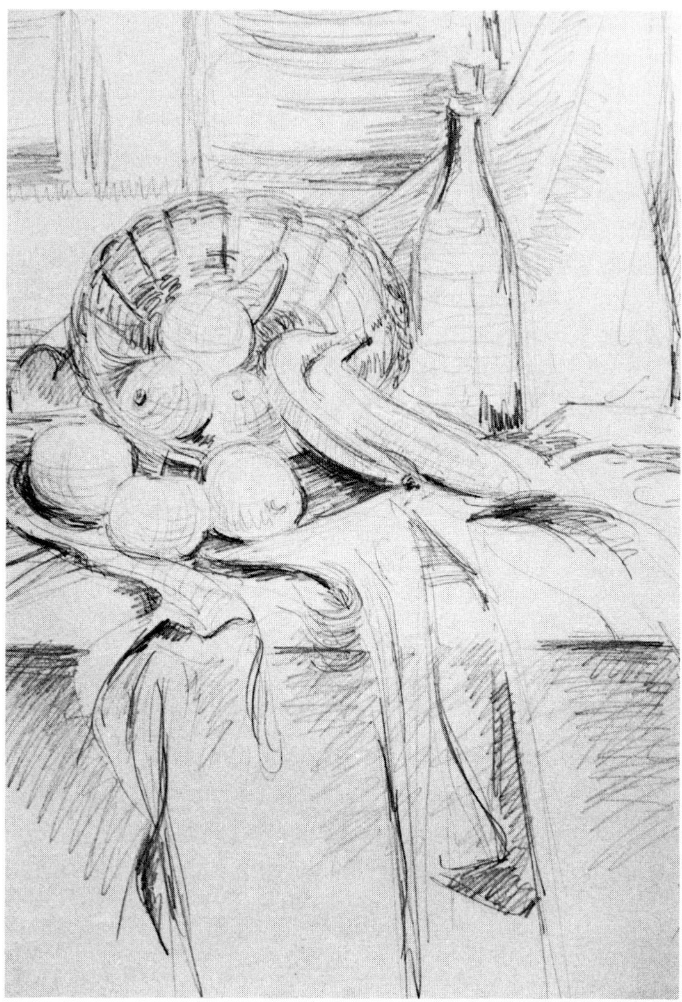

FIG 5 Schematic of Fig 4 (Pencil)

FIG 6 Construction drawing for Fig 4 (Pencil)

mentioned an eraser. I find it better not to correct marks that appear offensive, as often by being left in they make a contribution to the drawing. For this exercise it is best to draw with a 2B pencil. Remember to keep the drawing as light as possible. You may find it helpful to hold the pencil between the thumb and index finger as shown, as with practice this gives much greater control than the conventional writing position. With the schematic lightly drawn (Fig 5) you are now in a position to examine the structure of the components of the subject. To assist you, Fig 6 shows how the construction of the bottle can be dealt with regardless of its shape. I have indicated the construction of the whole drawing and the solidity of the items. Pay particular attention to the spaces between the components: these are as important as the components themselves. Try to think of all your drawings as shapes and spaces; this will help to stop you thinking of your picture's content in a figurative sense.

Now you have constructed the drawing with solidity in mind, enhance this aspect. Look at the subject through half-closed eyes; this will increase the contrast, enabling you to see the shadows on the subject clearly. When you are sure that you understand the patterns of dark against light, block in your drawing as shown in Fig 8. This part of the exercise is of great value in drawing and of even greater value in painting; it helps you to understand how important the shapes between the objects are when shadows are involved. Increasing the density of the contour lines in the shadow areas, as shown in Fig 7, will give the work an even greater register.

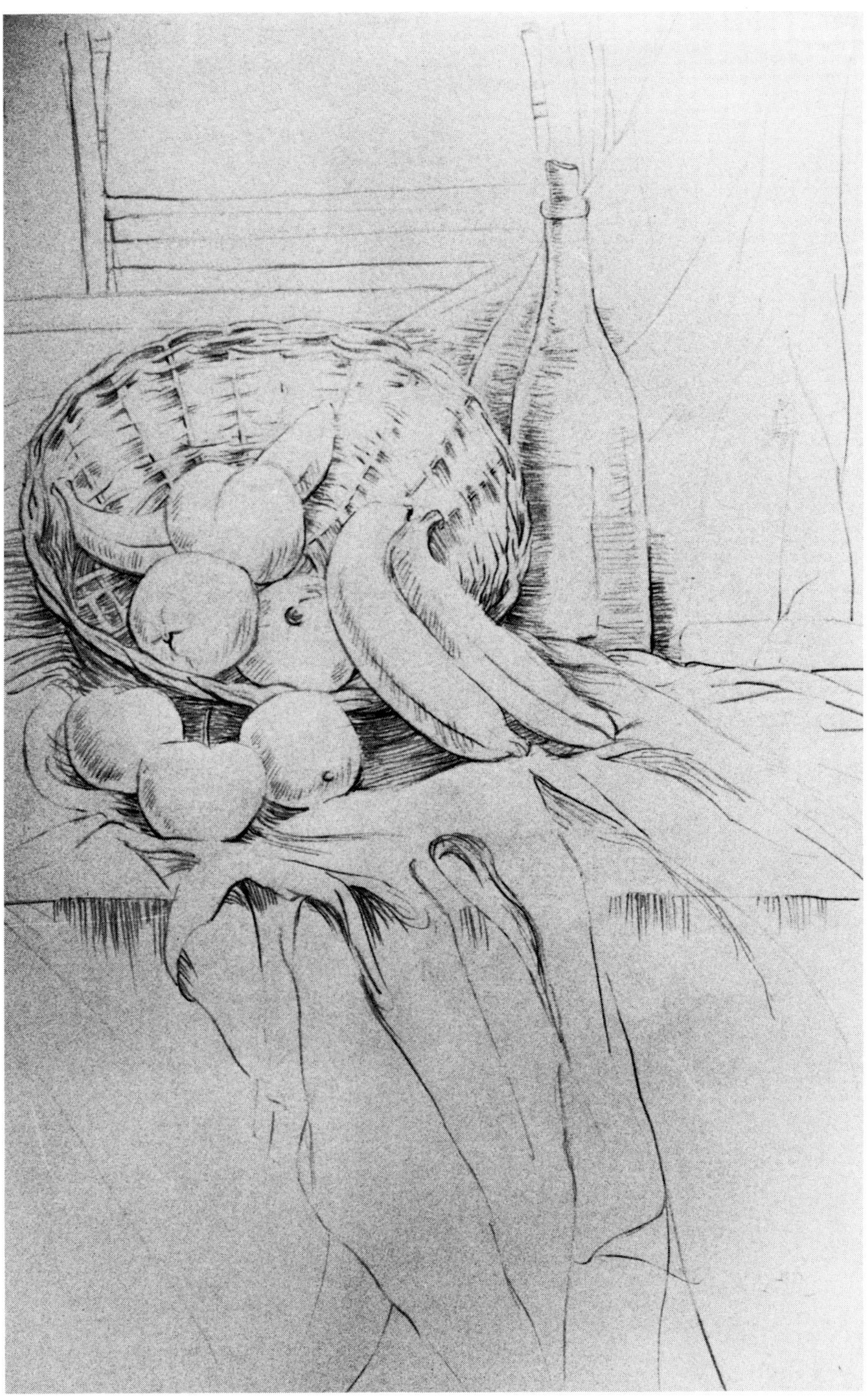

FIG 7 Blocking-in main shapes for Fig 4 (Pencil)

FIG 8 Ink drawing by Avril Darby
(18" x 14")

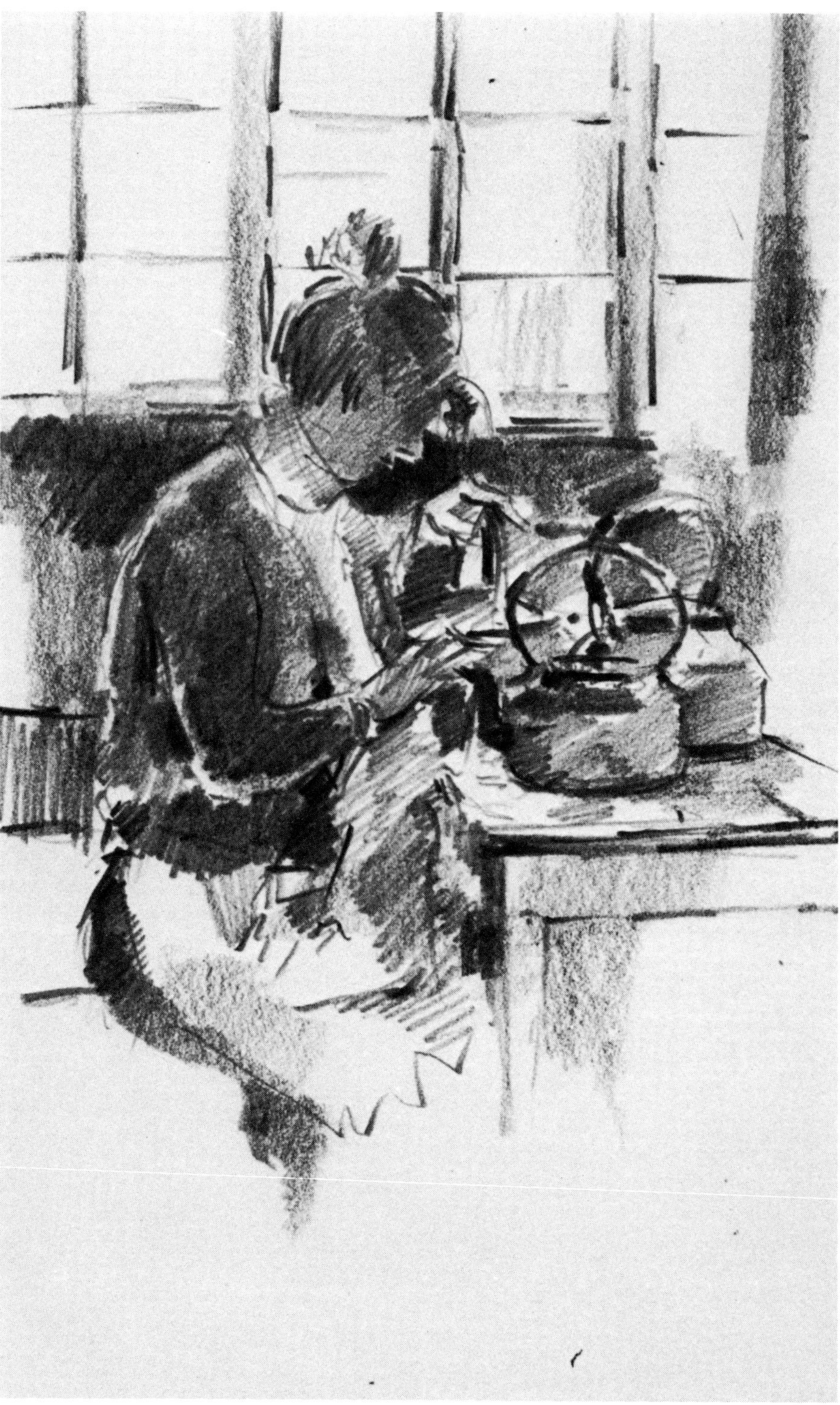

    In Fig 9 I have shown how this simple approach, using the methods
outlined, can be applied to a landscape. Fig 9a shows my doodle
drawing; Fig 9b shows the schematic with the basic geometric shapes
applied to the natural forms, and finally the finished drawing with such
detail considered necessary to get the correct register for the subject.

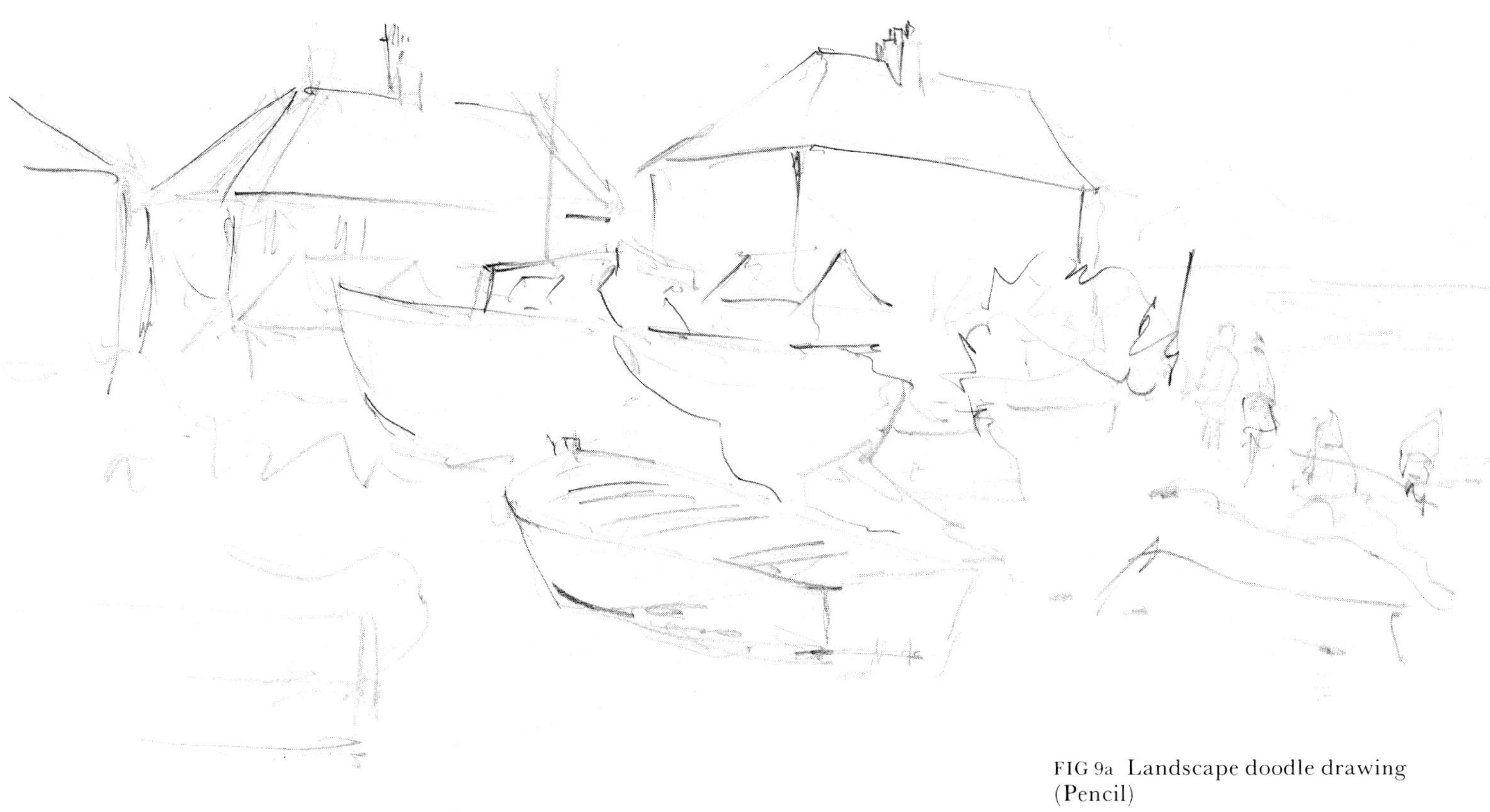

FIG 9a Landscape doodle drawing (Pencil)

FIG 9b Schematic drawing (Pencil)

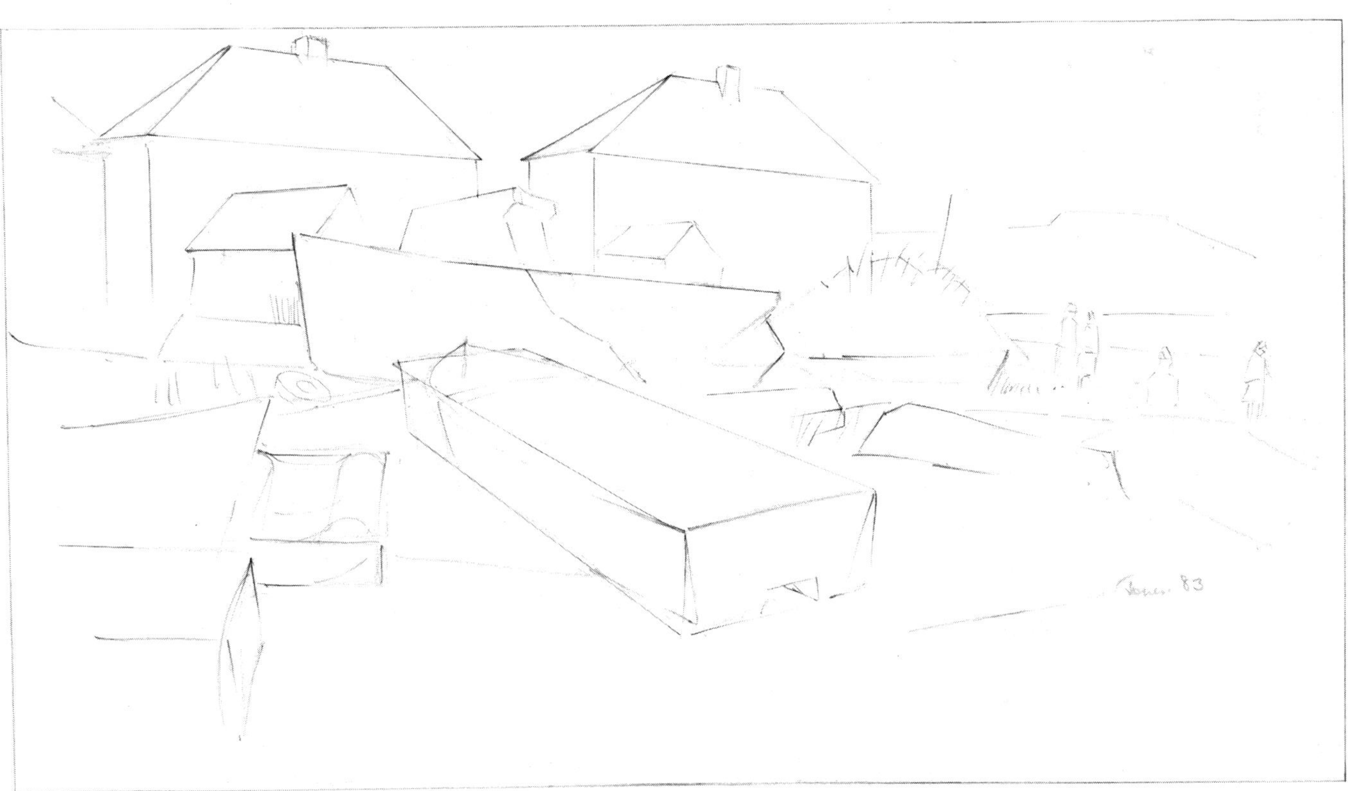

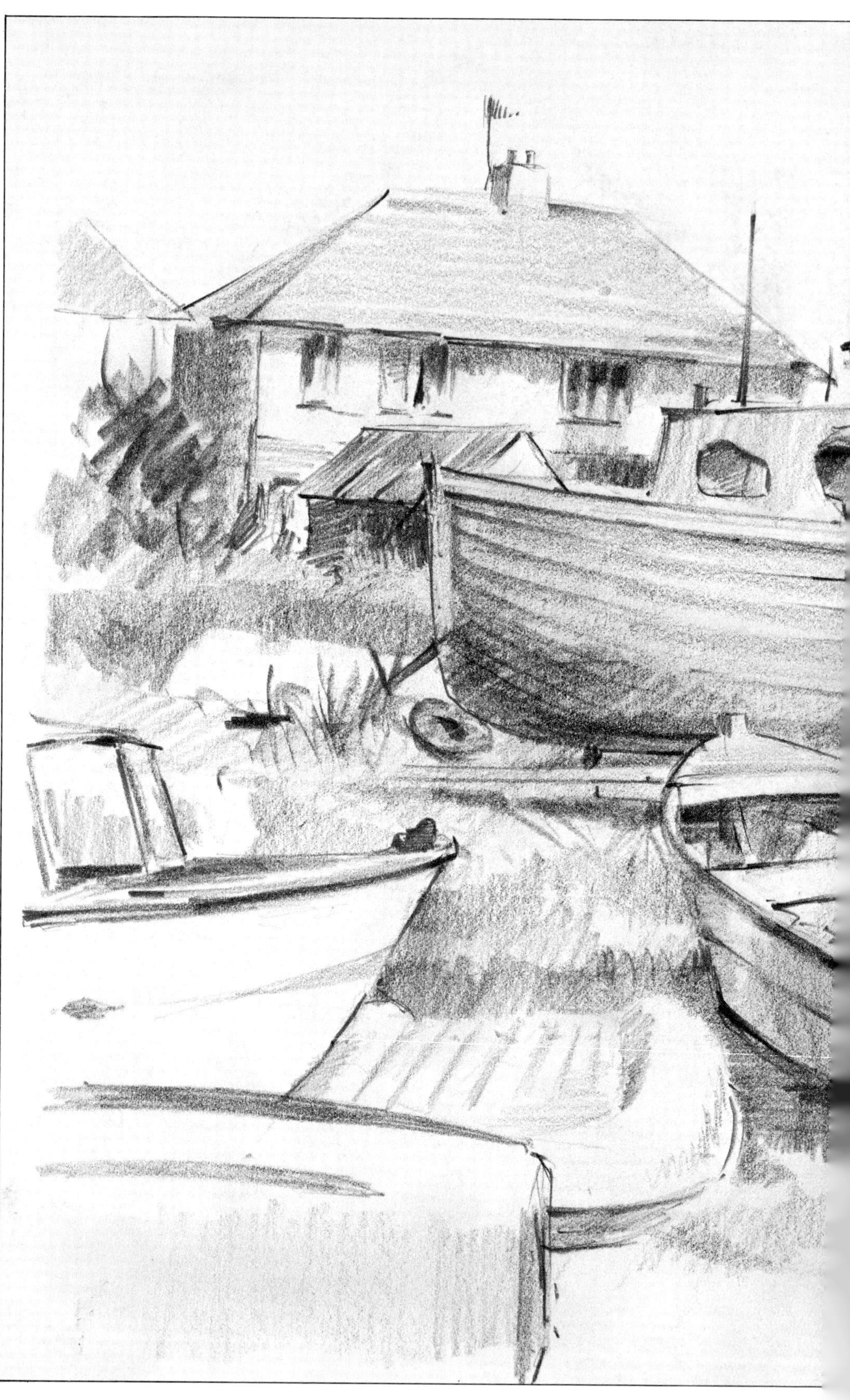

FIG 9c Finished drawing (Pencil)

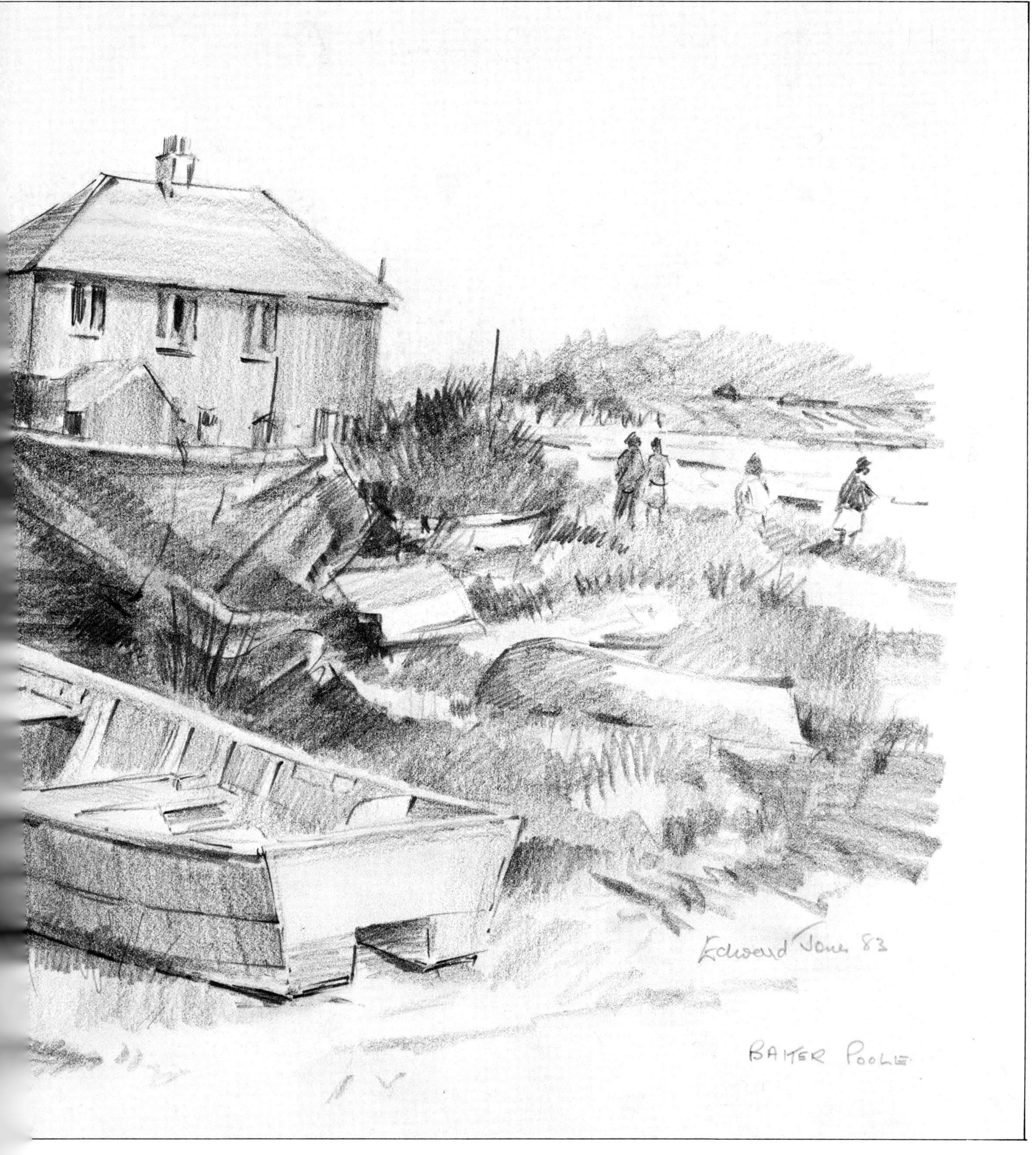
Edward Jones 83
BAITER POOLE

So far I have made no reference to perspective. It is without doubt one of the aspects of drawing that tends to inhibit beginners, but once again, with the right attitude of mind need not to be a problem. If you draw exactly what you see, you will in all probability achieve a drawing in reasonable perspective. In the simplest possible explanation, we can say that anything of which we can see the top is below our eye-level or horizon; similarly, any object we have to look up to is above the eye-level or horizon. It therefore follows that the first thing you must do is decide where on your sheet of paper the eye-level should be placed. There is no hard and fast rule for this, but if you refer back to the first two exercises, you will see that if the eye-level is very high in the drawing or even above the top edge of the paper, you will be looking right into or on top of the subject. So, as you can see, the decision is yours. This will be referred back to later, when design and composition are dealt with. The eye-level is in fact an imaginary line of infinite length, whose position in the picture frame is something you decide. You will have seen how parallel lines appear to converge to a common point in the distance – the best practical example of this is to look along

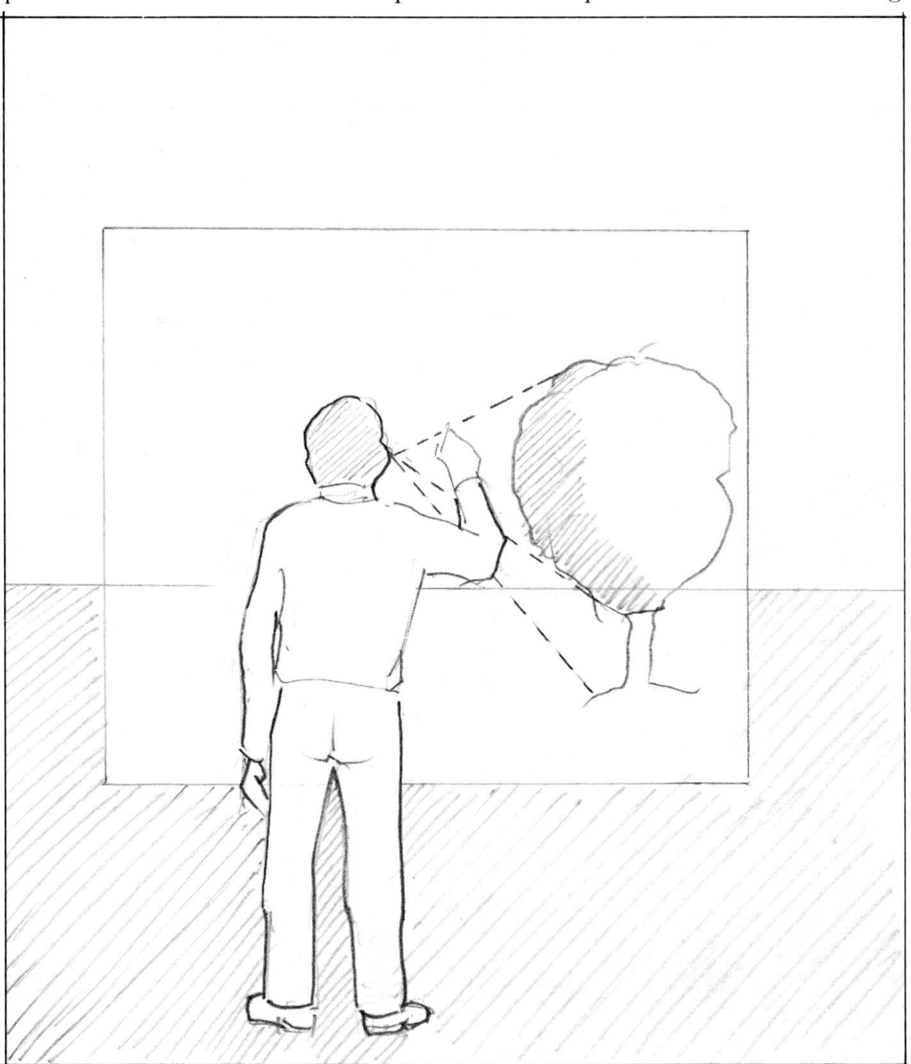

FIG 10 Perspective

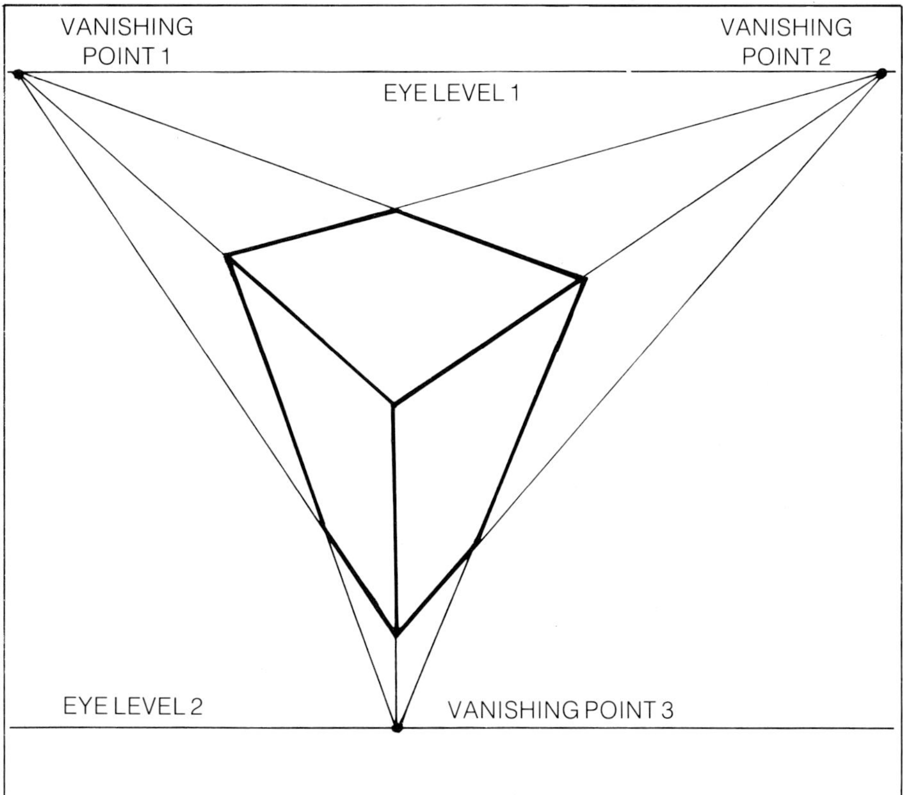

FIG 11a Three-point perspective

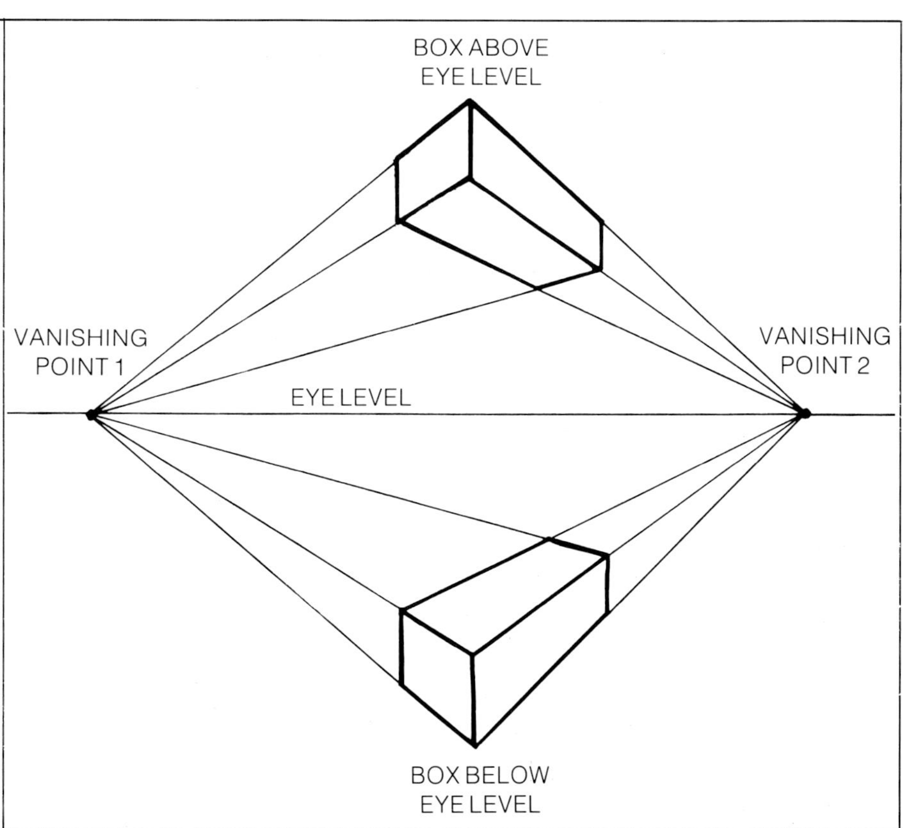

FIG 11b Perspective of objects above and below eye level

a railway track; not only will you see the lines converge to a common point, but also the sleepers appear to grow closer together.

This is *perspective*. The word is derived from the Latin *specio*, meaning to look. In a more practical sense, it means to look through from a single viewpoint. This approach was used by the ancient Greeks in their theatre set designs. They discovered that if you placed a small scene behind a large one so that there was a relatively small distance between them and a part of the small scene was visible, the illusion of a large distance between the two scenes was created. It was this that prompted Brunelleschi, a Renaissance architect, to create a mathematical formula which is the foundation of perspective as we understand it today. A more practical way of understanding perspective is to imagine that your paper is a sheet of glass and you are looking through it to the scene behind. If you were to trace on the glass the exact outline of the subject, you would be producing a perspective drawing (see Fig 10, which also indicates the eye-level).

Perspective assumes a fixed point of view, and you will see that all parallel lines meet at a common point on the horizon. To illustrate this more fully Fig 11 shows a number of boxes drawn in two and three-point perspective. When tackling this exercise it is better to use one of the sides on each box as the guide for evaluating the proportions of the other side. Fig 11 also illustrates a number of boxes in a random arrangement, above and below the eye-level. In Fig 12 I have shown the perspective of boxes and discs on the same eye-level. Three-point perspective is the odd man out, as it assumes two distinctly different eye-levels. In this case you look down upon and along your subject, the same view you would get from an aircraft flying over a city. When applying perspective it is, of course, essential to let the subject dictate

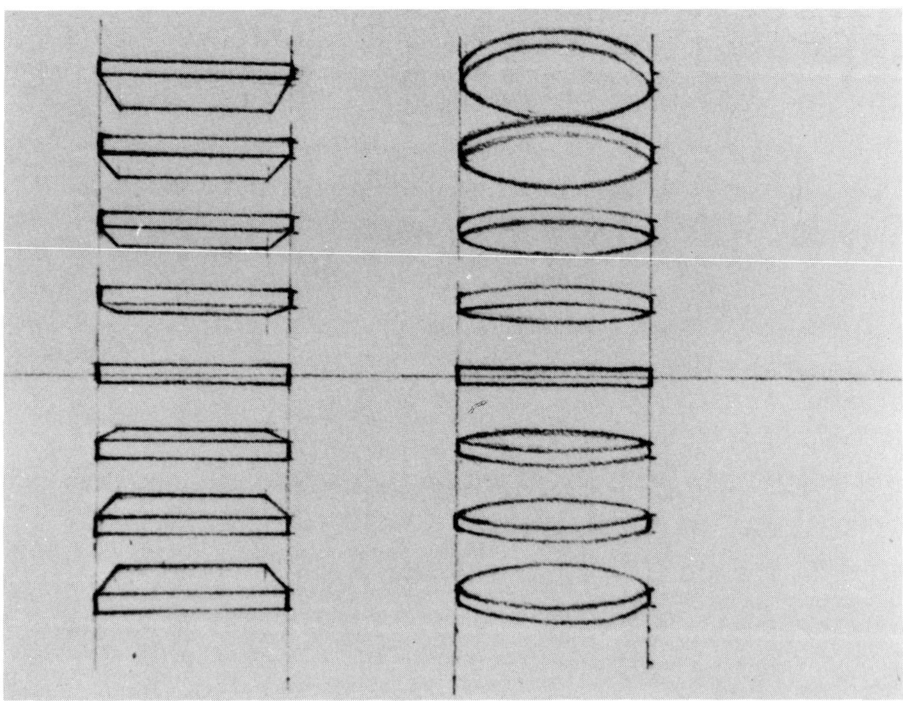

FIG 12 Perspective

the general approach as far as possible, but it is important to observe accurately the different angles of the picture's components. Each change of direction produces a different set of vanishing points for that component, as shown in Fig 11.

You will find from experience that the most valuable achievement is to find an acceptable register, and great artists achieve no more than that. The greatest register of spatial depth in a picture is achieved by moving from one plane to another – from front to back in one step without middle distance, the back plane being a simple picture behind a picture, and the forms expressed by contour lines. This projects the front picture, creating space and distance (see Fig 13).

Perspective has one other great attribute: it helps to relate shapes to each other in the right scale, which is very important. It can make us aware that it is not always necessary or correct to draw from a single viewpoint – indeed, many great twentieth-century artists dispensed with this attitude, and drew from many viewpoints in an attempt to draw right round their subjects. The works of Picasso and Braque are good examples of this. Picasso was particularly attracted to this method, which in itself was not new, but derived from Egyptian wall-painting, which shows that, irrespective of time, the language of drawing is unchanging.

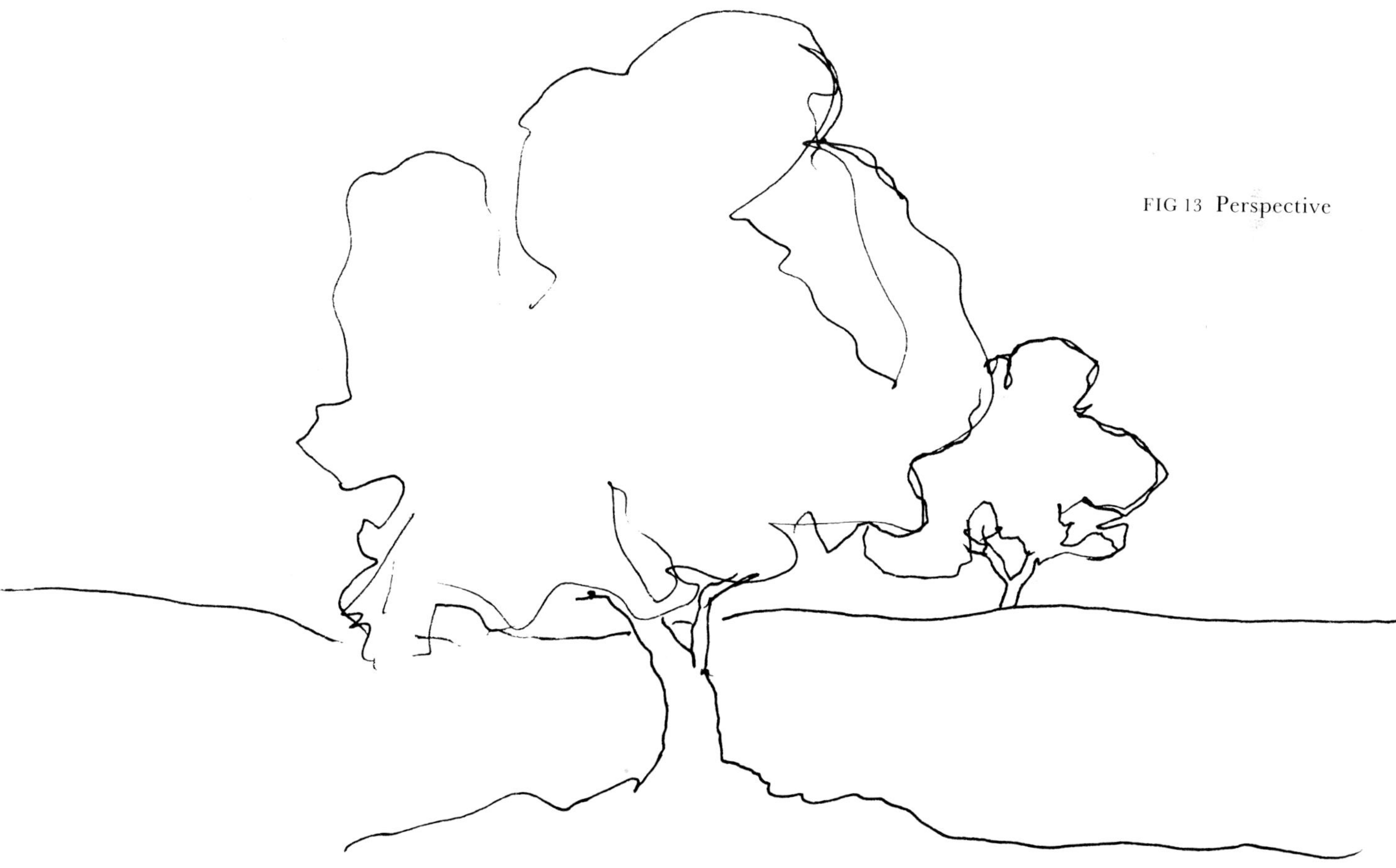

FIG 13 Perspective

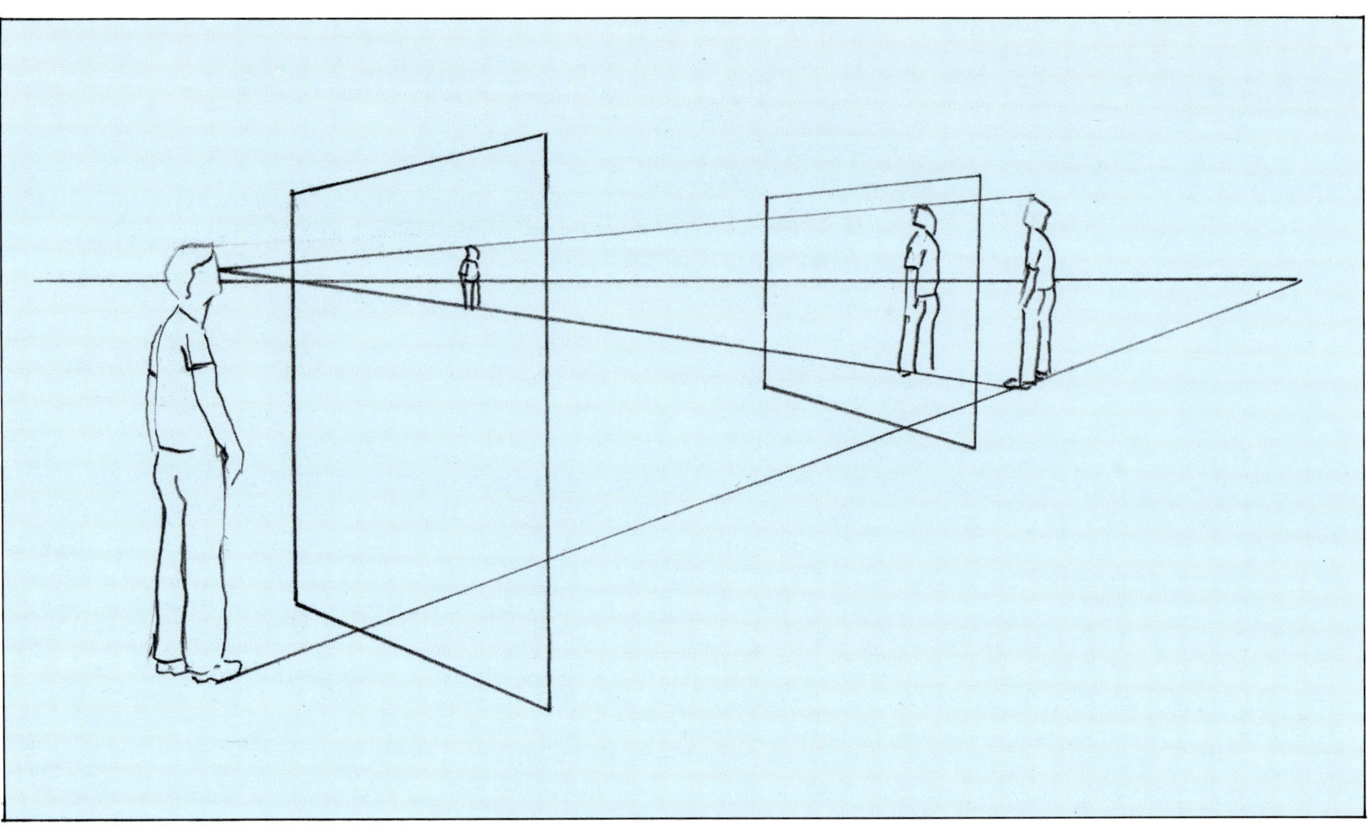

FIG 14 Perspective: positioning the picture plane

Returning to the idea of scale, Fig 14 illustrates how the content of a drawing becomes larger the nearer the picture plane is to the subject, and smaller the further away it is from it. Awareness of this aspect of perspective will be valuable when considering the composition and design of your work.

Linear perspective is only one way of perceiving space: there are many other ways of examining space and three-dimensional form. It will, however, help you to understand the complexities and geometric construction of natural form. Having examined the principal visual rules of drawing space and distance, let us now look at the other means which, when used in conjunction with an understanding of the linear rules, will enable you to perceive three-dimensional space more accurately and selectively. Focusing the eye gives an awareness of spatial relationship in terms of depth and distance. Atmospheric effects become greyer or neutral when depth is increased. Fig 15 shows the combined effect of the vanishing lines of the interior of my teaching studio coupled with the atmospheric effect. Note how, as we are led into the room, the background parts are grey and are drawn with little contrast, whilst the foreground is treated more vigorously and with considerable contrast.

When this phenomenon is observed and applied, it is called aerial perspective. The shapes of cast shadows tell us about the form and nature of the surfaces being drawn. The overlapping of foreground objects will also give further clues to depth. Texture and patterns appear more detailed when viewed close to, so that the drawing will

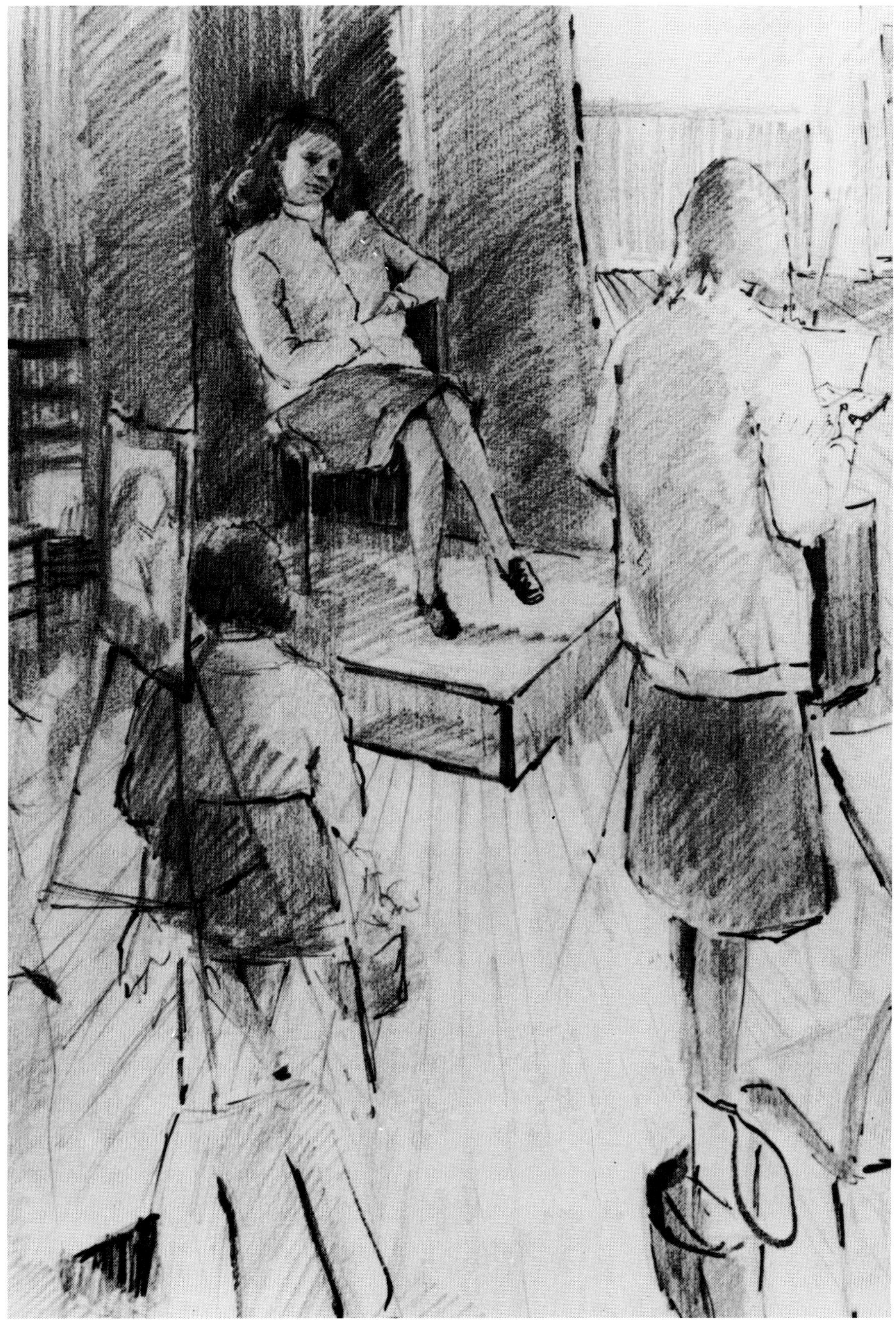

FIG 15 Perspective

FIG 16 Foreshortening

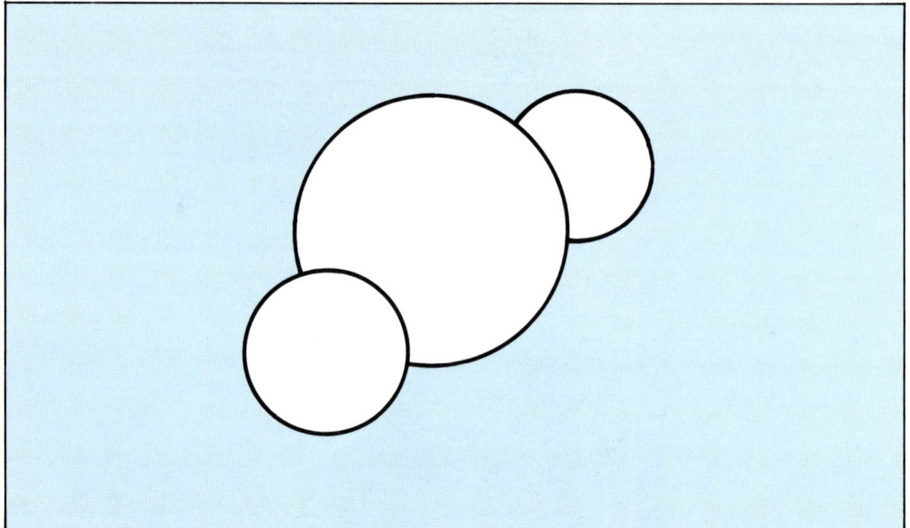

need more attention to emphasise the detail. These important points help to interpret three-dimensional space and can be applied in the drawing. Selectively can also play an important part, as it is not always essential or desirable to incorporate all these factors when making a representational drawing – it can even be quite uneconomic to do so.

Perspective and foreshortening are sometimes thought to be the same thing, indeed there is a similarity, as both are concerned with three-dimensional space. The main difference is that perspective makes things recede, whilst foreshortening makes things advance.

The essence of foreshortening lies in overlapping, placing one form in front of another, and showing that the front contours overlap the contours of the rear form. In Fig 16 I have drawn three different sized balls, viewed from the front and slightly from the side. Note that the smallest ball is at the front and the largest in the middle: this is a simple exercise in foreshortening. You will find that in three-dimensional drawing this is an essential part of your armoury for acquiring a correct register. It becomes necessary to make the branches on trees appear to be growing from all around the trunk, so some branches must come forward while others recede. Similarly, when drawing the figure, limbs will be in front of other parts of the body, which is achieved by foreshortening. Fig 17 shows foreshortening applied to a section of a tree. Notice how some branches seem to come out of the picture. Similarly, Fig 18 illustrates a method of drawing a foreshortened arm and hand built on the principle of overlapping shapes; in this instance I have used irregular shapes.

A major problem experienced by students faced with a foreshortened object is determining the size or scale of the nearest part. I always advise students to draw that part twice as large as they think it is. It seems that, for some unknown reason, we are able to reduce the size of foreshortened components when they are overstated, but we never seem able to enlarge them sufficiently when the opposite occurs. Always relate the closer object to the shape behind it when fixing the size of the nearer shape.

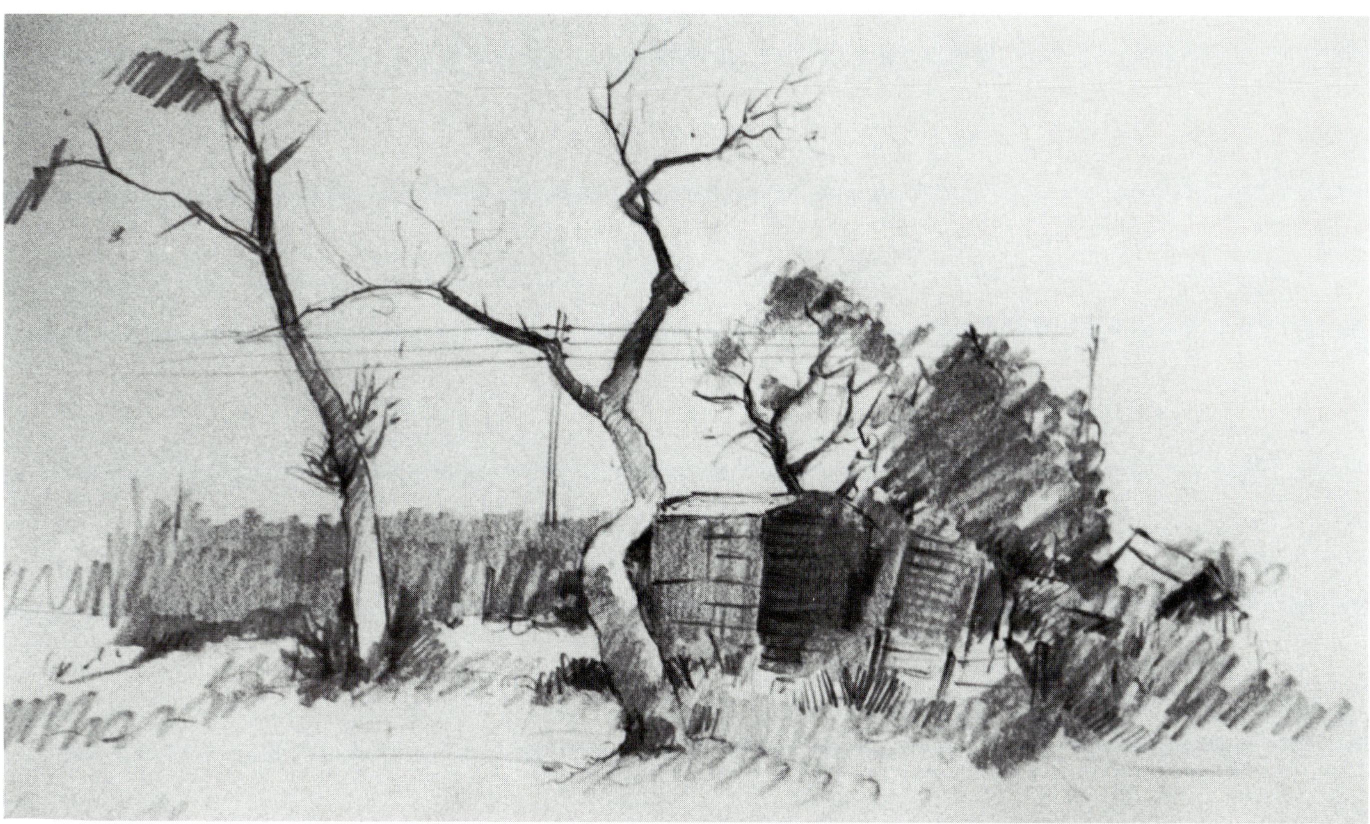

FIG 17 Tree (Pencil)

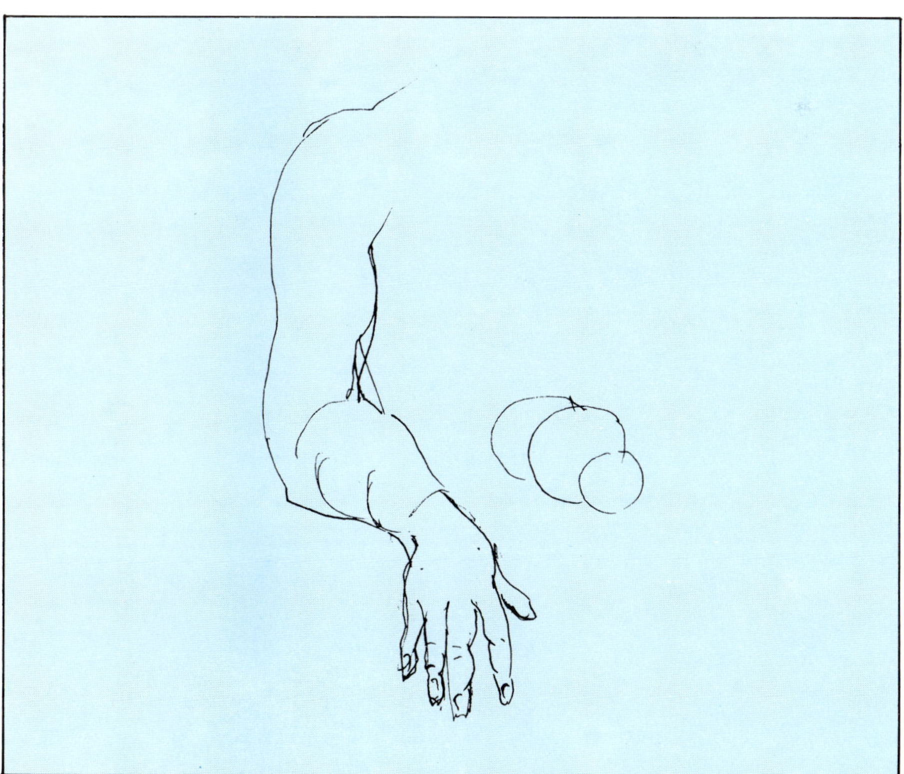

FIG 18 Foreshortening of arm and hand
(Pencil)

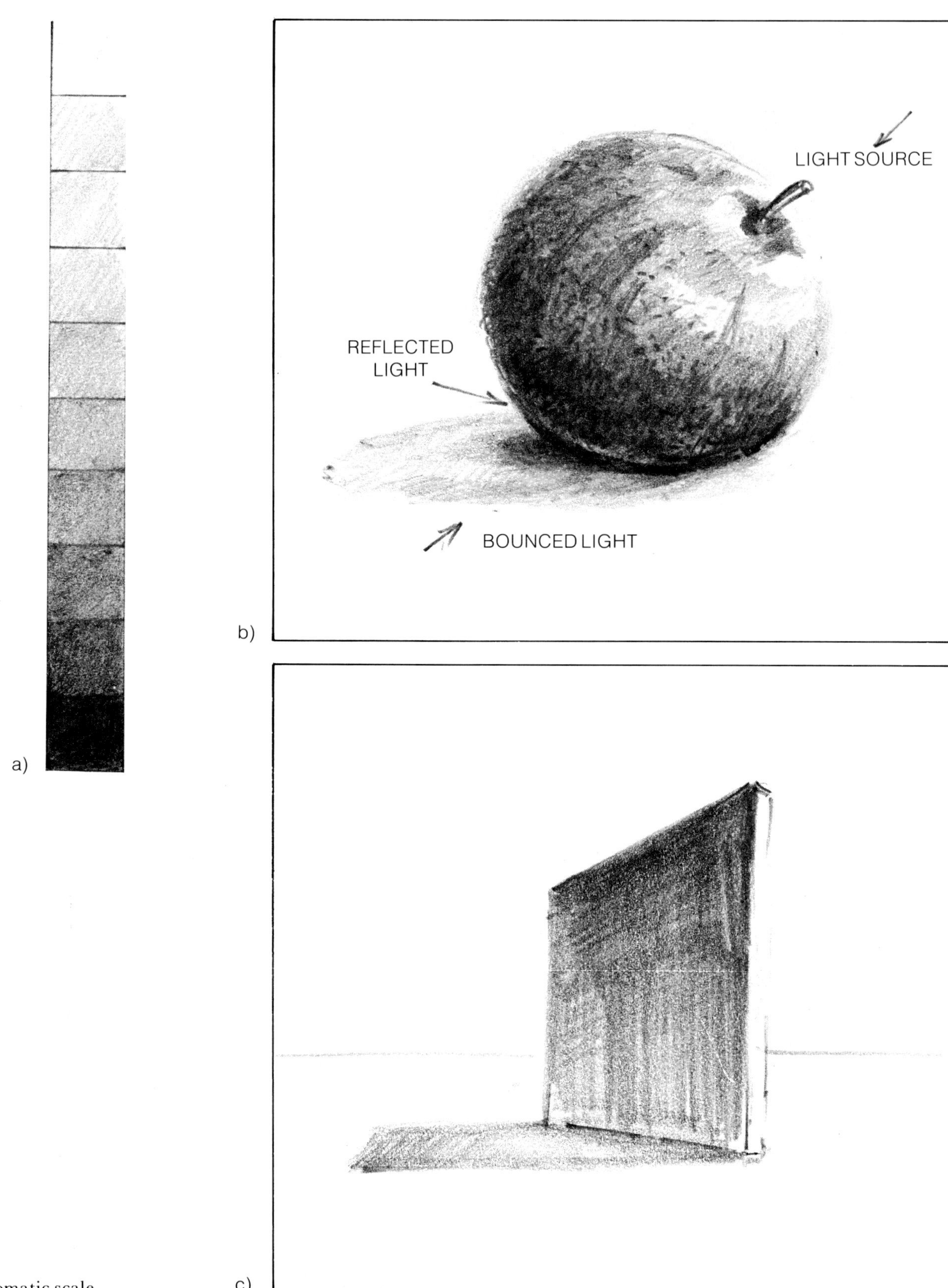

a)

FIG 19 Achromatic scale

Earlier, I suggested that you look at the subject through half-closed eyes to simplify the shadow areas. Before concluding this section, it is important to examine light, shade and tone more fully. Firstly it is essential to understand completely the achromatic scale; this is the scale in monochrome from dark through a progression of half tones to white. Fig 19 shows achromatic scales made with a range of media of different colours on white paper, although a coloured paper could just as easily be used. For the next exercise I have used white cartridge paper and a 2B pencil. The subject is a single apple, illuminated from the top right. This causes the bottom left of the apple to be in shadow, and also creates a cast shadow on that side. This is caused by the light being obstructed by the solidity of the apple. Light, however, is going past the apple and being bounced off the table, some of this bounced light being reflected back into the shadow side of the apple. This is called 'reflected light' and enhances the roundness of the fruit, giving a greater feeling of solidity. Reflected light occurs in most situations giving luminosity to the shadow parts of the subject. Fig 19 illustrates this feature in the drawing of a flat vertical plane, lit from one side only.

The rendition of light has been a constant preoccupation of artists for many centuries, and continues to be so today. It assumes even greater importance when painting and is further enhanced when related to tone. You may remember that, when discussing perspective, I pointed out how, in the drawing of the interior of my teaching studio, as the eye is led into the room, not only do the vanishing lines making the room recede but the greying and flattening of the contrast range also create a sense of recession. I called this *aerial perspective*. This is tone control. It teaches us that contrast and definition are at their strongest at the points nearest to us – we say the tone is *warmest* at this point. Conversely, at the furthest point in the picture, contrast and definition are diffused and tend to become lost – these are the *coldest* tones in the picture.

It will become apparent that warm and cold tones are more easily expressed in colour, although some expression in monochrome is possible. Tone control plays a very large role in creating the illusion of texture. In Fig 20 I have shown two pieces of bark, one from a pine tree and one from a beech, each with a different texture. Textures vary in practically every subject, none more so than in portraiture, with the large range of textures in flesh and in the drapes that subjects wear.

In Fig 21 is a completed pencil drawing of a wickerwork armchair with a variety of drapes. There is a magazine on the chair, and on the floor is a waste-paper bin with a screwed-up sheet of newspaper beside it. The floor is tiled, which helps to achieve a register of perspective. If you have practised the simple exercises so far, I would suggest that you set up a similar subject in your own room and draw it from life. Make sure you get a good arrangement at the right scale, and remember to construct your drawing around geometric shapes, having worked out your plan from several doodles. Observe the light and shade, and finally the tone values and textures.

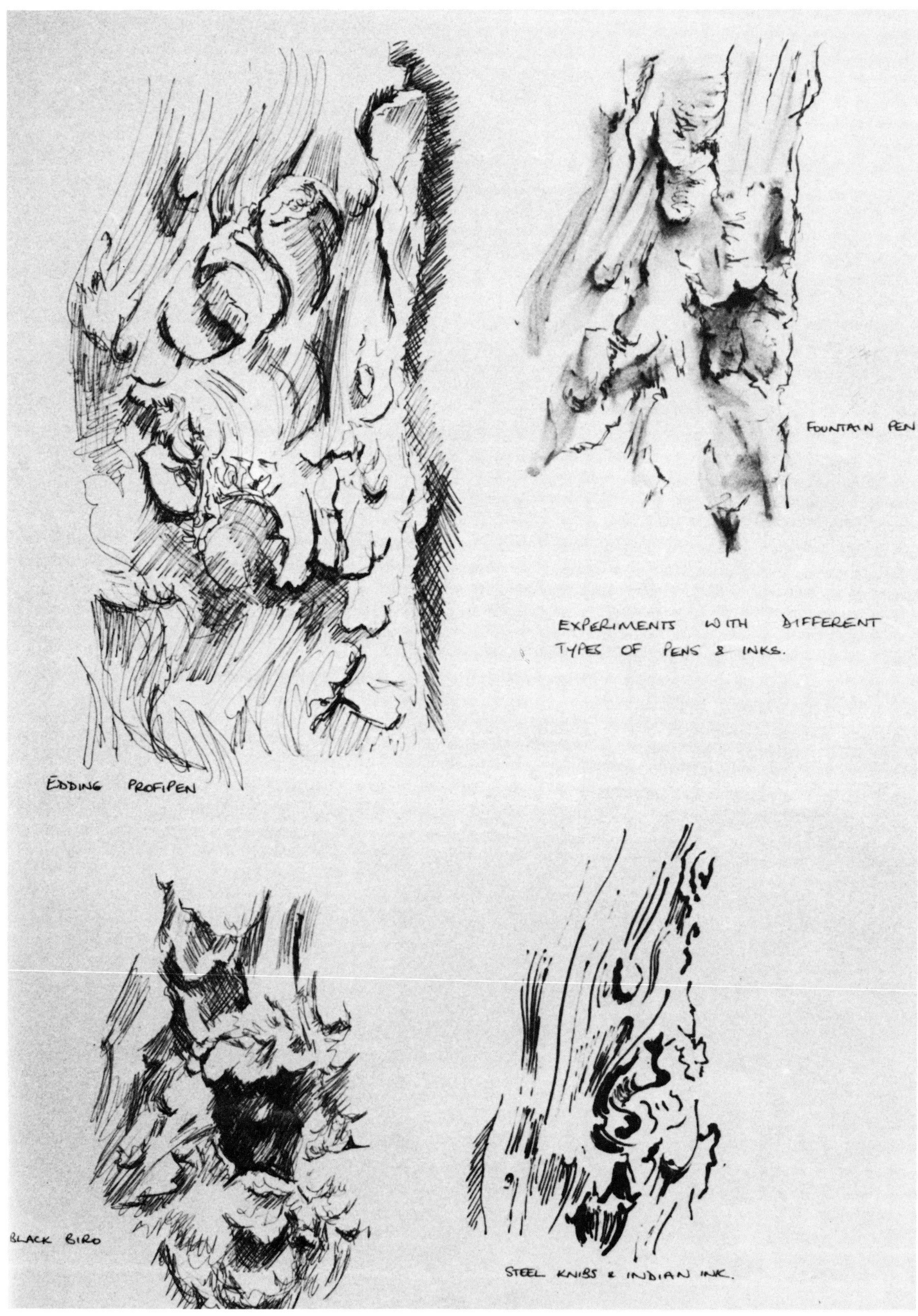

FIG 20 Study of various tree barks (Pencil
and inks)

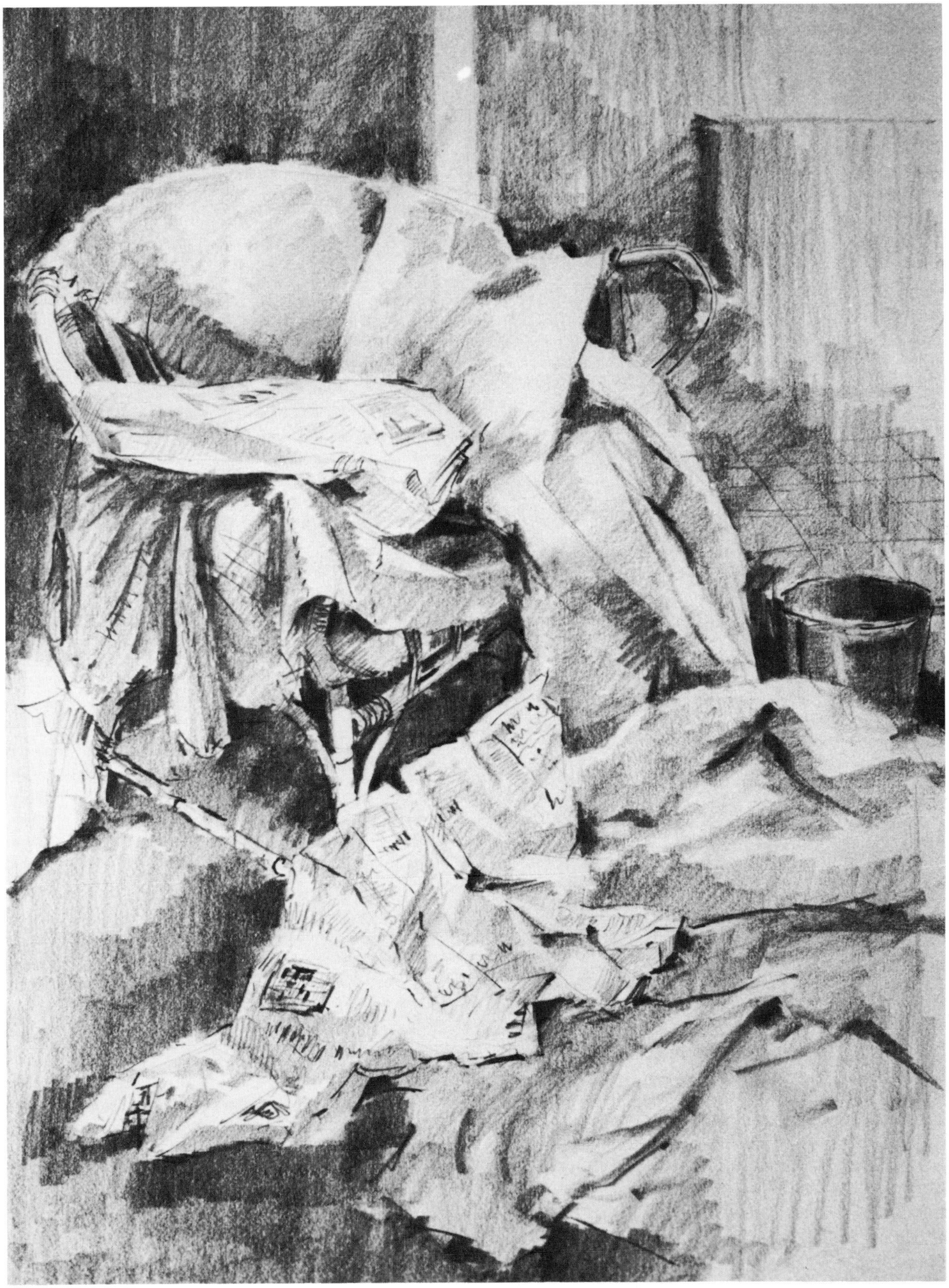

FIG 21 Wickerwork chair, drapes and textures (Pencil)

Now that you have been introduced to the language of drawing using a pencil, it is time to explore the other drawing media described earlier and to continue to advance your drawing skills. The basic disciplines used so far with pencil will always form the basis of your drawing, whatever the medium. Use of other media broadens the capability to express a subject more fully and in greater depth. Using the 2B pencil with its precision encourage you to draw accurately. Many of the other media, because of their softness and texture, are able to flatter your drawing. This facility will be to your advantage if you don't lose sight of the basic disciplines explained so far. The most commonly-used drawing medium is charcoal. It is also one of the oldest, and is available in a variety of sizes and hardness. More recently a new form, called compressed charcoal, has become available. This is somewhat darker in appearance and has the feel of a crayon. The methods of using charcoal are limitless, as are the surfaces on which it may be used. All paper with a slight tooth will accept charcoal, as will canvas, fine sandpaper and sugar paper (which is always a favourite with students as it is inexpensive).

As with any new or untried medium it is sensible to find out what it is possible to achieve. To this end, I suggest that you take a large sheet of cartridge paper and make some marks with charcoal, using all the different thickness availability. Try softening and shading the marks with a finger or a tissue. You will see they all differ slightly. Try also covering a large area using a fabric powder-puff. Fig 22 shows a range of different charcoals, with some of the equipment I have found useful when making charcoal drawings.

Fig 23 shows the range of tones and some of the textures and marks that charcoal can give. Because of its nature, charcoal will encourage you to draw boldly. Do not resist this, as it is a desirable feature. The

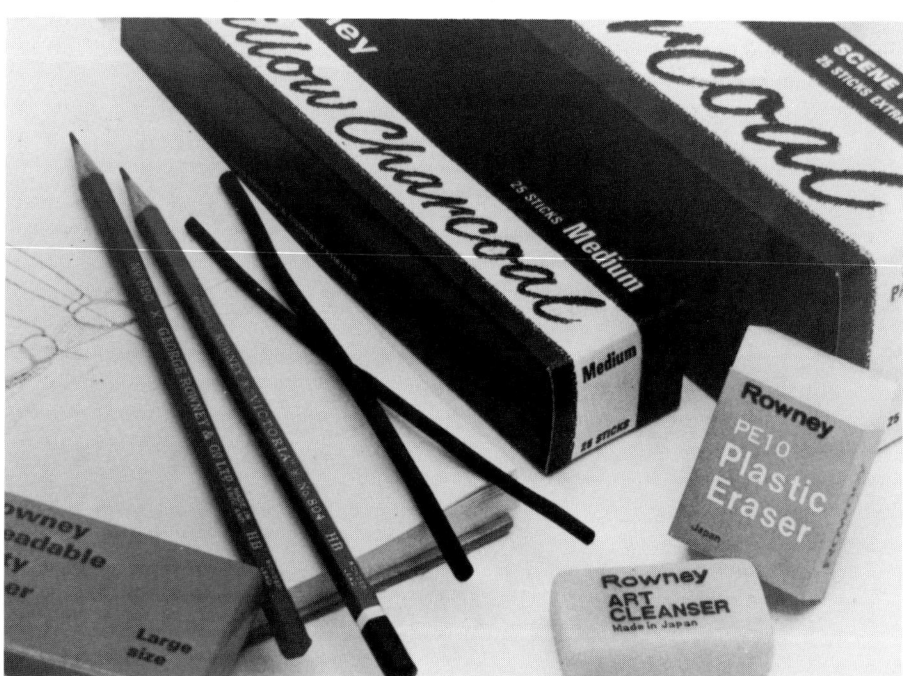

FIG 22 Types of charcoal

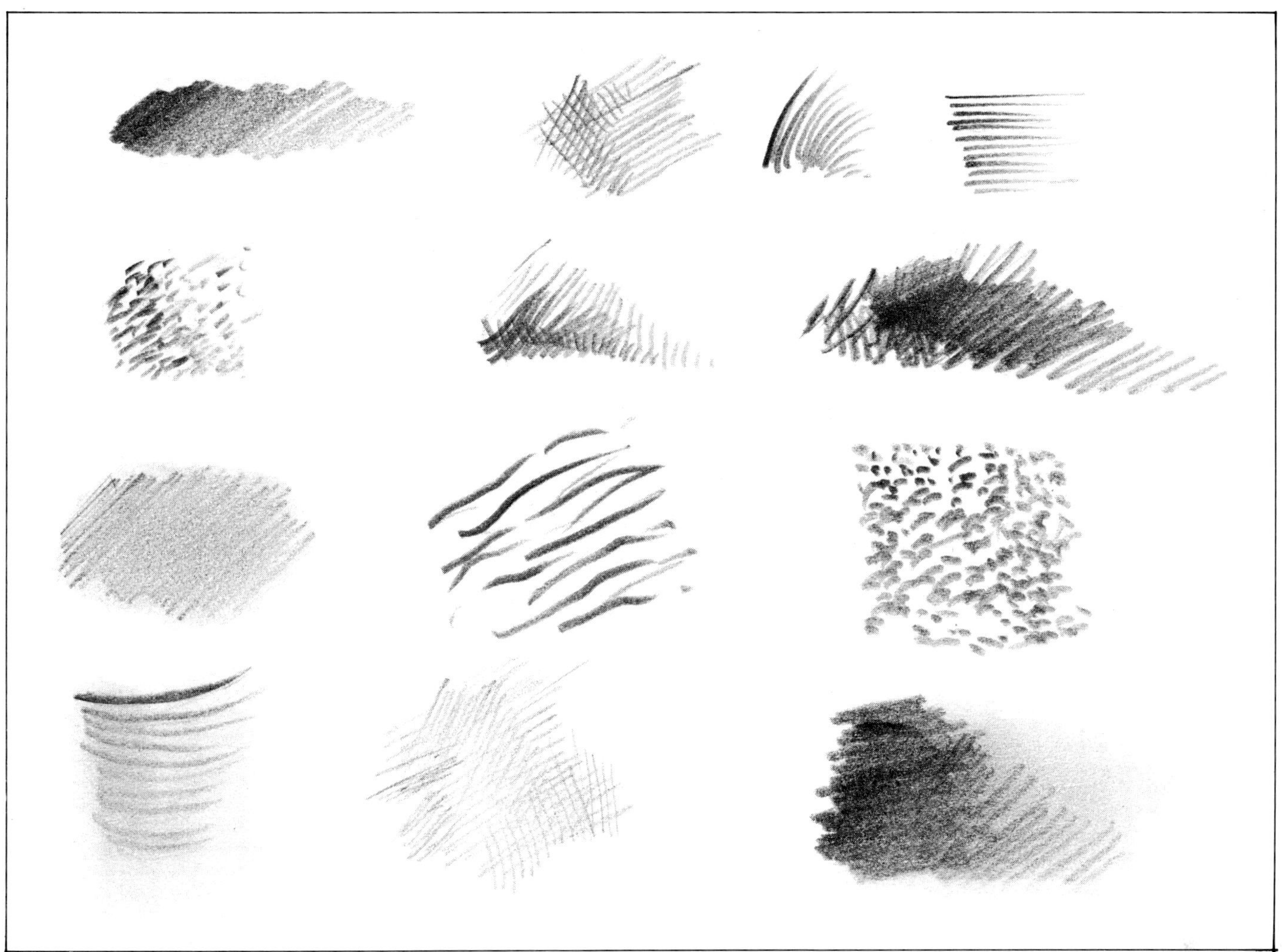

FIG 23 Range of possible tone and marks with charcoal

mobility of the medium allows you to adjust your drawing almost at will. This facility makes the initial doodle drawing an exciting exercise, as it is possible to modify as you doodle. In Fig 24, a still life of some of my painting hats, the method of approach was initially the same as outlined earlier. I doodled until the arrangement and scale reflected my reaction to the subject. The construction was then very lightly, but freely, established on a sheet of bronze-coloured Fabriano Ingres paper. With the construction complete, and using the powder-puff I was able to establish the dark areas, adjusting the tones with my finger where necessary. Not only does this give solidity to the components of the drawing, it lays the foundation to give texture to the surfaces. With this treatment covering the entire picture surface, as shown in Fig 24a, I could establish the pattern on the deerstalker hat and finally the stronger dark areas, bearing the tone values in mind. All that remained was to pick out the highlights using the kneaded or putty rubber, and generally to clean the drawing where the charcoal may have inadvertantly become smudged. In general, I prefer to work at an easel when using the softer media: the hand is less likely to touch the working surface if the paper is in a vertical position.

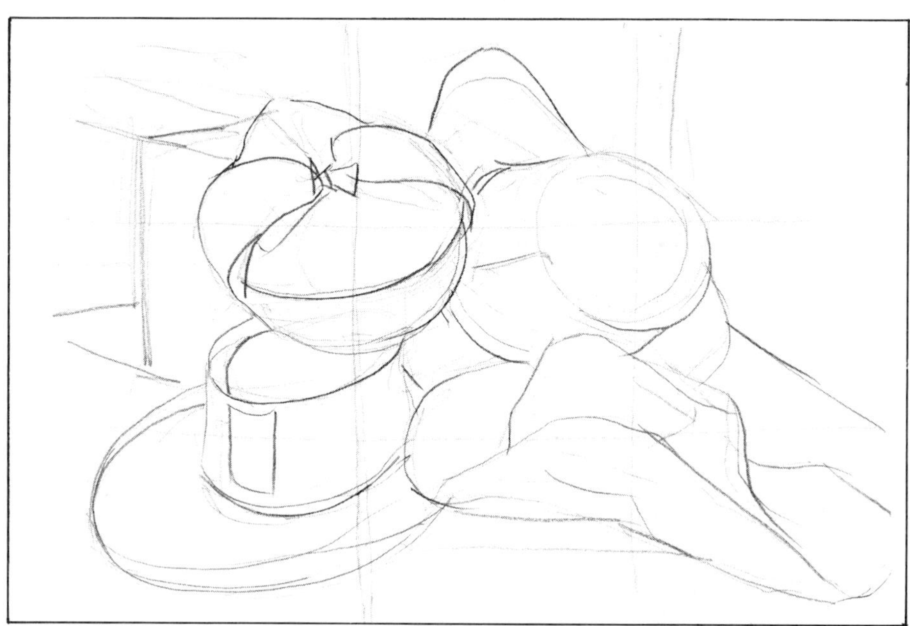

FIG 24a *My painting hats* doodle (Charcoal, 28" x 18")

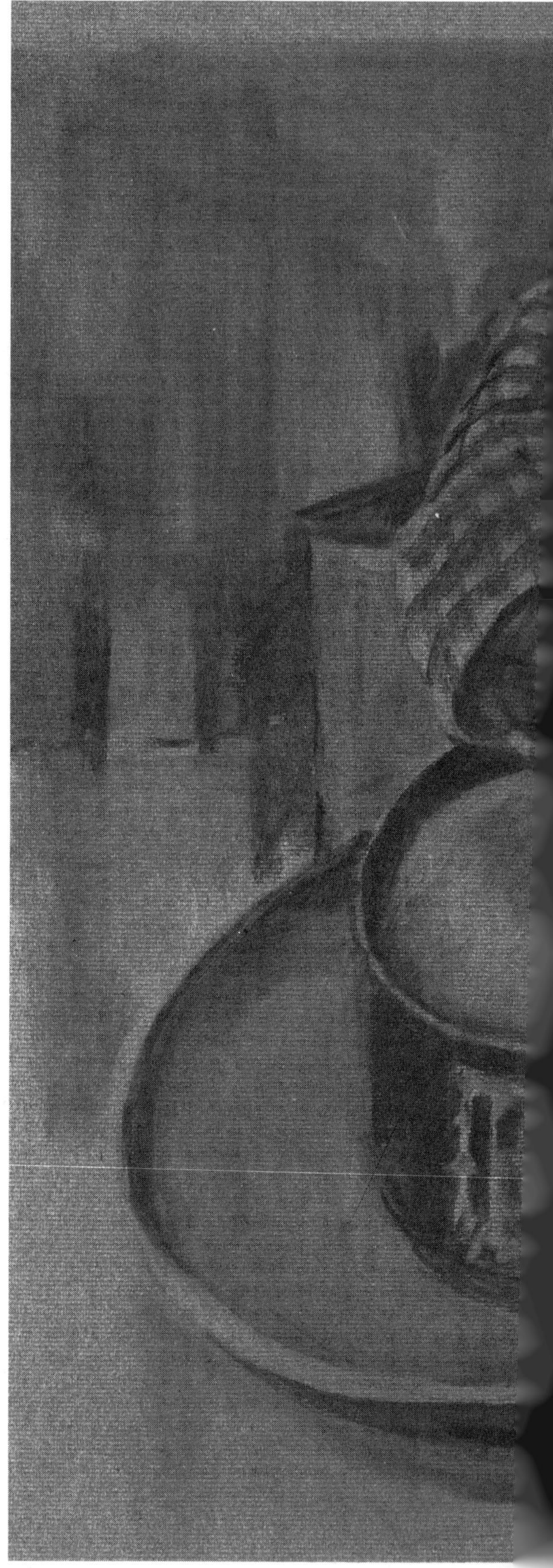

FIG 24b *My painting hats* (finished drawing, 28" x 18")

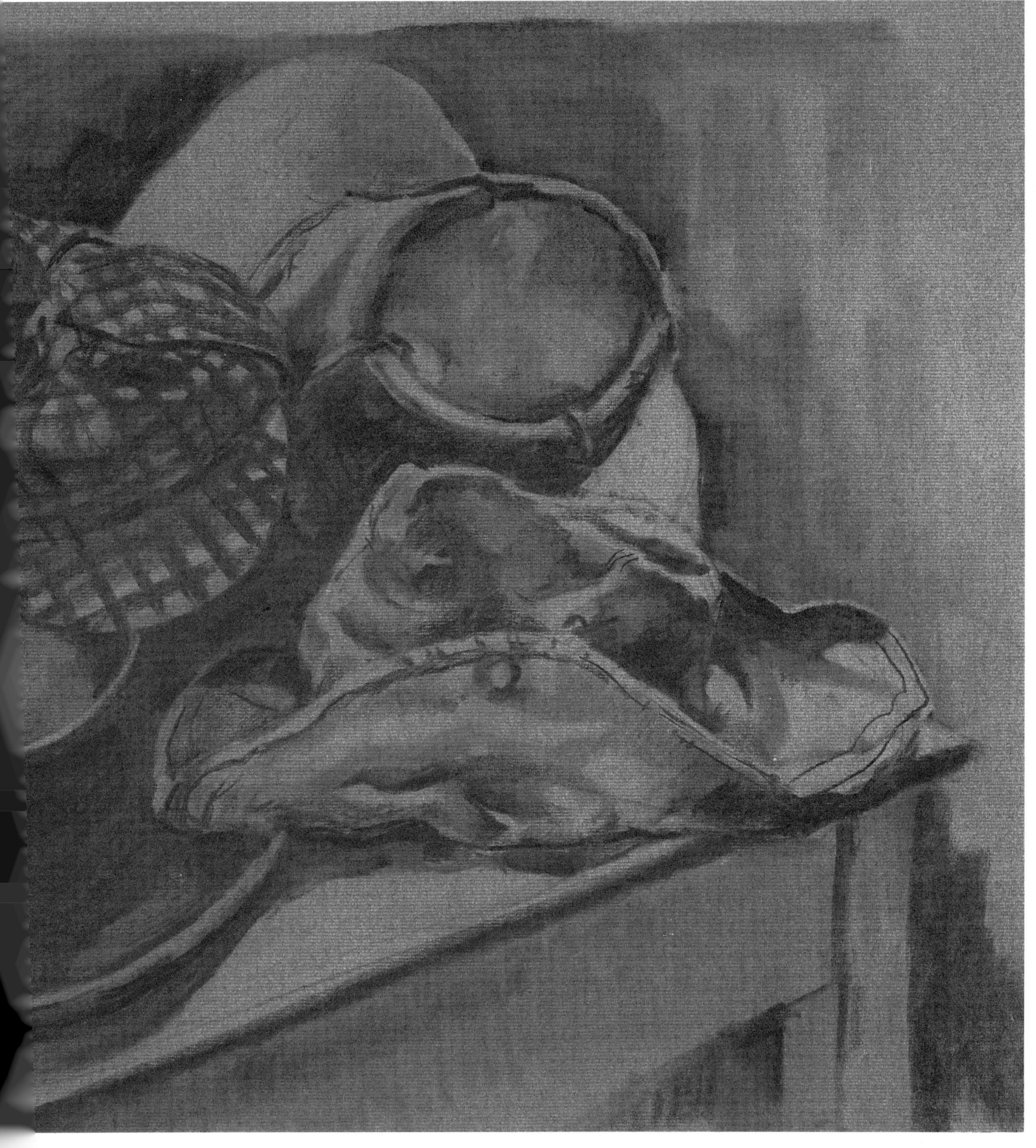

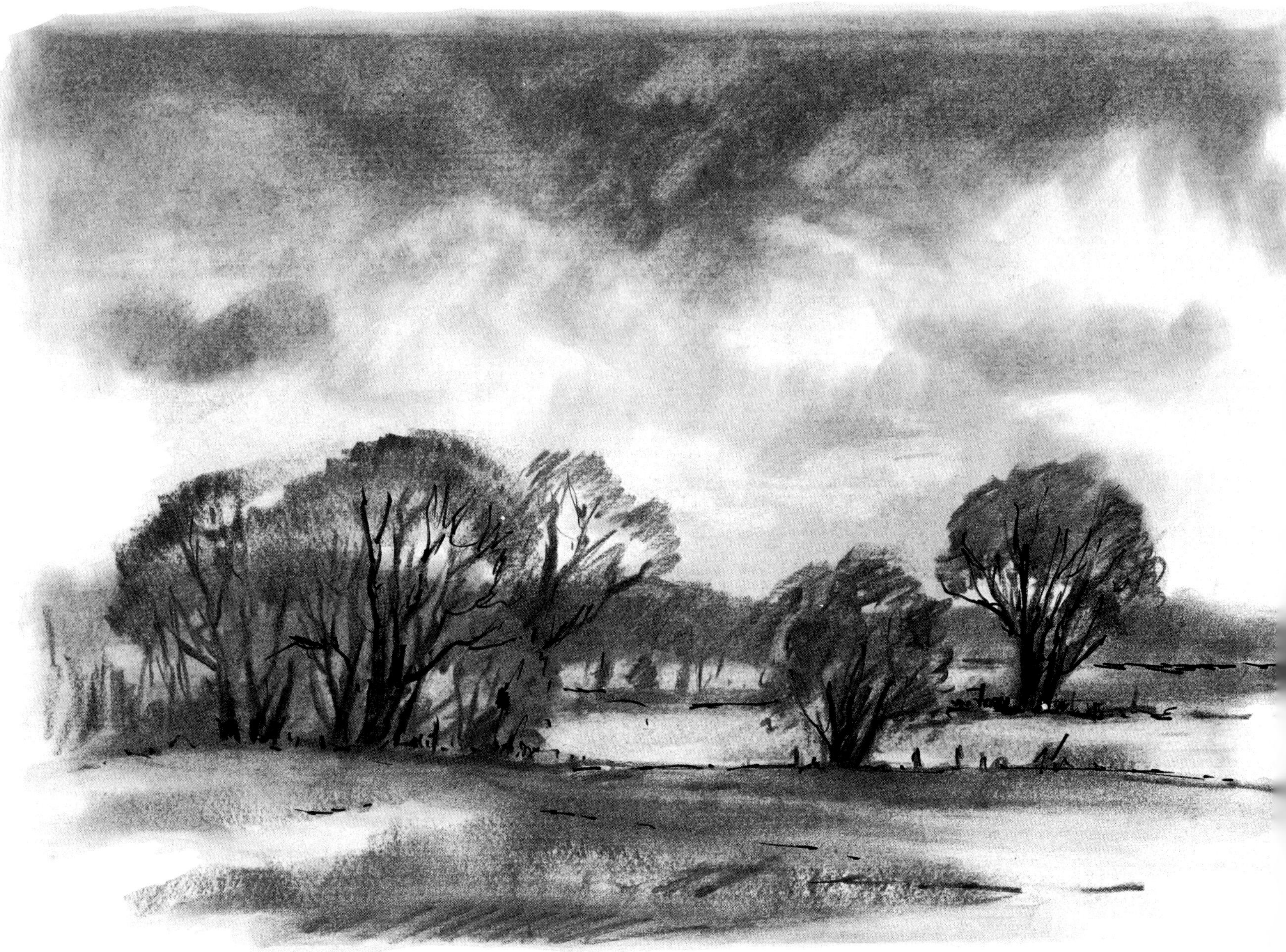

FIG 25 *Stormy landscape* (Charcoal, 18" x 13")

Because charcoal is liable to smudge, when your drawing is finished it must be protected by fixing. This is achieved using spray fixer, available in aerosol cans. To apply this, spray across the drawing, keeping the aerosol 18 inches from the surface, and moving continuously to ensure an even coverage without puddling and spoiling the work. Charcoal lends itself to all subject matter. Whilst it is not my intention at this stage to cover more complex subjects, Fig 25 illustrates a stormy landscape and Fig 26 shows a French townscape with people – two very different subjects which illustrates the remarkable scope offered by charcoal.

FIG 26 *French townscape* (Charcoal, 10" x 7")

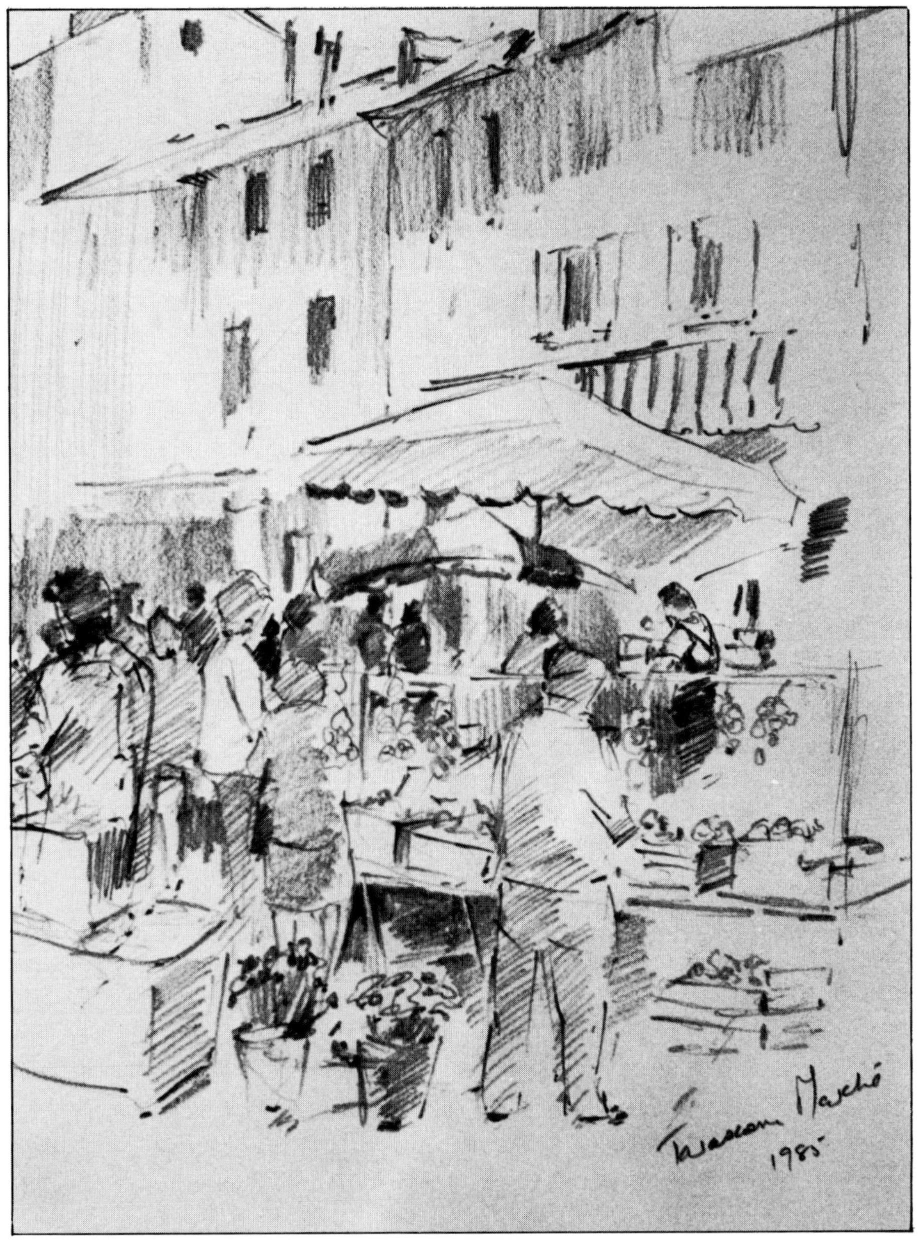

Charcoal can be used in many ways and on many surfaces, all of which are worth experimenting with. I enjoy drawing with charcoal on Bockingford water-colour paper. The texture is most exciting and attractive, and because I use 140 lb weight paper it is thick enough to try innovative experiments. Fig 27, a figure against the light, is one such picture. As in previous work, the idea was initially developed as a doodle, and the construction and visual scanning lines laid in very faintly with emphasis only where the dark areas were obvious. Having satisfied myself that the general arrangement and construction were to my liking, I blocked in the main dark areas using a powder-puff. On

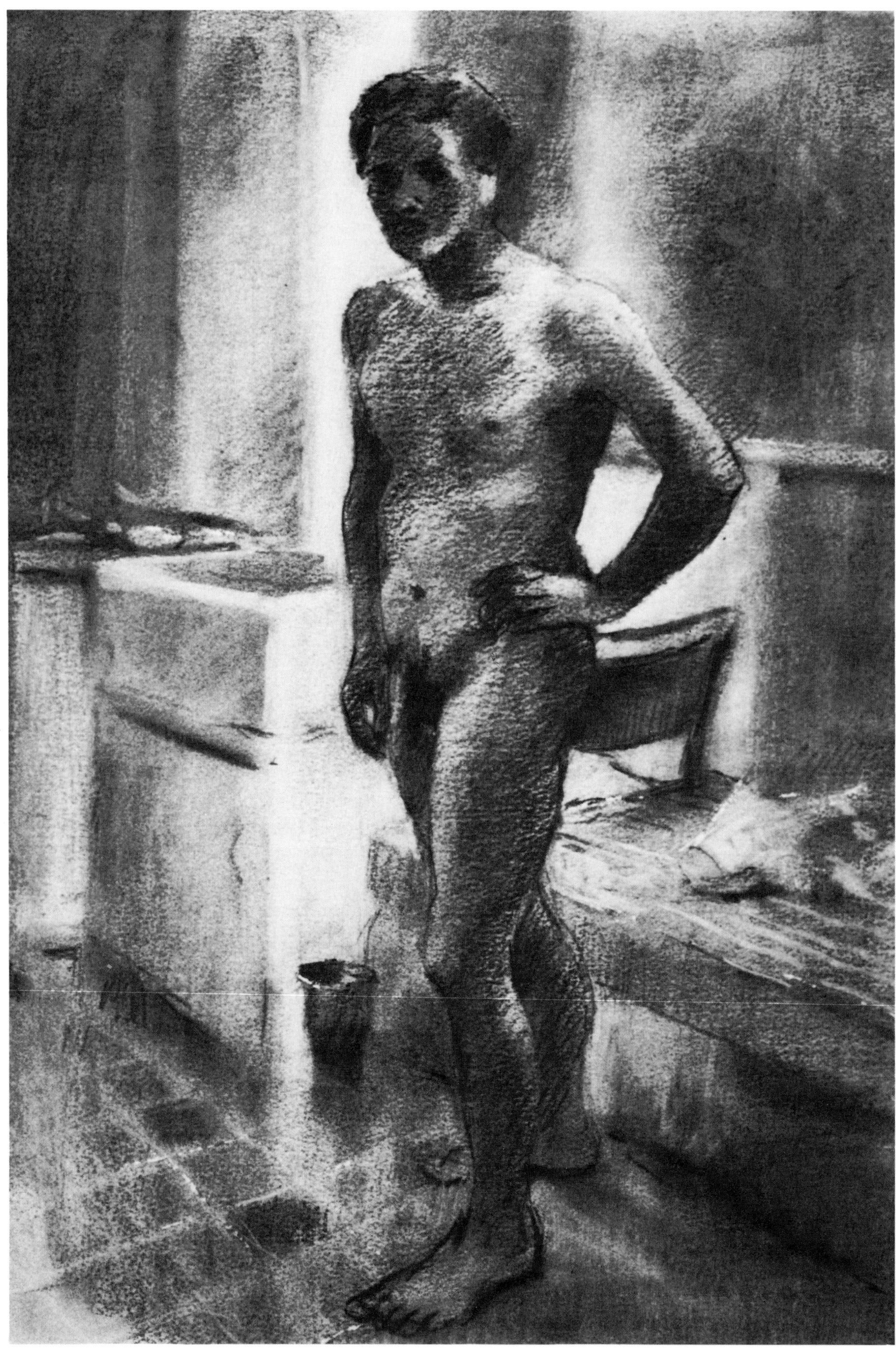

completion of this stage, the drawing was fixed. It could now be worked on further without fear of the drawing underneath being disturbed. You will notice that the white paper is the lightest part of the work, and that the progression is from light to dark. Because the drawing had been fixed, I was able to build on the dark sections, increasing their density. Conversely, should I have wished to remove some of the darks because of the thickness of the paper, I would have been able, with the use of a scalpel, to cut into the passage and restore the white paper. This gave the drawing a further dimension, as it was now possible to make a different texture. The drawing was then fixed again, and the final pulling together of the whole accomplished.

Drawing in any medium is only a collection of lines, marks and smudges arranged in such a manner as to create the illusion of the subject. Charcoal, by its very nature, encourages thinking in a language of marks, lines and smudges. It teaches us to look at the subject in this way – nature does not encompass form with lines. Neither is the subject entirely hard-edged – on the contrary, close observation shows us that edges are lost and found. The acknowledgement of these points, built on drawing of sound construction, will make for good register and pave the way towards making your drawings and paintings capable of expressing an emotional response to the subject.

As a further exercise, make another still life around the theme of the garden, using charcoal and white chalk on tinted paper. My illustration (Fig 28) shows a collection of earthenware flower-pots, wooden seed-boxes, some geranium cuttings, a trowel and gardening gloves, all on a bench in the potting shed. The drawing was begun by doodling a series of small sketches to determine the best arrangement to capture the mood of gardening. In the final arrangement I felt that the window of the shed should form part of the design so that the outdoor ambience of the garden could be conveyed.

The next decision, related to the design and composition arrived at in preliminary sketches, was which colour of paper to use. I decided on a blue/grey Fabriano Ingres paper.

I was now ready to commence the drawing. As I wished to convey the mood of the garden, atmosphere was a very important component in the work. It required freedom of handling of the medium, making full use of the paper and its colour. I therefore felt that it would be a mistake to attempt a small drawing, and so decided on a full imperial-sized sheet of paper.

A great deal of thought and time went into the construction and placing of the individual parts of the subject. Visual scanning ensured that the measuring and relationships were fully understood. Fig 28a shows the drawing once this stage was completed. You will note that so far the charcoal has been handled very lightly and in a linear manner. At no time has any correction been made with an eraser. Should any adjustment be necessary, I find that, with the drawing being so pale, I can make corrections using the powder-puff. This preserves the surface of the paper and, ultimately, the quality of the charcoal marks.

FIG 27 *Figure against the light* (Charcoal, 28" x 18")

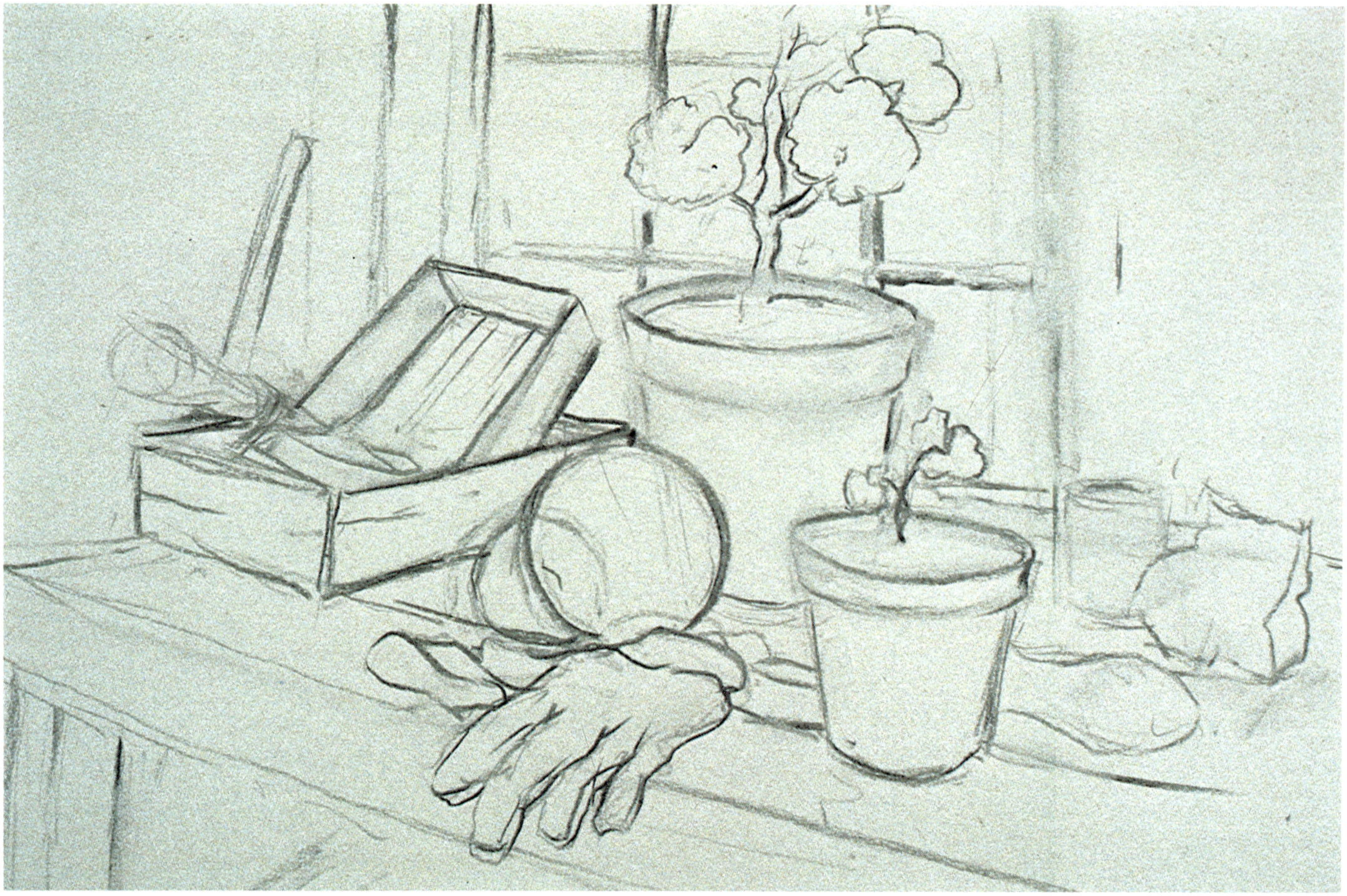

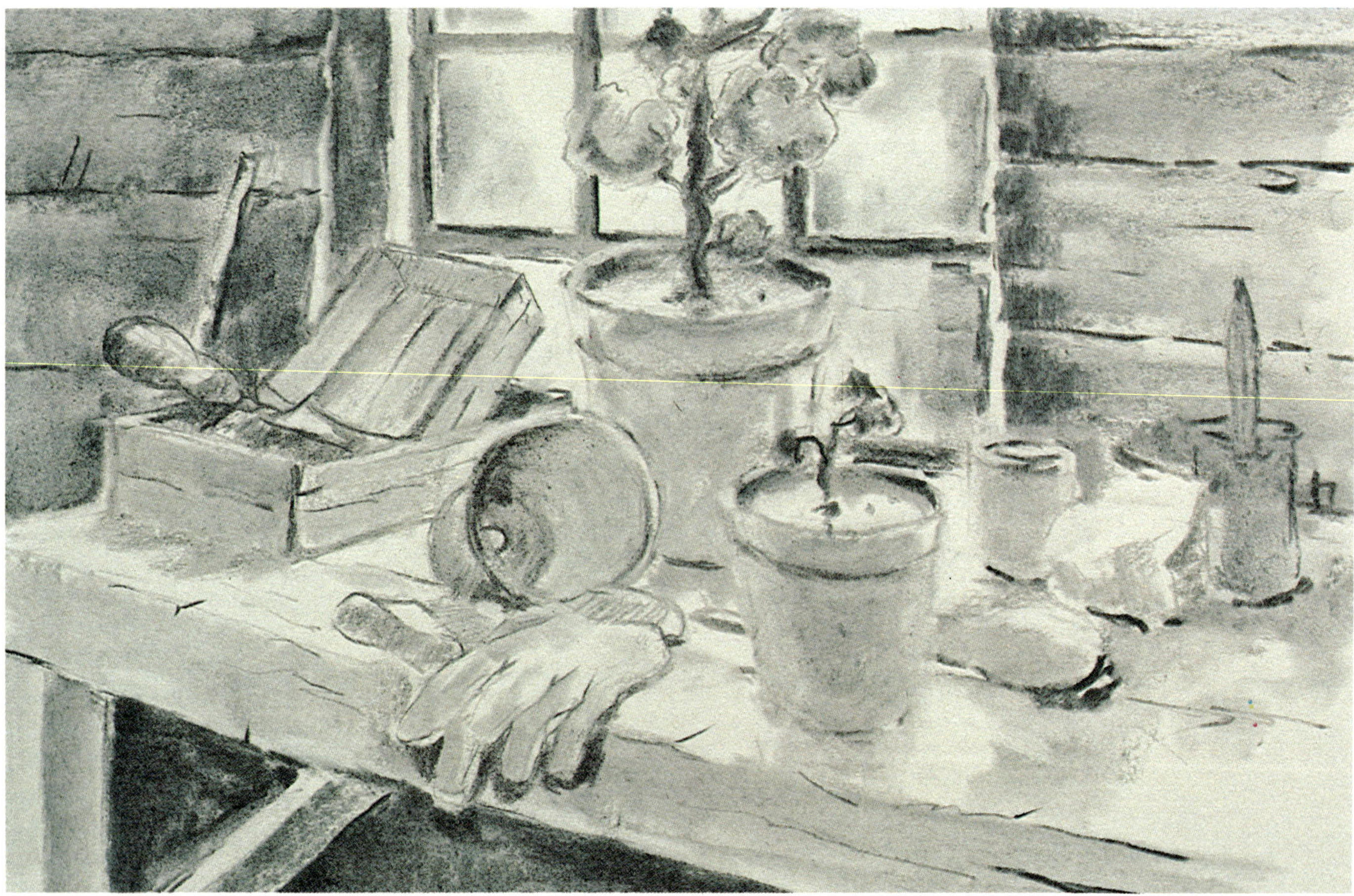

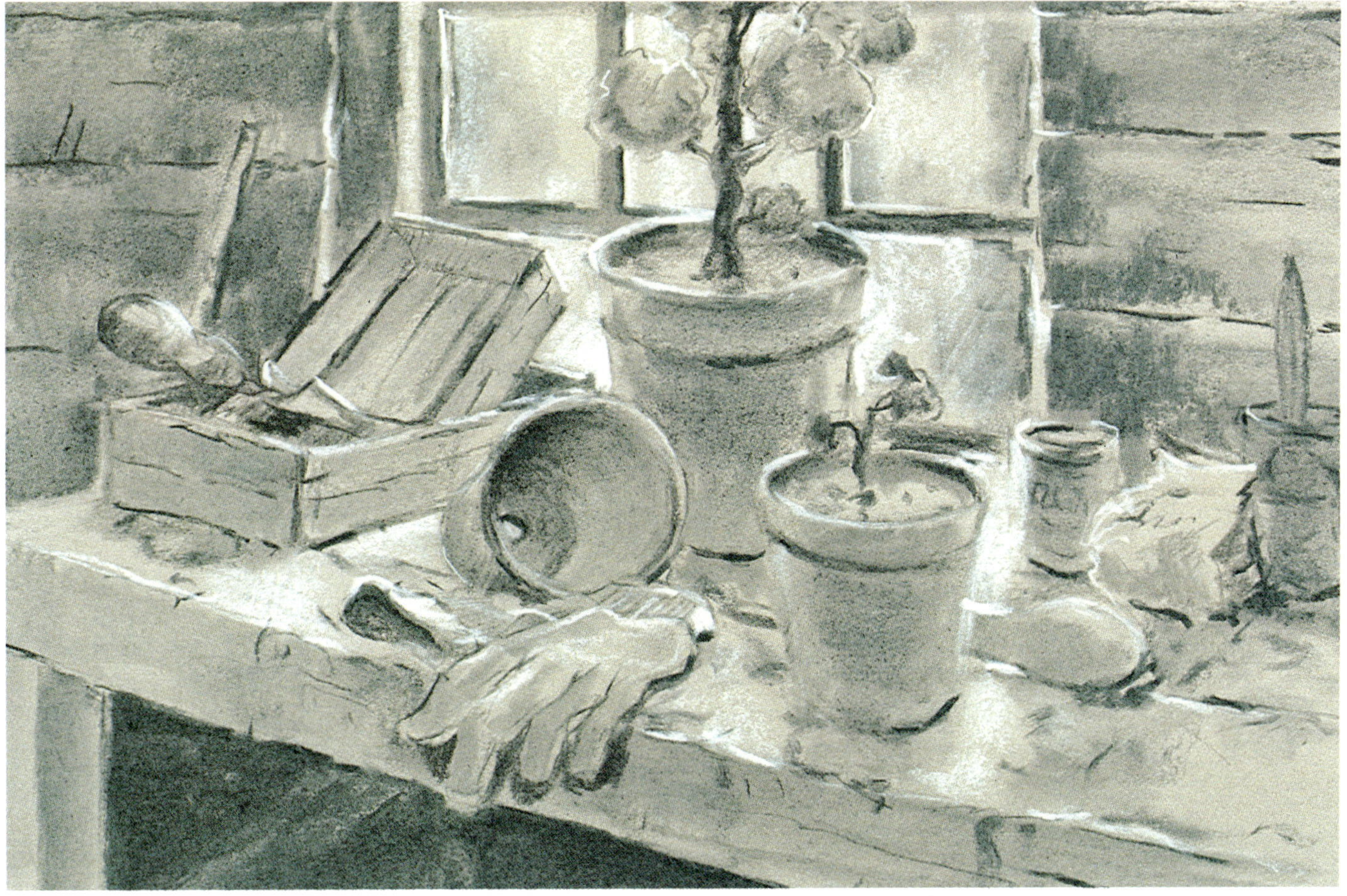

FIG 28a *The potting shed* (Charcoal, construction stage, 26" x 18")

FIG 28b *The potting shed*. Solidity and contrast stage

FIG 28c *The potting shed*. Completed

My next move was to establish the solidity of each component by blocking in the shadows. This included the shadow on the wall behind the bench, but care was taken not to interfere with the light through the window. This was emphasized by ensuring the density of the window bars was dark enough. At this stage the cast shadows were also indicated, bearing in mind that these can and should give information about the surface they are on as well as indicating and enhancing the volume of the object that makes them. Fig 28b shows the drawing at this point.

During the previous stage I had not consciously applied tone control. Although a certain amount of tone had crept into the drawing, it needed a much more conscious understanding of tone if a spatial content was to be developed within the work. The most valuable contribution that tone can make is the creation of space, not only through the picture but between the components of the subject. Tone also helps to give information about the textures of the materials of the subject. Although in this exercise I was working in monochrome, the idea of tone control applies as equally as when working in colour, which is why I have suggested that a good understanding of the achromatic scale is so valuable. Observation will show that objects nearest to you convey the greatest detail and contrast. As the eye travels through the subject, detail and contrast diminish: the darks are less dark and lights are less brilliant. When tone is applied to a landscape, where distances are greater, contrast can virtually disappear in the furthest points of a drawing or painting until all that remains is a cool, grey silhouette. It is this quality that needed to be introduced to the drawing of the *potting shed*. Tone plays an important role in focusing the eye of the spectator within the linear design. Here, I particularly wanted to focus attention on the arrangement of flower-pots and seed-boxes on the left-hand vertical third, and to balance this mass with the objects behind and to the right of the picture. After the drawing had reached this stage I felt it was somewhat bland and so, to bring some sparkle back to the work, I picked out the highlights with the putty rubber. As this developed, I found it necessary to increase the value of some crisp darks. All that now remained was to enhance the light through the window and allow some of that light to be picked up on the objects on the bench, which was done with careful use of white chalk. The drawing now needed to be protected, so a gentle spray of fixative was applied.

You will now see how important preliminary doodle sketches and construction drawings are in acquiring knowledge of the subject. I tend to think of these as 'enquiry drawings'. I cannot over-emphasize the importance of visual scanning. It must be applied to everything you draw and paint, as it is the best way to relate the shapes to each other in a pleasing manner within the format and design. Fig 29 shows the visual scanning lines I used for a drawing of the nude. You will see that the approach for this is identical to that for Fig 28a, the construction and scanning stage of the *Potting shed*. Note that scanning co-ordinates are not confined to the periphery of the subject; scanning embraces all measurement points both inside and outside the subject.

It may seem paradoxical to be told at one moment to observe and measure accurately, and at the next to be told not to copy nature. As you acquire more experience, it will become apparent that the more you know about your subject and the more accurate your observation is, the more sensitively you will be able to impose your reaction, interpretation and expression on your work. Distortion arising from lack of knowledge nearly always registers as a mistake, whilst distortion with intent will always have the right register. The approaches indicated so far will, with practice, enable you to tackle any subject with confidence. It is possible to apply these thoughts and methods to other media, modifying and adding to them where necessary.

These philosophies will allow us to explore a whole range of media, the first of which will be conté-crayon. I have chosen this because it is similar to charcoal in its handling and fluidity. Unlike charcoal, however, it comes in varying grades of softness, indicated in the same way as pencils, i.e B, 2B, 3B etc, and in a range of colours. For your purposes I think it is wise to limit the colours used to sanguine, bistre, black and white, although a good range of warm and cool greys available, and you may wish to try these a little later. Conté-crayon is available in either pencil or square stick form. Personally I prefer the stick form, as it can be used on its side for blocking in large areas, and I can shape the end of the stick to suit my drawing. Like charcoal, Conté can be used on virtually any paper that has a slight tooth. Among my favourites are cartridge paper, pastel papers and sugar paper. Certain

FIG 29 Visual scanning the figure (Pencil, 20" x 16")

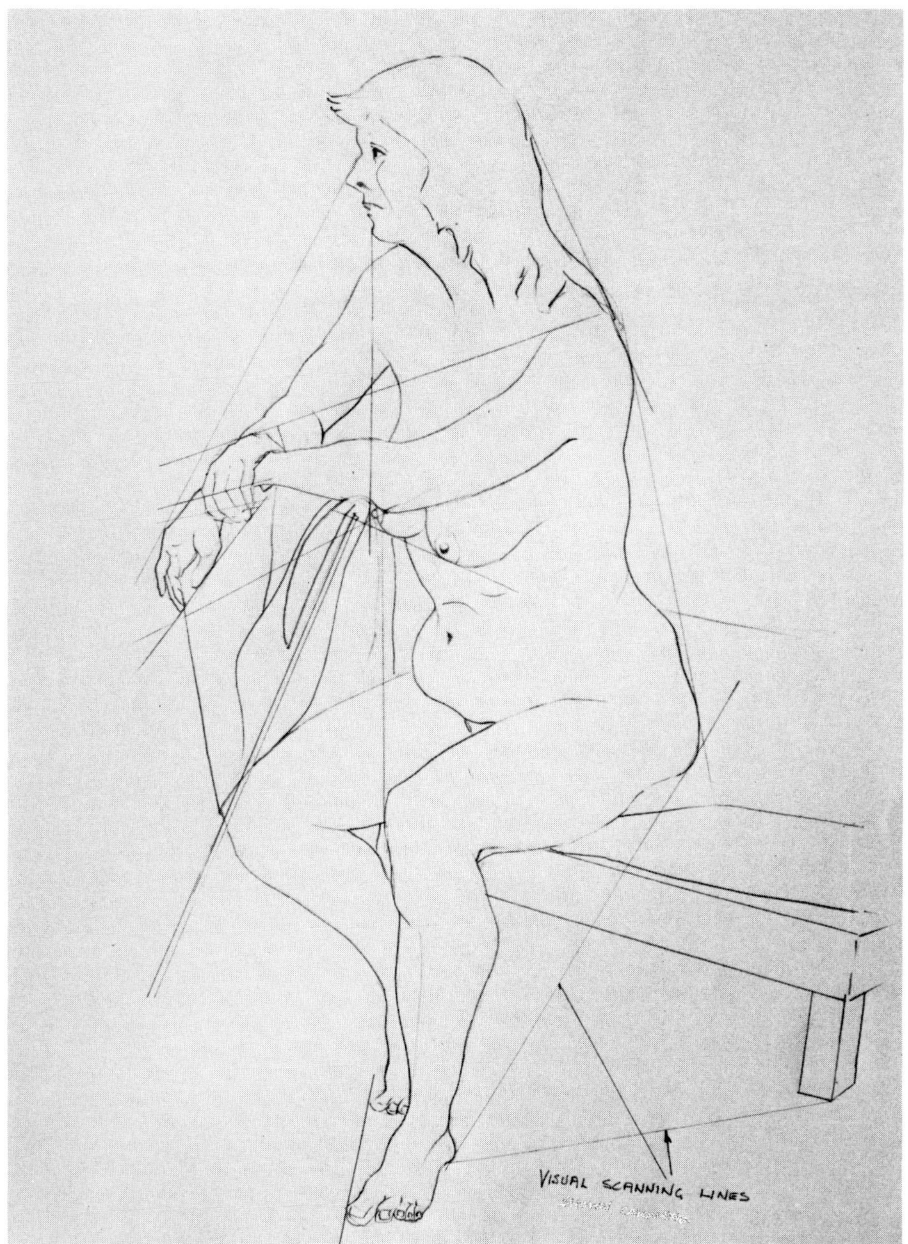

wrapping papers also provide an interesting surface to work on and, for the more advanced artist, the various water-colour papers offer a marvellous range of exciting textures.

The old masters made drawings in chalk, using the same colours that we have selected in conté. I recommend that you examine the chalk drawings of Leonardo, Michelangelo, Rembrandt, Degas, Toulouse-Lautrec and Cézanne, among others. You will see how they constructed their drawings and left the construction lines in the finished work. This invaluable evidence of their thought process strengthens us in our approach to the task.

Conté is not altogether sympathetic to erasing so, like the old masters, it is necessary to indicate your constructional drawing very lightly, as any attempt to remove conté is only partly successful, tending to change tone when an eraser is used.

Conté is an extremely sensitive medium. Because of this, I have always felt that it requires a sensitive method of handling, and so I tend to use it in a linear method. Whenever I think shading could be advantageous, I almost inevitably use a crosshatch method.

As with any medium, conté responds to touch in much the same way as pencil. Any drawing that does not have the quality of touch will, in all probability, be somewhat bland and insensitive. With quality of touch, much is intuitive, while some can be seen when looking at the subject: it is the ability to equate what we see in terms of what we are using. The strong dark on the underside of any object will need substantially more pressure on the drawing implement than the lost and diffused edge of a highlight, whatever the medium used.

Figs 30 and 31 show two entirely different subjects, each handled in a suitable manner. In the first, a landscape, the conté is handled in a broad fashion, the large tonal masses being applied with the side of the crayon. In the portrait, the entire drawing has been developed in a purely linear sense in order to bring out the sensitivity of the subject. Note how the line is sensitive and searching. The cross-hatching that has been used in very restricted, in keeping with the rest of the drawing.

FIG 30 *Landscape* (Conté crayon, 10" x 7")
FIG 31 *Portrait* (Conté crayon, 20" x 16")

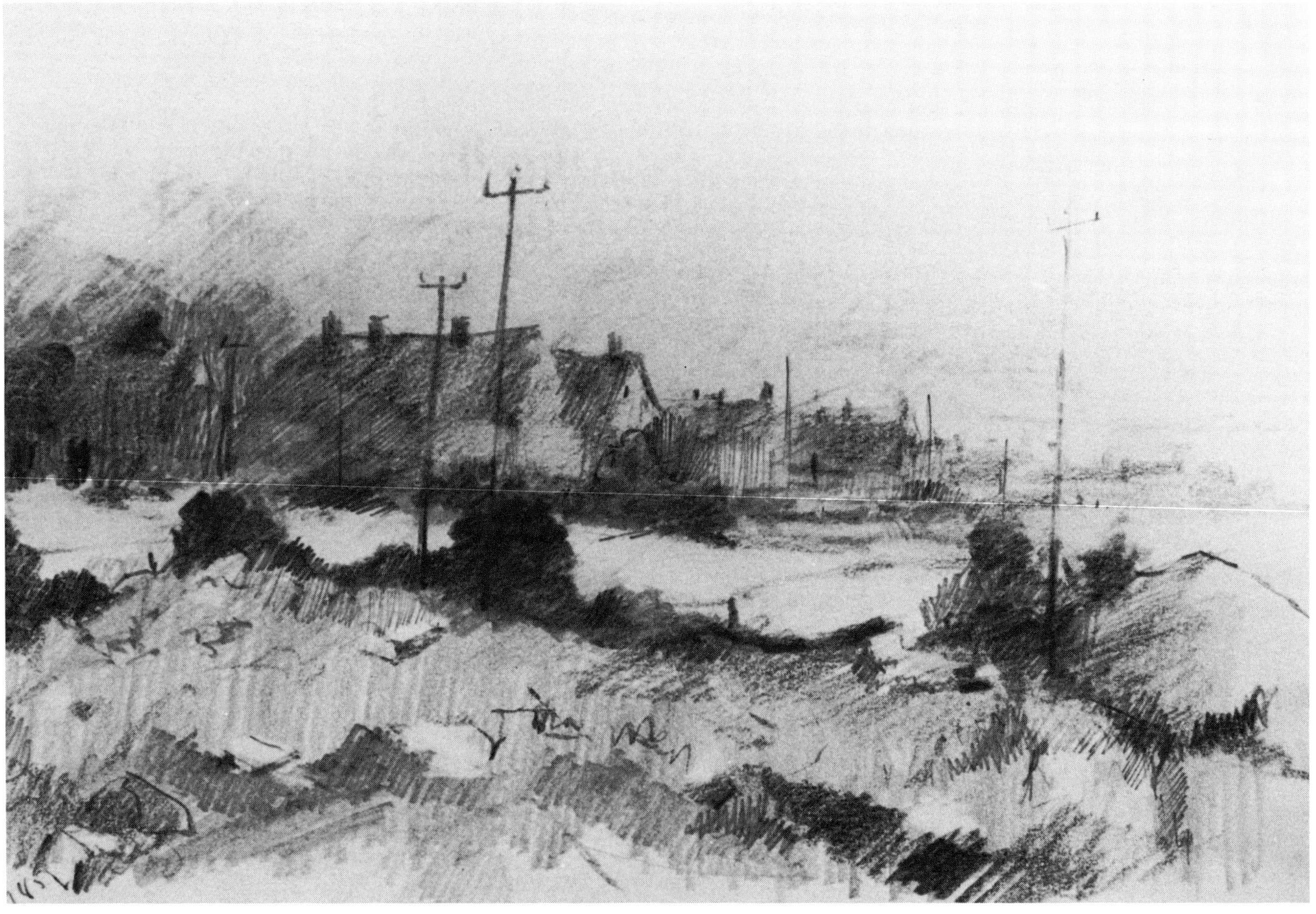

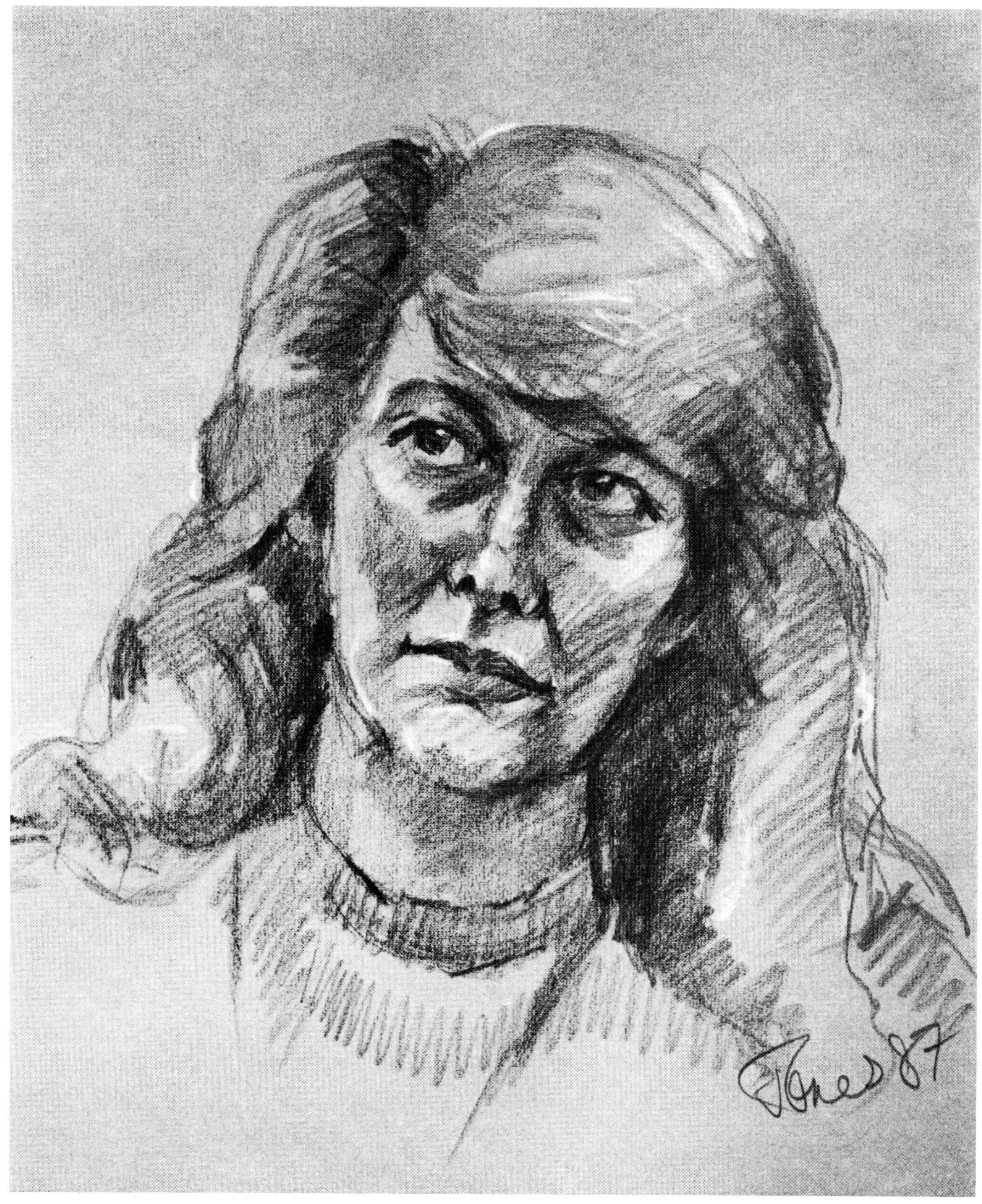

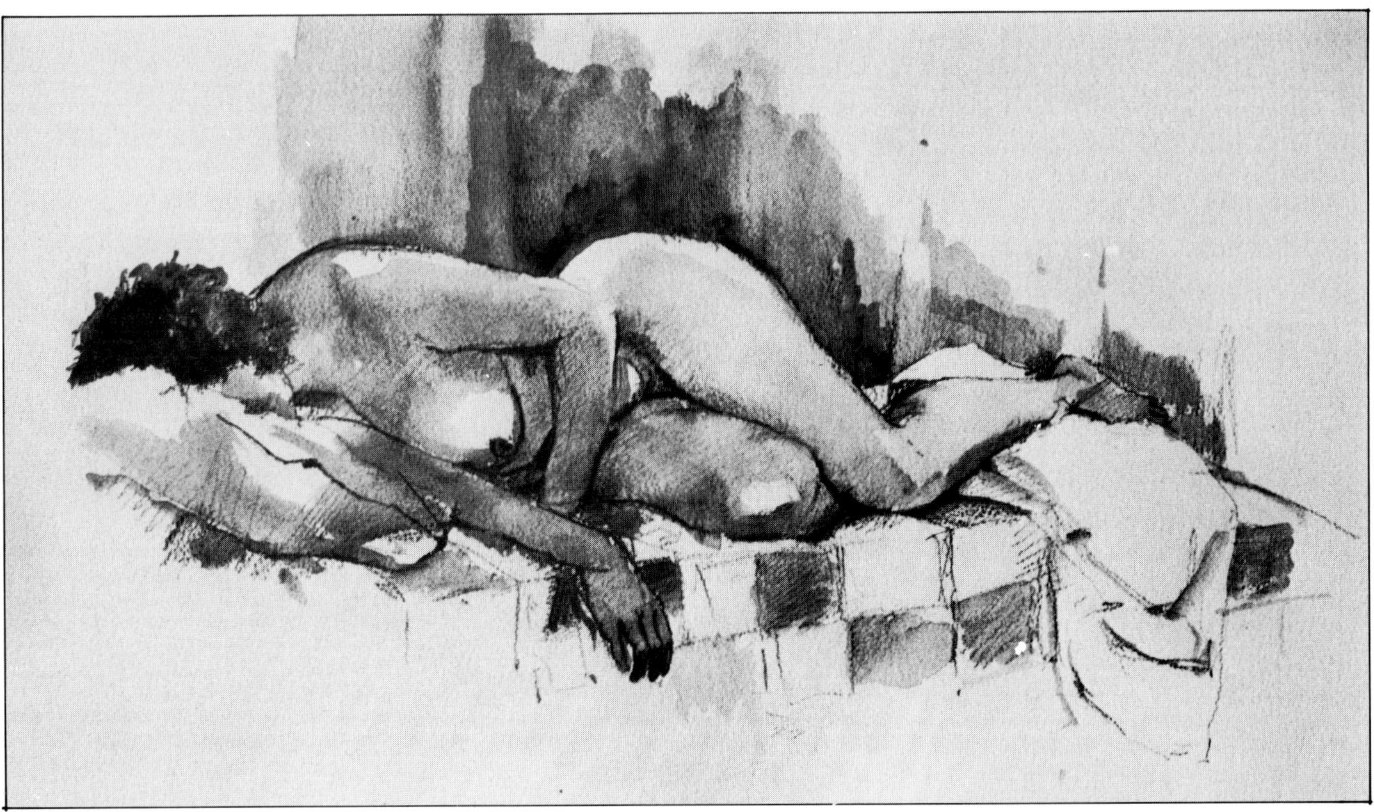

FIG 32 *Nude* (Conté and wash, 20" x 16")

It is not uncommon for conté-crayon drawings made on tinted paper to be heightened with white. I prefer to use white conté for this, although white chalk will suffice, providing the difference in texture is not important.

As with any drawing, it is necessary to protect and preserve the work. Conté, with its tendency to smudge, is like charcoal and so you need to use fixative. A word of caution: do not hold the spray too close to the work, or it may make the drawing run. Conté is very easy to move with any liquid and I have achieved an almost water-colour effect with a brush and water. I do not recommend trying this on pastel or cartridge paper, but some very interesting results can be achieved on water-colour paper. Fig 32 shows a conté wash drawing made in this way.

The next form we are going to explore is pen drawing. When we think of pen drawing we automatically think of ink. This is only one medium for pen drawing, however. There are many others with which you can develop your skills.

There are two types of ink: waterproof and non-waterproof. The type of mark that the ink will make depends on the nib used: personally, I prefer an ordinary Gillott drawing nib. Of course you are not confined to drawing with a nib; any object that can make a mark can be used with ink. Some of the things I use are: a cocktail stick, a matchstick, a ruling pen, a small brush and a goose quill, to name but a few. In fact, when I have been on a sketching trip and forgotten my pen, I have even used a stiff piece of grass or a twig. My favourite drawing tool in this medium, however, is a sketching fountain pen.

Unless I am going to apply a water-colour wash to the drawing, I always use non-waterproof ink, as I can then dilute the ink with water should I wish to make a brush drawing. Waterproof ink can also be diluted. Fig 33 shows a sketch drawn with the sketching fountain pen – a pen which is ideal for rapid drawing because of its constant ink flow. This small sketch was made very rapidly on one of my French painting

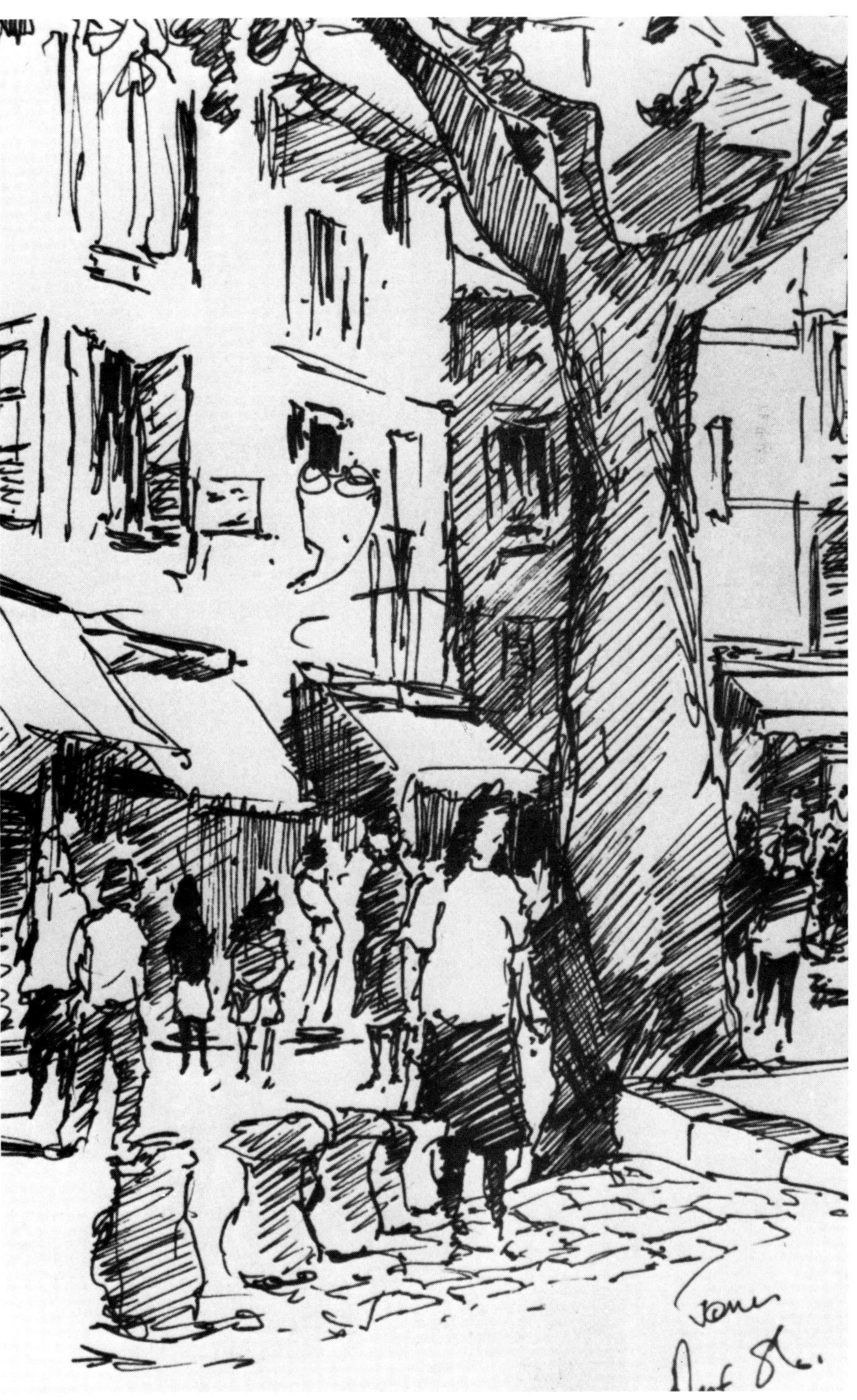

FIG 33 *Apt, Provence* (Ink, 10" x 7")

holidays. The next illustration (Fig 34) is a drawing of a stone quarry in the Purbeck hills in Dorset. For this I used rough-grained paper and applied the ink with both a cocktail stick and a matchstick to help convey the ruggedness of the landscape. In the next example, an interior with figures (Fig 35), I have used a No. 4 round Dalon watercolour brush for the entire drawing. The ink was diluted with distilled water, hence the tonal range of greys. This study, like so many of the others, was not begun until I was sure of my requirements. This meant making several pencil drawings. When I had finally clarified my thinking, the pencil was used lightly to position the drawing and to indicate the construction of the figures. I did not use any ink until I was happy with this. The ink was first applied in a linear manner, using the brush as a pen to establish the drawing. After the drawing had been loosely laid in, I applied washes of diluted ink where necessary, remembering to leave the white paper where highlights showed, and working from light to dark throughout the drawing.

You will see that working with ink can be a most exciting and rewarding experience. Because of its permanence, the medium does not allow for removal of any section; this alone makes us observe and draw accurately. Should a drawing need adjustment, there is no method of removing any offending passages. They have to be left and the correction or adjustment made without concern for the inaccurate statements. You will find that the corrected passage will not suffer because of this: on the contrary, the incorrect statement will often add to the drawing rather than detract from it.

Now you have been introduced to the basic drawing materials and the language of drawing, it is important to develop this understanding and apply it to shape. This means you have to learn to see: to train your eyes in much the same way that a musician's ear has to be trained to hear clearly. It is necessary to train the eye to see shape, volume, form, colour and tone, and then make the brain analyse this information clearly and simply enough to pass it to the hand and so to the paper. You need to understand that the eye, acting purely through light, sends a mechanical image to the brain. It is the brain that gives the power of selection and rejection of that information; it is therefore the brain that gives the ability to make decisions of emphasis and distortion. With the recognition of these facilities, it is possible to create on a perfectly flat, two-dimensional surface the illusion of the external world, which has three dimensions: height, width and depth. To translate what we see, we must use illusion to express depth and surface. Development of these skills is essential to the study of art and you will find that as time progresses you will learn to use your eyes more carefully and precisely than you ever thought possible. Through the development of this act of seeing the world will become a different place for you. Nature will become your constant companion; you will eventually look at everything with the discerning eye of the artist and you will find yourself mentally drawing and painting these visual experiences.

This will only occur when the understanding of the language of drawing and the act of seeing become second nature. Once this is

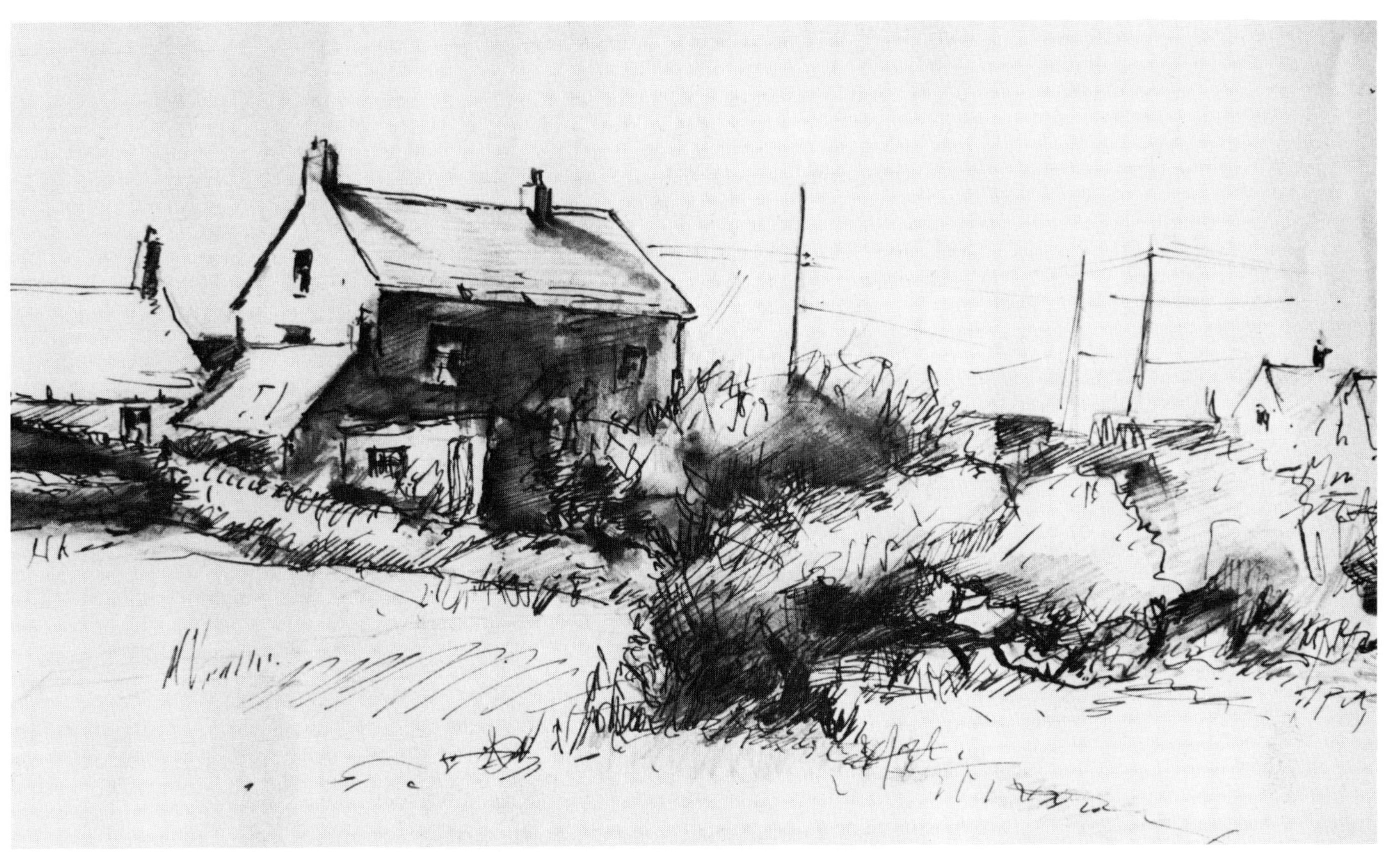

FIG 34 *Acton Quarry* (Ink, 10" x 7")

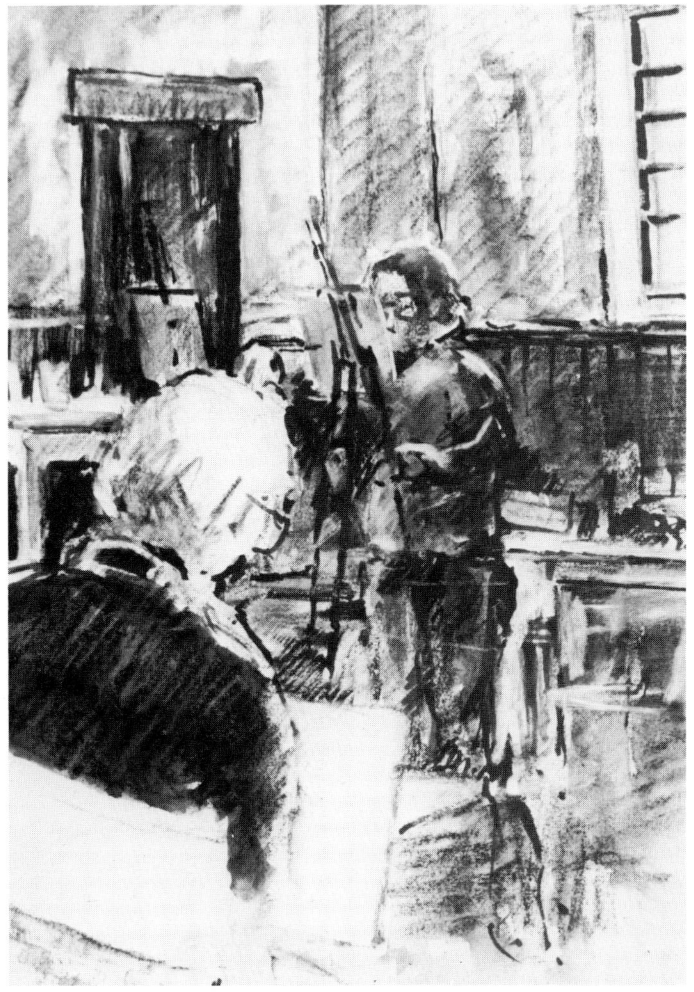

FIG 35 *Interior with figures* (Ink, 15" x 12")

achieved you will be able to concentrate all your attention on the subject and allow the methods and technique to come from the subconscious. After all, we only wish to draw and paint in order to express what we think and feel about the world around us.

The drawing process creates the need to develop a dialogue with ourselves. This is a two-part dialogue. The first part is questioning, and will in all probability go like this: what shape is that group of trees on that distant hill? What scale do they have to the foreground trees? Is the line through the shoulders tilted? In every case we have to question what our eyes tell us. All too often we draw what we think we know, and not what we see. Developing an internal dialogue helps to avoid falling into this trap. The second part of this dialogue is a critical one, and will apply after a drawing or painting has been made. This requires us to look at our work and question the correctness of the decisions that have been made. We will ask, is that leg correct in relation to the other, bearing in mind it is foreshortened? Does the position of that bush in the foreground contribute to the design and composition of the whole? Obviously the practical dialogue is the more desirable and should be developed and worked on all the time, but do not restrict it to the subject. Ask yourself, am I looking at the subject enough, or am I looking at the working surface too much?

With these questions constantly in mind, set yourself a subject: a pair of old gardening boots make a fascinating example. Start by looking at the contour shape, as in Fig 36. Continue with this; check that the contour shape you have drawn leaves interesting negative shapes.

FIG 36 Contour drawing of gardening boots (Pencil, 15" x 12")

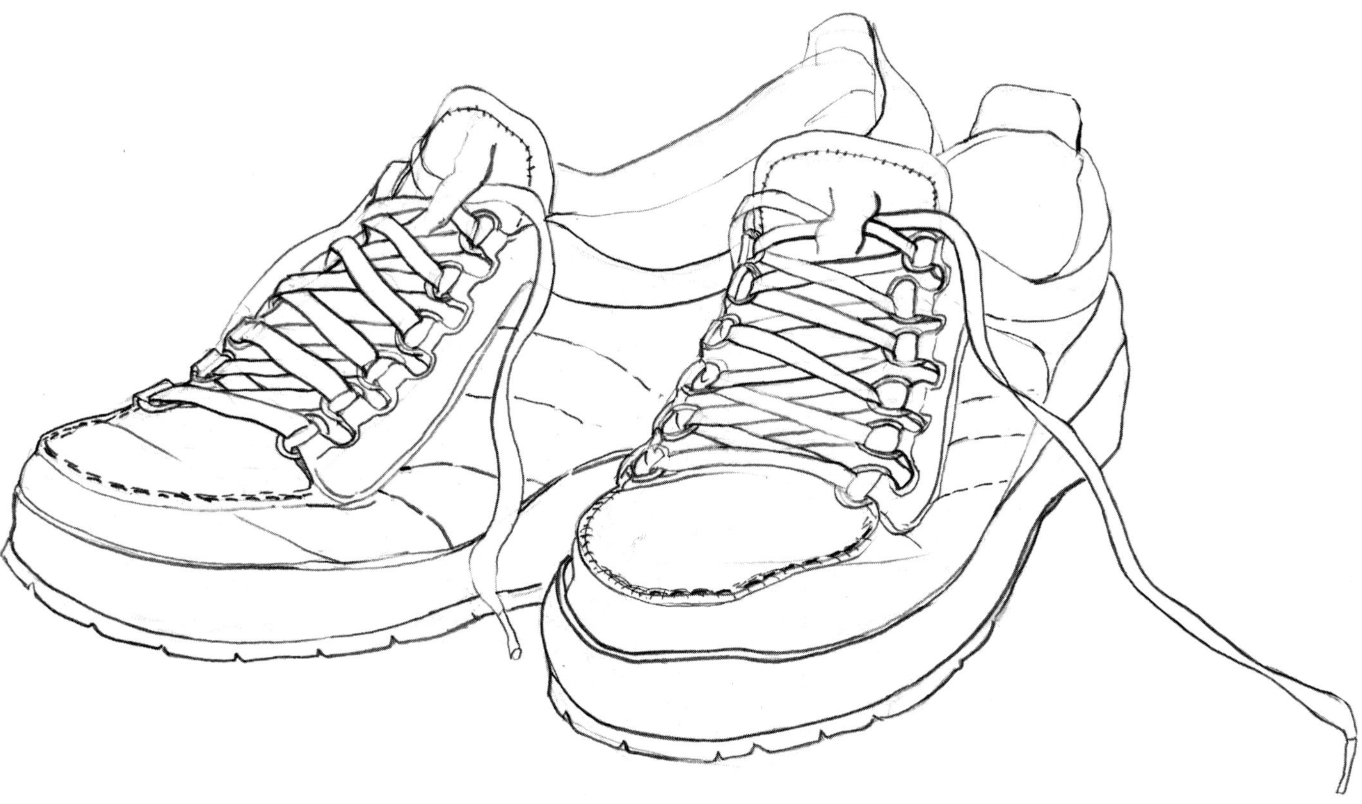

When you are satisfied, add detail to the drawing as required. During this exercise, try to make a contour drawing without looking at the paper – a word of warning here: it is important to keep the point of the pencil travelling at a constant speed, otherwise the results will be humorous, to say the least! This is a good exercise for ensuring that the subject is being constantly referred to and that you are not spending too much time looking at the paper. A good rule to remember is that you should spend more time looking at the subject than at the paper.

Before applying the language of drawing to more specific subject matter, it is necessary to have some understanding of design and composition. It is this aspect of the arts, coupled with the areas discussed so far, that will make your work pleasing and interesting to the spectator. Without composition and design, the message will be lost. It has always been said that the reason for producing the work must be apparent to the spectator. Composition, and the arrangement of the subject, makes this possible.

The positioning of the parts of the subject within the rectangle of the paper plays a crucial role in composition. It is necessary to know those areas of the working surface which can be used to achieve a pleasing arrangement. The old masters called these areas *golden sections*, and they were based on the Greek idea of the perfect parts of a line. From this, the perfect parts of a rectangle can be determined. In Fig 37 I have shown how this is arrived at on both horizontal and vertical formats. It becomes apparent that the golden section approximates to the rectangle being divided into thirds, as shown in Fig 38; generally speaking, this will meet most of your requirements.

Earlier, it was suggested that you doodle in order to understand the subject and to arrive at a pleasing arrangement. I suggest that your sheet of paper be squared in thirds, as shown in Fig 38. In the execution of the doodle sketches this will help to place the important parts of the subject in or near the important parts of the rectangle. You have now started to compose the work. During the course of the doodle it is now possible to try many alternative arrangements. I find that, having first drawn something fully as a doodle, it is helpful to apply a number of smaller rectangles of the same proportions as the anticipated final work and place these on different areas, as shown in Fig 39. This reduction of the scale can often give a design that is more in keeping with the reason for the work.

Whilst it is impossible to give an absolute formula, a good design will ensure that the empty shapes left by the subject matter will be as pleasing as the subject. Remember always to compose your picture around the large shapes: it is these that determine the overall design. This will assist you when deciding what to include and what to leave out. The selection/rejection process in picture-making is most important and makes a substantial contribution to design and composition.

The large areas of light and shade, balance and harmony are all part of the scheme of things and must be considered. In Fig 40 I have shown a typical doodle from my sketchbook, in which all these points have been considered.

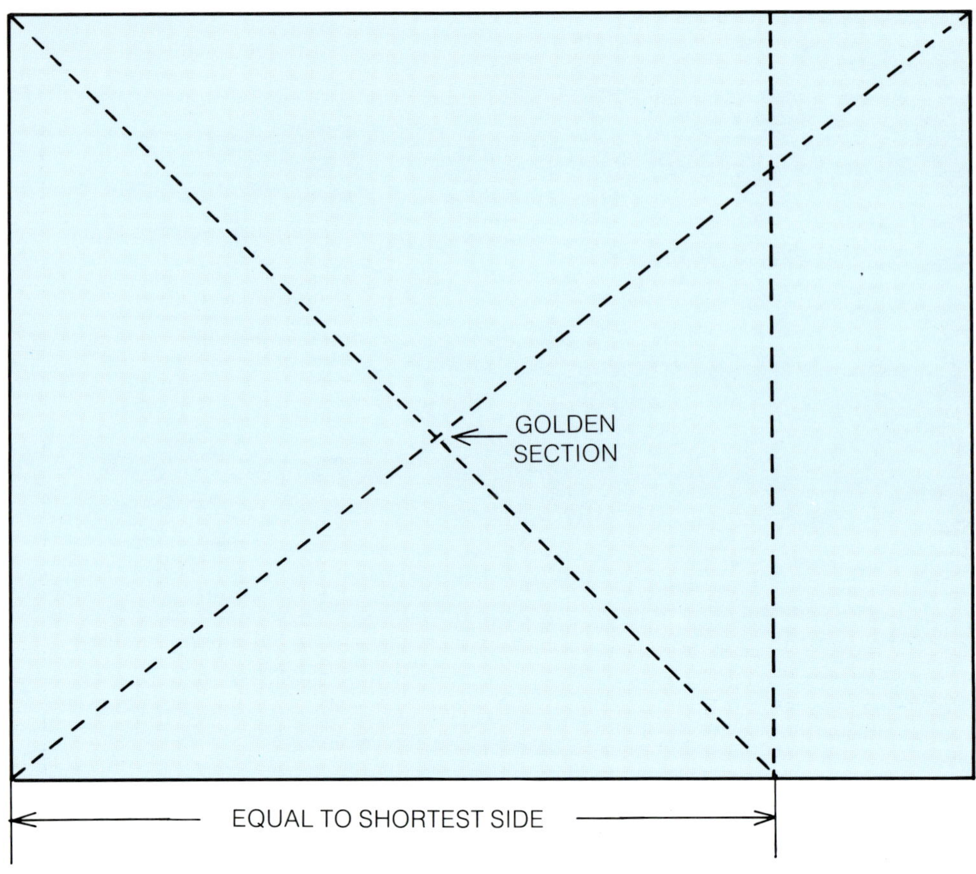

FIG 37 Golden Section

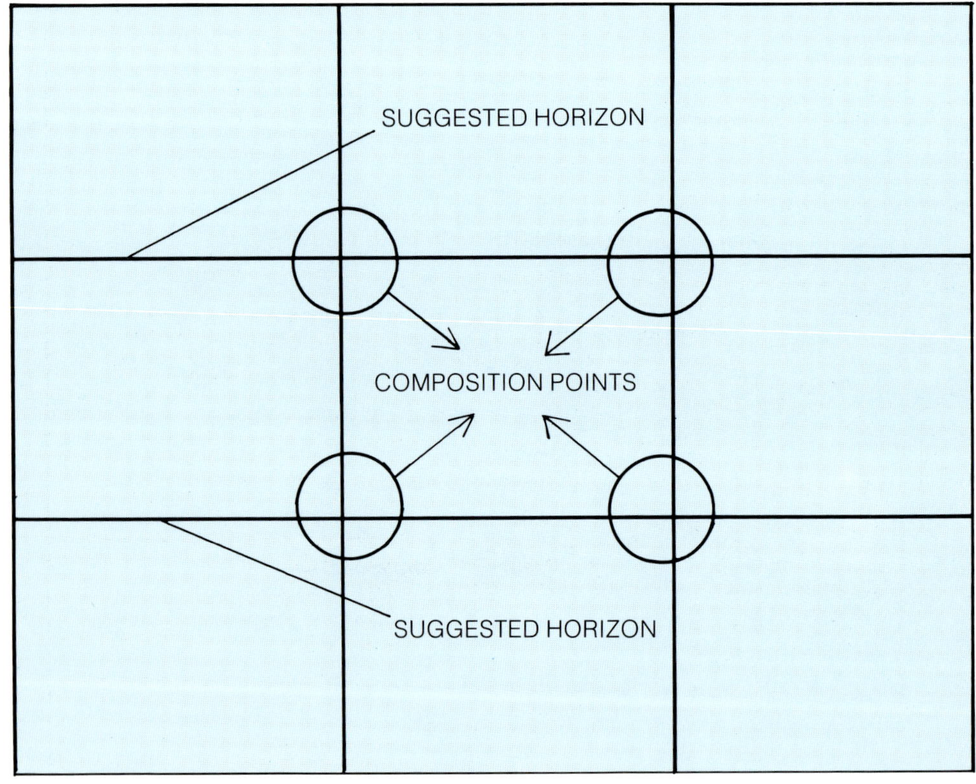

FIG 38 Composition grid of thirds

FIG 39a Doodle sketch showing
compositional rectangles
FIG 40 Doodle sketch of light and shade
(Pencil, 10" x 7")

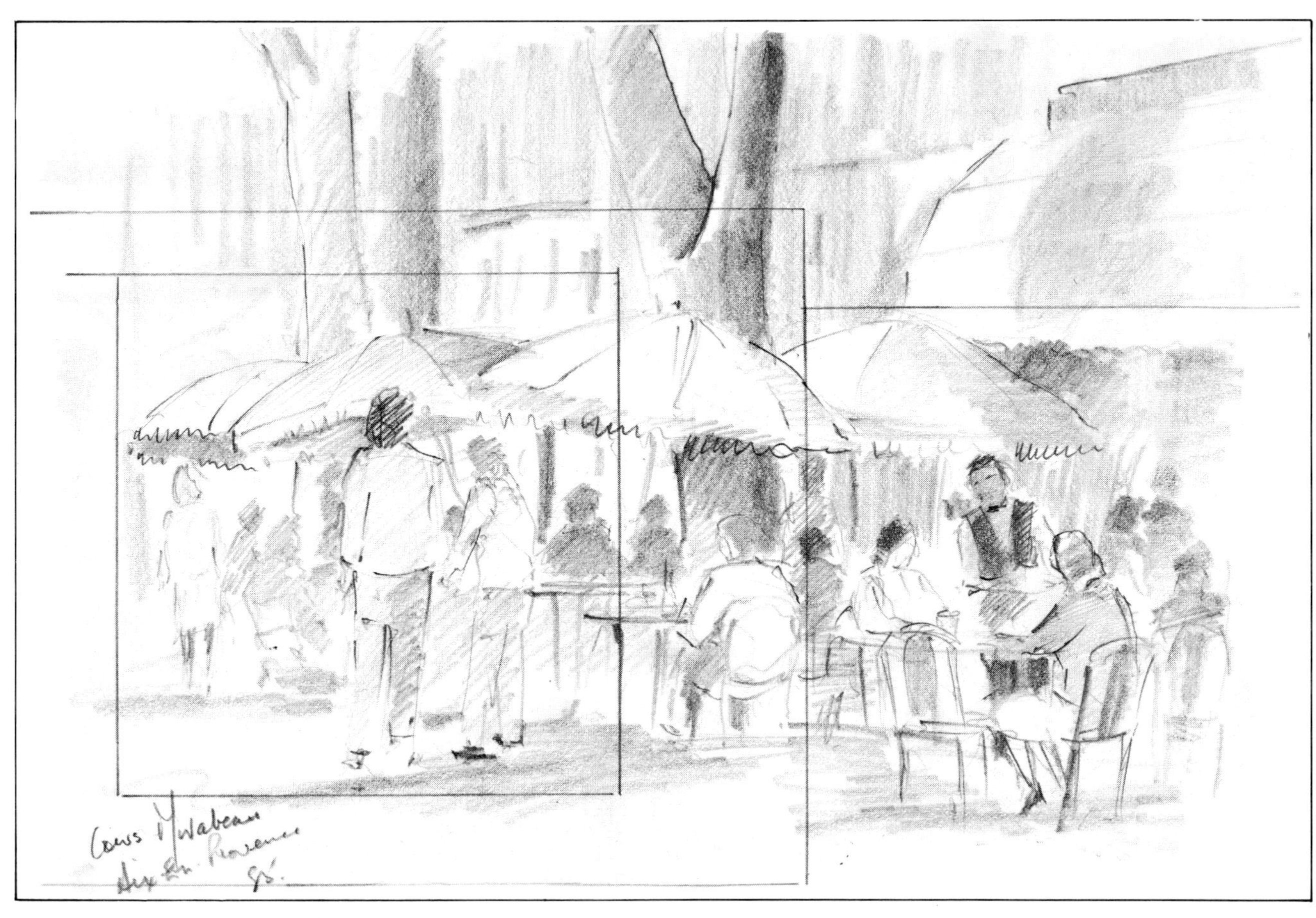

Cours Mirabeau
Aix en Provence
85.

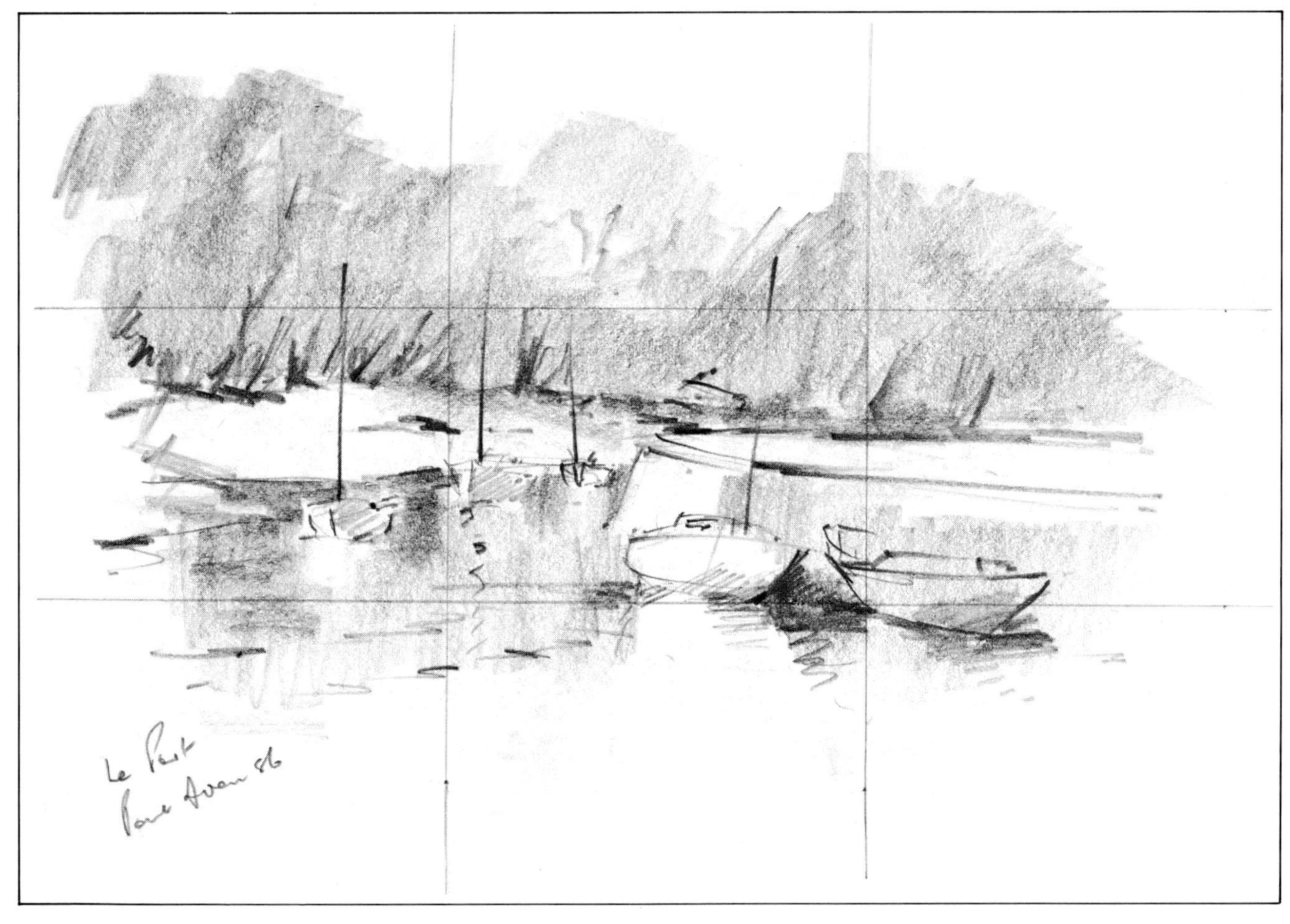

Le Port
Pont Aven 86

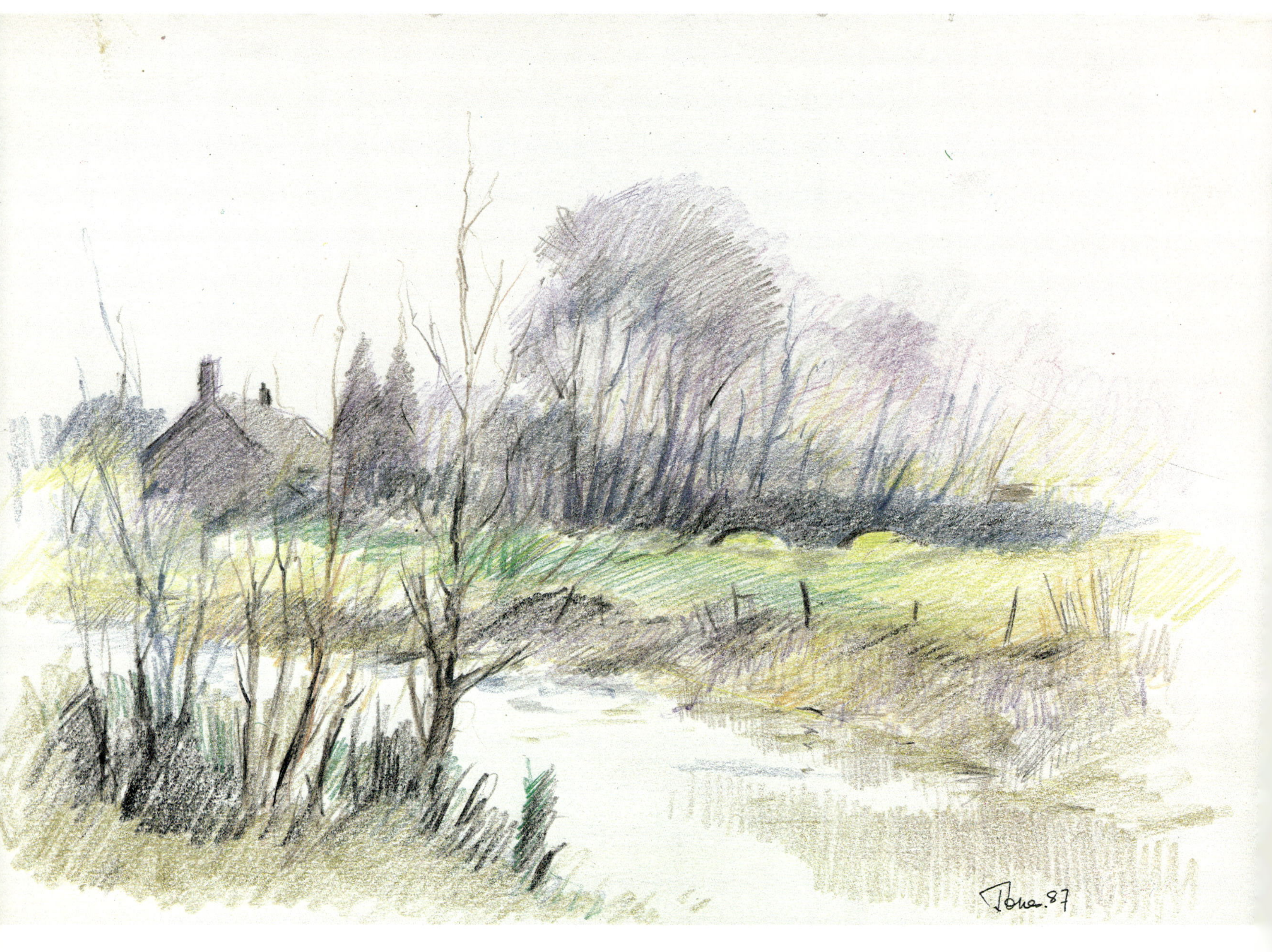

FIG 41 *The River Stour at Wimborne* (Pencil, 12" x 8")

Viewpoint and scale play an important part. The first of these is often forgotten. It is difficult to break away from conventional viewpoints, but when this is done the results can be most stimulating. Most of us will look at a different angle when using a camera viewfinder, so why not when drawing or painting? It may help to make a viewfinder: I use an empty transparency mount, which is always in my sketching bag. When I find a subject to my taste, I look at it through the viewfinder from above and below the horizon or eye-level, as well as from the eye-level.

Using the format in thirds can be of immense help in landscape drawing and painting. The horizontal thirds make a good guide for positioning the horizon and remove the risk of it being placed in the centre of the rectangle, which would divide the work into equal areas.

My water-colour, *The River Stour at Wimbourne* (Fig 41), shows the upper third used as a guide for a higher eye-level, in order to emphasise the river and not the sky. The main group of trees placed on or about the right-hand vertical third is balanced by the bridge and buildings on the left-hand side.

A further approach which I have found helpful is to silhouette all the main shapes of the subject against the lighter shapes of the surrounding spaces. This is of special value in preparing working drawings for landscapes, portraits and figure studies, as we are able to see the large abstract relationships, which must exist between all large areas if the composition is to have any impact.

I mentioned earlier the occasional need to reduce the area of vision to improve the design and, at the same time, to give dominance to that part of the work which was the reason for the exercise. With this in mind, it really does not matter if, in the achievement of the aim, parts of the work are cut by the frame or mount, as long as a simple thought is observed: if the eye is taken away from the picture, there must be a means of bringing it back.

It will be seen how important it is to have worked out mentally what needs to be done if the work is to have any chance of succeeding. It can be argued that such a philosophy can kill the creative instinct; this would certainly be so if it were applied only as suggested. This is not my intention: on the contrary, I am advising you to think of these points before and during the preparation of the preliminary drawings, but to work quickly and surely, so that spontaneity and immediacy can reflect your pleasure and emotional reaction to the visual stimulus. If you have any doubt at all that the composition is reflecting your aims, think of the subject as a stained-glass window design. You can do this by encompassing all the components of the work with a heavy dark line, so that each section appears to be defined with lead, as in a window. This allows you to see the overall design in much clearer terms.

So far we have considered the contribution of geometric shapes, linear shapes and contrast as a part of a two-dimensional arrangement. There is one further element to consider: that of tone. The use of tone in composition allows for design in the third dimension. It will be apparent that this is essential if the work is figurative. It therefore becomes necessary to involve the spaces that exist between components in the receding plane. This was touched upon earlier, and what was said then still applies, but with the added control given by the understanding of tone (that is, the enhancement of the spatial concept in the work). Recognition of this feature will not only help in the design of the composition, but will also make the volumetric content of the work play its part.

With this understanding of composition and design, coupled with the language of drawing, you will be able to apply these disciplines to all the drawing media discussed so far. In the next sections these will be applied to drawing a range of subjects and themes, many of which require specific knowledge before the introduction of the use of colour.

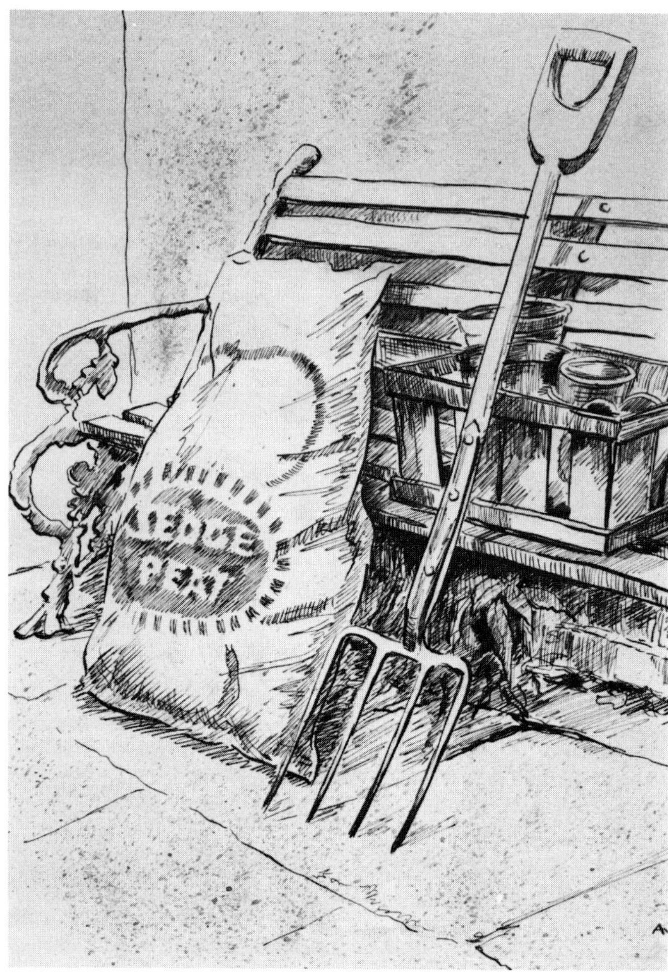

Ink drawing by Avril Darby (18" x 14")

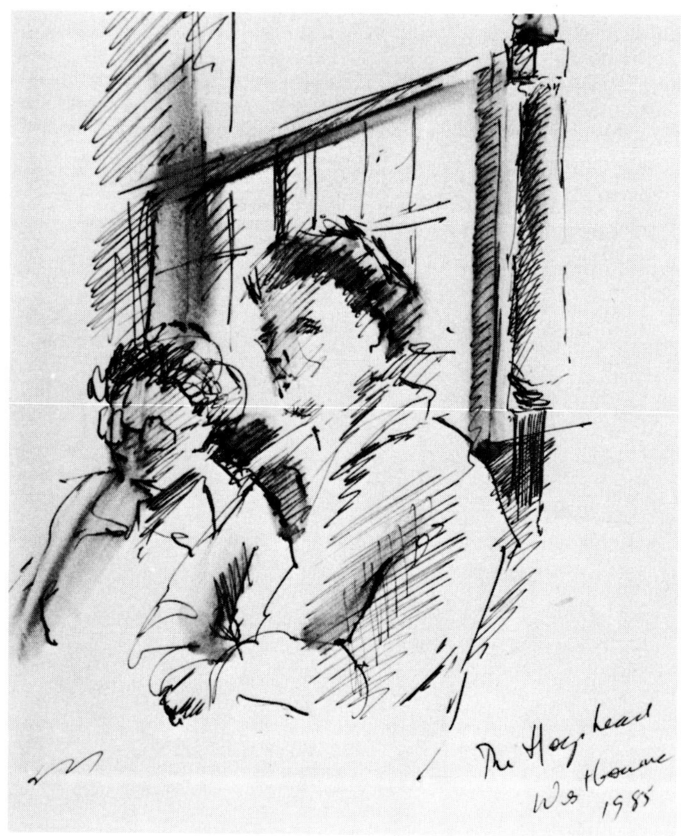

In the bar (Ink, 10" x 7")

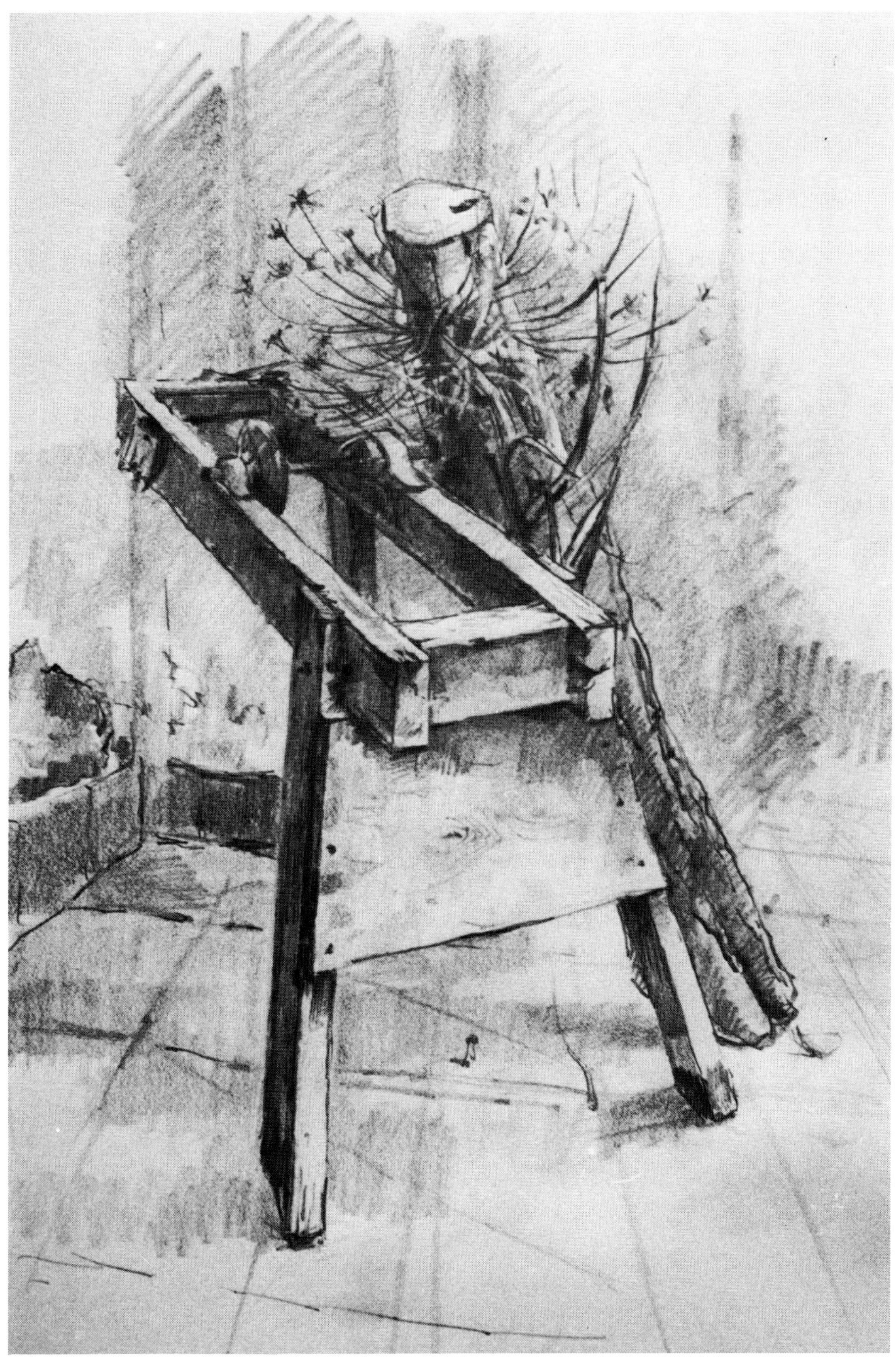

Unrelated wood (Pencil, 22" x 18")

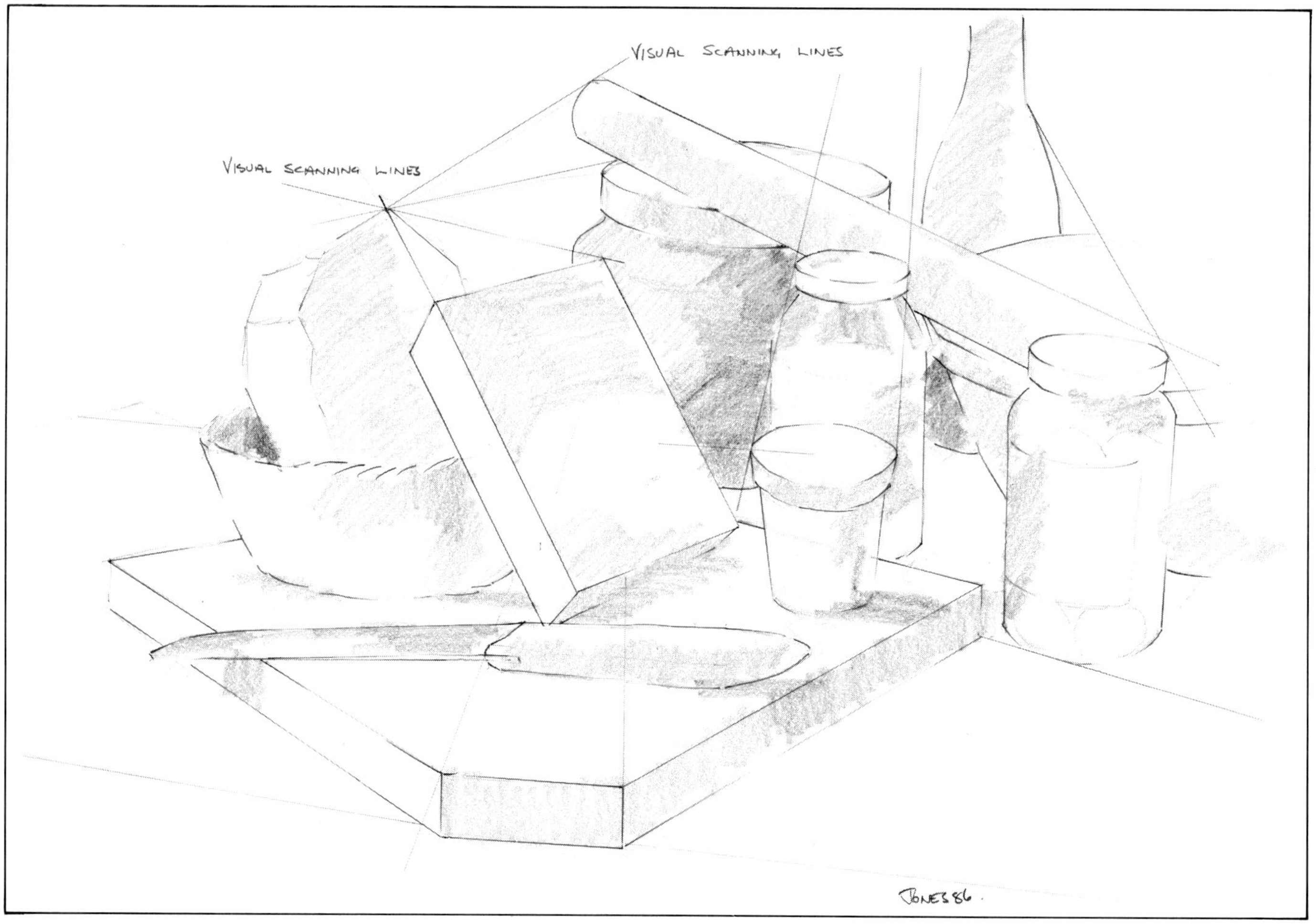

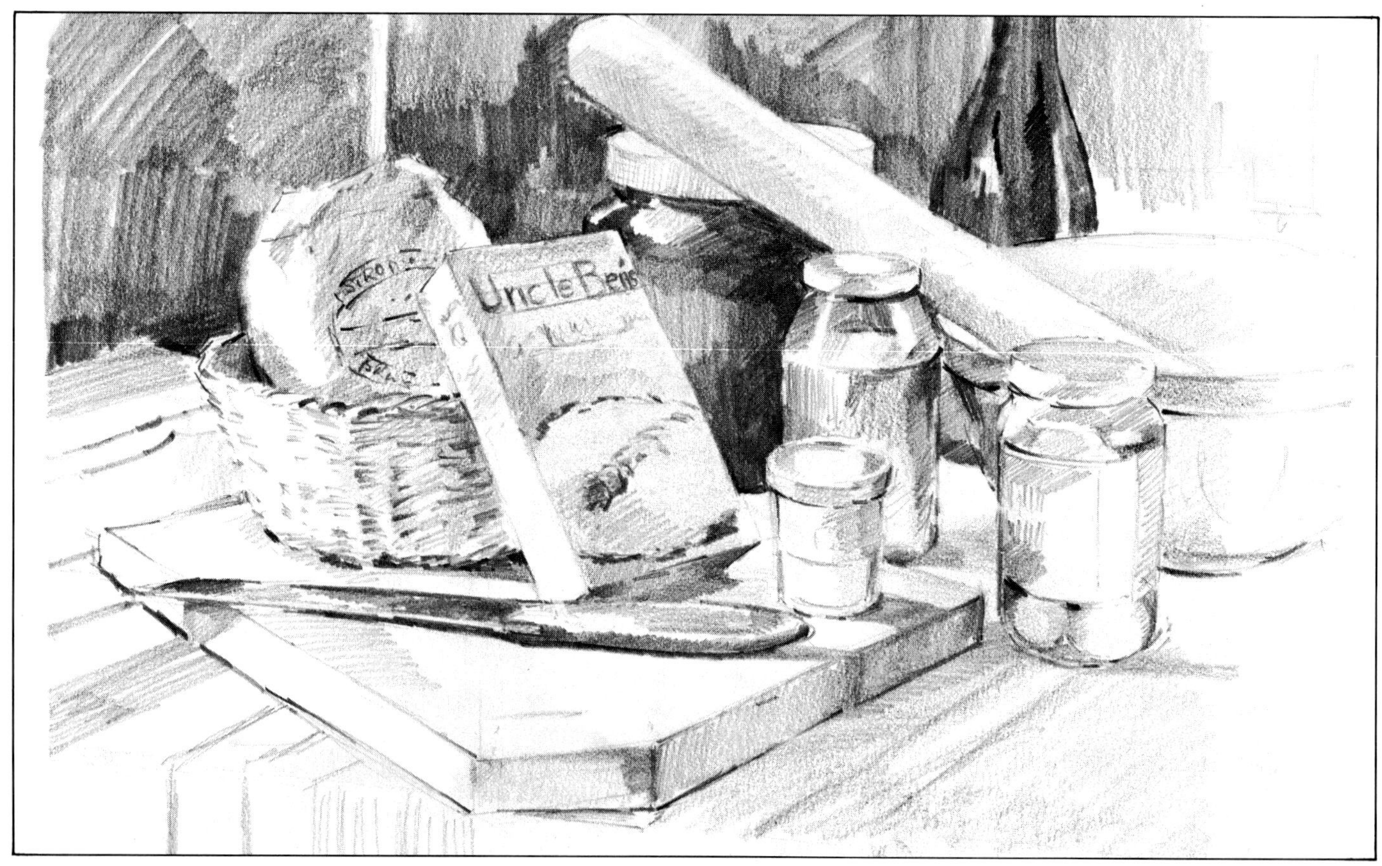
VISUAL SCANNING LINES
VISUAL SCANNING LINES
JONES 86.
Uncle Ben's

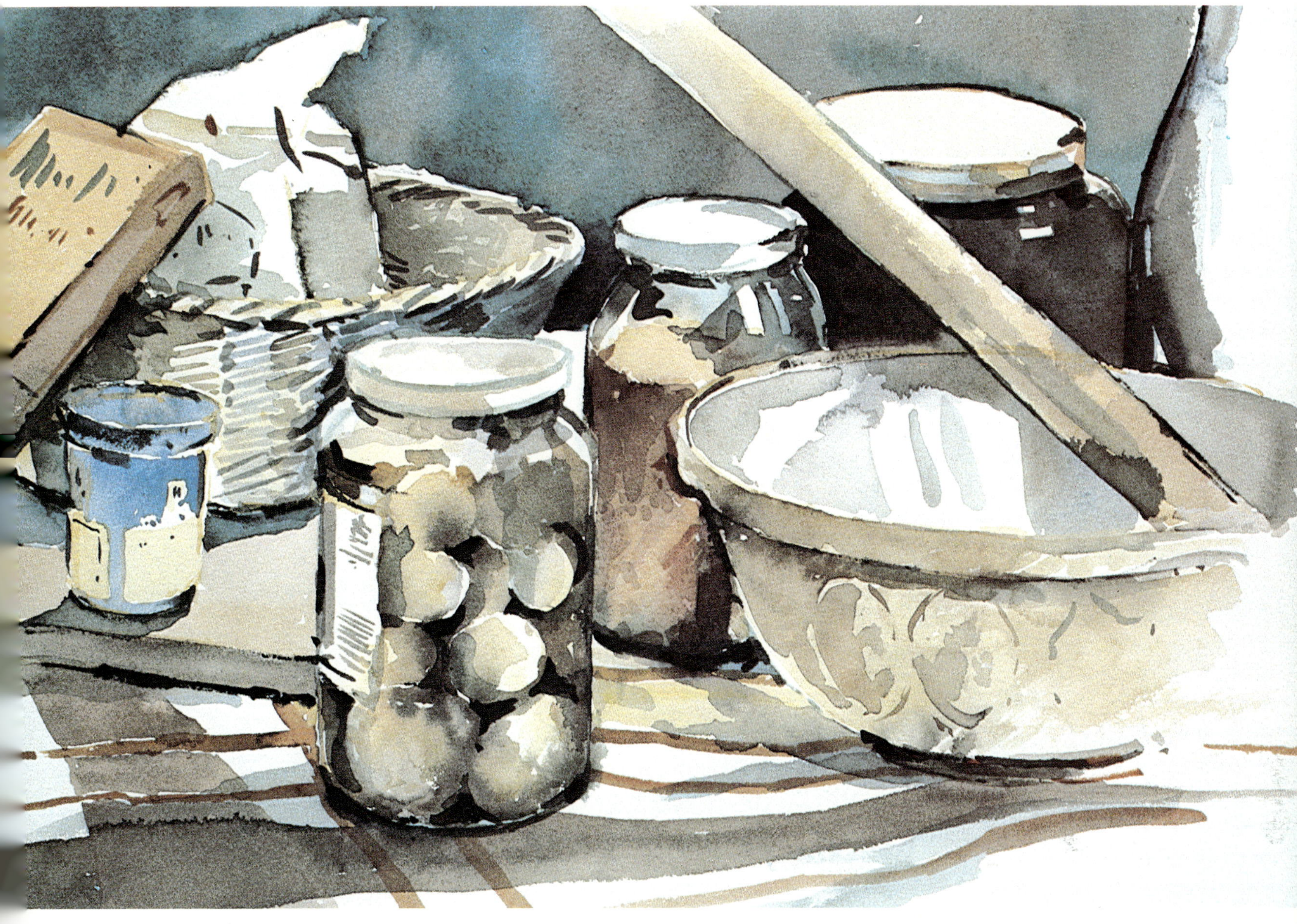

Kitchen still life composition and
scanning drawing (Pencil)

Water-colour of kitchen. Still life based
on above drawings (15" x 11")

Finished drawing (Pencil)

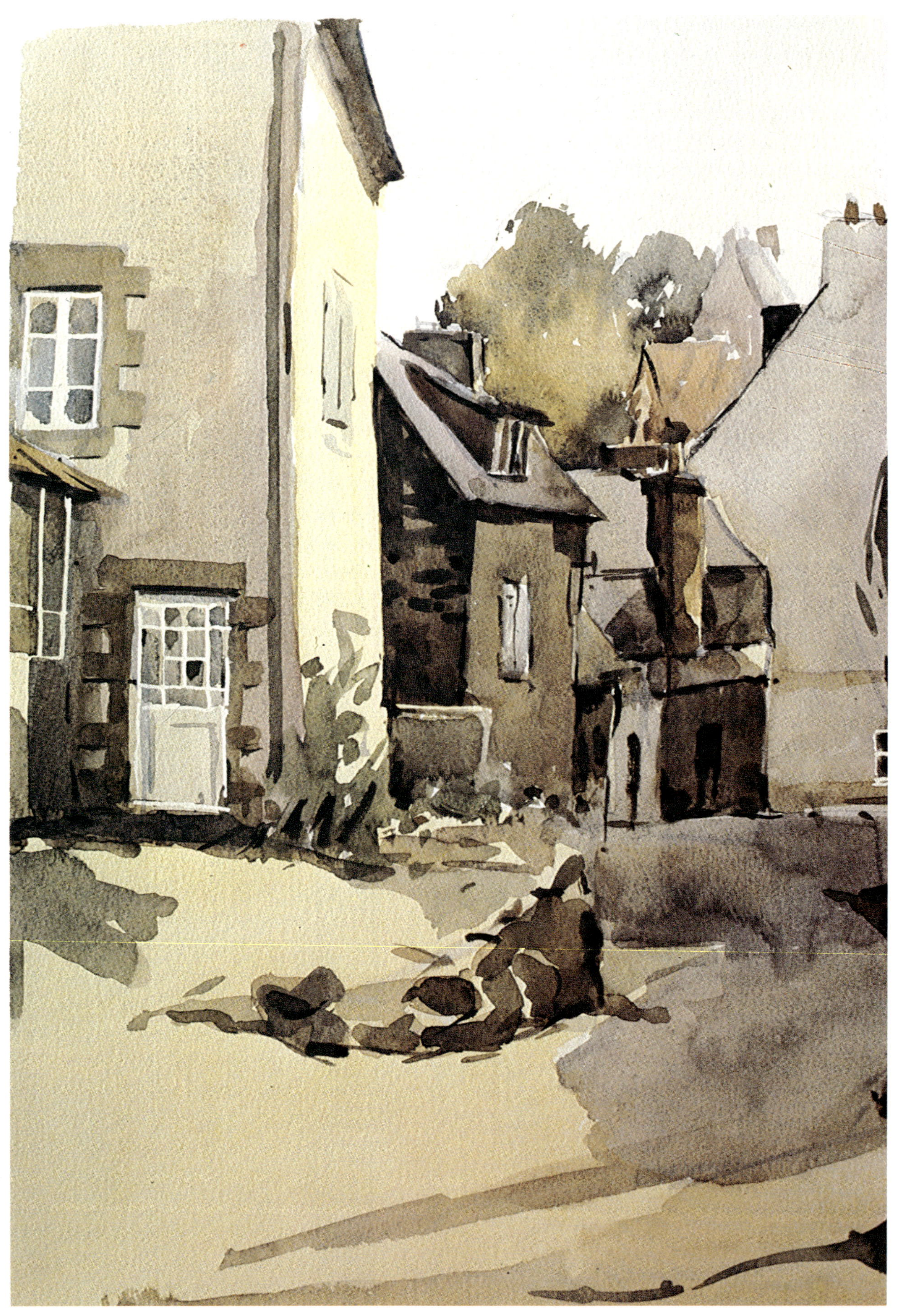

2. GENERAL SUBJECT MATTER

There are many approaches to the drawing and painting of still life. It may involve arrangements of related or unrelated components, which can in turn be treated in a figurative sense or, in the other extreme, as a total abstraction.

Many students seem to resist painting and drawing still life subjects. This is difficult to understand, as here is a subject that remains absolutely constant: it will not move, neither will the light change a great deal; and it can be left set up to work from over long periods, thus providing a facility for prolonged periods of study without distraction.

Still life subjects were a source of inspiration for many of the great masters, particularly Paul Cézanne, who not only made still life into a lifetime's study, but used the knowledge gained from it to broaden his handling and perception of many other fields of painting. It requires an ability to understand and interpret texture regardless of medium and use of knowledge to the advantage of the subject. This will prove invaluable when you come to paint or draw any subject.

This section deals with the problems of drawing in a variety of media. In this context, I advocate letting the subject determine which media are used. The range of subject matter is infinite: still life is not necessarily confined to an arrangement set up in the studio; there are many arrangements to be found, for example, in the garden, the tool-shed, the greenhouse and in the countryside. Indeed, many years ago I remember exhibiting a painting of the sunlight on a galvanised dustbin against an old brick wall. It is because of this variety of content and location that still life becomes such an excellent area of study. For our first exercise let us take a very simple and yet homely subject: *A brown teapot* (Fig 42). In this drawing the subject has been set against the light and although the teapot is the focal point of the subject, it is the light which is the dominating factor. For the example I used pencil and, during the course of the drawing, it became apparent that the construction of the table and chair with the teapot was important if the diffusion of light was to have any meaning in the final work. An understanding of the construction of the components is essential, whatever medium is used. In Fig 43 the same subject has been drawn with charcoal. The fluidity of charcoal meant that it was easy to gloss over the need to construct the drawing: beware of this, as it will be obvious in the finished work.

Pont-Aven (Mixed media, 15" x 11")

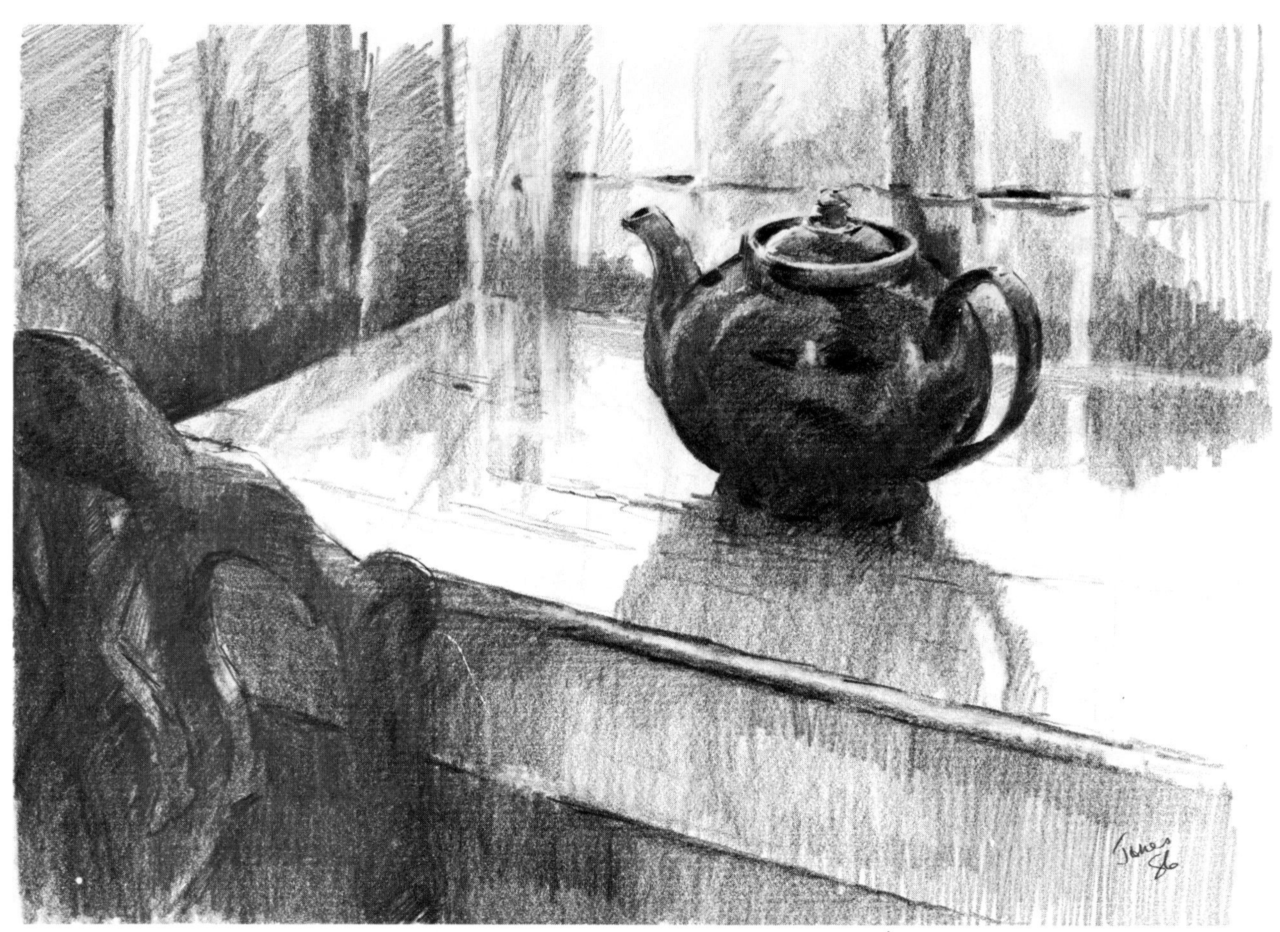

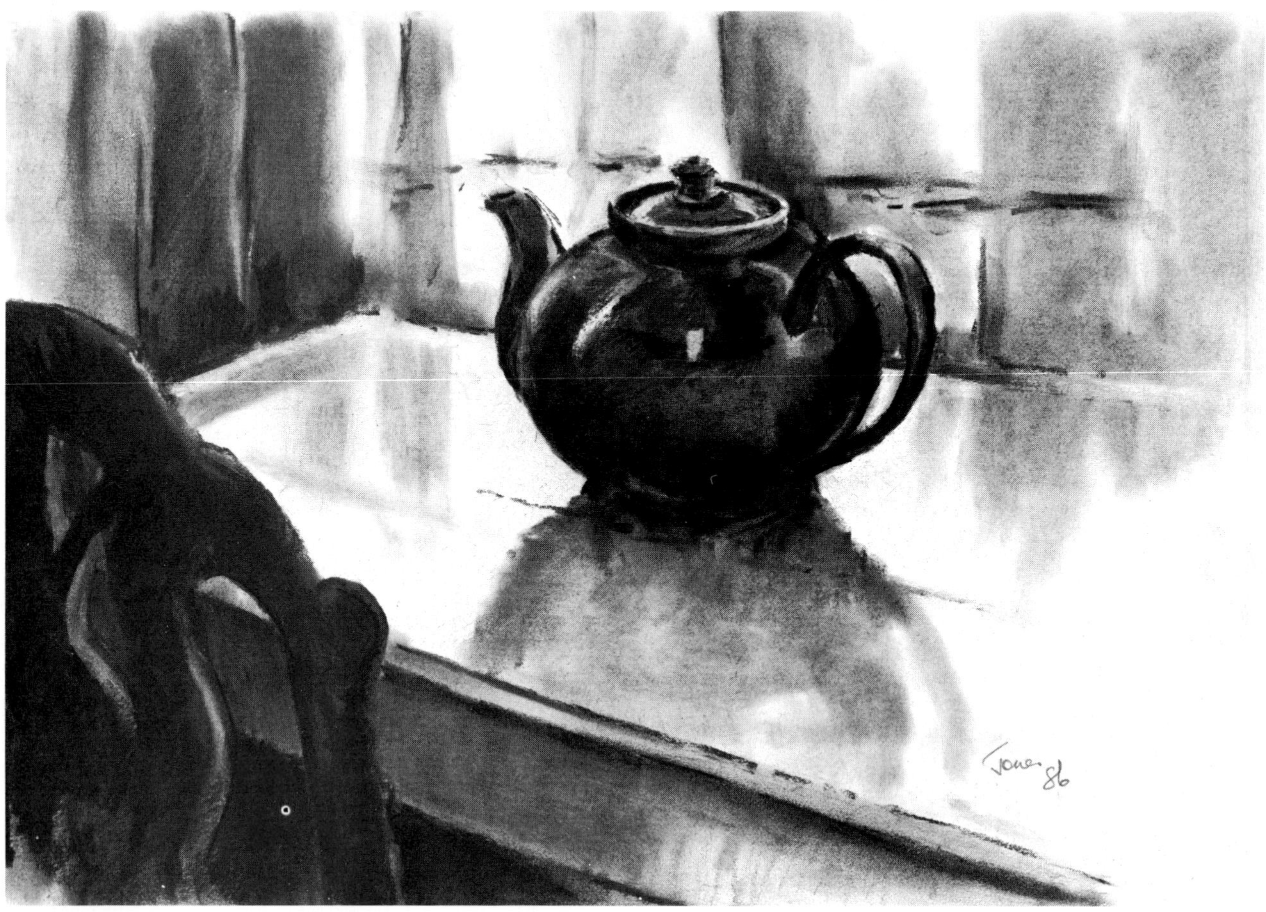

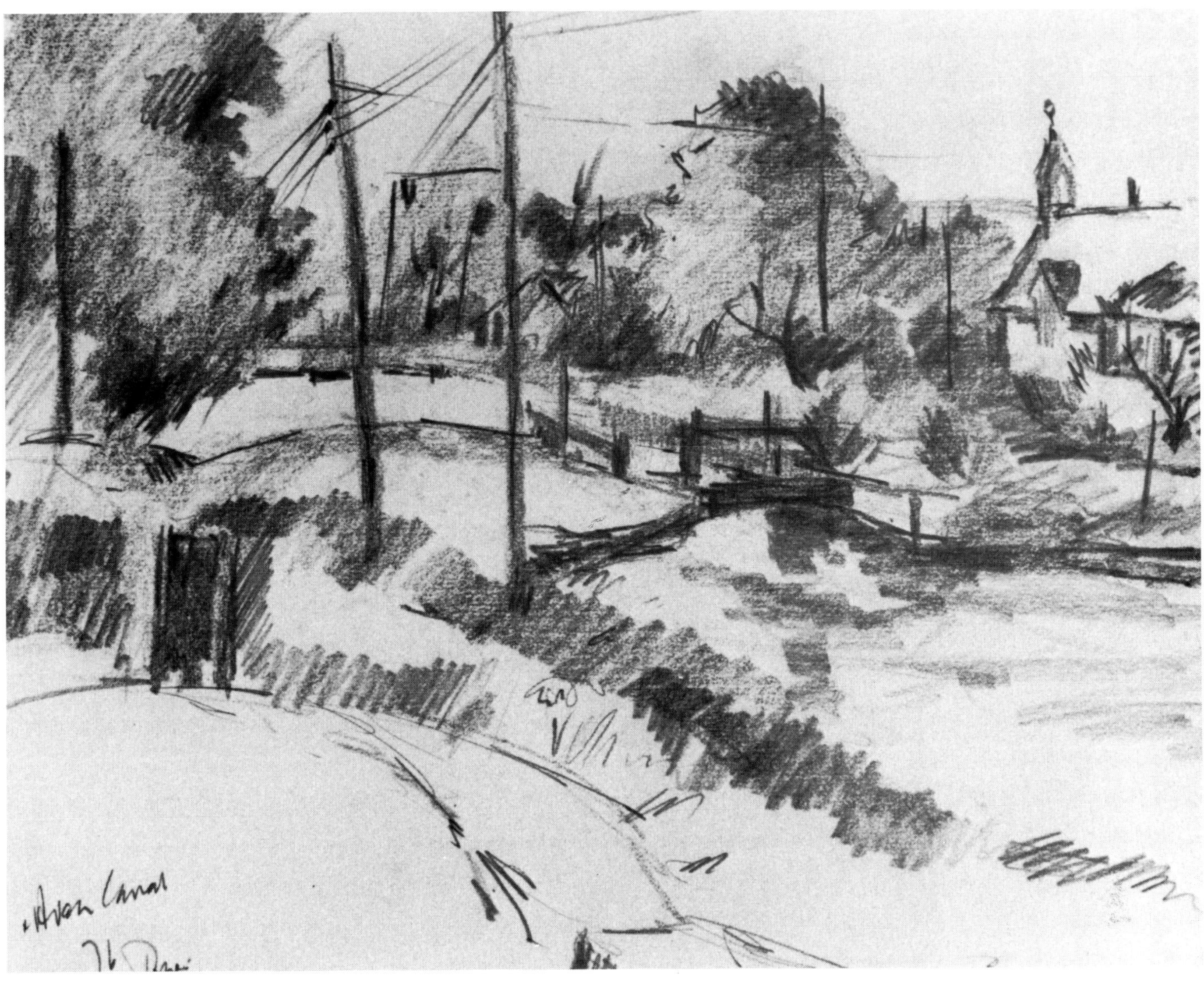

FIG 42 *The brown tea-pot* (Pencil, 15" x 12")

FIG 43 *The brown tea-pot* (Charcoal, 15" x 12")

FIG 44 *Tone study* (Pencil 10" x 7")

You will see that in the two different studies the texture appears consistent. The highlights on the teapot are made to work by their relationship with the extreme darks. You will also see that the medium has mainly been used vertically. It is this, together with an accurate observation of the relationships of contrast, that conveys the illusion of a glazed surface. Each drawing is of course different: much of this is because of the different media used, which gives support to the idea that the subject should be the final arbiter in the choice of medium.

Where the subject is more complex, involving a large number of items, other factors must be considered. Whilst it is always a major consideration, here the design needs to be paid much greater attention. The spaces between the various parts appear as valuable as the objects that made them. In Fig 45, a drawing called *Bric-à-brac*, the complexity of the subject meant that a number of preliminary sketches had to be made before I was able to decide on an arrangement that I felt did justice to the relationships between the various components. Producing

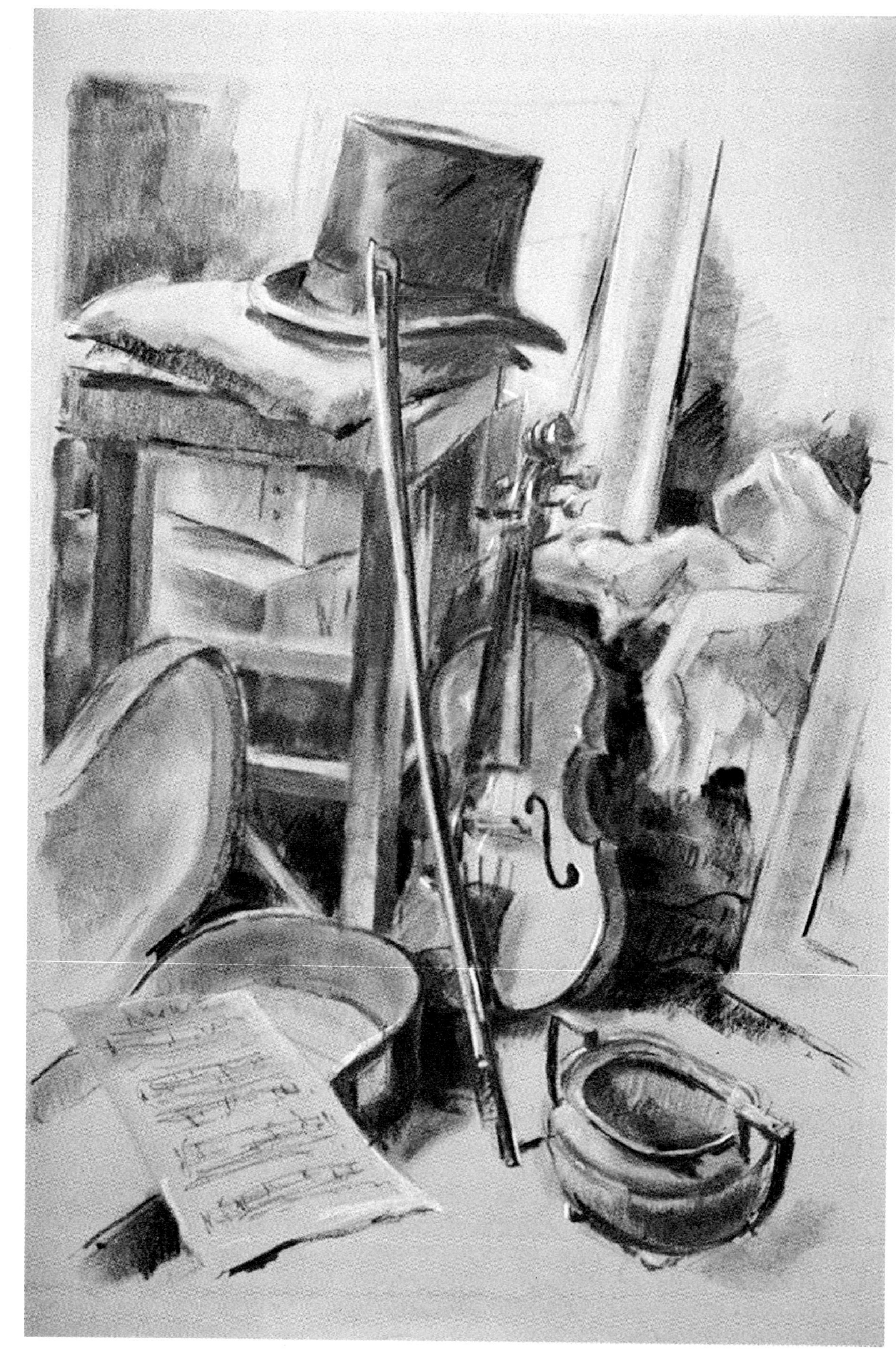

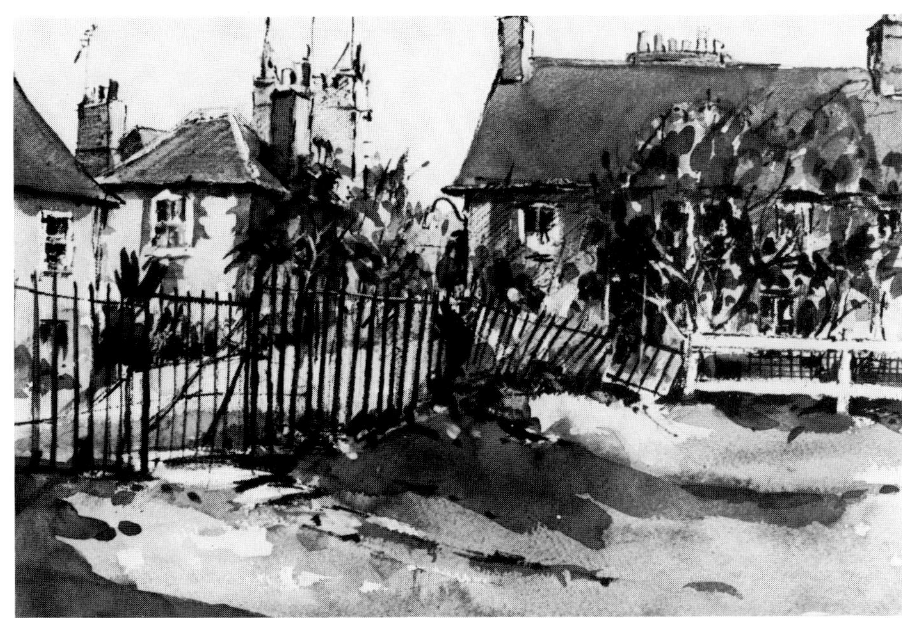

Dorchester (Ink and wash, 16" x 12"). Ink applied with a match-stick

The kitchen garden (Mixed media on tinted paper, 22" x 18")

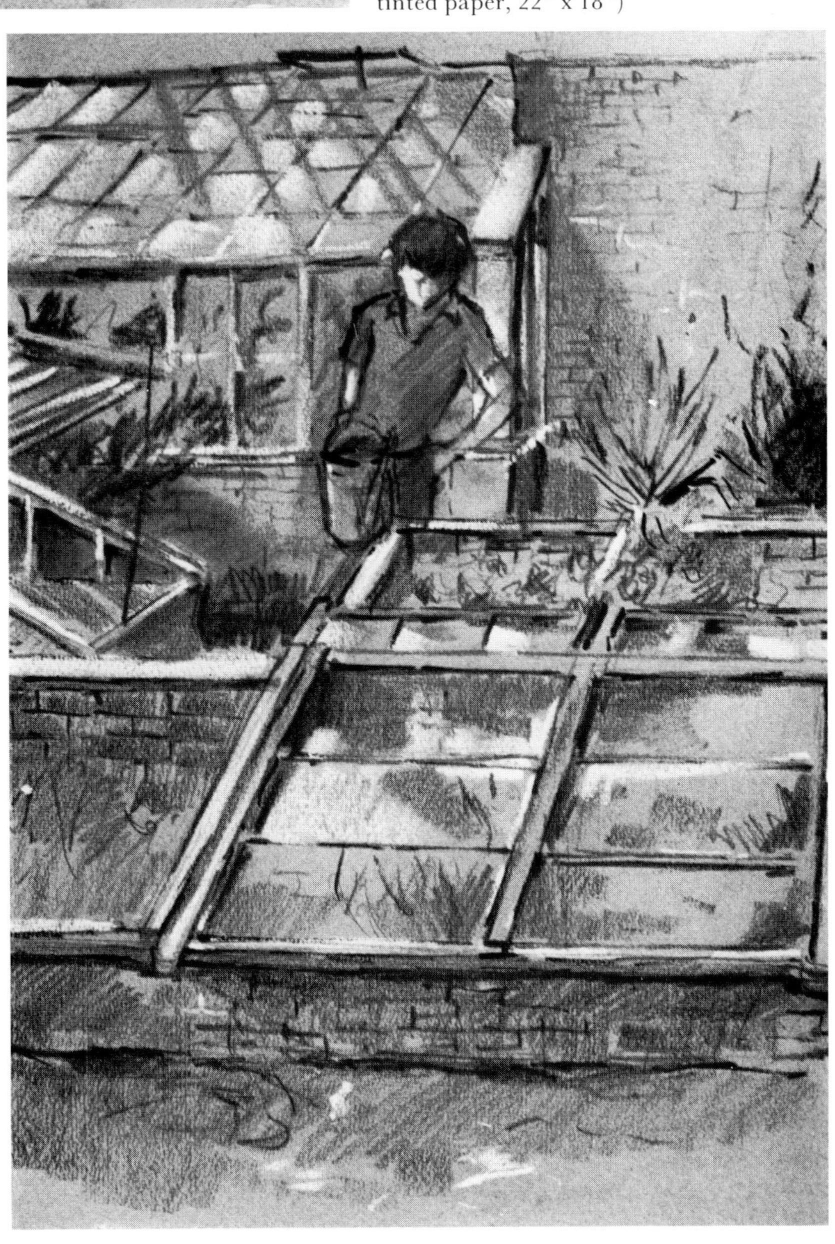

FIG 45 (**left**) *Bric-à-brac* (Mixed media, 26" x 18")

the working sketches also helped to decide how the final drawing should be handled and which medium would be best for exploring the different textures involved. I concluded that mixed media – charcoal, compressed charcoal, conté-crayon and graphite – would best suit my requirements. In view of the fact that the contents were not related in a material sense yet needed to be related aesthetically, I selected a stone-coloured heavyweight Fabriano Ingres pastel paper for this study.

As the preliminary sketches developed, the violin and top hat emerged as the focal point, with the rest of the bits and pieces acting in support. The spaces between the contents were essential to the composition, conveying the feeling of confusion and general untidiness which can only be achieved pictorially if order is used in the arrangement. I commenced the final drawing by lightly laying in the composition with the graphite stick. The next step was to block in the shadows with charcoal; these were subsequently knocked back with the powder-puff. It was now possible to assess the work as a whole by viewing the shapes of light and dark areas. It generally follows that if these shapes are pleasing as an abstract design then the composition will work. The drawing was taken a stage further by intensifying certain shadows with charcoal, and then it was fixed. As the work progressed, it became obvious that it was looking too neat and tidy. I decided that this could be rectified by drawing into the work with black conté-crayon and compressed charcoal, taking great care not to destroy the highlights. The drawing was then fixed again. All that now remained was selectively to put in such detail as was warranted, such as the violin strings, the dents in the metal tankard and the detail of the top hat.

If the highlights need lifting at this stage of the drawing, as on the pewter pot, this can be done with a little white conté or chalk. A word of warning: be careful not to overdo it, as if used to excess it can make the drawing appear wooden and lifeless. Fig 48 is a still life of a copper kettle and a collection of china and earthenware pots. In this work the kettle has been made the focal point, both in its positioning and its treatment. The medium in this case was charcoal, used on water-colour paper to give the textures I felt were needed.

As previously stated, still life subjects abound and need not necessarily be contrived studio exercises. Fig 49 is a page from my sketchbook and shows a still life I stumbled upon in an outbuilding on a country estate. As you will see, it is obviously the inside of a glory-hole: an old dustbin, sacks, and a window covered in cobwebs with old milk bottles on the window-sill. The interior was very dark, apart from the light from the small window, which illuminated much of the content of the picture, making the contrast most dramatic. On this occasion I had only a pencil and a sketchbook with me, but fortunately the pencil was a 6B and so I was able to achieve the range of contrast required. I think this shows the potential of still life as a subject for pictures. Fig 50 is another example, of farming implements drawn on site in mixed media, using precisely the same approach as for the drawing of *Bric-à-brac*.

FIG 48 *Still life* (Charcoal, 26" x 18")

FIG 49 *The glory hole* (Pencil, 10" x 7")

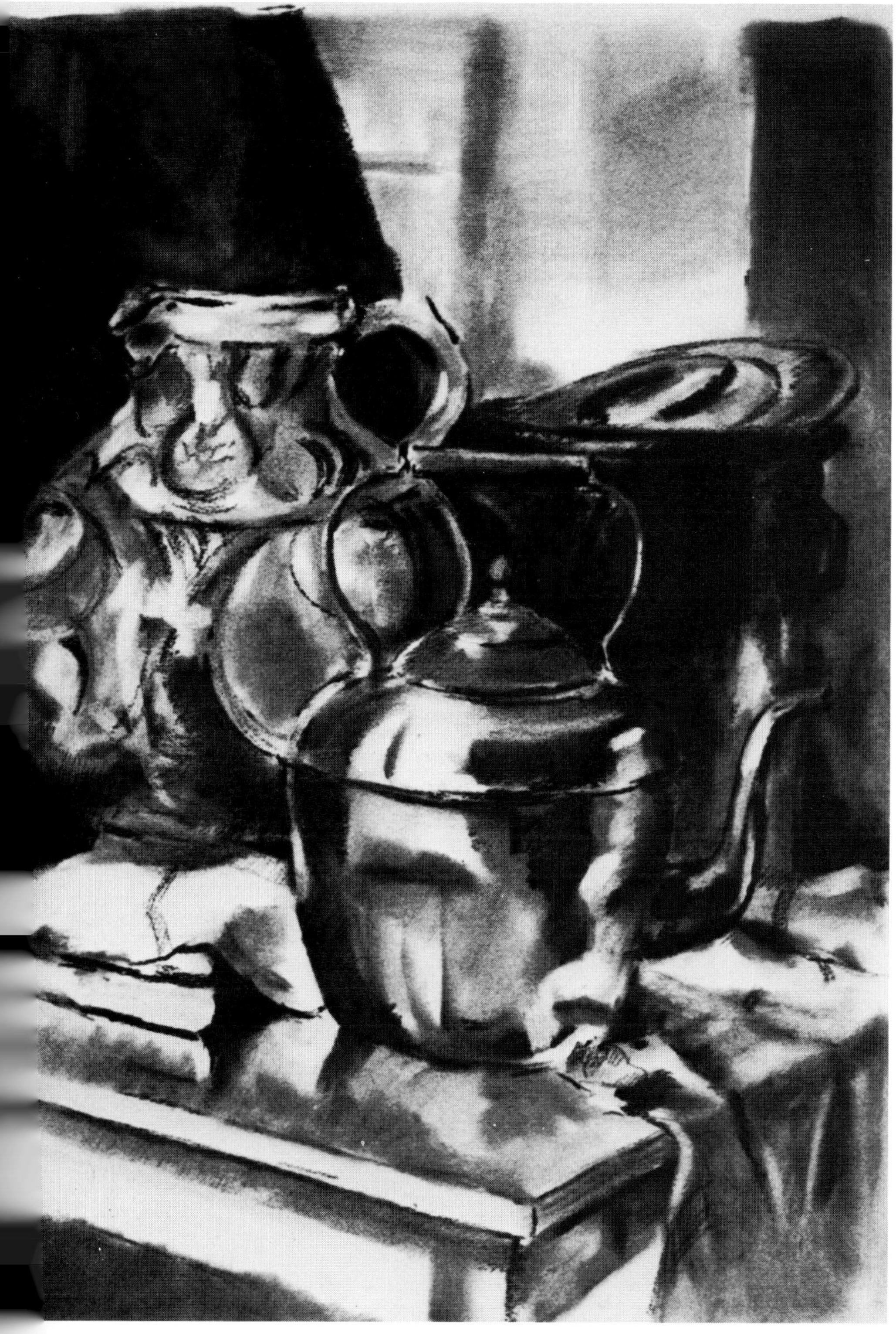

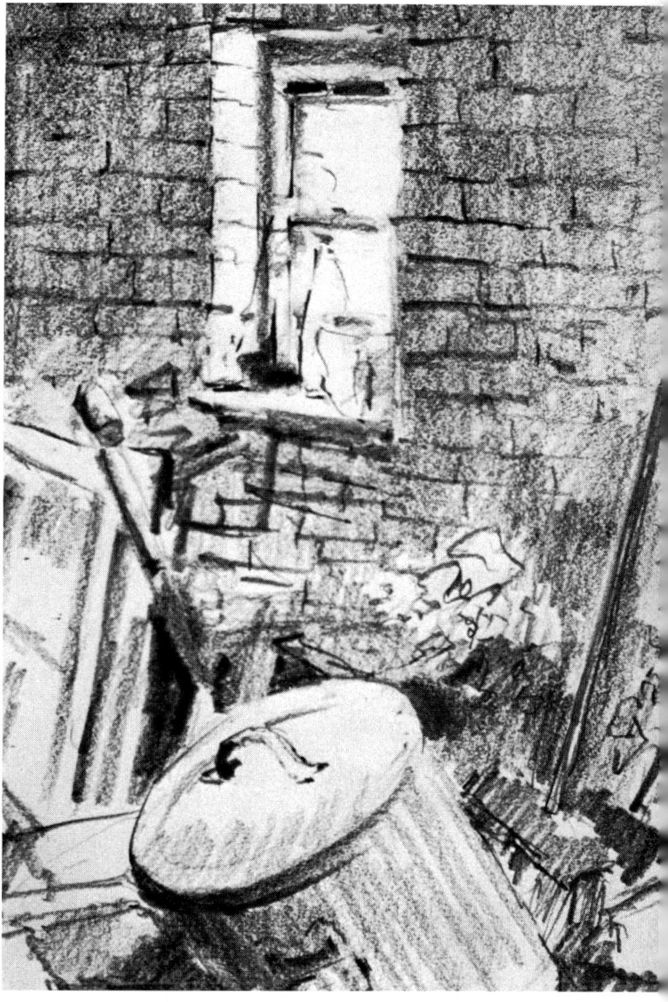

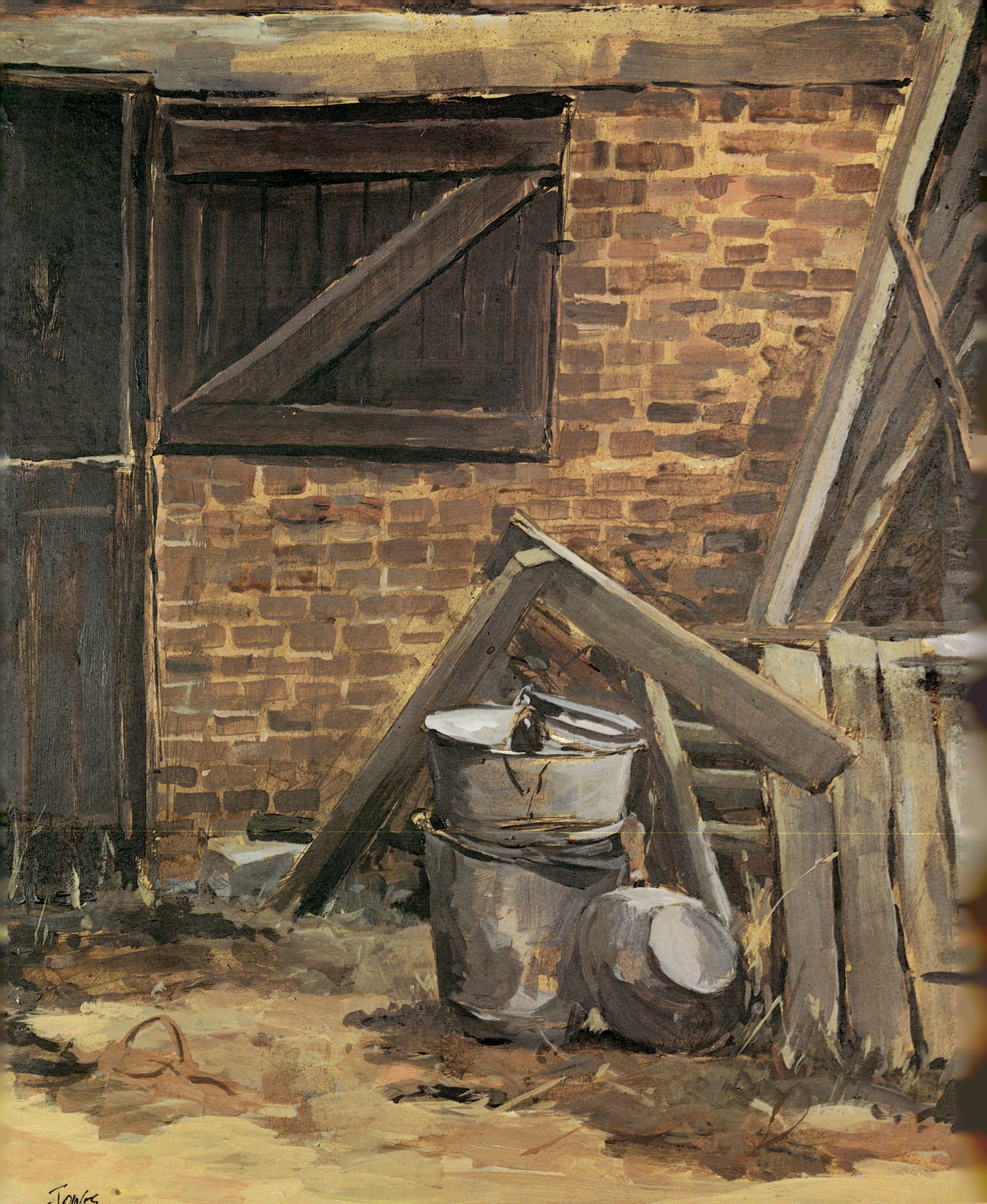
Jones

FIG 50 *Farming implements* (Mixed media, 25" x 18")

It is necessary to understand what you are looking at and to construct your drawing from that knowledge whatever the subject, but never more so than when flowers and foliage are introduced into the work. Once you understand how plants are constructed it becomes easy to make quick sketches such as Fig 51, a study for a still life with plants (Fig 52). It is important to remember that the natural shapes of flowers and plants can only be made to work if the posture is observed and recorded accurately at the start of the drawing. These natural shapes can be rendered in a variety of ways, such as in free-flowing linear marks that give an impression of shape and movement. Blocks of tone can be added to give a general description of the hues and shades, or a careful detailed drawing made which examines the exact construction of all the parts that make up the plant or flower.

For your early attempts at this type of drawing choose a plant with a simple structure, preferably with large leaves and single flower heads. Pick two or three specimens, and keep them in water away from the sun (they last longer that way). Take a medium-hard pencil (a B will be fine: make sure it has a good point, and sharpen it frequently as you work) and a sheet of cartridge paper. Begin by drawing the stems, which will establish the posture, and the rough outlines of the leaves and flowers. Now examine how all the parts fit together. During this detailed examination note how the leaves are attached to the stem and how the petals wrap around each other and overlap; see how the pistils, stamens and sepals are constructed. Finally, look at the leaves. Do they have a smooth or rough texture; is there a main rib; is the tracery of veins feathery or symmetrical? Above all, try to put down what you see in flowing lines rather than in a hesitant manner. Finally, add small details, such as serrations on leaves, hairs and thorns on the stems, as necessary.

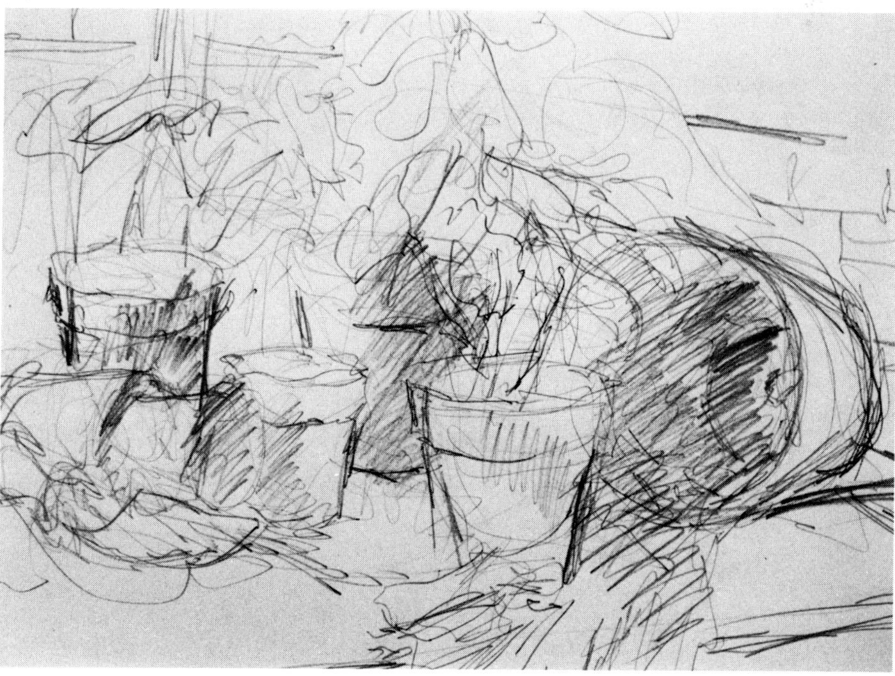

FIG 51 Study of plant and still life (Sketch in pencil, 25" x 18")

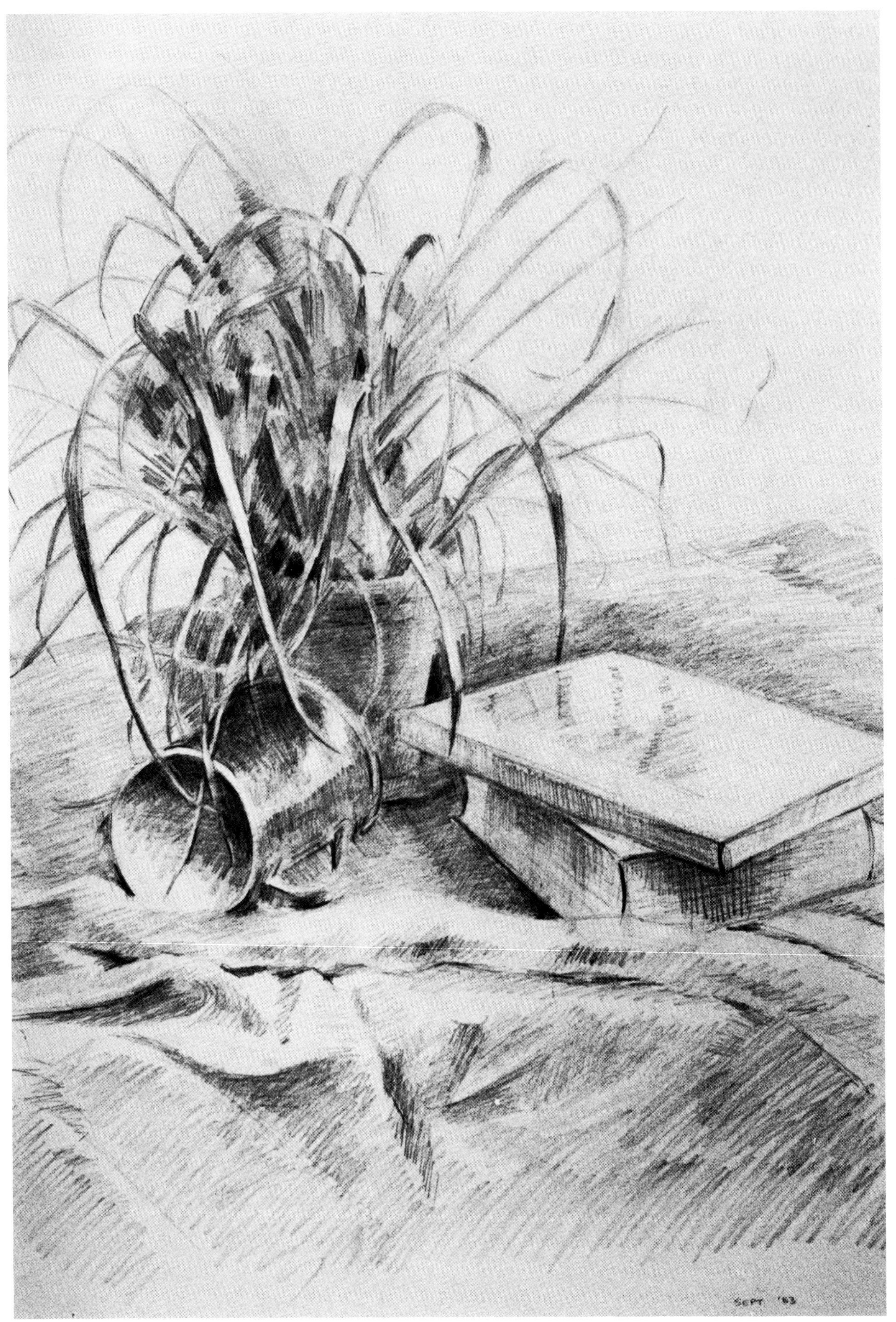
SEPT '83

FIG 52 (**left**) Final drawing of plant and
still life (Pencil, 25" x 18")

FIG 53 (**right**) Study of plant (Brush
drawing using dilute ink, 13" x 10")

FIG 54 (**below**) Section of hedgerow
(Conté crayon and charcoal, 16" x 14")

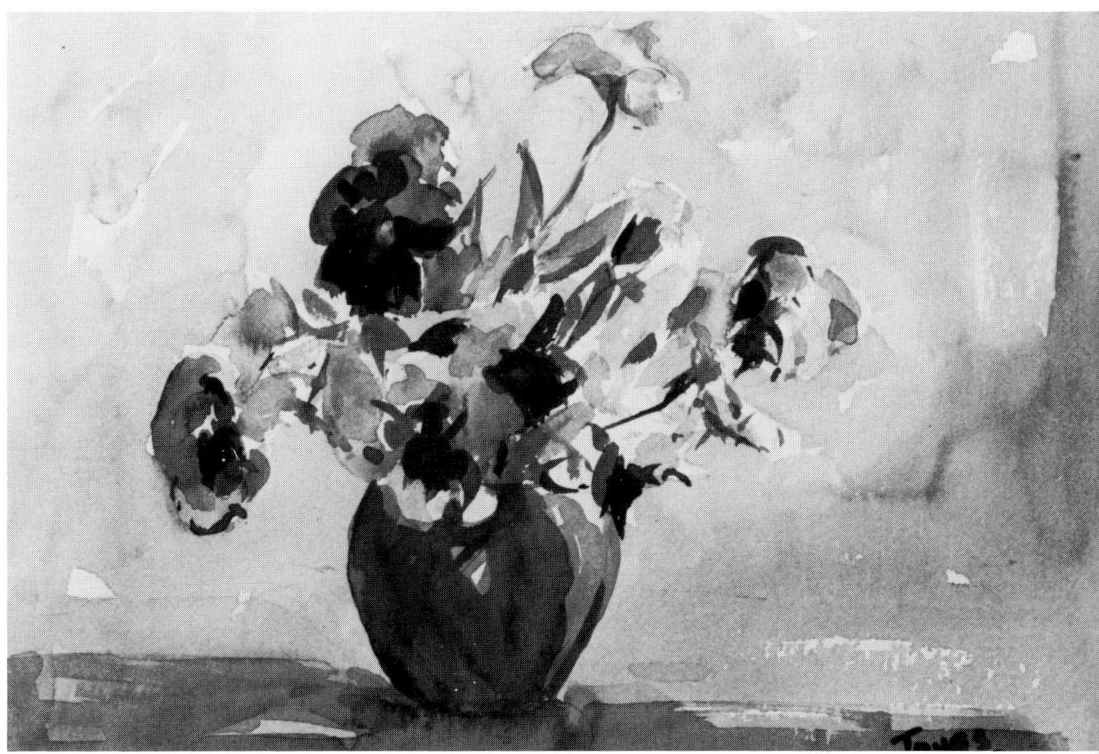

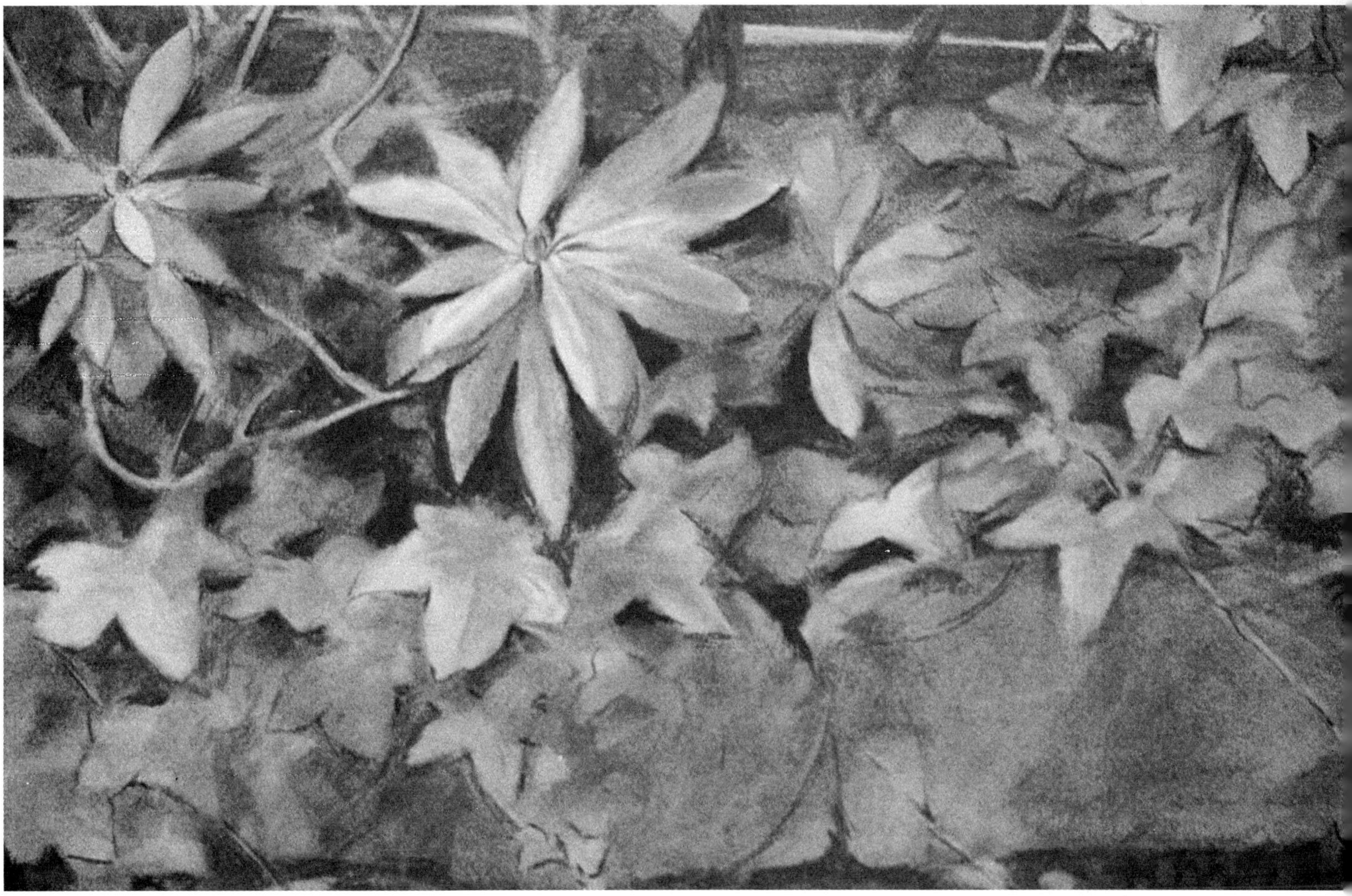

As I have already said, the medium selected will be determined by the species of flower or plant being drawn and the type of drawing you wish to make. Fig 53 is a study of a plant drawn with a brush using diluted indian ink. As with pencil drawing, the main posture lines and the large leaves were positioned using very diluted ink and, as the drawing progressed, the ink strength was increased to give contrast and tone control, creating space within the plant. You will see that within the large masses of leaf formation the edges of the individual leaves appear lost and found. In this case the effect was achieved by using ink of the required density applied with a pen, drawing into the washes to create an edge. The detail was added in a similar way.

Conté-crayon, charcoal and pastel can all be used to good effect for the expression of flowers and plants. Whatever the medium, and whatever form you wish the drawing to take (e.g. a botanical illustration, or a free drawing which sets out to capture the subject and its mood), it is essential that you have a good understanding of the construction and rhythm of the large shapes. It can be of great help to examine the drawings of flowers and plants by Leonardo and Rubens. From these you can see how the drawing has been built up. From here it is only a small step to draw the foliage of the landscape. The approach is exactly the same as for drawing flowers and plants: the choice of the manner of drawing and the medium will be governed in part by the subject and your reaction to it. In Fig 54 I have shown a section of a hedgerow. I chose to do this drawing in charcoal and black conté-crayon on buff pastel paper. The foliage was handled in the same way as the plants, with the addition of branches and their textures. The conté enabled me to express the texture of bark and grasses, as I was able to draw into the charcoal in much the same way as I did with the pen and brush drawing (Fig 53).

In landscape drawing and painting you will be continually confronted with the challenge of portraying leaves. Once again you will do well to see them as a problem in shape organisation. Always look for the large masses at the start of your drawing, paying particular attention to the grouping of light and dark areas. I use a very simple back-and-forth tone stroke to establish the masses before moving on to a different approach that will reflect the textures of the leaves.

Consistency of handling while allowing for variation should be your method when dealing with complex leafy surfaces. The method of handling should of course suggest the type and character of the foliage you are drawing, and that will be greatly influenced by how far you are from the subject. To give credence to your statements, it will be essential to articulate some of the leaves and branches. When doing this, remember to draw following the direction of growth. Trapped shapes of light and sky-light popping through the foliage will contrast well with the strokes of the leafy shapes and help to create movement.

Tone values play an important role in this type of drawing: they provide a way of looking through the foliage. These values can be enhanced by observation of the patterns of light, remembering that concentrated areas of light against a dark background will always

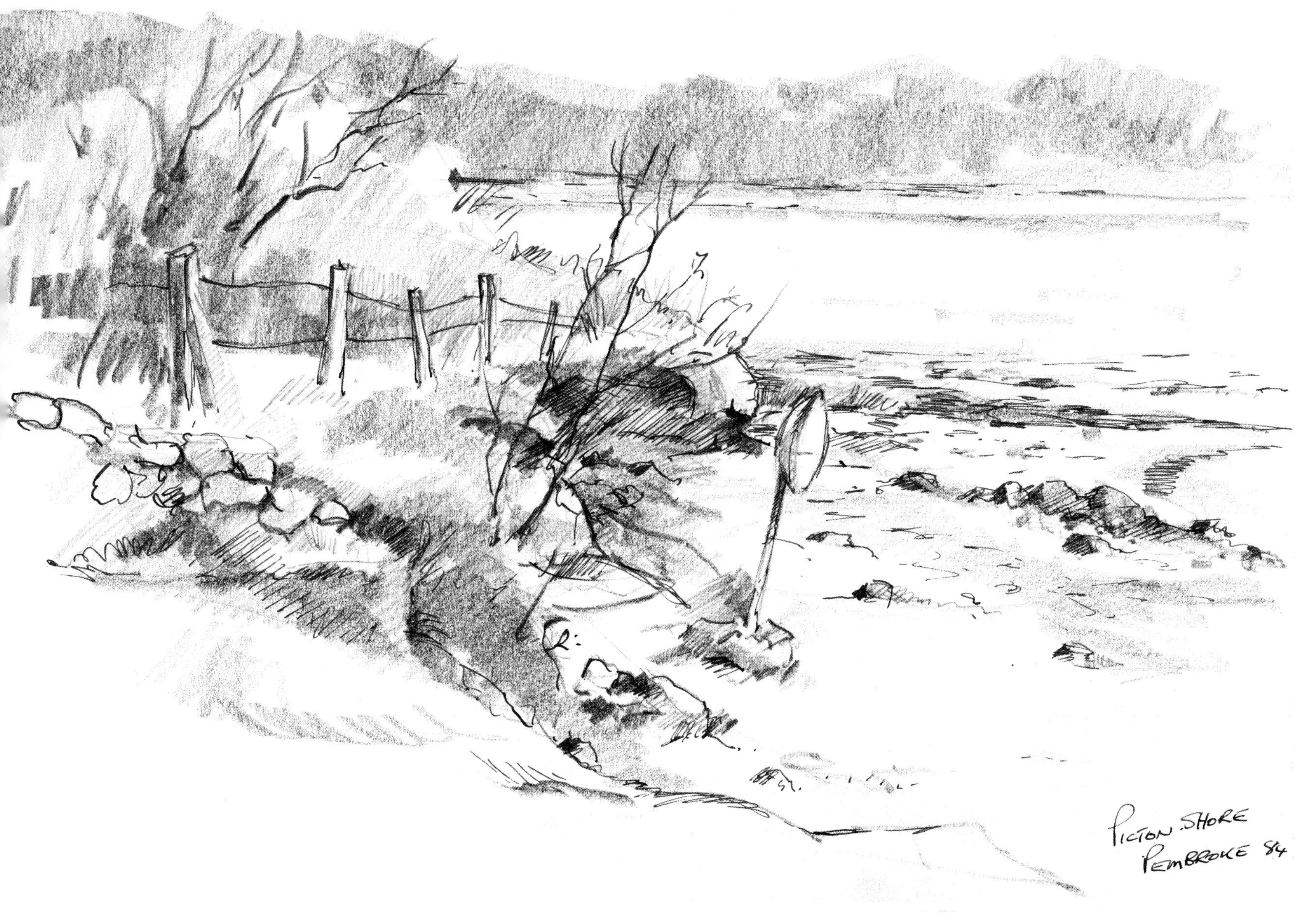

FIG 55 Landscape study showing tonal masses (Pencil, 10" x 7")

project forward. This can be of value, providing a visual lead to take you into and around the drawing in the manner you desire, thus aiding composition and design.

Silhouette will also allow you to depict branches and individual leaves, and is a useful aid to identifying the species of foliage. Finally, with complex subject matter such as this, always explore the full potential of the relationship between the large masses and their tone values. Fig 55 shows a landscape study expressed by the large tonal masses alone. The simplicity and economy of this drawing allow the space and mood of the landscape to come through. Landscape is not restricted to rural scenes devoid of human association: old farm buildings provide an infinite variety of subject matter, as do villages, towns and cities.

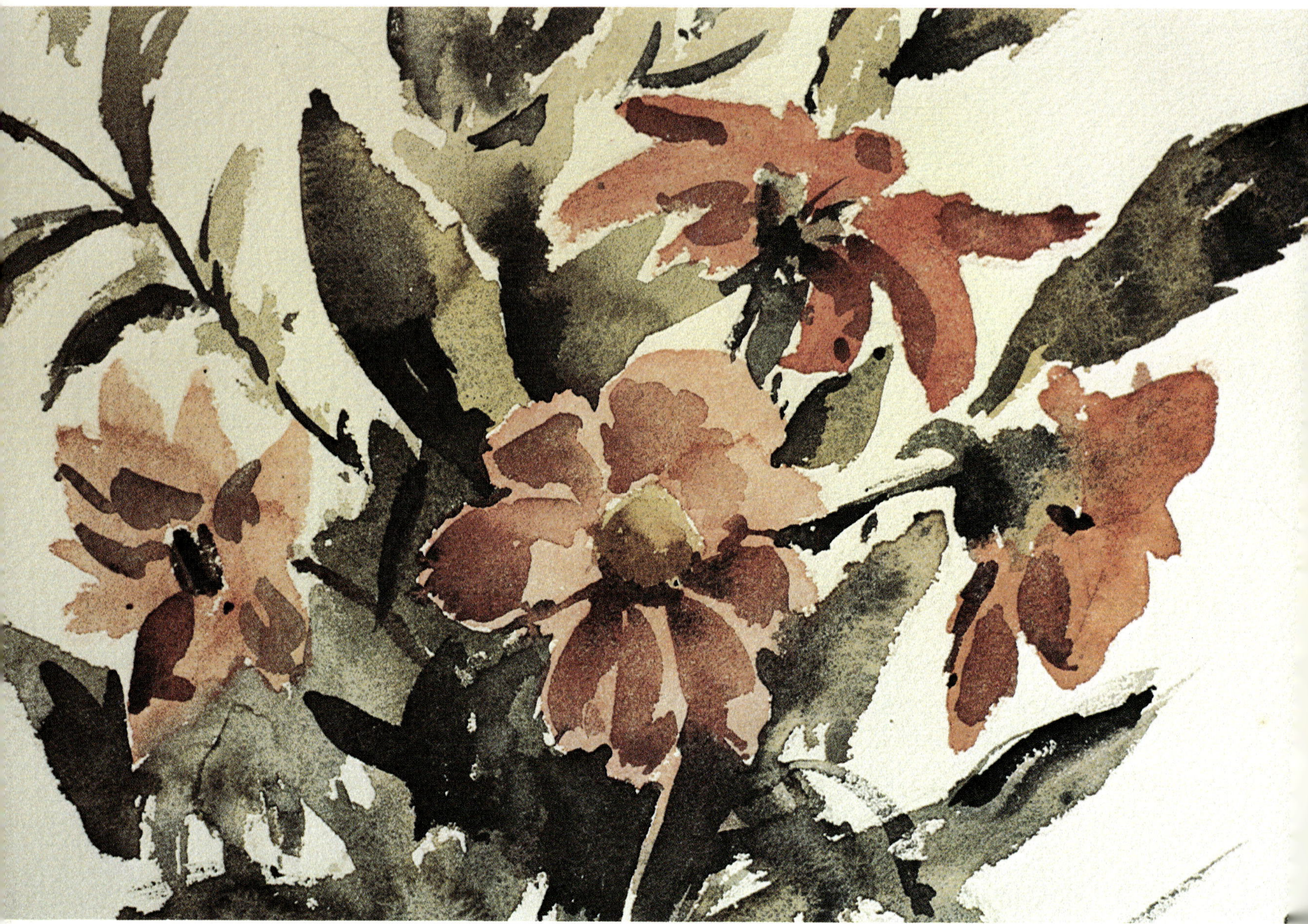

Flowers (Water-colour, 15" x 12")

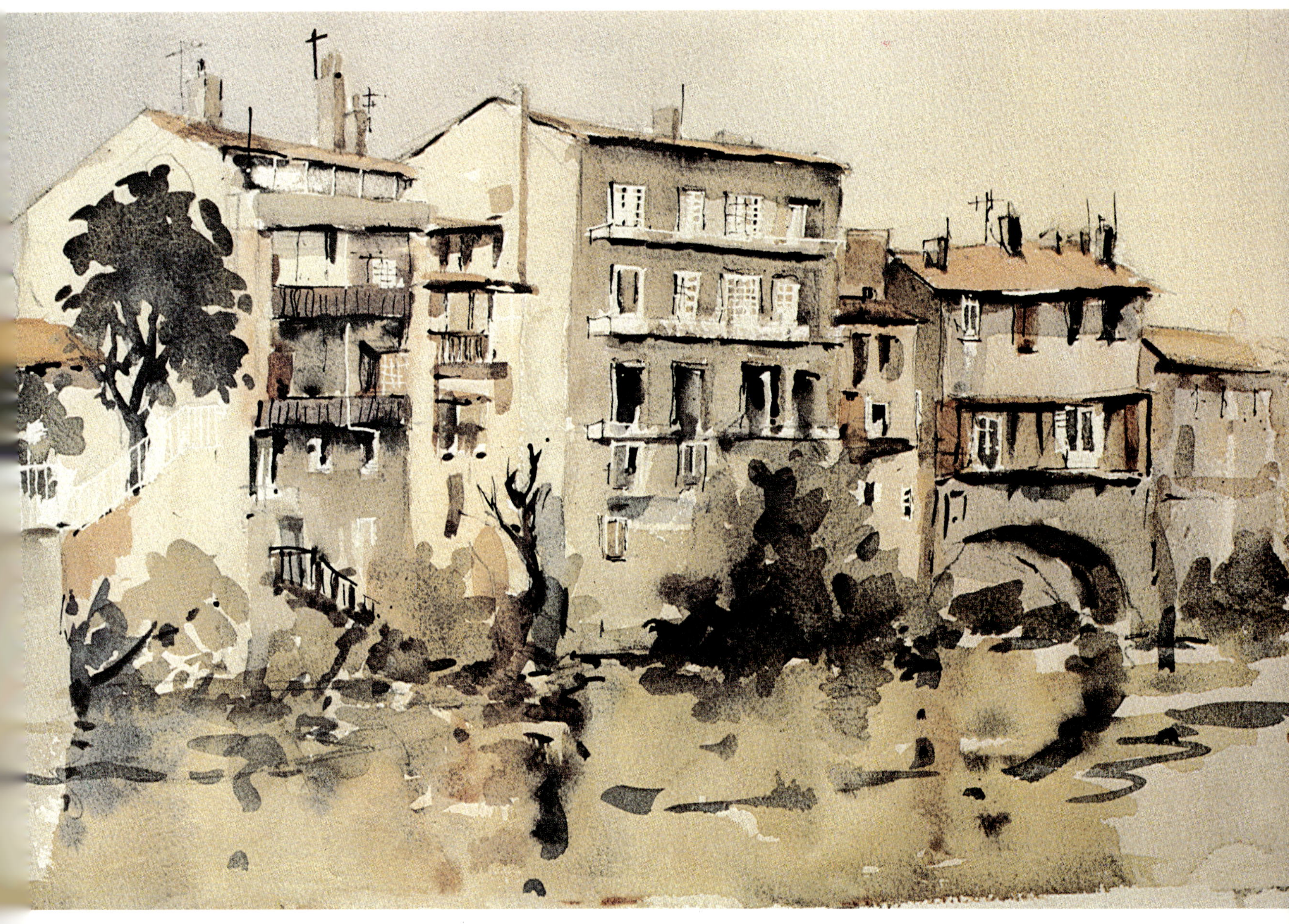

Castres (Water-colour, 15" x 11")

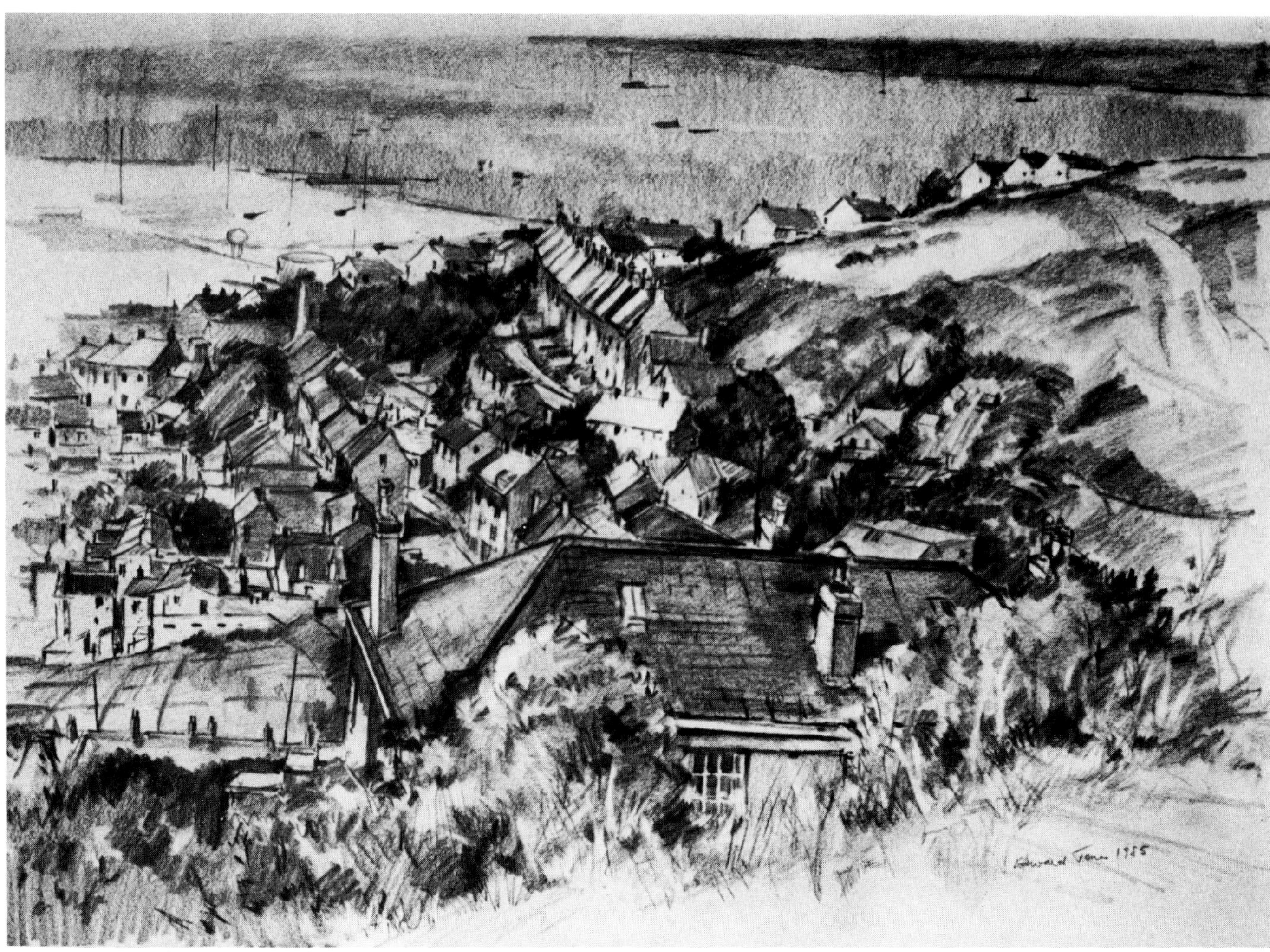

FIG 56 View from upstairs window
(Pencil, 28" x 18")

Drawing and painting buildings demands an understanding of perspective. The language of drawing dealt with earlier will stand you in good stead when working with this subject matter. As with any other subject, you will need to do some preparatory work. Make quick pencil and ink sketches of the shapes, noting the large shapes and their relation to the square or rectangle of your working surface and their relationship to each other. A building seen face-on creates a square or rectangle in relation to the support, whilst the same building viewed from another angle will create a strong diagonal movement against the rectangle. Always think of the direction and mass of shapes in your composition.

Often the position that gives you the best composition allows very little room in which to work – you may find yourself jammed in a doorway or against a wall (this will limit the size of your drawing). It often means that you are too close to the drawing: when this occurs, put the work down and walk back from it so that you can see it as a whole.

Many interesting views of buildings can be seen from upstairs windows. Buildings drawn from a high viewpoint provide a good exercise in perspective. In Fig 56 I have drawn the view from an upstairs window, looking across the gardens to the houses beyond. In this work it is essential to register the changes in scale as well as in the amount of detail, especially that apparent in the nearest buildings. This will assist you in giving these details the correct amount of register in your comprehensive sketch. Remember that most communities have at least one interesting building – a church, a barn, or even a building site. Careful study of these single buildings will enable you to observe and understand architecture without the confusion of busy urban life and its environment.

Pure perspective can be misleading. This applies to all buildings, but especially to old ones. Buildings are rarely absolutely straight: they often have distortions which create strange angles (this also applies to the streets). Examine the relationship of windows to the wall they are in. Fig 57 illustrates the method and construction principles I apply to ensure that the windows not only relate to the wall they are in, but have the correct perspective for it. Explore the shapes and texture of walls, fences and gates to discover the various ways that you can use drawing media to achieve different textures.

FIG 57 Construction of windows in wall (Pencil, 10" x 7")

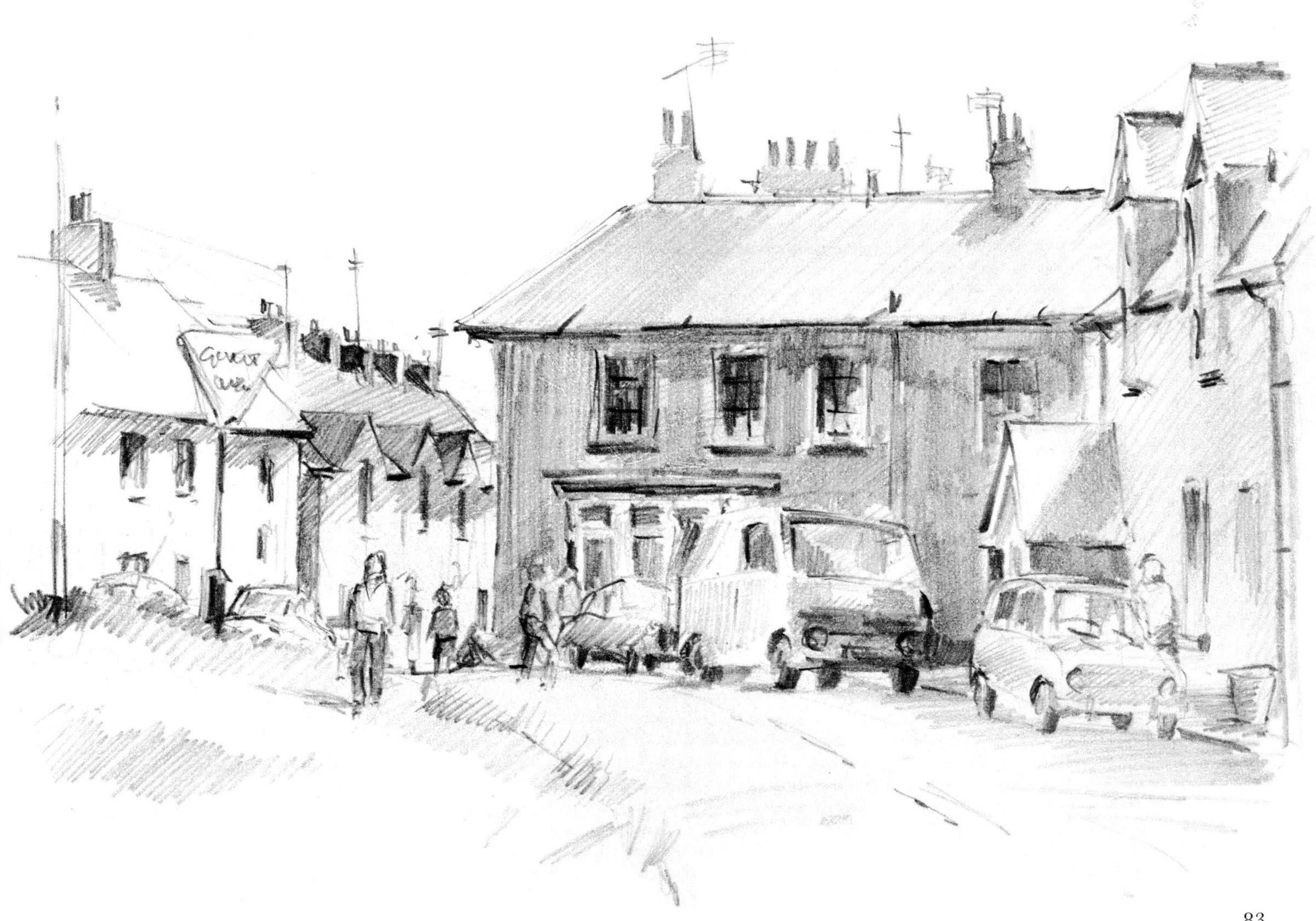

Bridges, railway and bus stations and factory complexes all make excellent subjects, as perspective and emphatic changes of scale are all greatly accentuated. Scenes such as these generally contain precise vertical and horizontal lines. Let the tonal scale be determined by the linear perspective. Such compositions have strong shadows: I have found that when making sketches out of doors it is important to fix the position of shadows sooner rather than later in the creation of the sketch. Once they are fixed, do not change them, as to do so will alter the entire concept of the work.

Drawings of buildings, villages, towns and cities are representations of the habitat of people. Because of this, they will need to include people, and although the drawing and painting of figures will be dealt with later, I feel it will be a worthwhile exercise for you to suggest them in your drawing. This will greatly assist in determining scale. It is helpful to place one figure near a door that must be drawn, so that the person can pass through it. As people move constantly, it becomes essential to make rapid studies in the sketchbook. These must be made quickly and should aim to capture the shapes and masses as they move. Draw and redraw in order to create an impression of the figures by the use of essentials. (See Section 3, *Drawing people*)

There is one further aspect of drawing landscape that must be considered: areas of water. Outdoors the world we see is never static: this is even more apparent when it contains moving water. Water can be the subject in its own right, but more often it is only the physical support for the main component, such as a boat or a group of old piles. The surface of water can be very still and mirror-like, reflecting a scene and the sky – this is often seen in puddles, lakes, and slow-moving rivers. Alternatively, it can be restless such as a harbour, fast-flowing river, rough sea, or weir, providing us with one of the most exciting of subjects and one of the most difficult to capture.

When making studies from direct observation of water, the main problem is how to represent movement, to show its character or to freeze one fixed moment of it. Water moves and can reflect a moving sky. I suggest that you concentrate on one aspect; look for an enclosed area of water, such as swimming pool, where there is seating. Use either charcoal, conté, or wash with diluted ink using a brush. Fig 58 shows a very rapid sketch, using a combination of charcoal and ink-wash. For the washes I used a No. 6 sable and, with the wide range of subtle tones from pale grey to almost black, I was able to create the movement and depth of the water. The lines on the bottom of the pool were instrumental in giving an idea of the movement.

The handling of the medium will of necessity change according to the degree of movement of the water. It is a constant source of surprise. On occasions it reflects the light from above and behind the spectator rather than the sky, so that against a dark sky it appears light and luminous. You will find there are days when the horizon is sharp and clear and others when the sea and sky merge; sometimes the serration of waves is visible on the horizon, and then there are the days when the sky seems painted on the surface of the water.

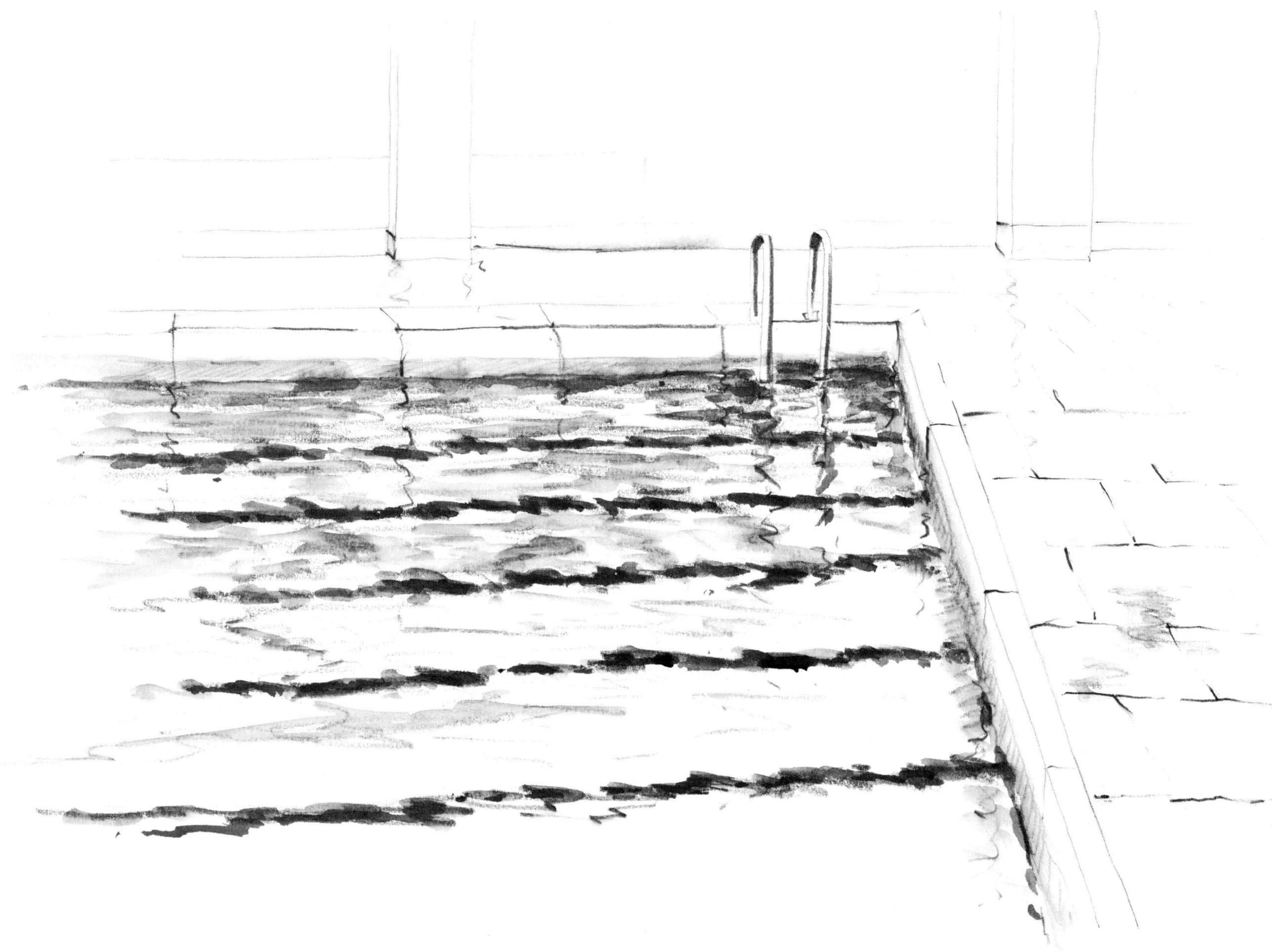

FIG 58 Water movement in swimming pool (Charcoal and ink wash, 15" x 11")

Reflections in water, no matter how still the surface may appear, require you to train your eye to look for the most significant ones and put them down quickly. Fig 59 is a quick charcoal sketch of trees reflected in water. This produced a compound problem: not only was the water moving, changing its surface, but also the trees were moving, as the wind moved the leaves and changed the light with each gust. If you watch carefully, you will see two different patterns of movement: the rhythmic swaying of the trees creates an irregular movement whilst the ripple movement of the water is quite regular.

Try to visit the venue in different weather conditions and produce drawings for each circumstance. Do not concentrate too much on the trees in your early attempts. In your early landscape sketches, you will have many studies of foliage and trees to refer to. It will, however, be

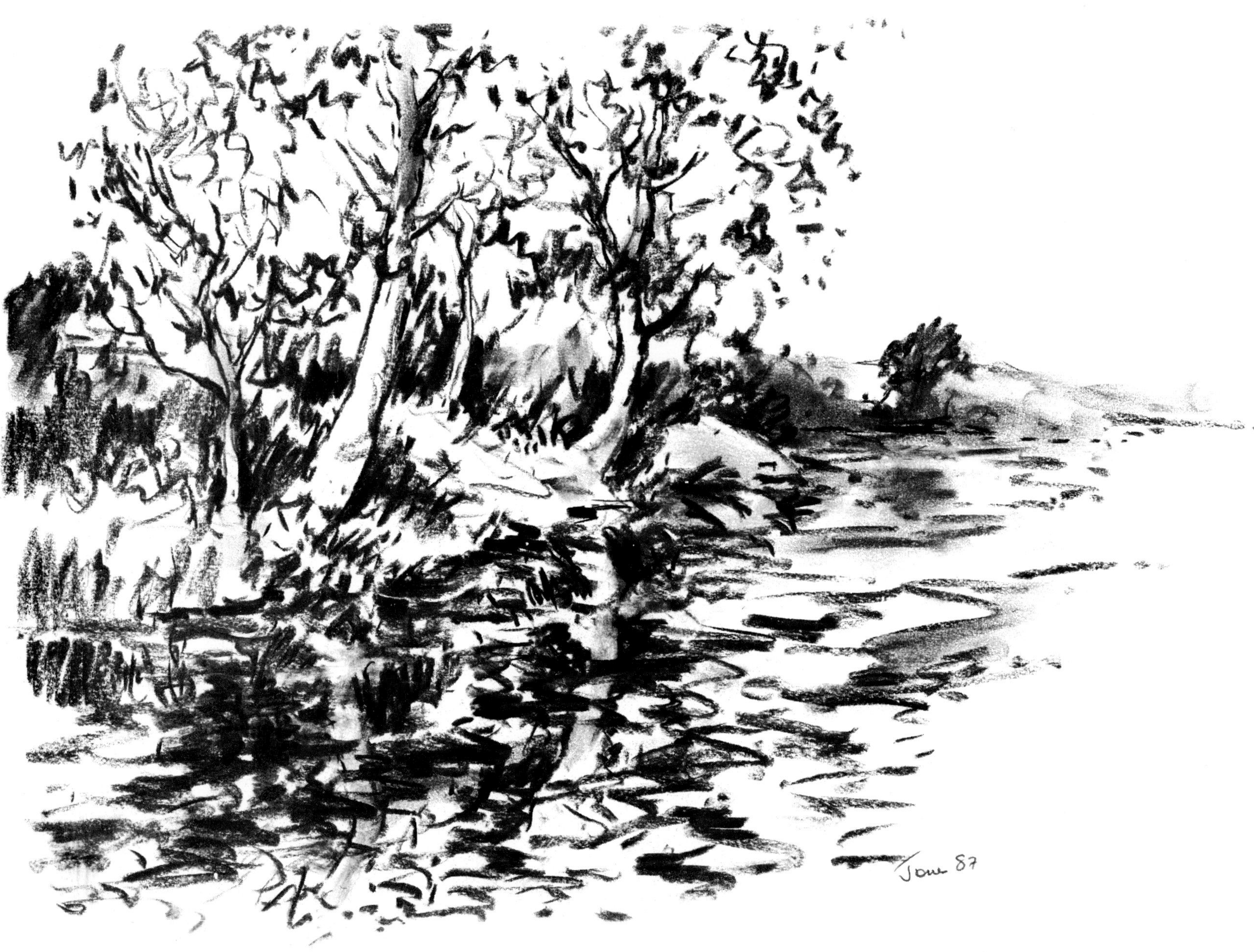

FIG 59 Reflections of trees and movement
(Charcoal, 15" x 11")

both helpful and interesting if you make studies of various species of tree that you find near water, such as willows and poplars.

When looking for a subject containing water most artists will be drawn to harbours and marinas, access to which is usually easy. They are relatively comfortable to work in but, most important of all, they are attractive to draw and paint. Boats and boat-builders' yards are usually full of fascinating subjects. Boats are extremely difficult to draw as their shapes are awkward to determine because of the viewing angle. This is further complicated by the changing curves in the hull. When superstructure is involved, the problem is made more acute by the mass of lines and forms which seem to defy understanding.

In Fig 60 I have shown how I construct a boat using the language of drawing. The hull is built into a rectangular cube. The centre line drawn through the length of the cube represents the keel; the sides, bows and stern are then built into the cube around the centre line. Any superstructure that may exist can now be added in the sure knowledge that the perspective will be correct. Keep a sketchbook with you to make notes of the structure of any craft, whether on water where the reflections must be observed, or on the shore where you can see the vessels above and below the waterline. Make sketches of sailing-boats (which do not sit and pose for us): observe the effect of the wind in the sails and the angle at which they heel; look constantly for those essential posture lines, for it is only through continual observation that

FIG 60 Construction of ships and boats
(Pencil, 15" x 11")

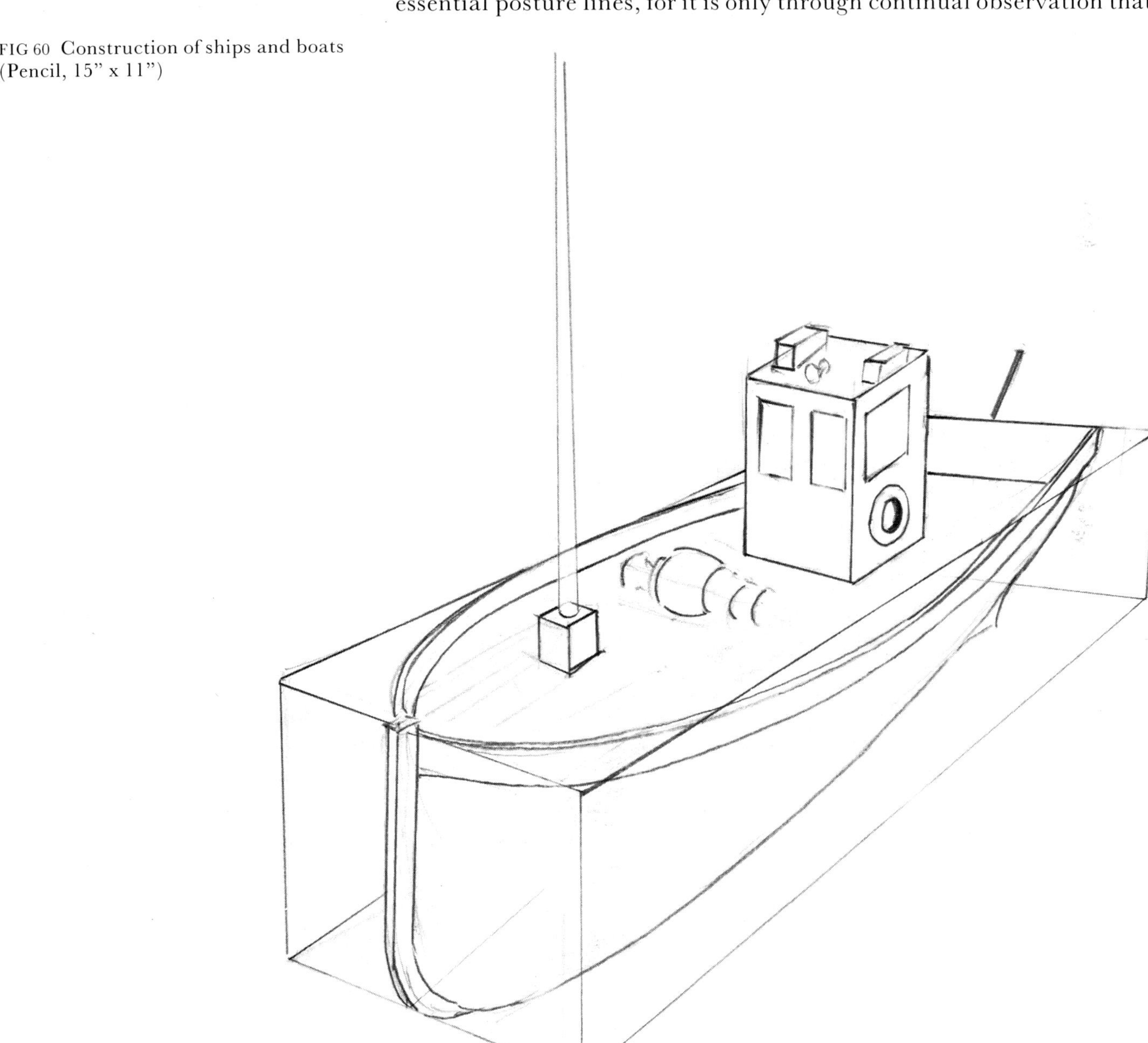

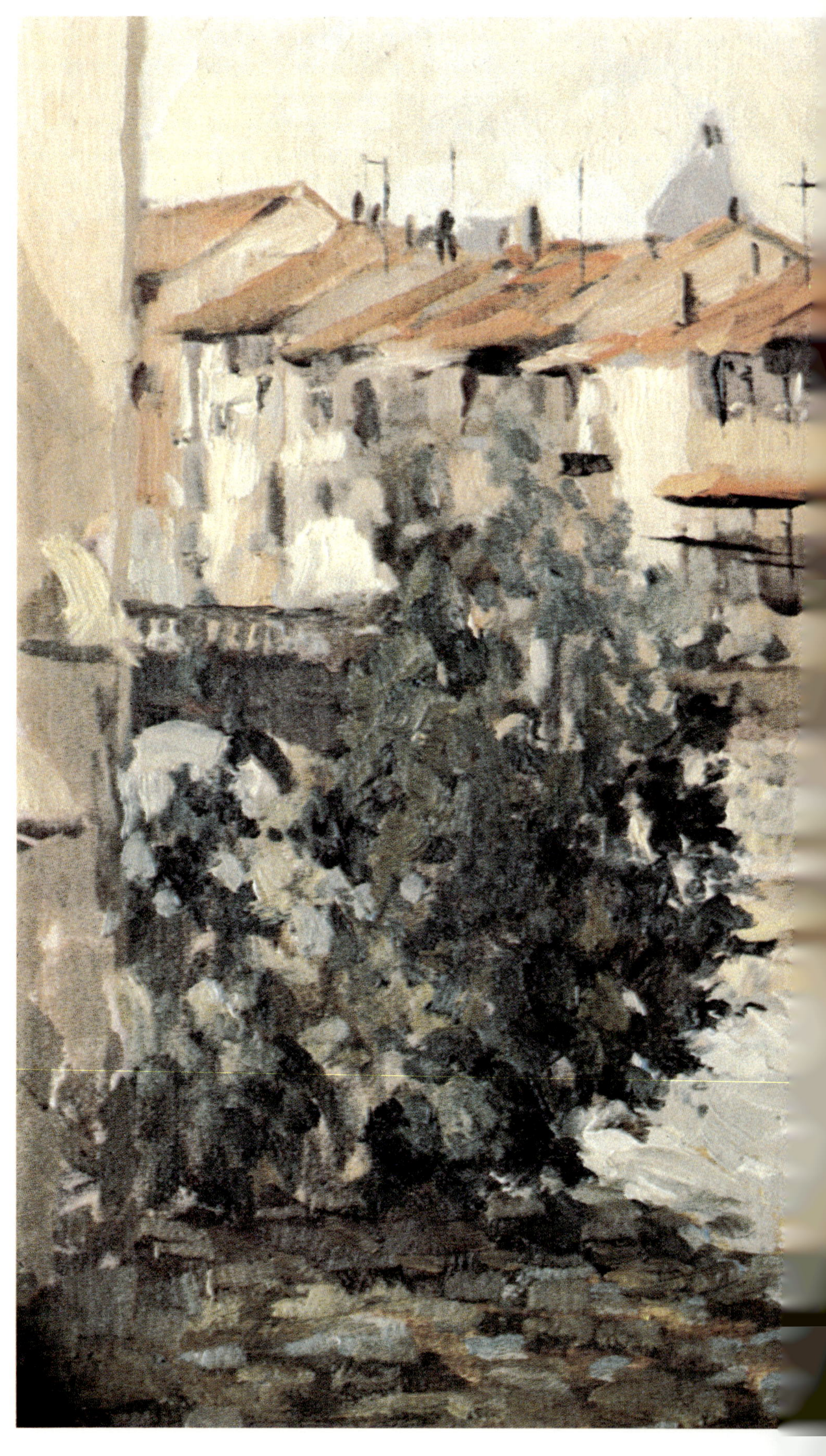

Castres (Oil, 22" x 18")

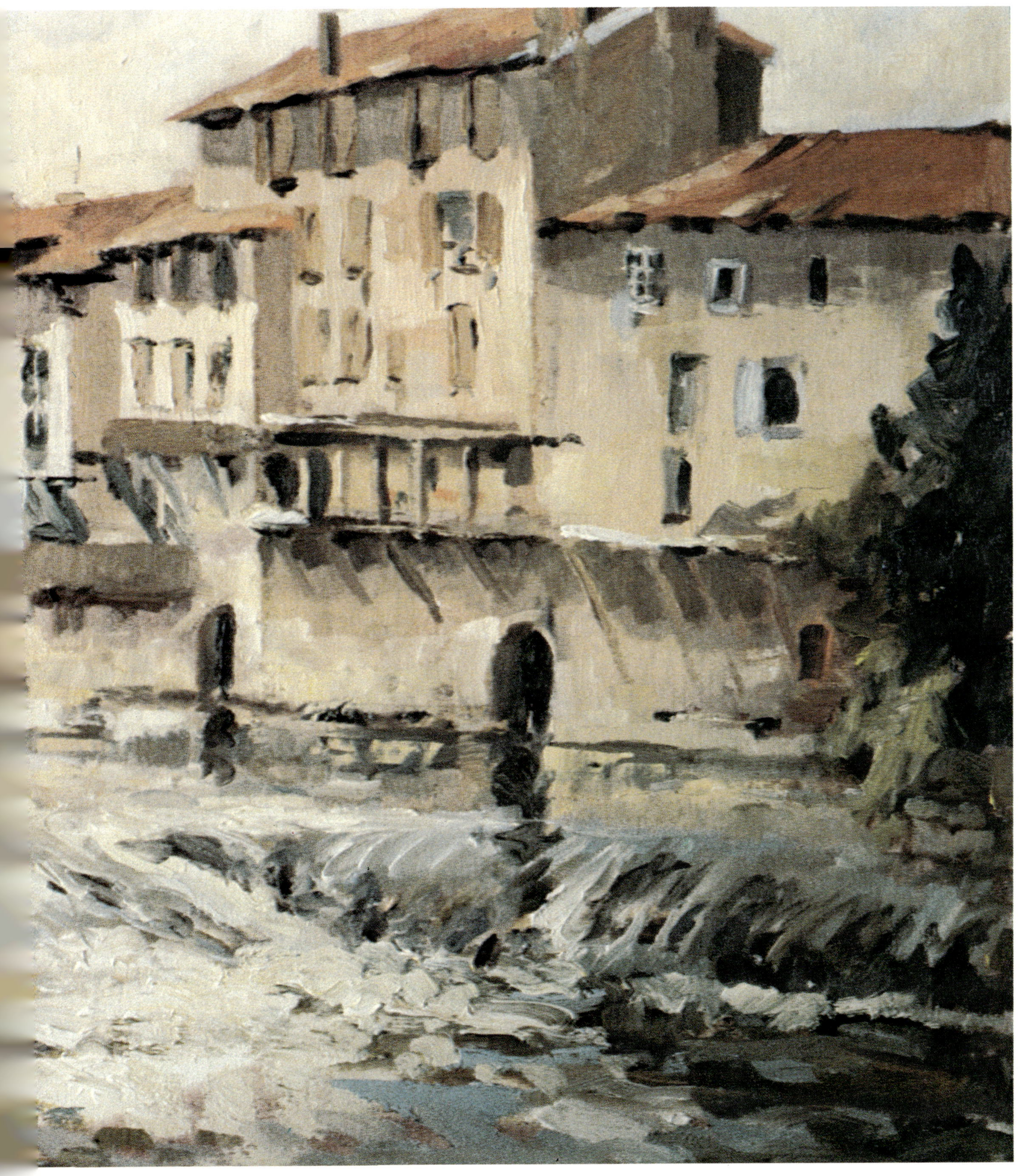

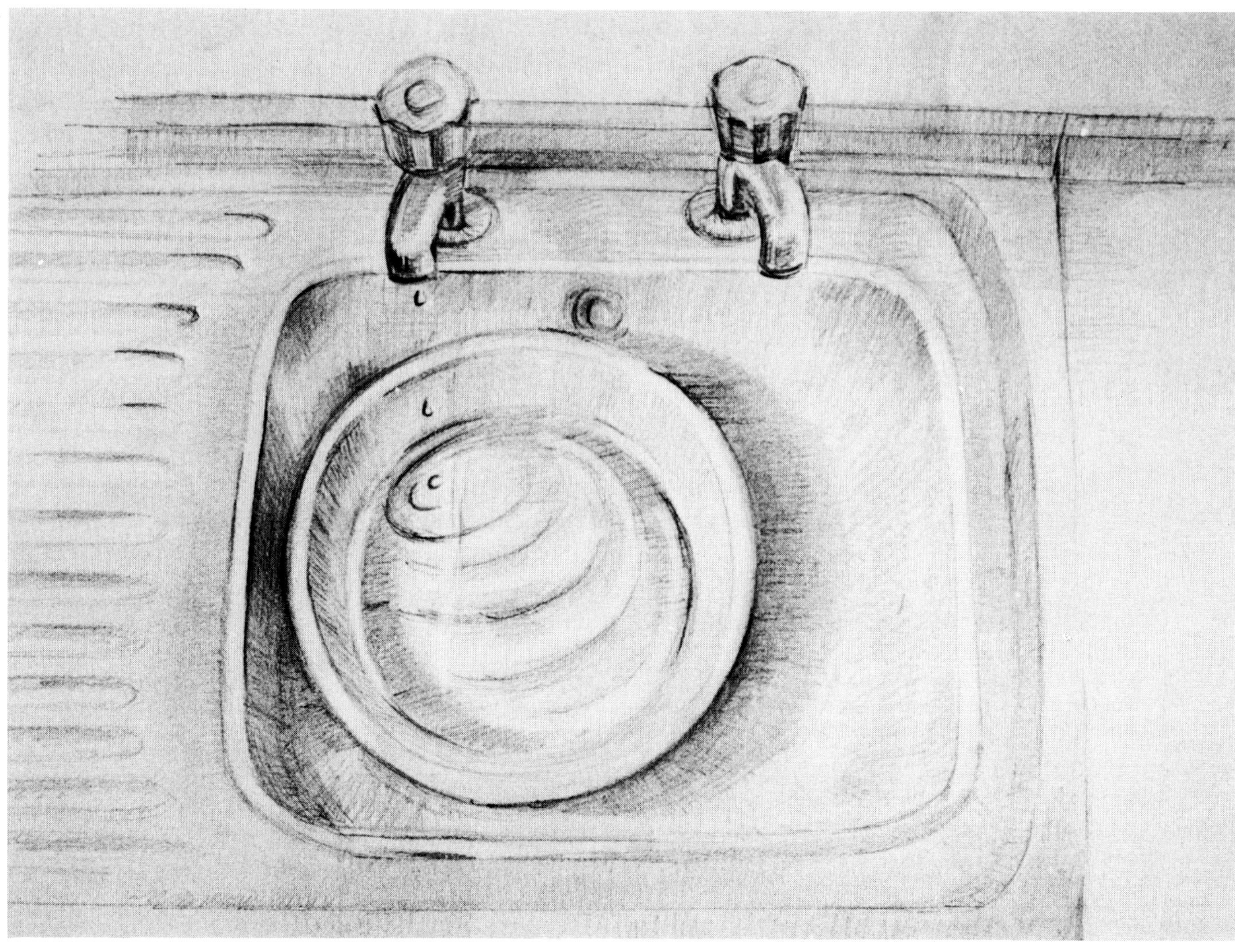

you can build a visual library. Another worthwhile exercise is to draw
moving water. In Fig 61 I have shown water falling from a tap into a
bucket (this could just as effectively be a washbowl or bath). Ensure
that the rate of fall makes an interesting pattern – observe how the
ripples and reflections conform to the shape of the bucket. This exercise
will be helpful when drawing and painting the movement and
reflections around the hulls of boats, buildings and trees. As your
experience grows you will be able to bring together many of the things
dealt with so far into a more complex marine subject such as a busy
port. There you will find many different craft, warehouses and marine
paraphernalia. Vessels are often moored in groups, which helps to
make pleasing compositions. Draw them in a variety of media, and
finally use your experience to make a larger pen-and-ink drawing, such
as that illustrated in Fig 62, which was drawn on pale buff paper.

With all these exercises, never lose sight of the construction of your
subject and remember to relate that construction to perspective.
Remember that the plane of the water surface is identical to the plane
of a table surface: a cup and saucer on a table has to be drawn in the
same plane as the table; the boat on and in the water has to be treated
similarly, as illustrated in Fig 63.

FIG 61 Student drawing of water falling
from tap (Pencil, 14" x 12")

FIG 62 *Southampton Docks* (Mixed media,
26" x 18")

FIG 63 *Boats on water* (Pencil, 15" x 11")

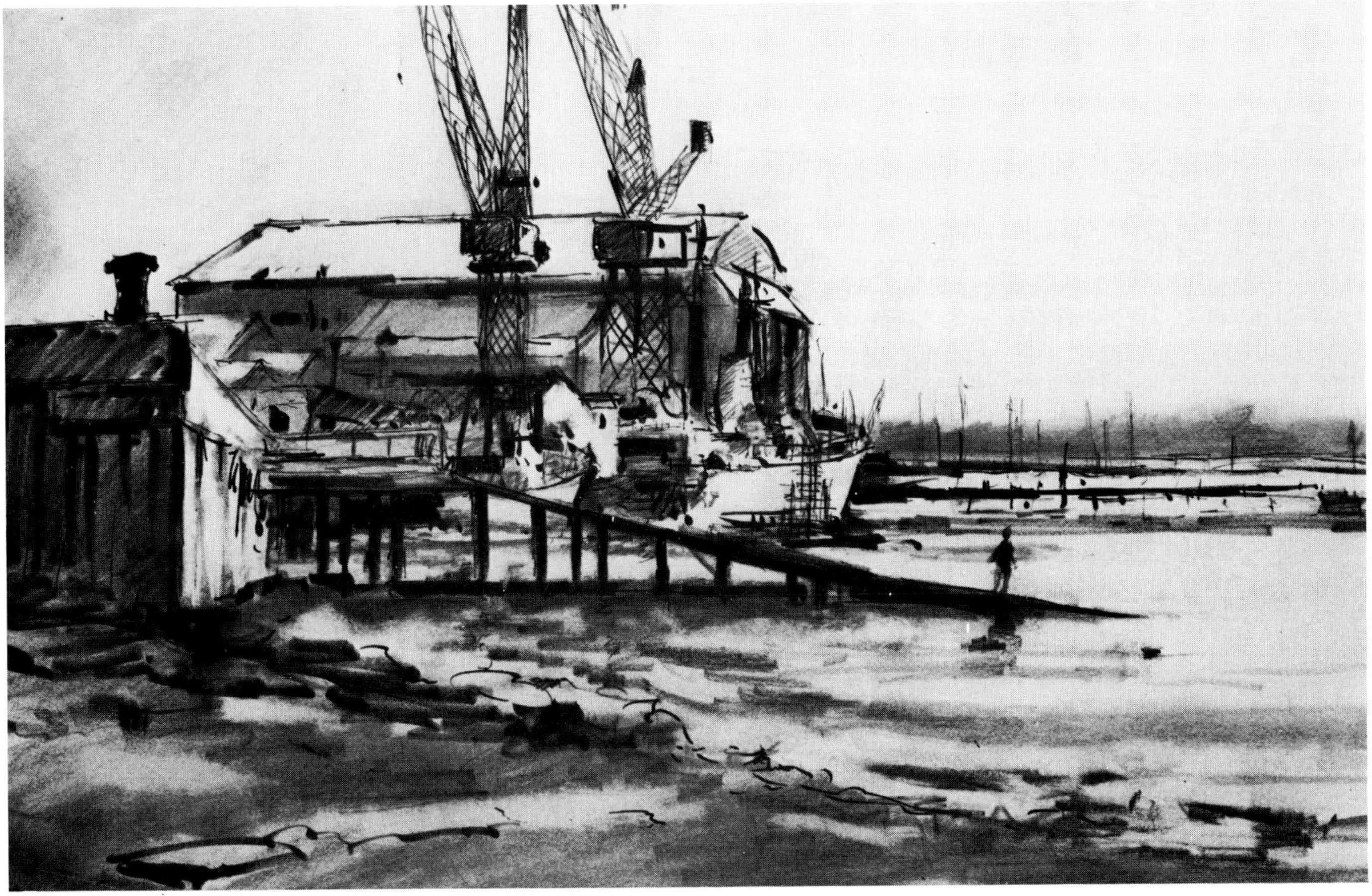

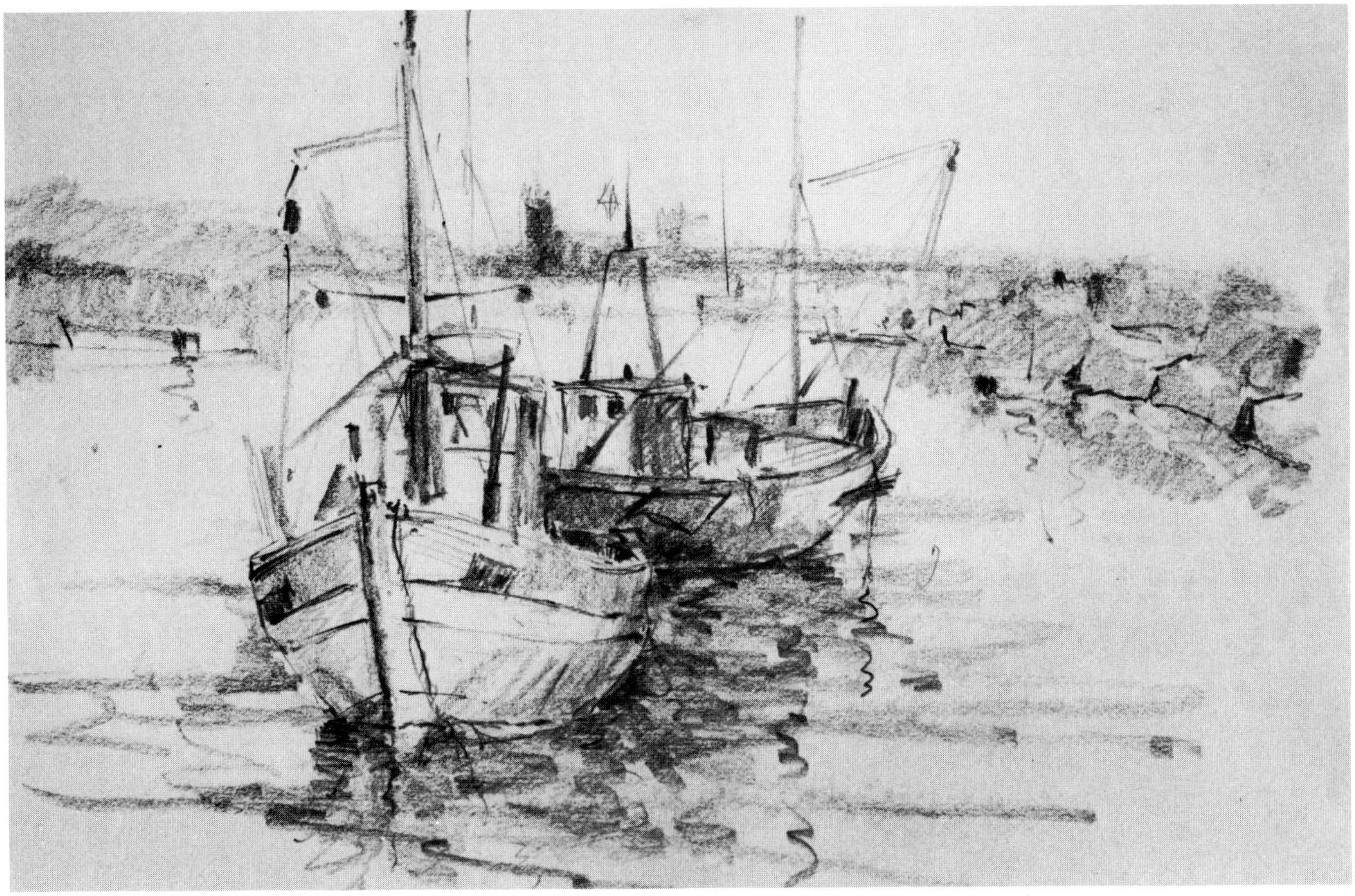

When drawing water which has strong movement, such as the sea, look for the construction and pattern of the wave forms. Water with heavy movement has tremendous weight and power: this can only be conveyed if the direction and volumetric form of the waves are understood.

With complex subjects, such as ports, it is necessary to be very selective in the arrangement of the component parts of the picture. It is possible to overcrowd the work, making it confusing for the onlooker. Tone values will play an important role in directing emphasis. The observation of light and shade, especially on the water, will assist greatly in the composition of such complex subject matter.

Dorset Stour, Throop (Water-colour and candle, 15" x 11"). Candle being used to create sparkle on water

Study of Olive tree (Pencil, 10" x 8")

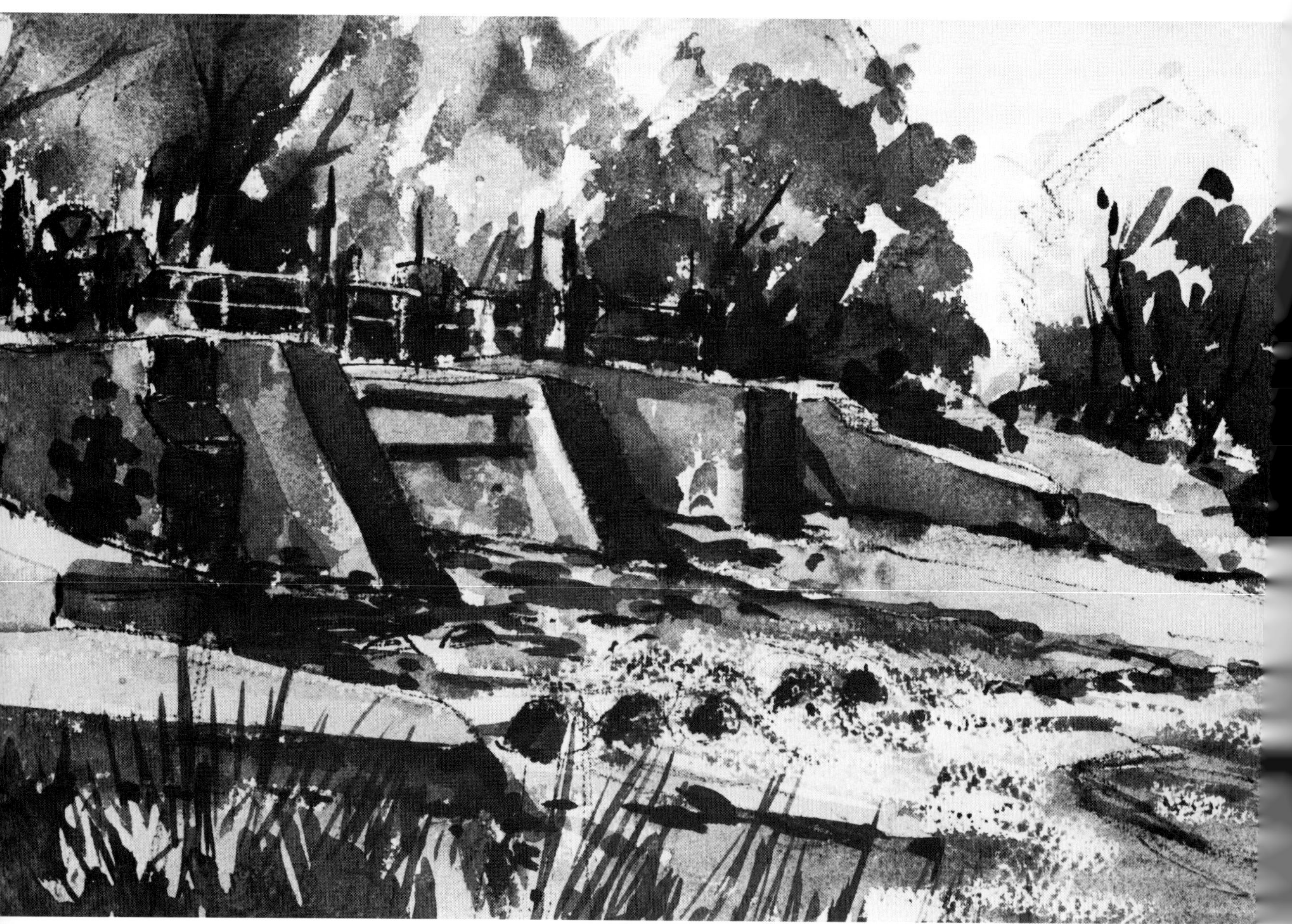

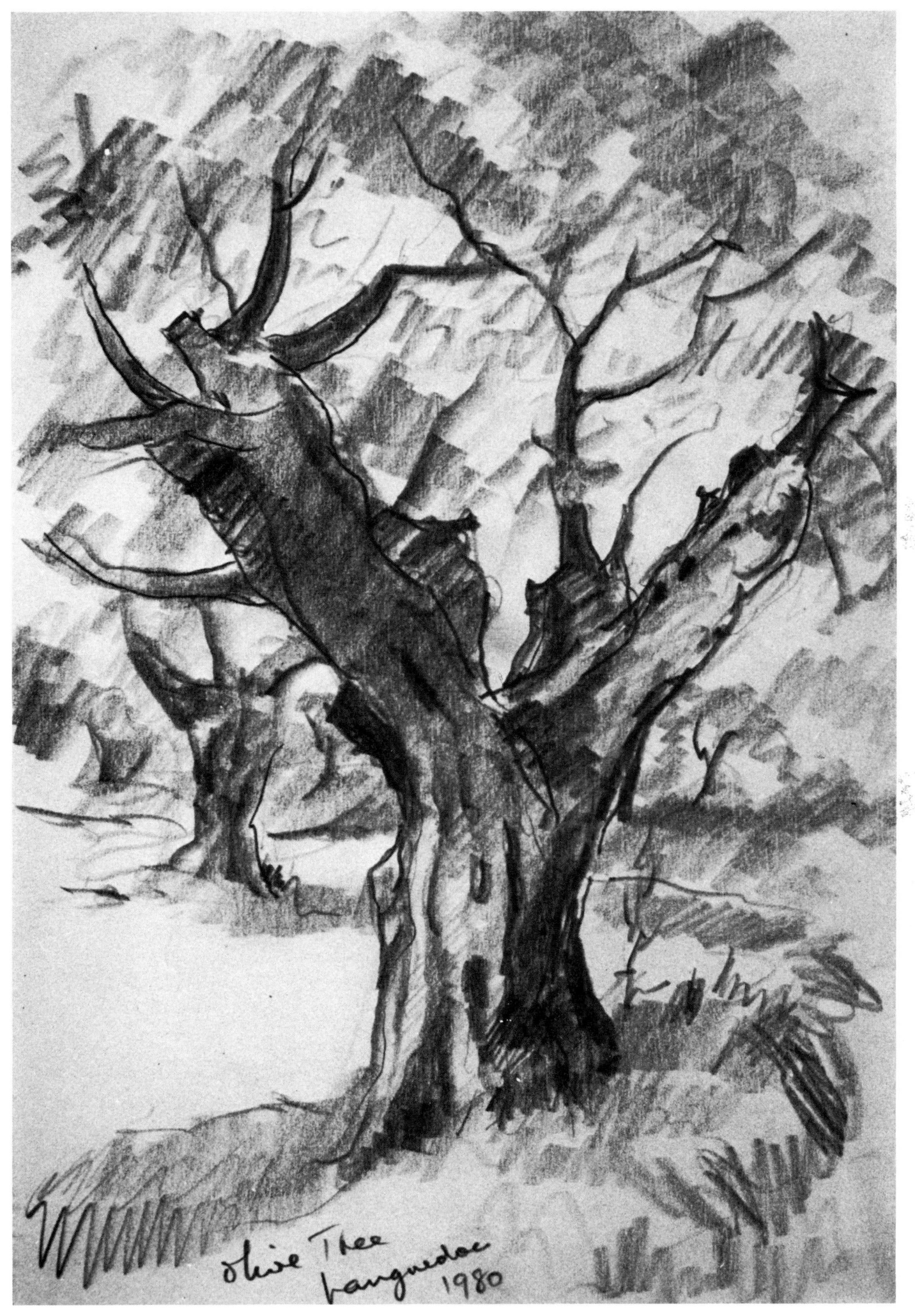
Olive Tree
Languedoc
1980

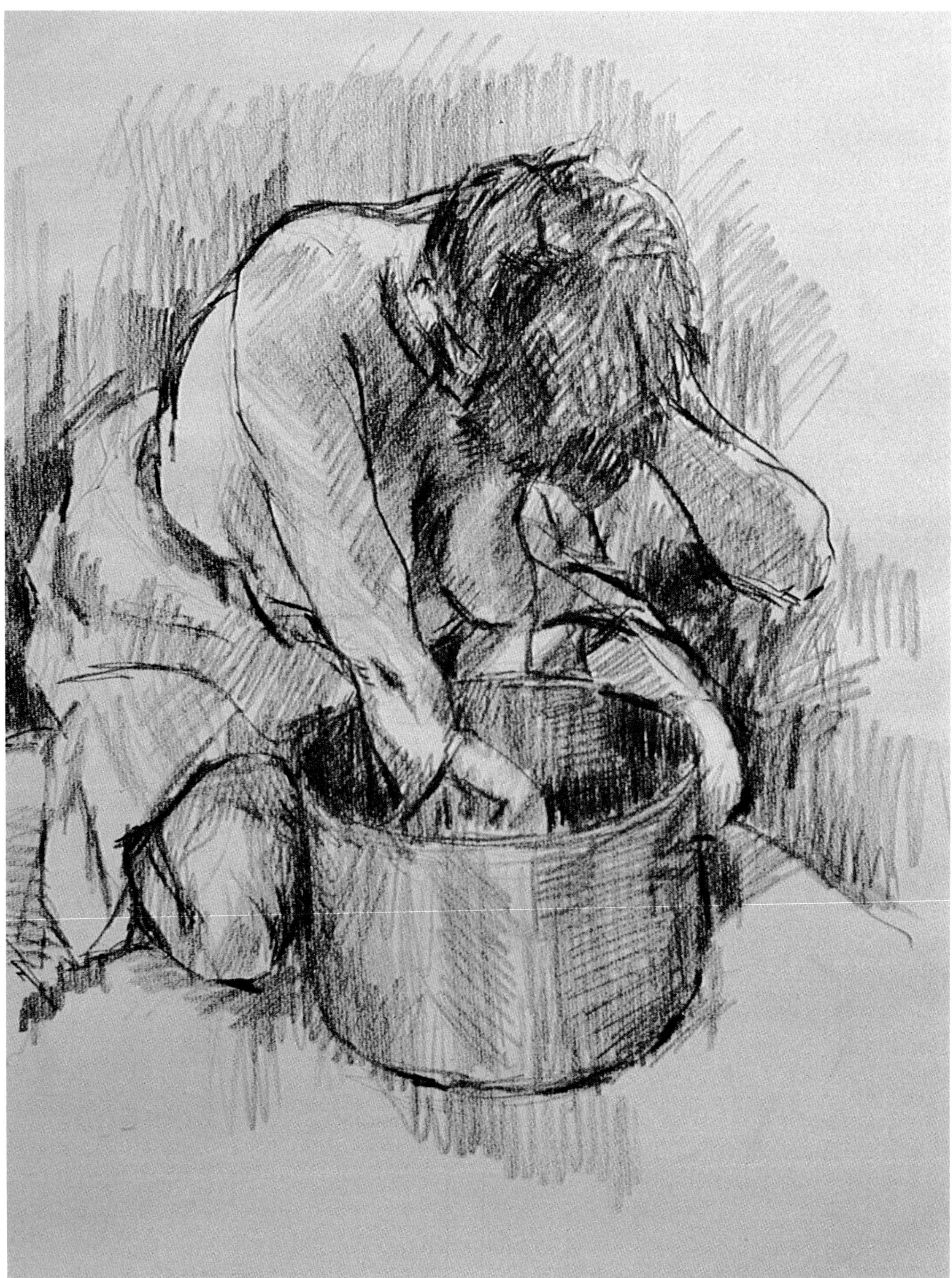

3. DRAWING PEOPLE

Wash day (Conté crayon, 24" x 16")

When drawing people, it is helpful, though by no means essential, to set aside as a studio a room which will be large enough to allow you to tackle either the full-length figure or just a head and shoulders portrait. For the latter, I recommend you acquire a rostrum. Fig 64 shows the construction and dimensions of a collapsible rostrum which can be folded and placed against a wall when not in use. Lighting is important: we are often told, quite correctly, that a north light is desirable. Unfortunately this is not always possible in the room available, but it need not be a problem if the rostrum is placed so that there is a good side light on the model, and the easel so that there is sufficient illumination without cast shadows. For working during the long winter evenings a photographer's flood lamp can be useful for lighting the subject. Remember to replace the photographic lamp with a conventional 150 watt bulb (these last longer). Much of this equipment will of course also be helpful, although not essential, for much of the other work you may wish to do.

FIG 64 Construction of rostrum

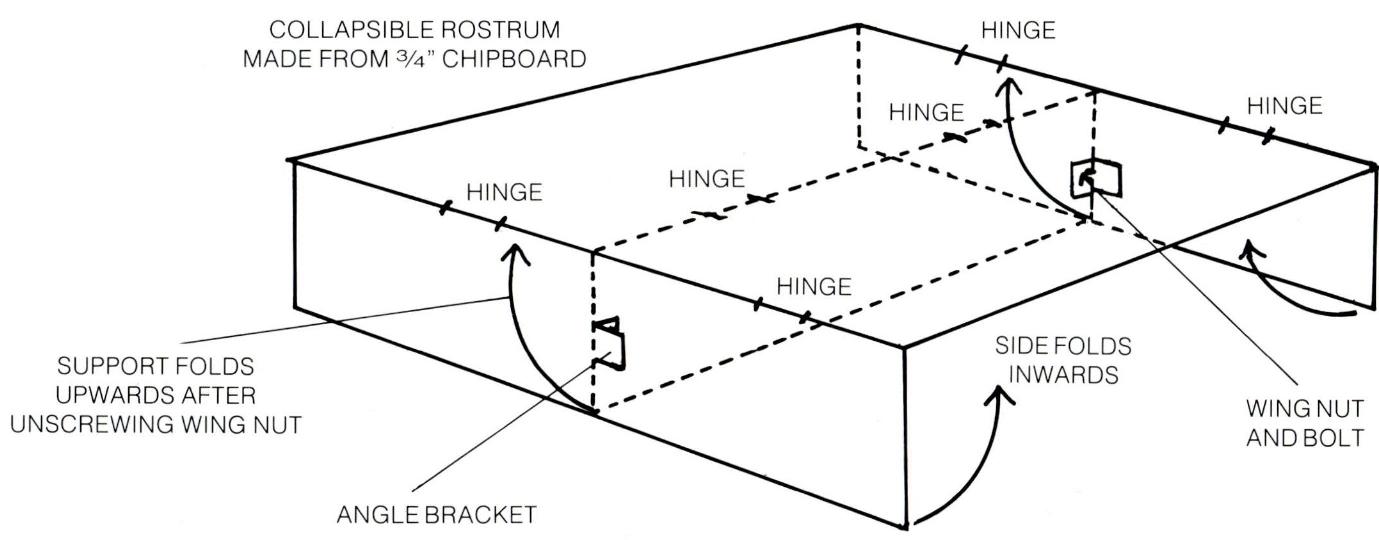

The right mental approach is necessary for all aspects of drawing and painting, especially when drawing and painting people. I often hear my students comment on the difficulties of a pose and saying, 'I can't do it'. This is a negative approach, and will always end in failure. In this section I shall constantly be imploring the student to look, look and then look again. Ninety per cent of drawing and painting is looking. Having taught drawing and painting for many years, I am still surprised at how infrequently students look at their subject. It is an inescapable fact that a tree is a far more complex object to draw than the human figure if the same standards of observation are applied, yet the figure is still considered the more difficult. The reason for this is that we identify more closely with another human being, setting ourselves much higher standards of visual accuracy. Remember the subject, in this case another human being, is our greatest asset. The model's comfort must be a major concern – if the model is uneasy this will reflect in the work. Allow the model to rest for at least five minutes after each twenty minutes spent posing. During rest periods, take stock of your work in readiness for the model's return. At the beginning of a pose, the model will take a little time to settle and relax into position. It is therefore unwise even to contemplate working during this period, so use this time for looking at and mentally drawing the subject, deciding on the composition and arranging the various parts in a pleasing order on the working surface. This is always time well spent, and is conducive to achieving the right attitude of mind.

Drawing and painting people gives an opportunity to put the language of drawing into practice. It enables us to explore the infinite number of aesthetic reasons for producing work around one subject (in much the same way that Rembrandt did with his large number of self portraits, and Monet when he painted the façade of Rouen cathedral some 20 times, each painting representing a different time of the day and different season).

To begin drawing the figure, there is no need to do more than apply the disciplines already explained. With the subject in front of you, make a doodle that will explore the surface of the sheet of paper. Use a 2B pencil for this. Look at the model as you doodle: try to see the posture and capture the rhythm of the pose. Vary the quality and density of the line: make it sweeping and rhythmic one moment, and staccato and angular the next. If a form begins to suggest itself, allow it to develop, emphasise it and, above all, work rapidly. This exercise creates confidence and broadens your skills and knowledge by igniting the creative instinct. It has been said that when artists stop doodling they stop work. This 'doodle' approach to drawing, when applied to a subject, forms part of drawing for enquiry. It is exploratory by its very nature, and the line will be tentative and searching, exploring the surface of the subject (just as in doodling Fig 65 shows an enquiry drawing of a semi-draped figure). Such enquiry drawing encourages you to draw mentally – I rarely draw anything on paper without having first drawn it in my mind. By doing this, the selective process is being made to work; the parts of the subject that do not reflect your emotional

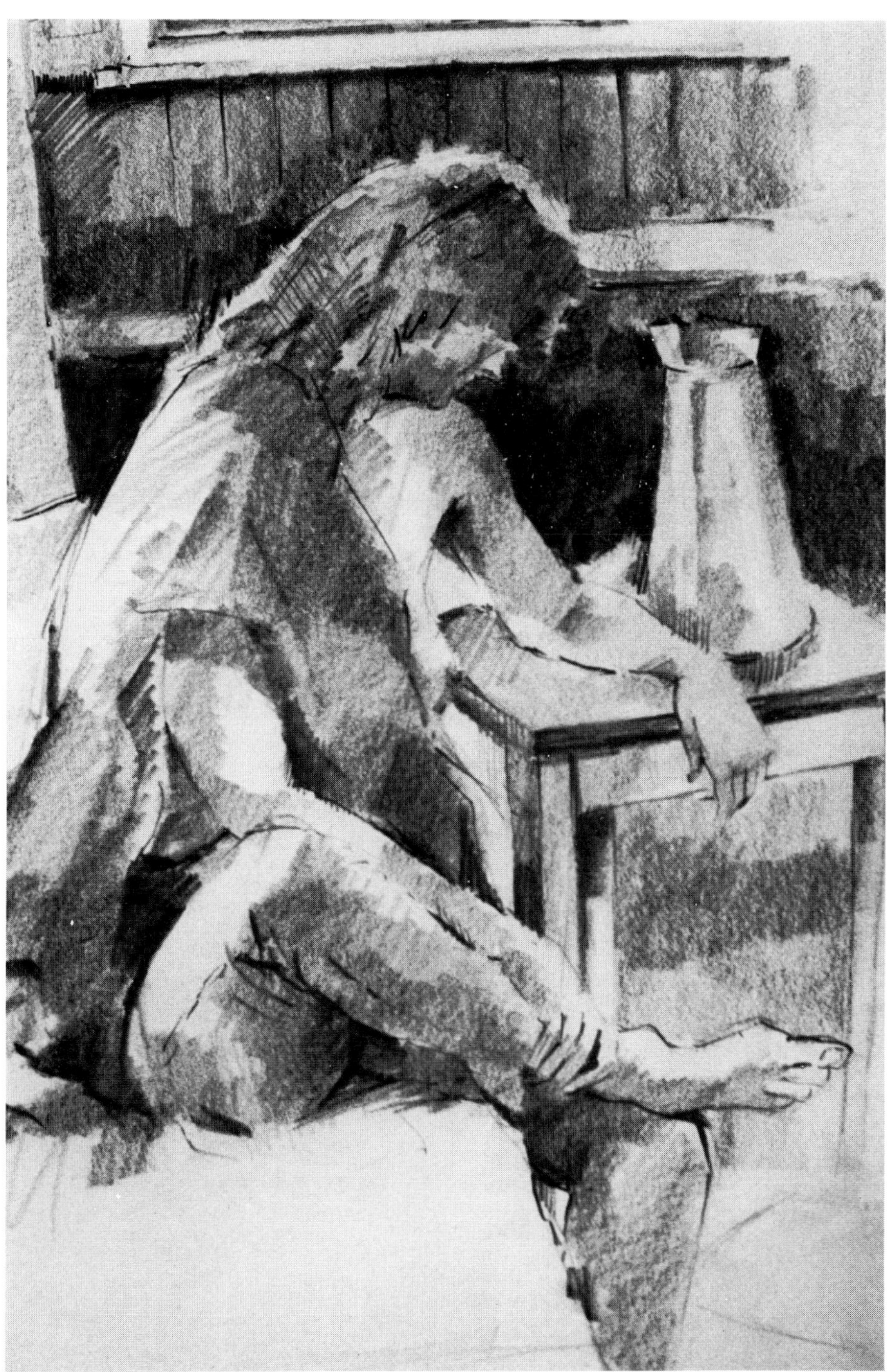

FIG 65 Enquiry drawing of draped figure

response can be rejected. Drawing in this manner will encourage you to look at the subject honestly, which, with the language of drawing, will then enable you to make a truthful statement.

Initially the drawing will inevitably be inadequate but, even if it is somewhat feeble, it will create the desire to develop it further, making the drawing self-generating. I have heard it said that when this really happens it is as if the picture draws itself, or there is a force beyond us which seems to take over.

By using geometric shapes, it becomes obvious from the beginning that the volume of the subject can be developed, creating an awareness of the underlying structure of the forms being drawn. It was in the Renaissance that artists first became aware of the need to understand form if an illusion of three-dimensions was going to succeed. It is this understanding that forms the foundation of sound painting. The great French artist Ingres said, 'Go on drawing for a long time before you think of painting. If one builds on a solid foundation one sleeps untroubled: for it is only from sound drawing that painting can grow'. Fig 66 shows a contour drawing of the standing nude with a geometric construction drawing of the same pose which illustrates the volume of the figure. I cannot over-emphasise the importance of understanding the volume of all the things you wish to draw. It is an essential requirement of both objective drawing and drawing for record purposes.

Perspective will also have a part to play in the drawing of people, particularly crowd scenes or a busy street. When drawing buildings, you saw that perspective helps to relate the figures to each other and to their environment, e.g. the buildings, the room, furniture, etc. In other words, perspective enables us to assess the relationship between shapes at the right scale, and this is of paramount importance in the drawing and painting of people.

Painting and drawing from life is one of the oldest and best established traditions of fine art. It requires total concentration of powers of observation, and it provides us with a tremendous variety of shapes and angles from which we can begin to understand three-dimensional form. A further advantage of working from the model is that as the pose is changing slightly all the time, it offers the advantage of studying the play of light over the form of the figure.

Commencing with the drawing process, try to draw the figure as a set of simple volumes, using the geometric shapes outlined earlier. This will help in understanding the basic structure, as Fig 67 shows. Note that in this drawing the point of weight distribution is indicated. If you have difficulty in determining this, find a true vertical or, if this is not possible, use a plumb line and relate the pose to it.

The human figure is a solid object existing in space. It divides into seven main volumetric areas: head, neck, torso, two arms and two legs. Each of these areas in turn subdivides: into upper and lower arms incorporating the hands and fingers; the legs divide into thighs, lower legs, feet and toes; the head into eyes, nose, ears, and mouth. In simple terms the first thing you must do is work out the volumetric characteristics of these parts. To simplify this, think of the larger parts as being cylindrical, each with a central axis. The axes are the key to analysis of the figure. Correct analysis of these axes will determine the direction in space of each part, and the volume it represents. Unfortunately other parts do not fit in with this form of analysis, as they are not all cylindrical in shape. The use of directional lines will help to deal with these parts. In order to see and establish these, ask, in which direction do the parts of the figure move in space, and what are the

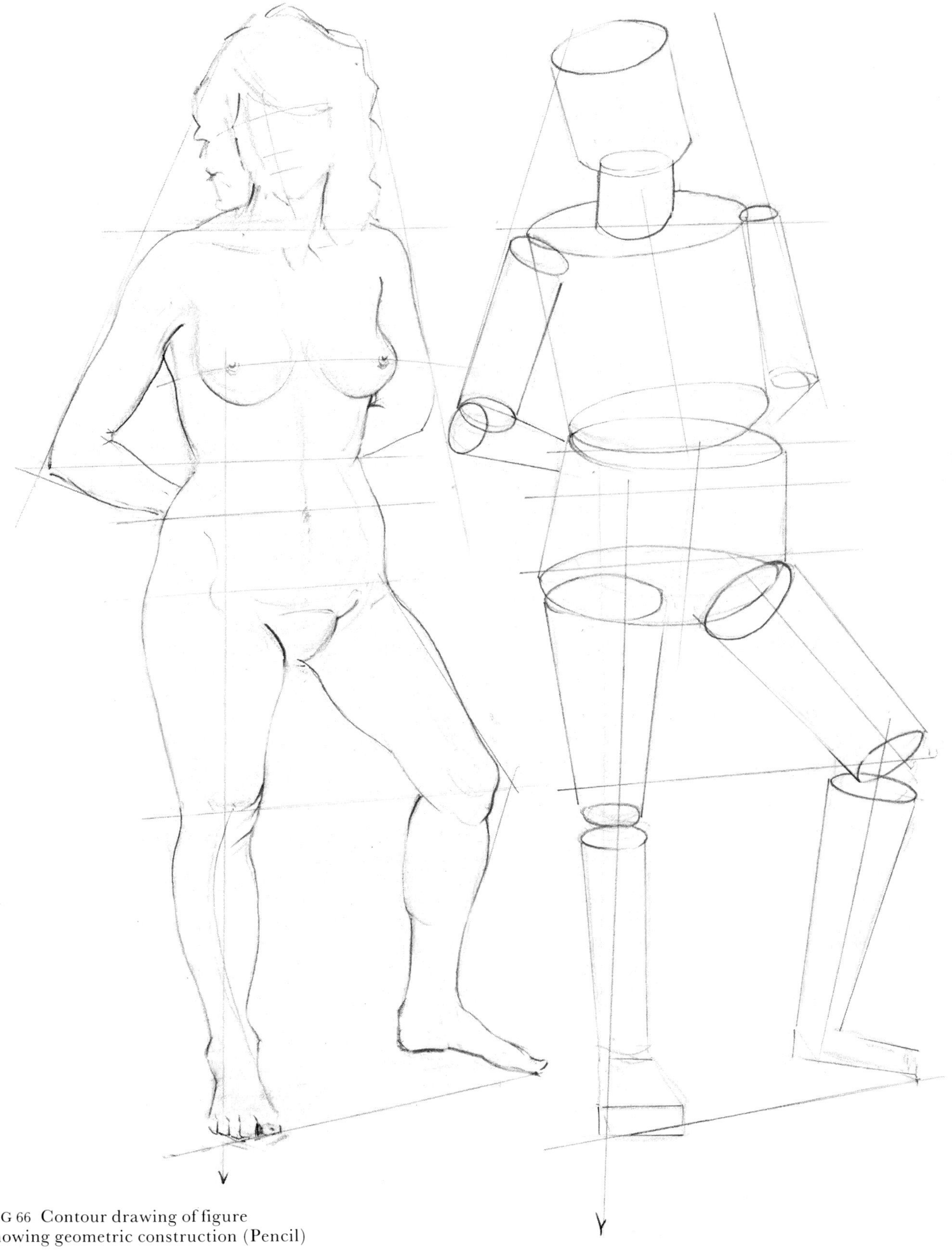

FIG 66 Contour drawing of figure
showing geometric construction (Pencil)

FIG 67 Weight distribution in drawing
the figure

FIG 68 Posture line

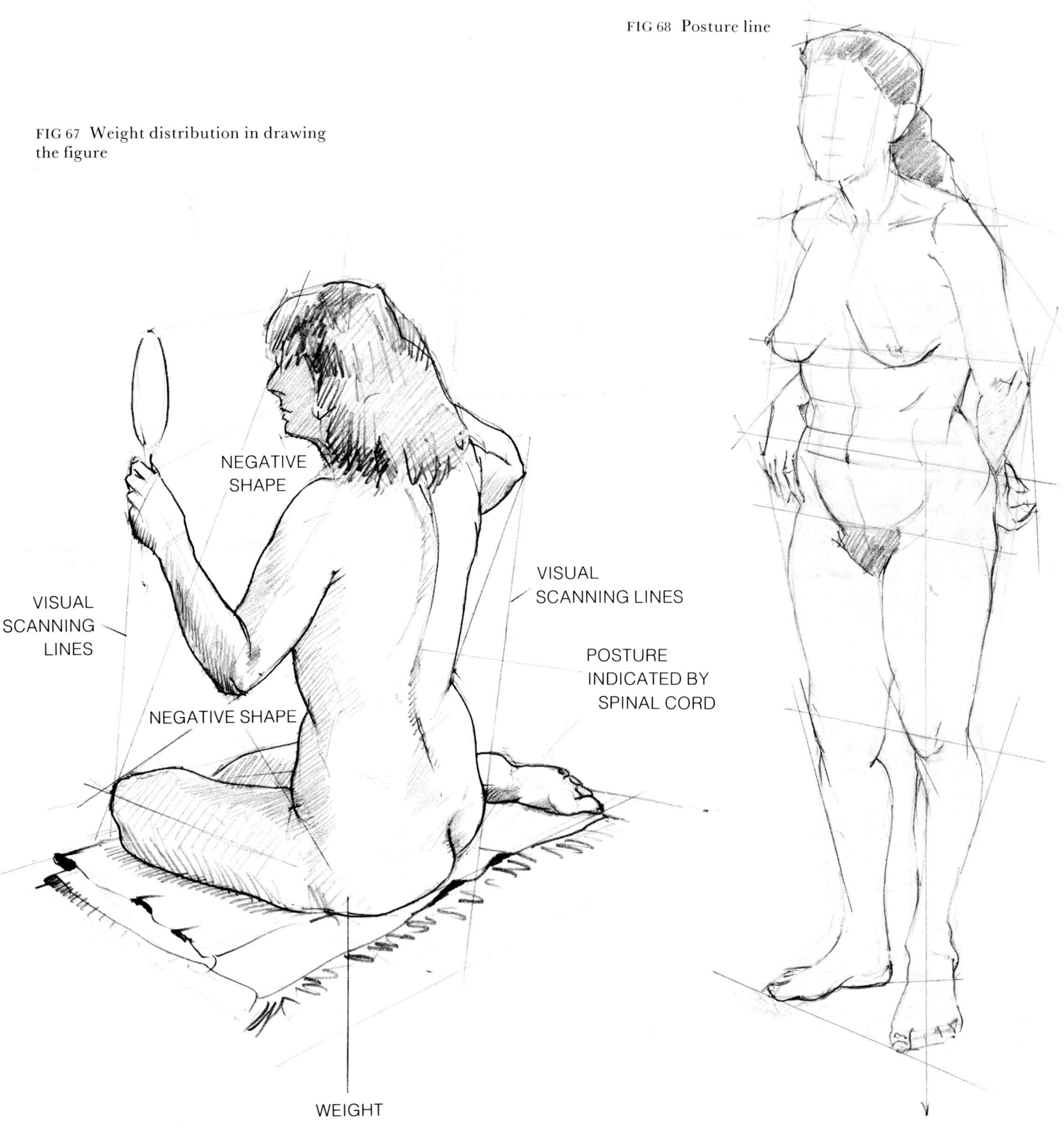

angles of inclination in relationship to each other? Look also at the negative shapes – that is, the holes between the shapes. A point to remember here: when drawing the hole left by a shape, do not start by drawing the shape; draw the hole, as to do otherwise will certainly leave the wrong shape. The combination of these factors will help to establish the position of a volume in space. A further step towards overcoming the difficulty of representing volume on a flat surface is to understand the cross-section of the figure. The use of the cylinder in figure drawing shows that in order to suggest volume it is helpful to draw around the form. When used in conjuction with lines indicating length and direction, this shows the three-dimensional state. It follows that the more complex the forms, the greater the number and the more varied the cross-sections will have to be in order to convey the volume.

Of course drawings of the figure do not normally have the cross-sections drawn on them, but you will see how helpful they are in understanding and exploring the structure of the figure.

The torso is the largest part of the figure, and it is here that your drawing can begin in earnest. It comprises two sections connected by the spine. The spine is a flexible pipe which allows the chest and hips a degree of related movement. These movements are forwards, backwards, sideways and semi-rotational, clockwise and anti-clockwise. In all free-standing natural poses the movement between the parts of the torso, around the centre of gravity of the figure, have a major bearing on the head, neck, arms, and legs. To establish these dispositions I find it necessary to indicate the posture by means of a single line following the centre of both upper and lower sections of the torso. Fig 68 shows how the posture line runs through the centre of the thorax and abdomen. The posture determines the distribution of weight. In Fig 69 I have shown a standing figure with the weight mainly on the right hand-side – note how the pelvis is pushed upwards and the shoulder drops towards the hip to compensate for the shift in the centre of gravity. This tends to compress the torso on this side of the body, with the result that the forms on the opposite side are stretched. You should always look for action and reaction when painting and drawing the figure. All of these movements are indicated in the spine. The spine continues into the neck, and any movement of the torso is again compensated for by a counter-shift in the position of the head. In this pose the left leg is not supporting much weight, so the muscles are relaxed and the knee flexed. These movements are known as *contra posture* and make a major contribution to the poise and rhythm of the figure.

As all drawing requires observation and the assessment of measurements, proportions and relationships, it is helpful to use visual cross-references. The best way to achieve this is to visually scan the figure, using straight lines to connect the various parts together. Fig 70 illustrates this in practice, and you will see how some of the lines travel across the figure whilst others move from one point to another, cutting the space between the points (head to knee, hand to hand, foot to hand, and so on). Whilst using visual scanning, remember to repeatedly

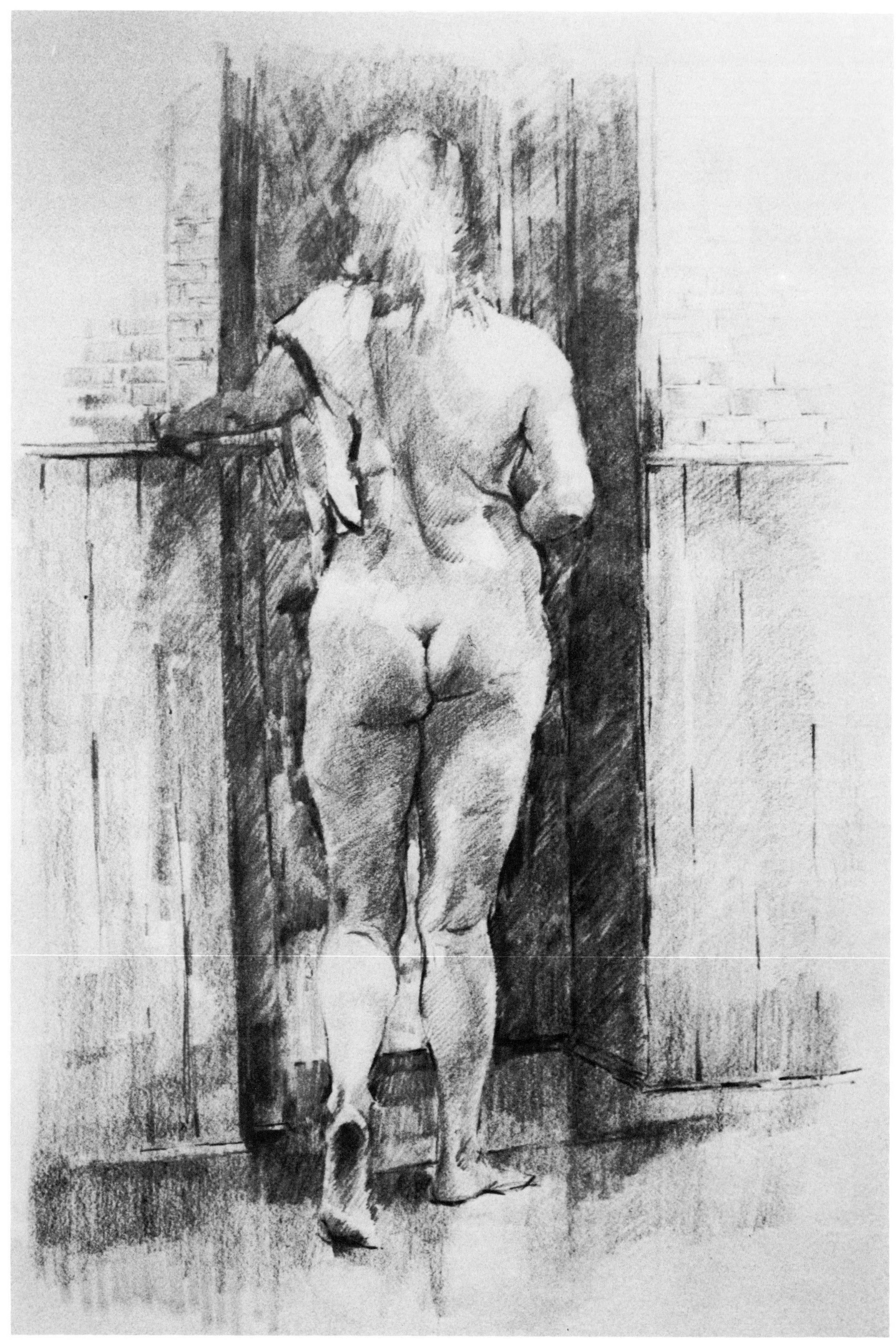

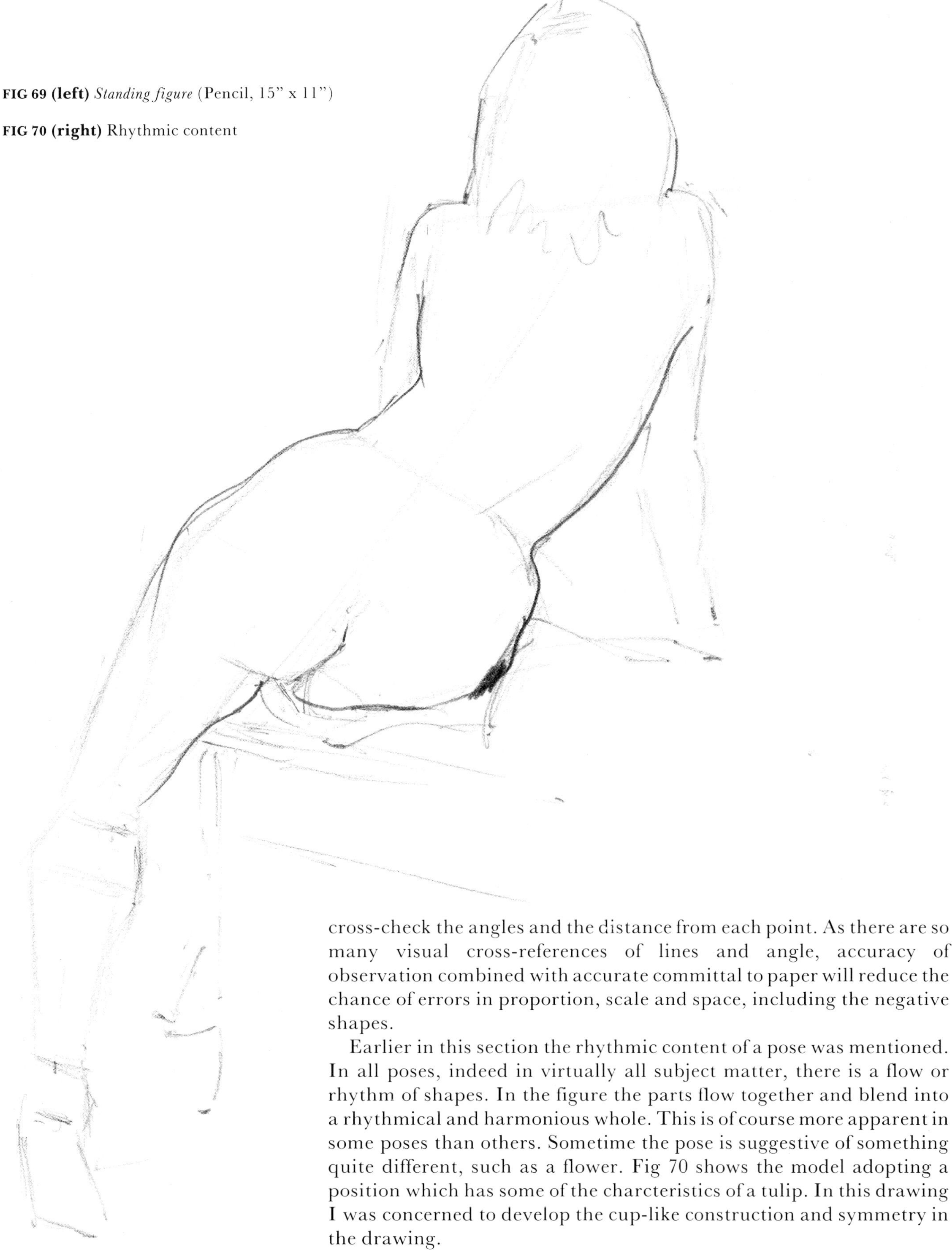

cross-check the angles and the distance from each point. As there are so many visual cross-references of lines and angle, accuracy of observation combined with accurate committal to paper will reduce the chance of errors in proportion, scale and space, including the negative shapes.

Earlier in this section the rhythmic content of a pose was mentioned. In all poses, indeed in virtually all subject matter, there is a flow or rhythm of shapes. In the figure the parts flow together and blend into a rhythmical and harmonious whole. This is of course more apparent in some poses than others. Sometime the pose is suggestive of something quite different, such as a flower. Fig 70 shows the model adopting a position which has some of the charcteristics of a tulip. In this drawing I was concerned to develop the cup-like construction and symmetry in the drawing.

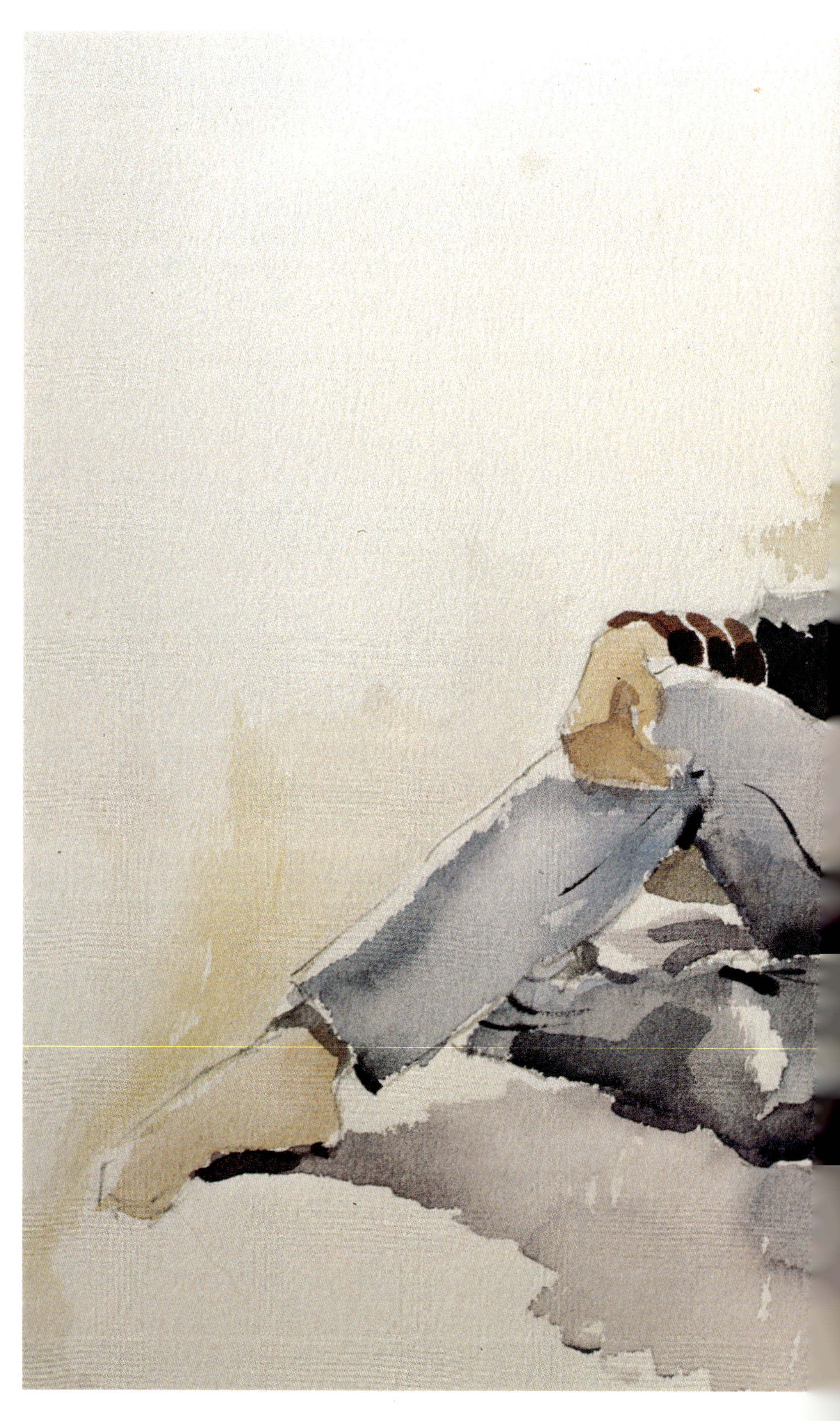

FIG 71 *Reclining figure* (Watercolour,
18" x 15")

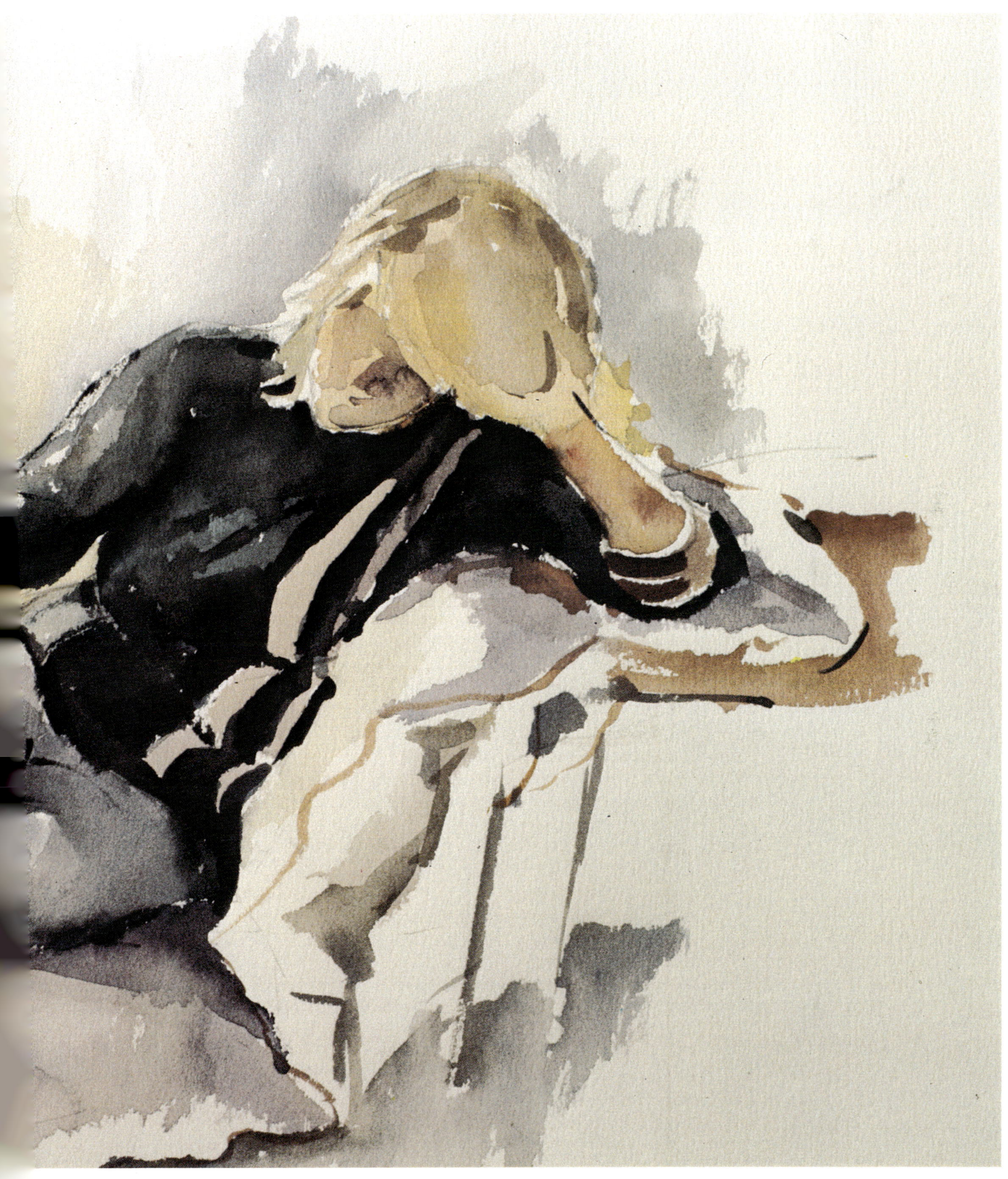

Essentially, try to remember to consider the entire figure. After all, it will be a fruitless exercise if all the different parts are drawn correctly, but do not fit into the whole. If you do not give your primary attention to evaluating the entire pose so that you understand the rhythm and movement, the relationship in space and the position relative to the eye-level, there will be no point in carrying out any further investigation of the structure. Eyes and mind are all too ready to involve us in detail, but this must be resisted. The eyes and mind must be disciplined to respond to the larger and main issues, and be constantly checking and rechecking the arrangement and position of the whole figure. Imagination and inventiveness are necessary in our response to the subject and you should, in the interests of freedom of expression, be prepared to experiment and innovate in the handling of the subject. In this way you will be developing the potential for aesthetic exploration by the manner in which you express the forms you are drawing.

There seems no doubt that in order to produce aesthetically pleasing figure drawings it is important to acquire an understanding and an appreciation of the figure as a number of rhythmically-related volumes in space, coupled with a spontaneous natural response to the perception of the subject. This will be instrumental in capturing the life and vitality of the subject as well as in developing your own sensitivity towards the work, in tune with the medium being used. Ultimately, you should be able to synthesise all these elements into a language which suits your own ability and interests.

Rapid drawing is an exercise that should be practised. It develops the powers of concentration, and encourages the assessment of pose, spatial disposition and areas of tension and relaxation. You can practise by setting up short poses in the life room. Starting with a ten-minute one, reduce them gradually to one minute. Try moving poses – these can be useful in making the mind retain visual impressions. Perceptions have to be recorded whilst the figure is walking, twisting, reaching, stooping, and so on. The movement should be repeated a number of times so that the mind can retain the visual image. When the image is firmly imprinted on the mind and the retina of the eye, then an attempt to draw it can be made.

Another worthwhile exercise for developing concentration is to draw the subject without looking at the paper. Contour line drawing is best for this, and you may check your drawing where lines cross, such as in the overlap of forms. Fig 72 is an example of this manner of drawing. The line should be encouraged to follow the contour of the figure and give expression to movement and volume. To do this, try to imagine the drawing implement actually following the edges of the model. During this exercise it is necessary to draw at a constant speed to avoid getting mismatches of contour. Feel free to move the contour lines, or even to draw a further line inside or outside the initial line; in other words, do not feel inhibited. The results usually look quite strange at first but, as with all the arts, practice makes perfect, and if concentration can be maintained some lively and interesting results may emerge.

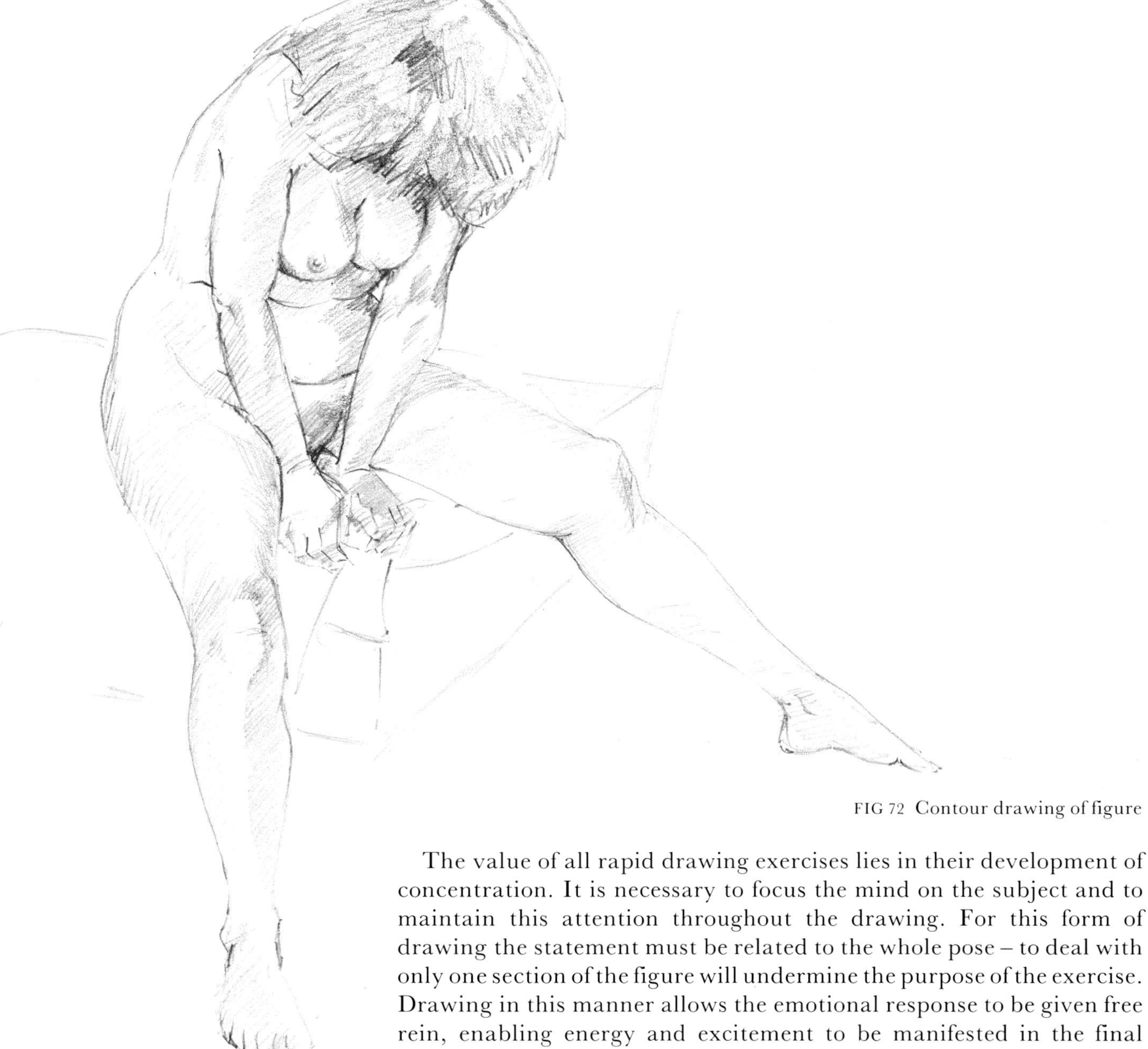

FIG 72 Contour drawing of figure

The value of all rapid drawing exercises lies in their development of concentration. It is necessary to focus the mind on the subject and to maintain this attention throughout the drawing. For this form of drawing the statement must be related to the whole pose – to deal with only one section of the figure will undermine the purpose of the exercise. Drawing in this manner allows the emotional response to be given free rein, enabling energy and excitement to be manifested in the final result.

Thus far our attention has been concentrated on the whole figure. It is now important to study the various components of the human form in greater depth, commencing with the head. As with the whole figure, the posture is critically important. It is the first mark that is made and it is the first step towards getting a likeness. You will remember how the posture of the head is dictated by the posture of the torso. This is of major importance when making a head and shoulders portrait. All too often we see portraits where the head and neck relate, but the shoulders and neck do not. In most instances this has come about because the postures of the head and torso have not been observed accurately.

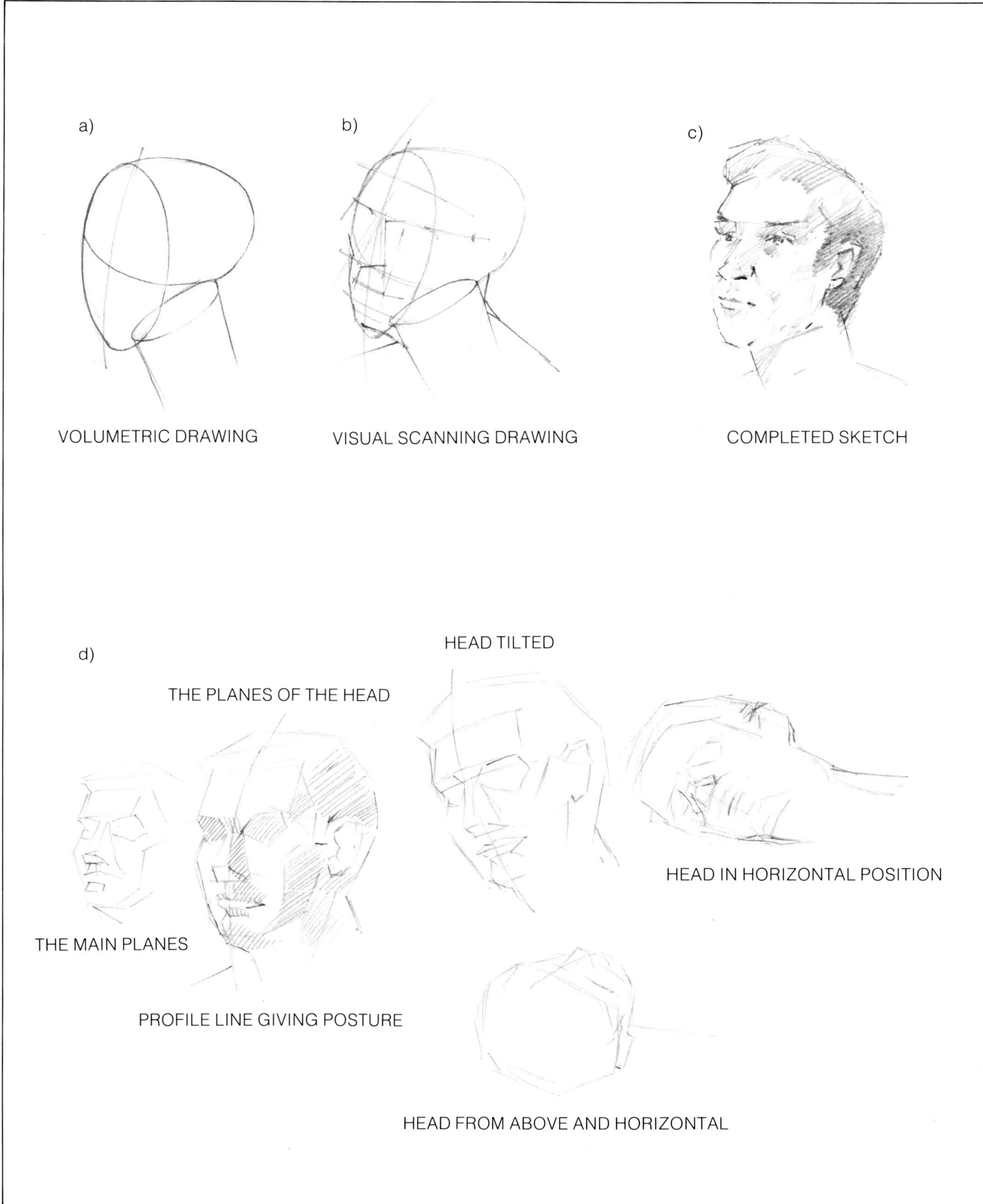

a)
b)
c)
VOLUMETRIC DRAWING
VISUAL SCANNING DRAWING
COMPLETED SKETCH
d)
HEAD TILTED
THE PLANES OF THE HEAD
HEAD IN HORIZONTAL POSITION
THE MAIN PLANES
PROFILE LINE GIVING POSTURE
HEAD FROM ABOVE AND HORIZONTAL

FIG 73a-c Structure of head

FIG 73d Structure of head

In Fig 73 I have shown the stages of a structural drawing of the head in a three-quarter view position. Fig 73a is a volumetric study using two spheres and a cylinder; this drawing helps to develop an awareness of the solidity of the head, enabling you to draw it as a solid object in space, relating it to the surrounding environment. Fig 73b shows the visual scanning lines I find helpful with the head in this position. In Fig 73c the picture is completed. Portraiture requires accuracy of observation and an understanding of the construction of the head and its composition. All this will be to little effect, however, if you are unable to position the eyes, nose, mouth and ears correctly. Visual scanning is the way to achieve this within the framework of the head, as shown in Fig 73b.

To be able to make an expressive statement about any subject requires understanding, and this can be gained through drawing. To draw the eye requires a knowledge of how the eye is made and how it works, and particularly of how these factors affect the surface form. Fig 74 shows a basic drawing of the eye socket, complete with eyeball, the position of the eyelids and the muscles that operate them. It is often, mistakenly, thought that the eyes are a mirror image of each other. Nothing could be further from the truth: there is always a difference, this being one of the contributory factors that create likeness. The eye also reflects the sitter's feelings, as the changes of its shape indicate many emotional responses. We as artists must be aware of this and be able to use it to the benefit of our work.

FIG 74 Drawing the structure of the eyes, nose and mouth, posture, geometric planes in various positions

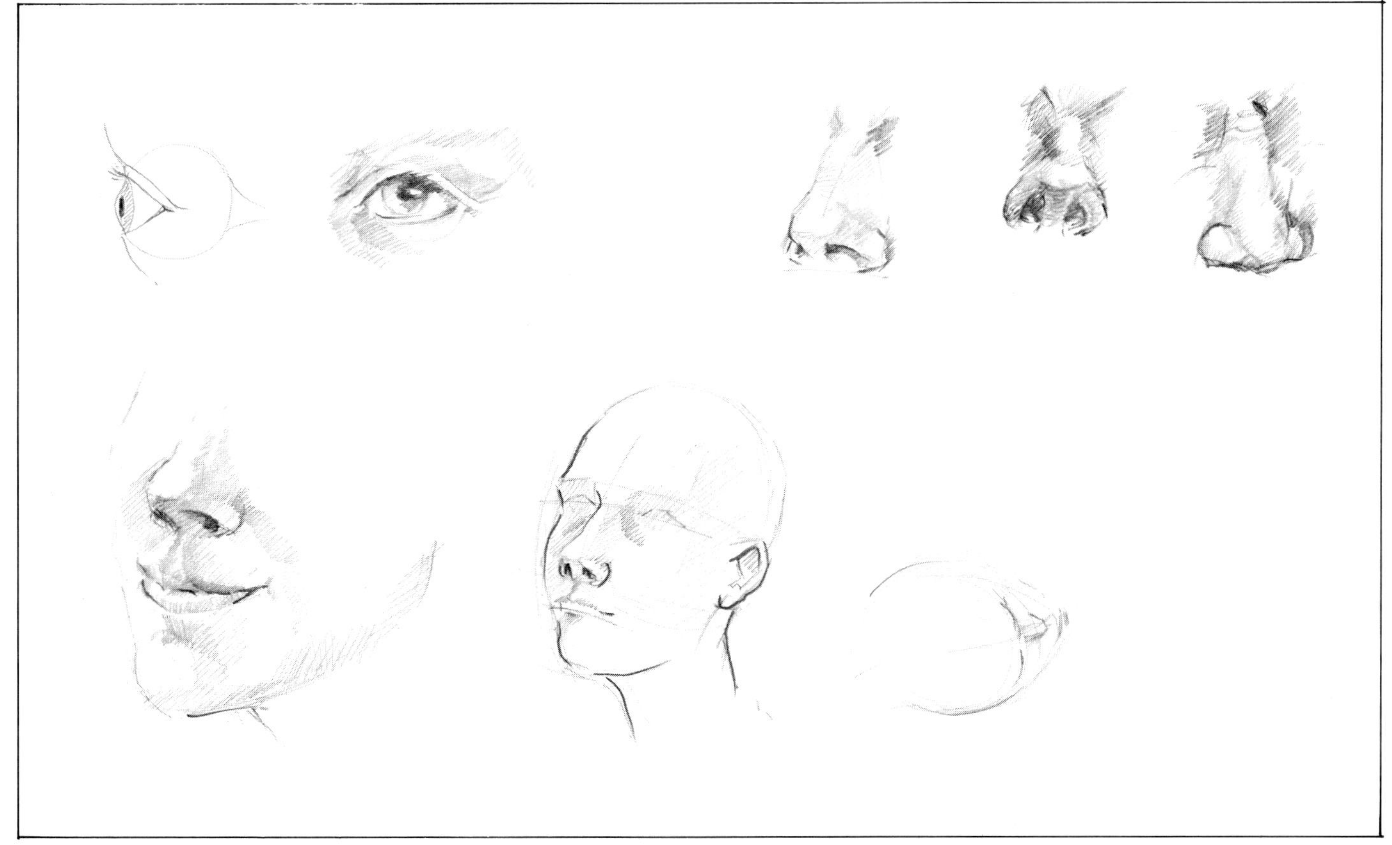

As all the components of the head are inter-related, it is logical to deal next with drawing the nose, its construction and its relationship with the eyes and mouth. Fig 73d shows the head as a series of geometric planes. Each of these represents a change in direction of the surface form. You will see from this drawing how each of the planes conforms to a change of direction on the surface of the head. You can also see the major changes of the surface planes of the nose, its basic shape being a rather lopsided pyramid.

Fig 73d also illustrates the movement of the profile or posture line and the change of position of the eyes, nose, mouth and ear, as the head is rotated through 180 degrees. At any point of movement, vertical or horizontal, the perspective of the components and the planes of the head change. Fig 73d shows the head drawn from a number of different viewpoints: above, below and from the side.

The construction of the mouth and its relationship to the nose and chin must also be understood. The mouth, like the eyes, reflects emotion. It does this by changing its shape. In the smile, it broadens and turns up, whilst in unhappiness it tightens and turns down. It can be relaxed or tense; it can be laughing or crying. All these aspects must be observed and registered if the portrait is to have any real meaning.

FIG 75 Drawing the lips and the mouth

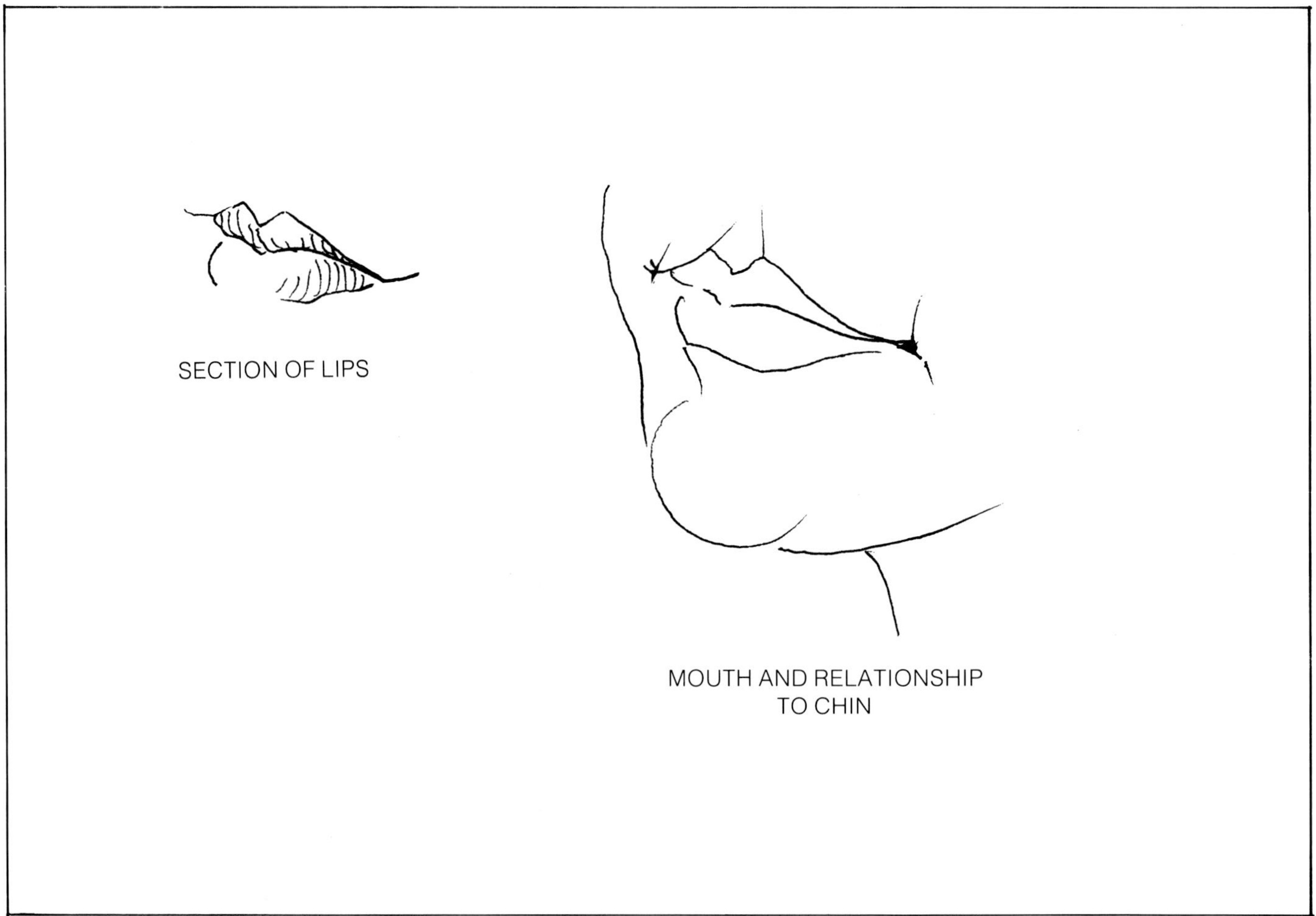

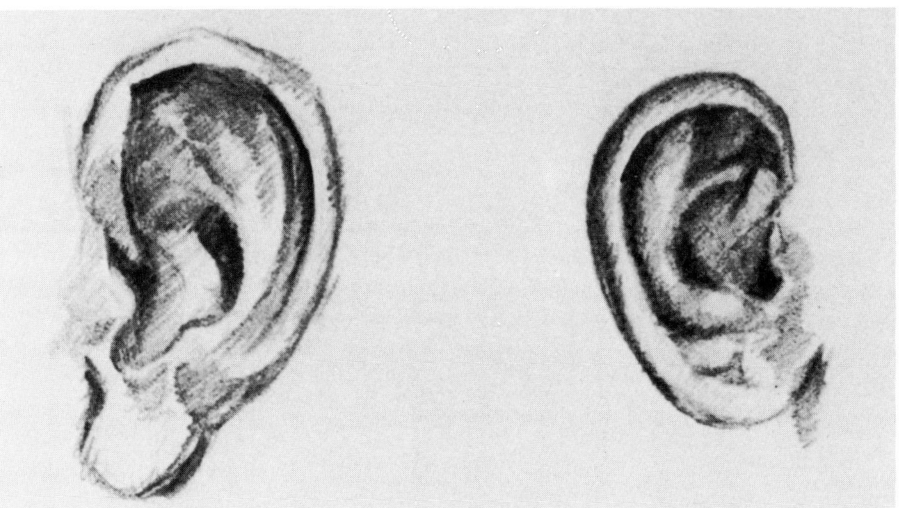

FIG 76 Drawing the ear

Far too often one sees portraits where the mouth is depicted as a static line: in reality, this is most certainly not the case. If you examine the shape and form of the lips you will see that the section is quite curved in the centre of the mouth. As the mouth curves round the head, the cylindrical section of the lips becomes smaller and flat. Fig 75 shows this in section. Of course, these illustrations are shown only as hypothetical guidelines: each subject must be dealt with on an individual basis, and the sitter's characteristics developed. The mouth's relationship to the chin is important and the shape and construction of the chin and jaw should be noted carefully. Fig 75 shows the ball-like shape that is the dominant feature.

There remains one further component to consider: the ear. All too often the ear receives little or no attention, but as a most complex organ, it requires a great deal. The construction comprises a series of cylinders, hills and valleys, and the whole is attached to and projects from the side of the head. In Fig 76 I have tried to show the construction of the ear and its relationship to the head, using the other components as measuring points. Note how the position changes when we look from above or below eye-level.

So far little has been said about likeness. If you have observed the shape of the head and its components accurately and related them to each other and to the whole, you will have a static likeness. What is wanted, however, is a living likeness. For this you have to find (when looking at your sitter) the common shape factor of the head – by this I mean that some heads are round, some are angular, some people have long faces, while others have short ones. Whatever the common shape factor in the head, you will discover that shape repeated more or less throughout the other components – so a person with a long angular face will have a long angular nose, the overall shape of the eyes and mouth will be angular, and the ears will likewise probably be long and angular. Selective emphasis on these shapes will help to capture a living likeness. Finally, confidence shown in the handling of the selected medium will impart a quality of life and movement to the drawing, which adds a further dimension to capturing the living likeness.

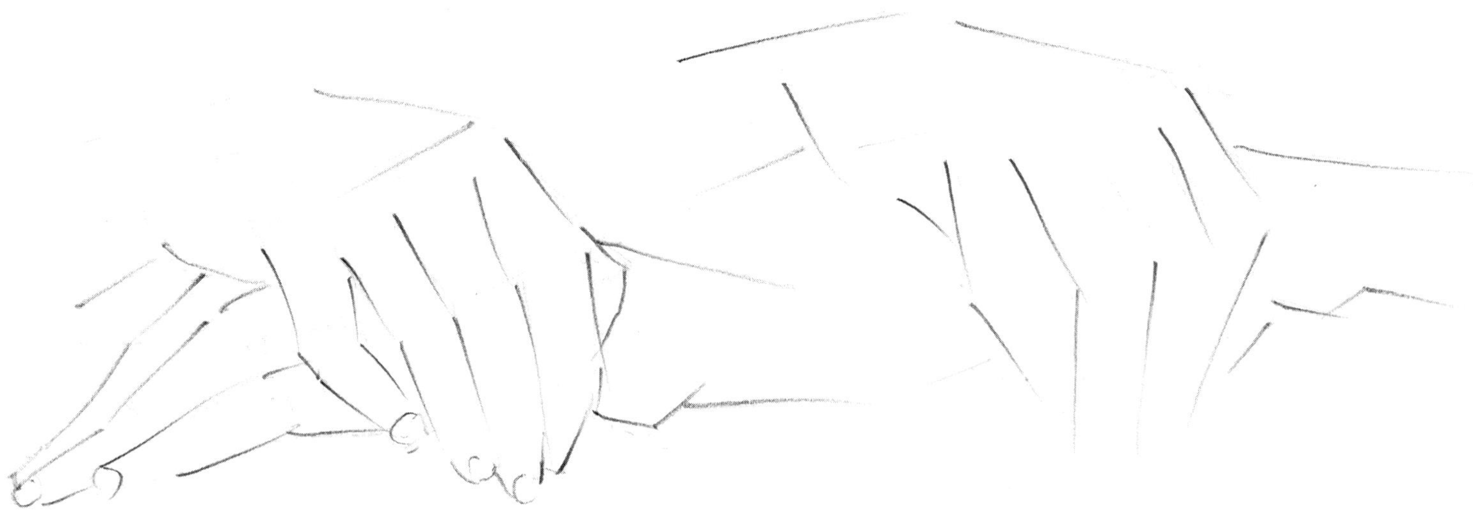

FIG 77 The scanning and structure of the hands

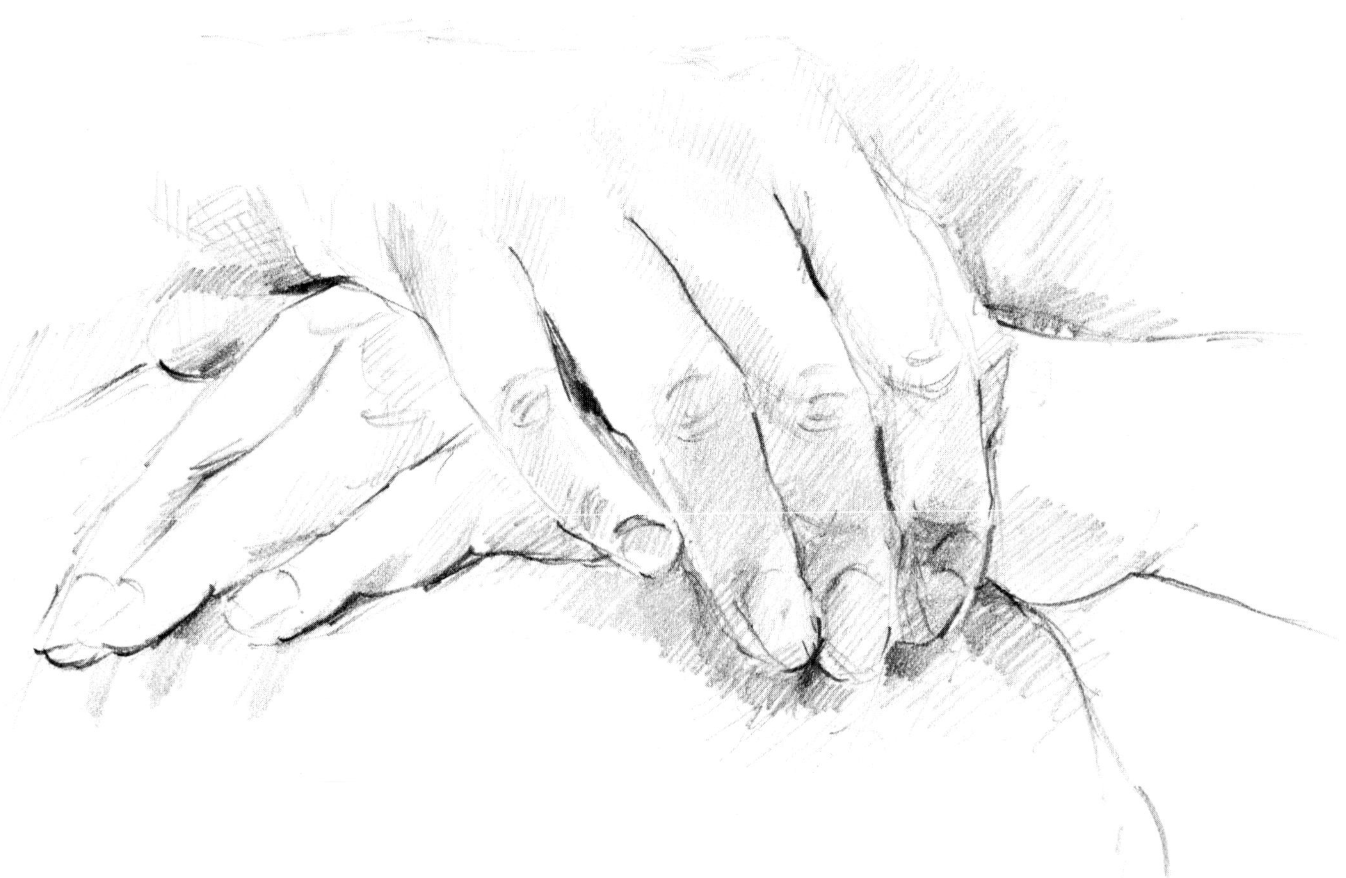

FIG 78 Completed drawing of interlocked hands

Likeness does not stop at the head. The hands and feet also play an important role in the registering of likeness. The hands, especially, can reflect character and profession, and in certain instances can convey more about the sitter than the facial likeness. You will see from this how valuable it will be to be able to draw hands and feet sensitively and expressively. To commence a drawing of hands it is, as always, necessary to see them as a whole. Fig 77 shows the volumetric drawing with visual scanning lines of a pair of related hands. Visual scanning lines will help you to see and measure the many angles and lines, as well as the many changes of direction that occur. In Fig 78 the drawing is completed and the cylindrical shapes of the fingers developed. Note the importance of the reflected light between the fingers, and how convex curved lines create an illusion of roundness.

The same approach may be applied when drawing feet, although I feel the problem here is not so complex. Fig 79 shows the three stages of development. The volumetric construction here is much simpler, using a cube, which is a sympathetic shape for the foot, and which enables the perspective to be easily registered. The scanning exercise is necessary for assessing the angles of the instep, ankles, and toes. One final and critically important point: do relate the hands and feet to the whole work. It is a common weakness for these components to be drawn too small. As a rough guide, remember that the hand is nearly as big as the face and the foot, when viewed from the side, is approximately as long as half the lower leg.

FIG 79 Construction of the foot

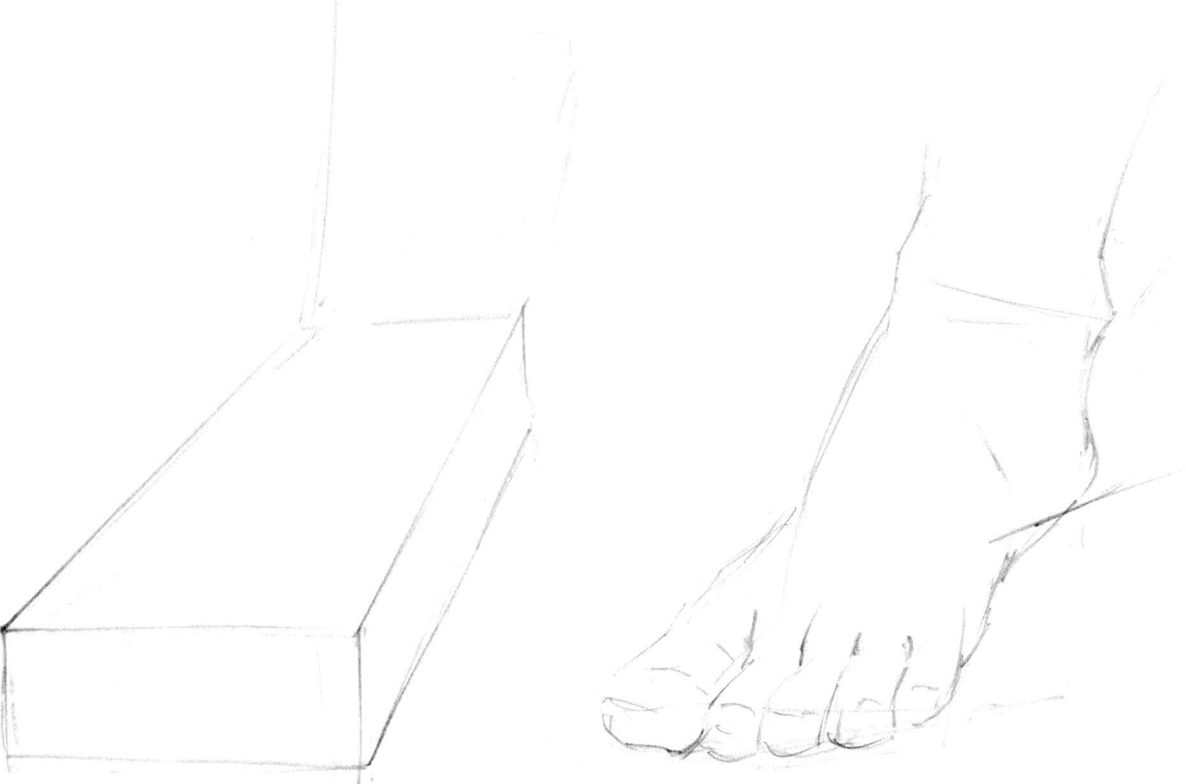

VOLUMETRIC DRAWING OF FOOT   VISUAL SCAN DRAWING OF FOOT

A final word about drawing and painting people and the figure in particular: I find it helpful to commence my final drawing from the centre of the figure, as it is from this area that the scale of the work can be determined and, being the largest section, it is helpful in arriving at a sympathetic composition. I have deliberately avoided any deep discussion of the anatomy of the figure in this section, because painting or drawing the figure is essentially an observation experience. This does not mean that a knowledge of human anatomy should be ignored: on the contrary, a good understanding of the body, used in conjunction with visual experience and a knowledge of the language of drawing, will inevitably assist you to produce work of greater register and perception. There are many good and authoritative works on anatomy for artists, which give insight into the subject, but remember there is no real alternative to using your eyes.

Animal life

Animals should be drawn using the same basic principles as those used for drawing the human body, or any other subject for that matter. As with the figure, a knowledge of anatomy of the various species that interest you is to be recommended, as this will ensure that a correct register is achieved.

Many museums have preserved examples of animals and will allow artists, on application, to make studies of them. This is a worthwhile exercise, as it will be of tremendous value when drawing from life. Apart from domestic animals, which are readily available in our homes and the surrounding countryside, many useful studies can be made in zoos and wildlife parks. This is an opportunity to couple photography and drawing in order to obtain as much information as possible so that work can then be developed in the studio.

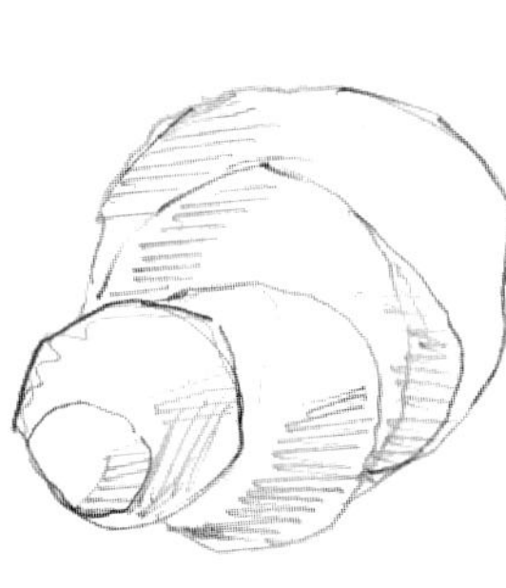

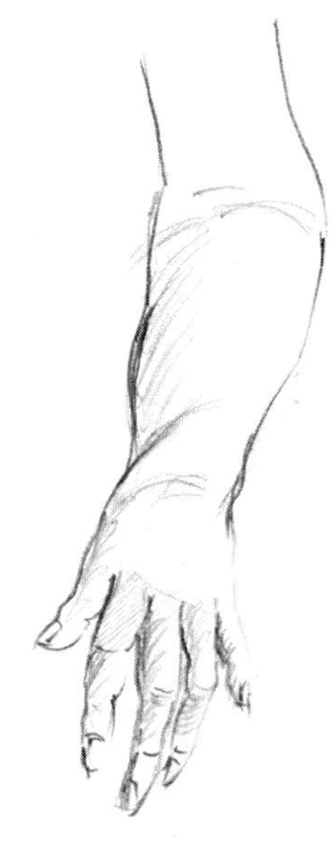

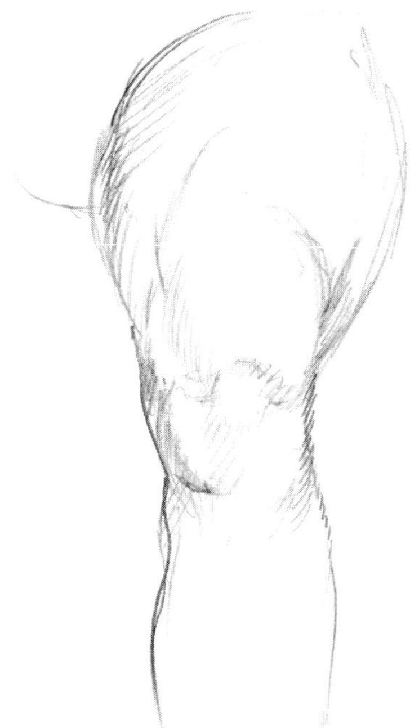

Foreshortening (Pencil)

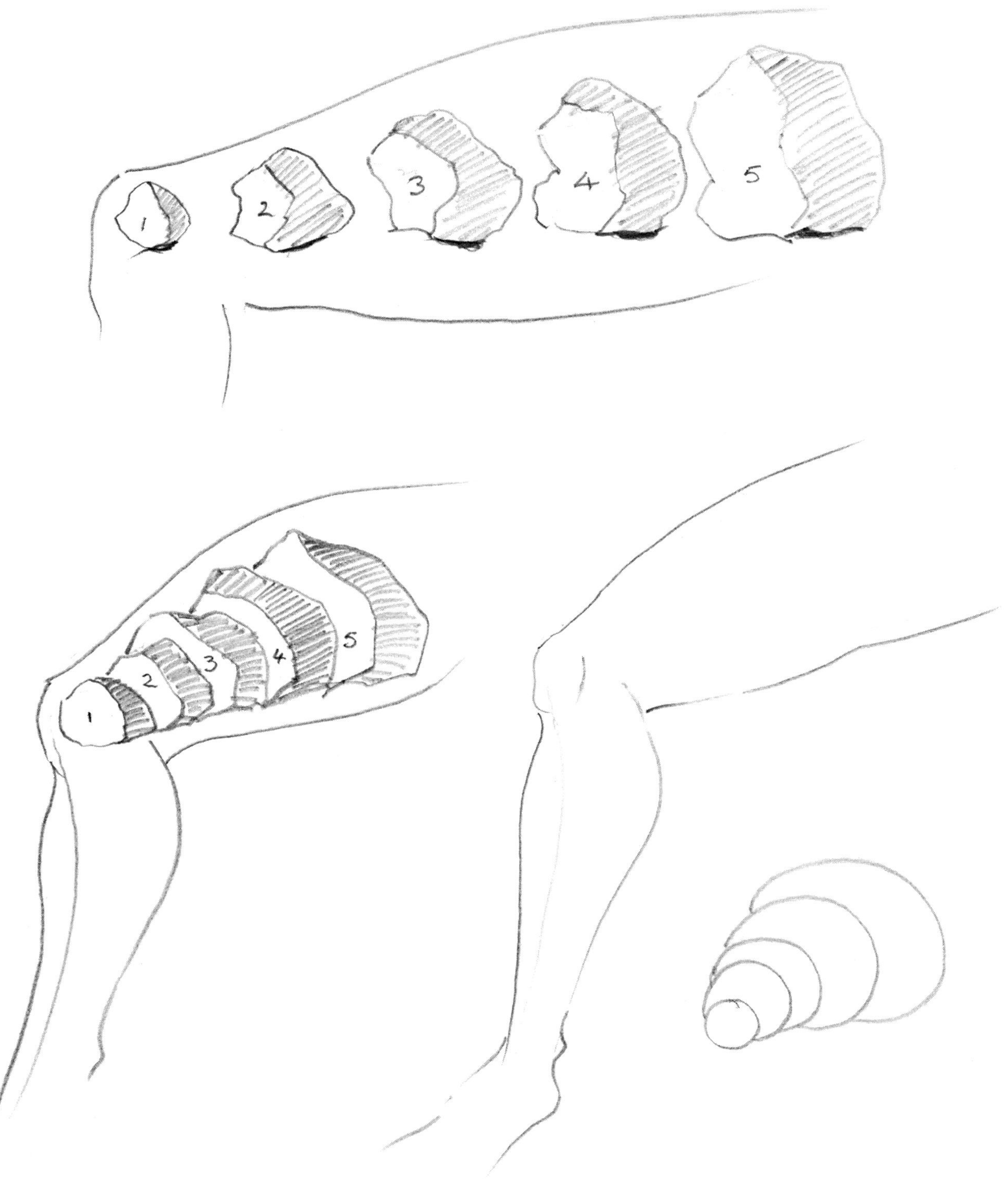

Principles of foreshortening using
overlapping shapes

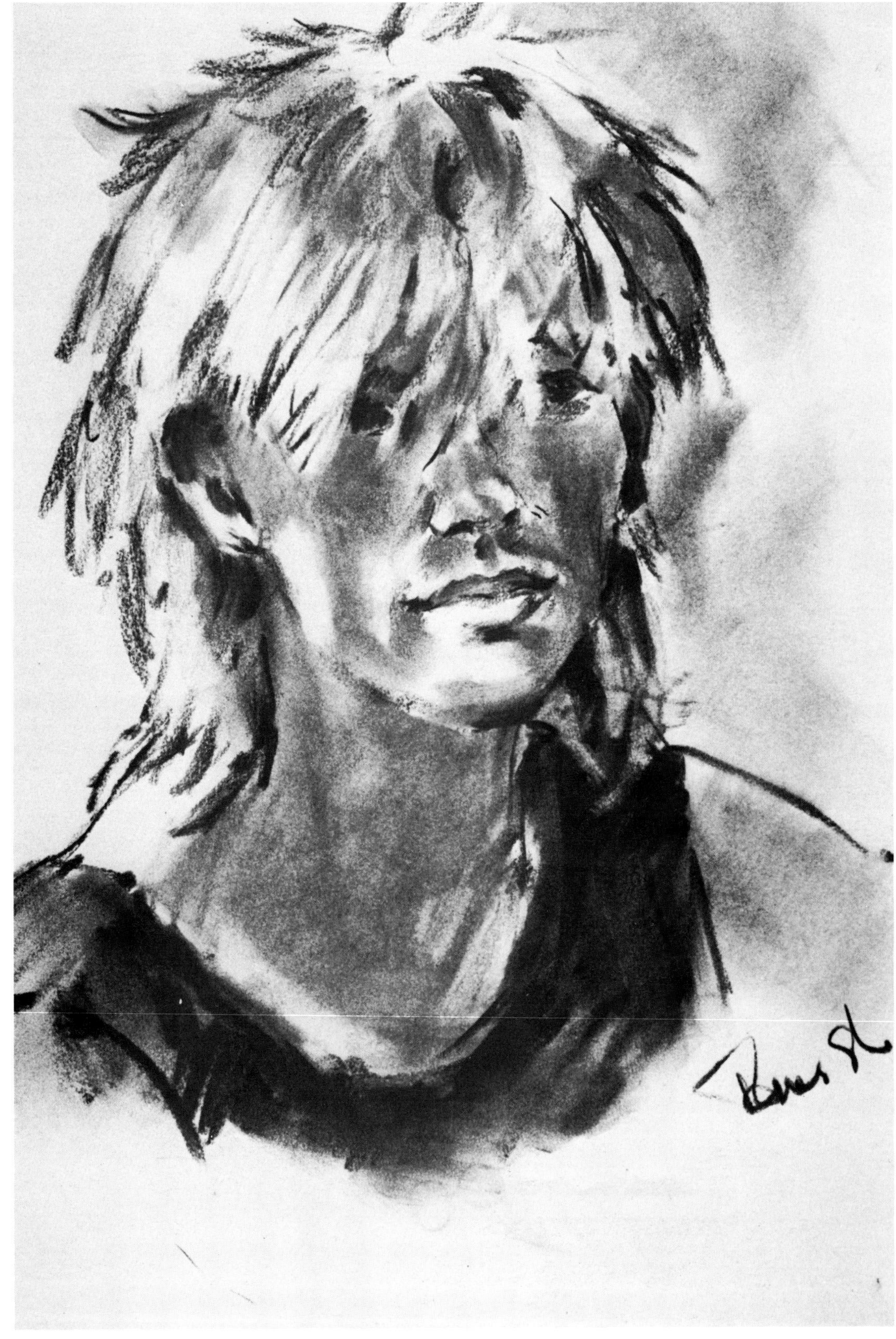

Charcoal portrait (20" x 16")

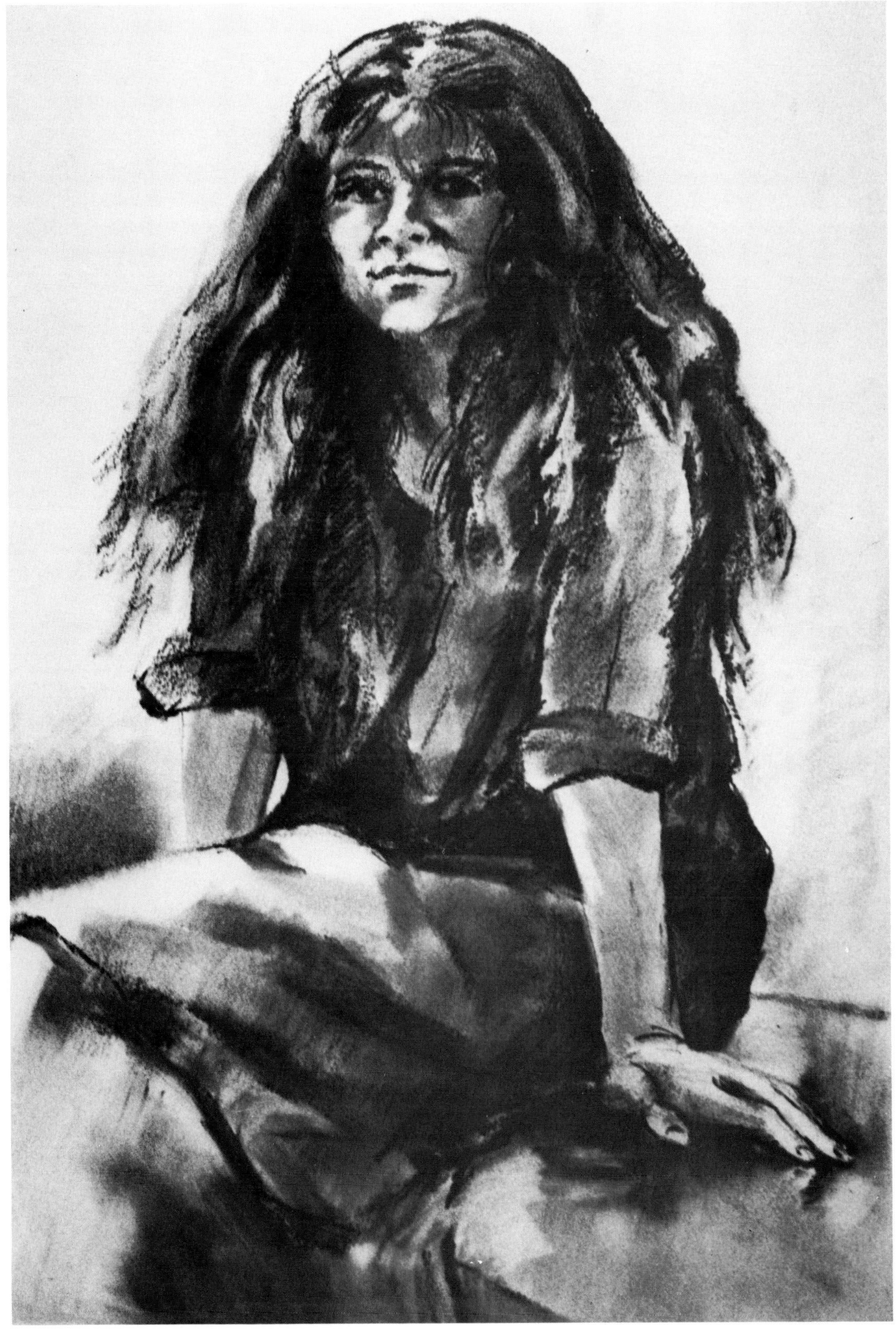

Anne. Seated figure in compressed and standard charcoal (23" x 17")

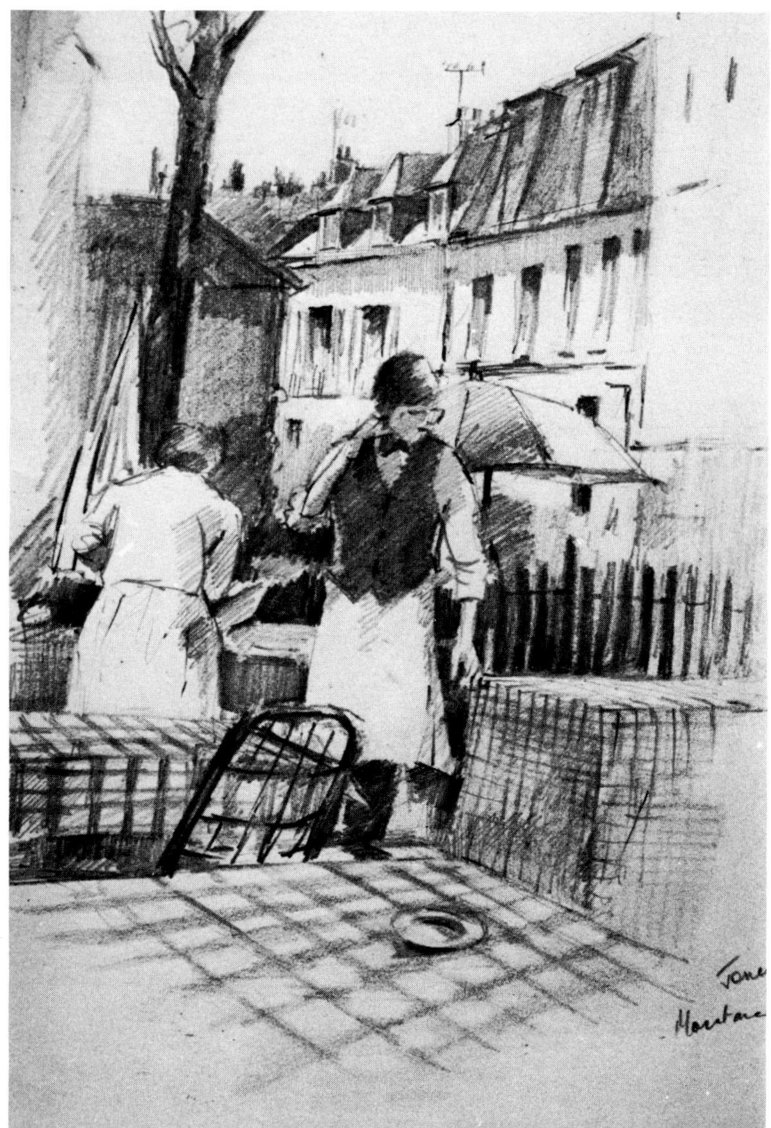

The waiter (Pencil, 10" x 7")

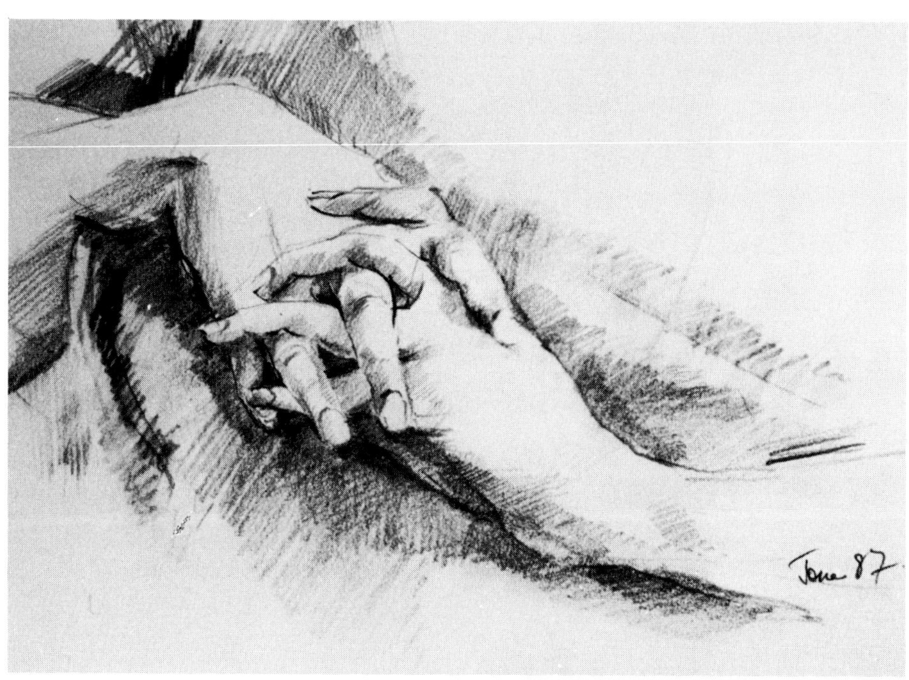

Study of hands (Pencil, 10" x 7")

Study of dogs' heads (Pencil, 16" x 12")

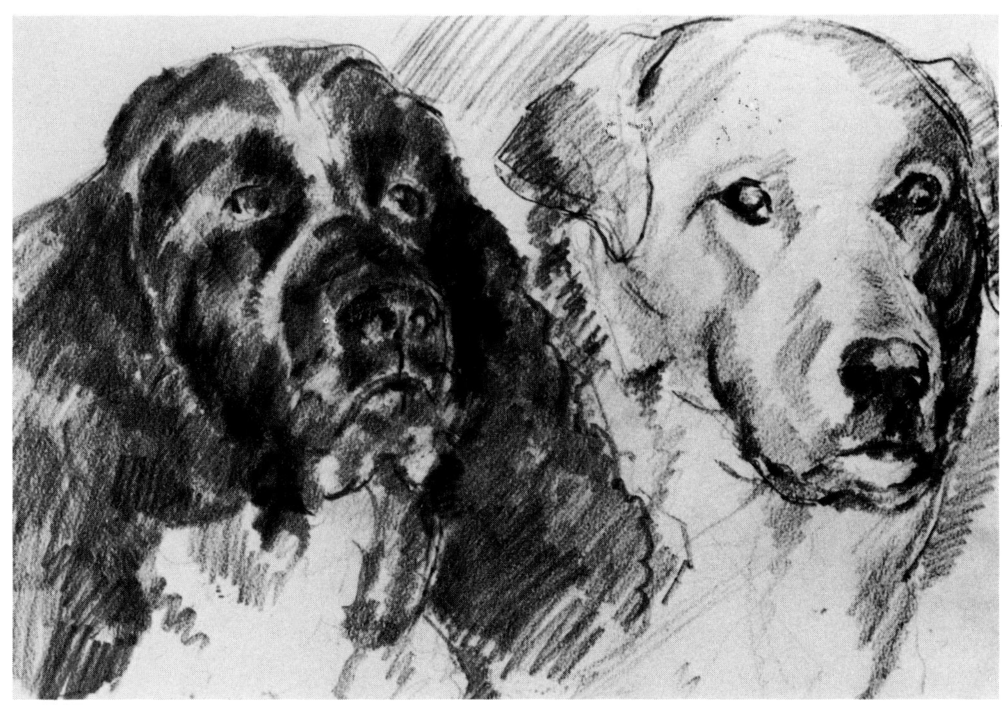

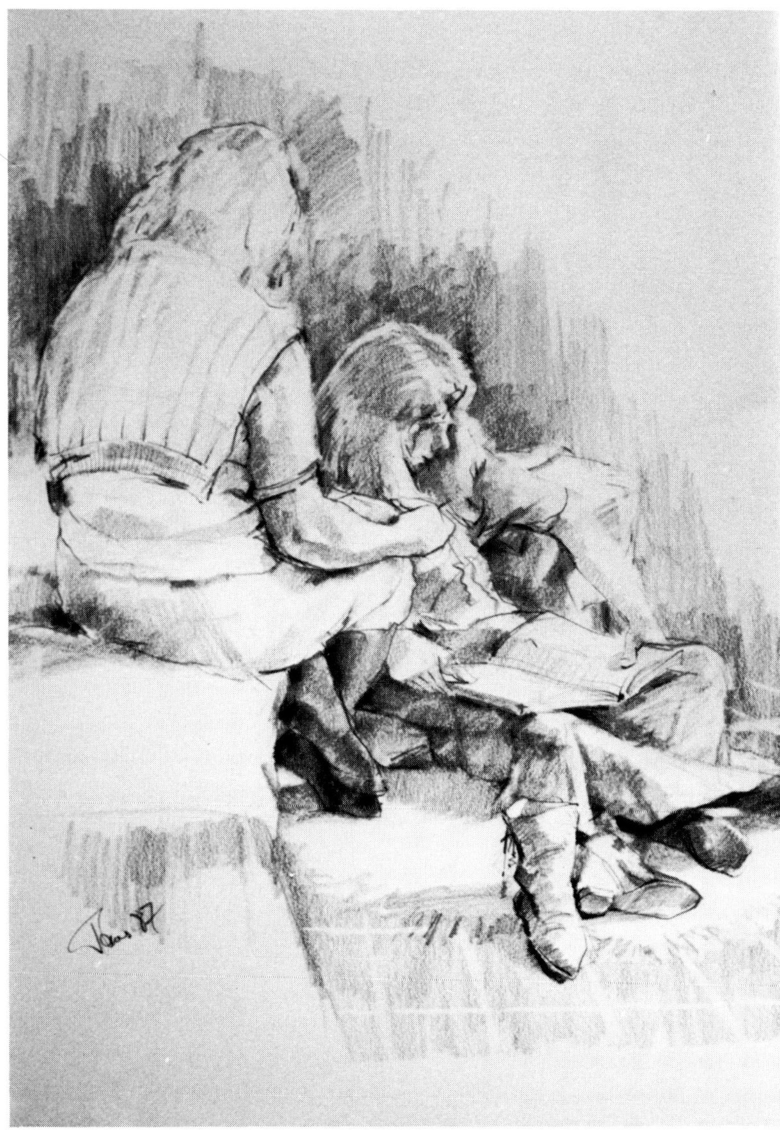

Sunday afternoon (Pencil, 22" x 18")

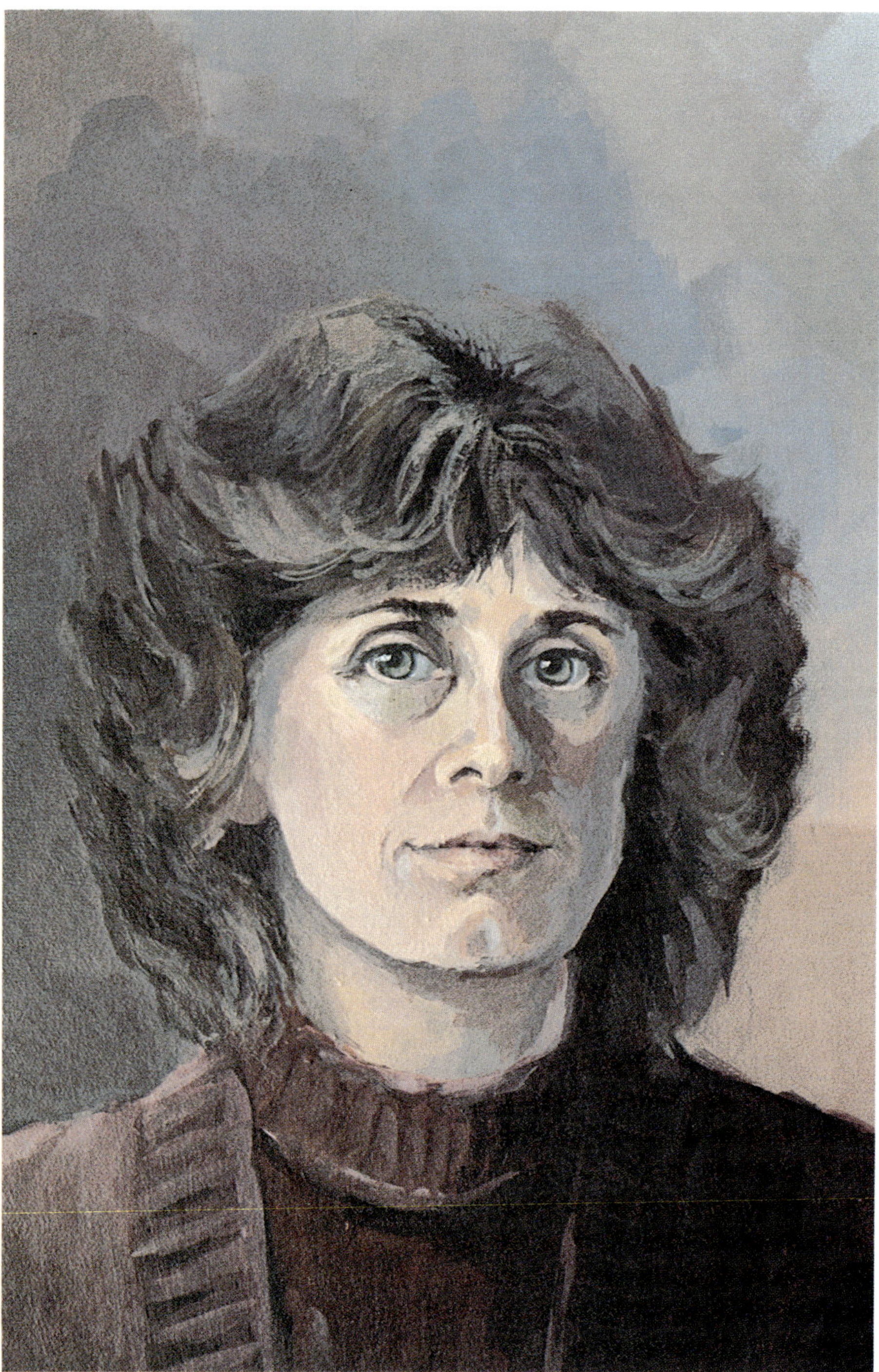

Self-portrait by Daphne Speight (Acrylic,
18" x 14")

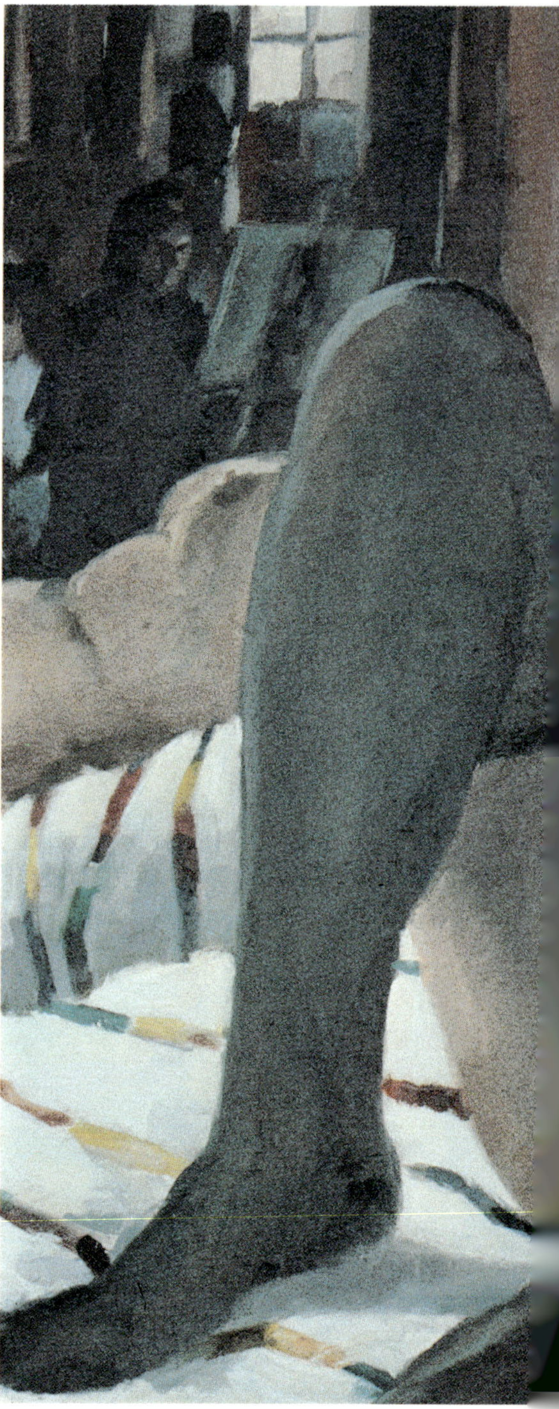

Reclining figure (Oil, 36" x 25")

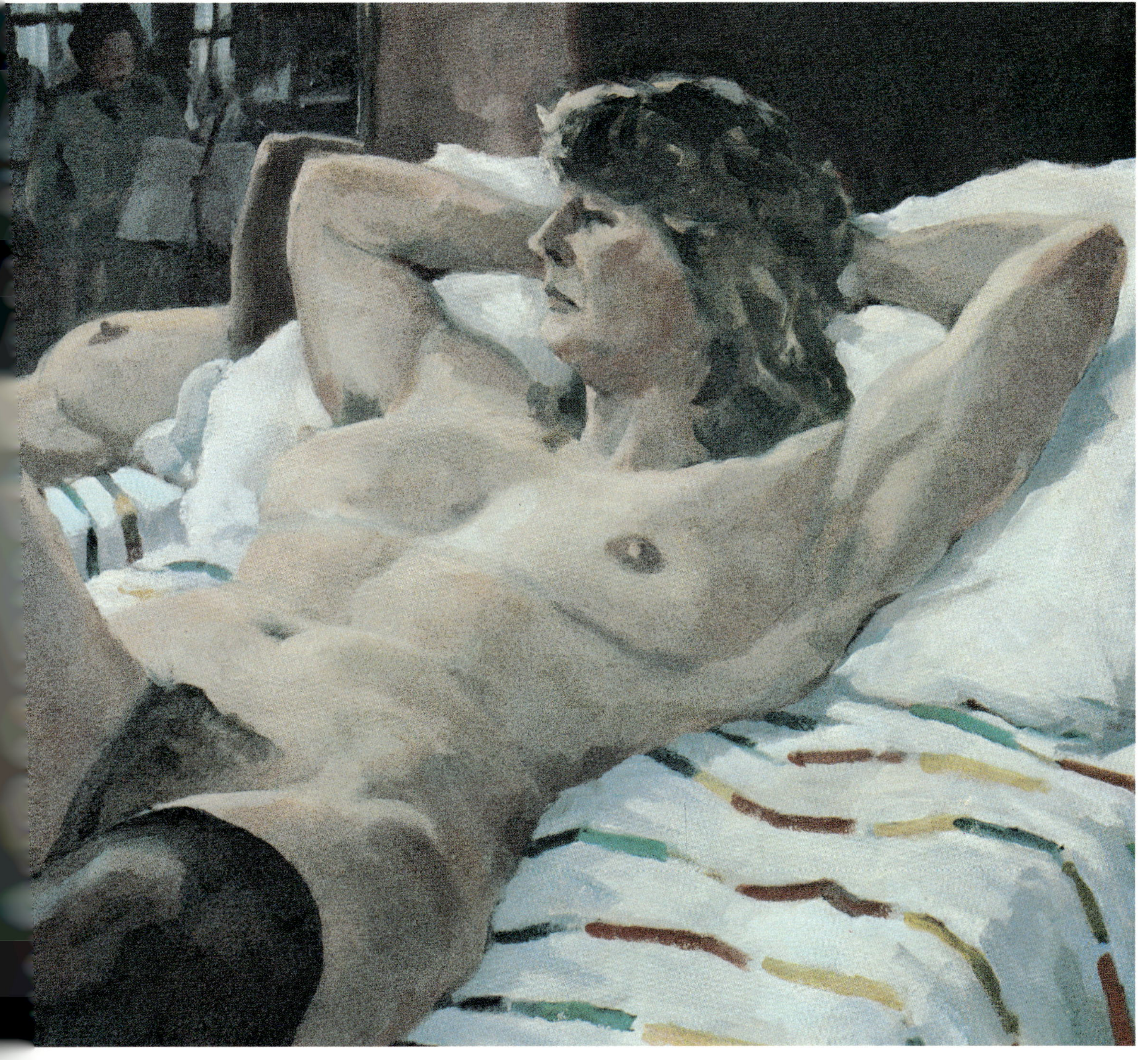

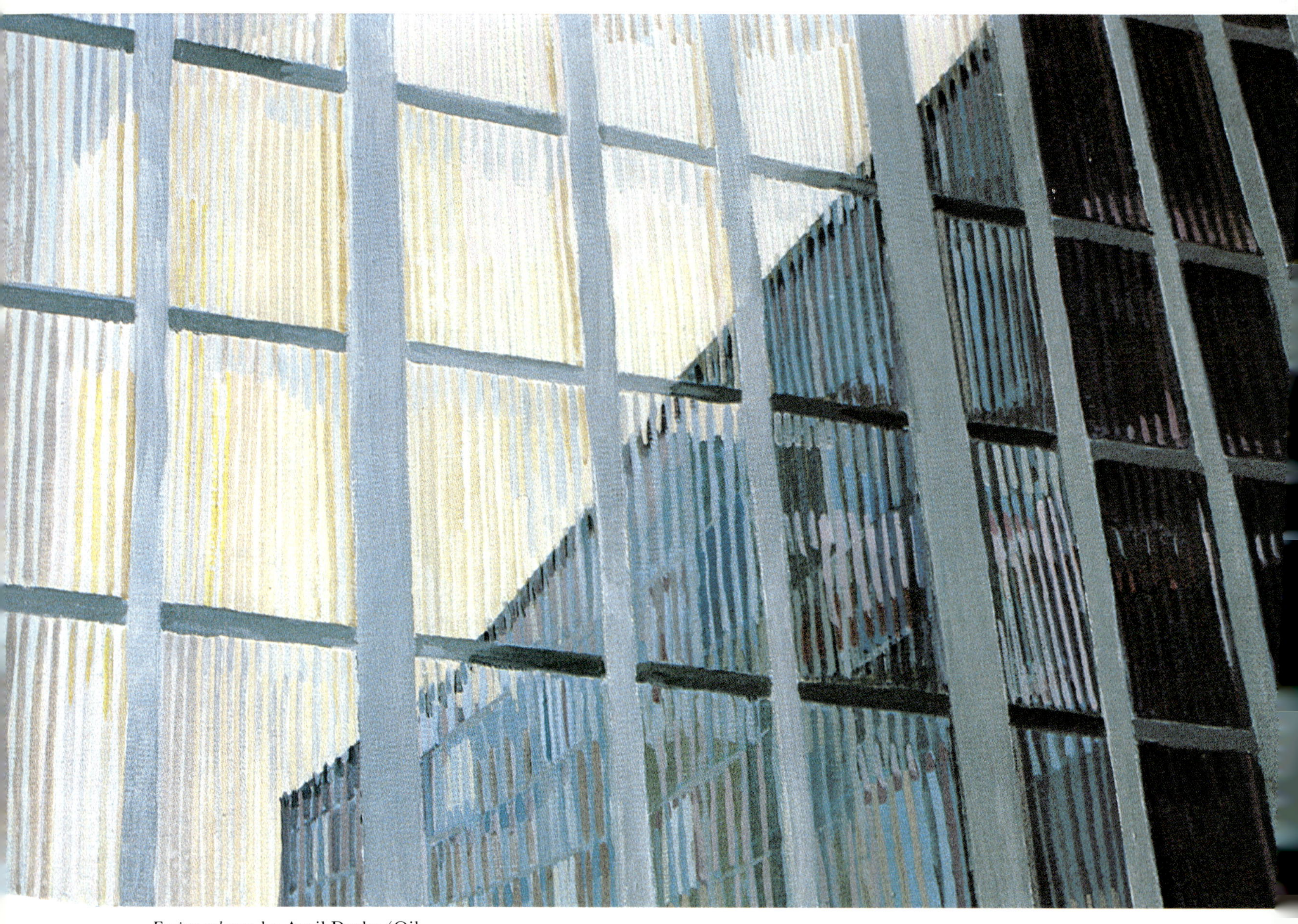

Fusing colours, by Avril Darby (Oil,
24" x 20")

4. COLOUR THEORY

Before you can consider using your skills of drawing and applying them to painting, you need to understand, in simple terms, basic colour theory and its application to tone. Colour is life; a world without colour would appear dead. Colour is the product of light, which reveals to us the spirit of the living world. Colours are forces that affect us positively or negatively, whether we are aware of it or not. The effect of colours should be experienced and understood, not only visually, but also psychologically and symbolically.

Artists are interested in the effects of colour from an aesthetic aspect, and therefore need both physiological and psychological information. Relationships between colour agents and colour effects debated by the eye and the brain have always been a major concern of the artist. The effects of contrast and their value to us are a proper starting point for the study of colour aesthetics. These can be classified under three headings:

(1) Impression (visual)
(2) Expression (emotional)
(3) Constructon (symbolic)

For an understanding of the effects of and the comparative brilliance of pigments look at Fig 80. This illustrates the problems of chromatic light/dark contrast. In this illustration the twelve equidistant steps of the achromatic scale from white to black have been repeated for each of the twelve hues of the colour circle (see Fig 81) in equal brilliance to the corresponding grey.

The question most commonly asked by students is, 'what is that colour and how do I get it?' For the painter, the decision as to which pigments to use to achieve the visual interpretation is always the most difficult. The problem becomes even more difficult when it is understood that it is virtually impossible to be objective about colour. Constant experiment and analysis of the results is necessary to develop knowledge and skill with colour. To assist in the development of these skills, take the simple route. There are only three primary colours: red, yellow and blue. These are the colours of the pigments. The mixing of pigments is known as *subtractive mixing*. Mixing similarly-coloured light is known as *additive mixing*. In the former, mixing the three primaries will give black, whilst mixing similarly-coloured light will give white.

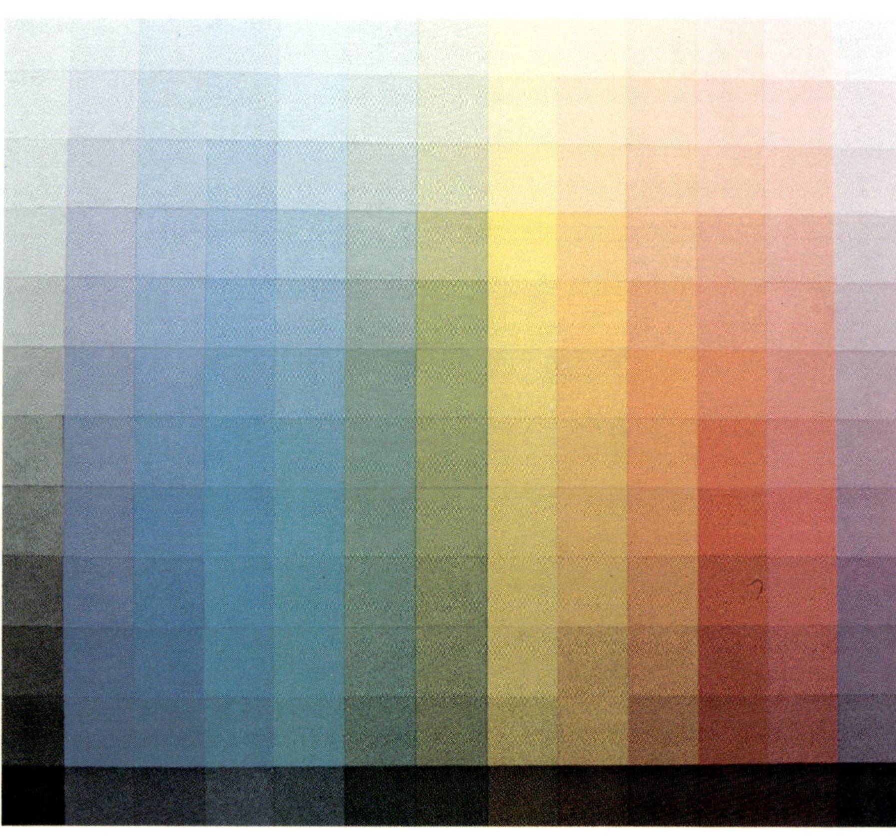

FIG 80 Chromatic light/dark contrast
scales

Armed with this information, you are now able to make a colour circle as shown in Fig 81. This illustrates how the mixing of any two primary colours will produce a secondary, so red and yellow = orange, yellow and blue = green, red and blue = violet. The colour wheel can now be completed by the addition of red/orange, orange/yellow, yellow/green, green/blue, blue/violet and violet/red.

It is necessary to examine some of the possibilities colour offers in terms of *hue, chroma, tone,* and the effect of combinations. *Hue* describes a colour so that it can be distinguished from another. *Chroma* is the term used to describe the intensity of a hue or its staining power. *Tone* describes the colour temperature of a colour – the addition of any part of the achromatic scale to any colour will change its tone value; similarly, the mixing of any pigments can make a warm or cold tone. Fig 81 shows the colour wheel, comprising primary and secondary colours. It is a good exercise for the student to see how many variations of secondary colours can be made. You will see that in this exercise it is not possible to make a pure violet, and so it will be necessary to add other pigments. The red/blue scale shows the greatest discrepancy between theory and practice.

Before progressing further it will be beneficial to understand more fully the implications of tone. Fig 82 shows the achromatic scale in global form, the bottom of the globe dark, rising through the greys to white. Imagine the colour circle placed within the globe as shown, and you will see that the result is the comparative brilliance chart (Fig 80)

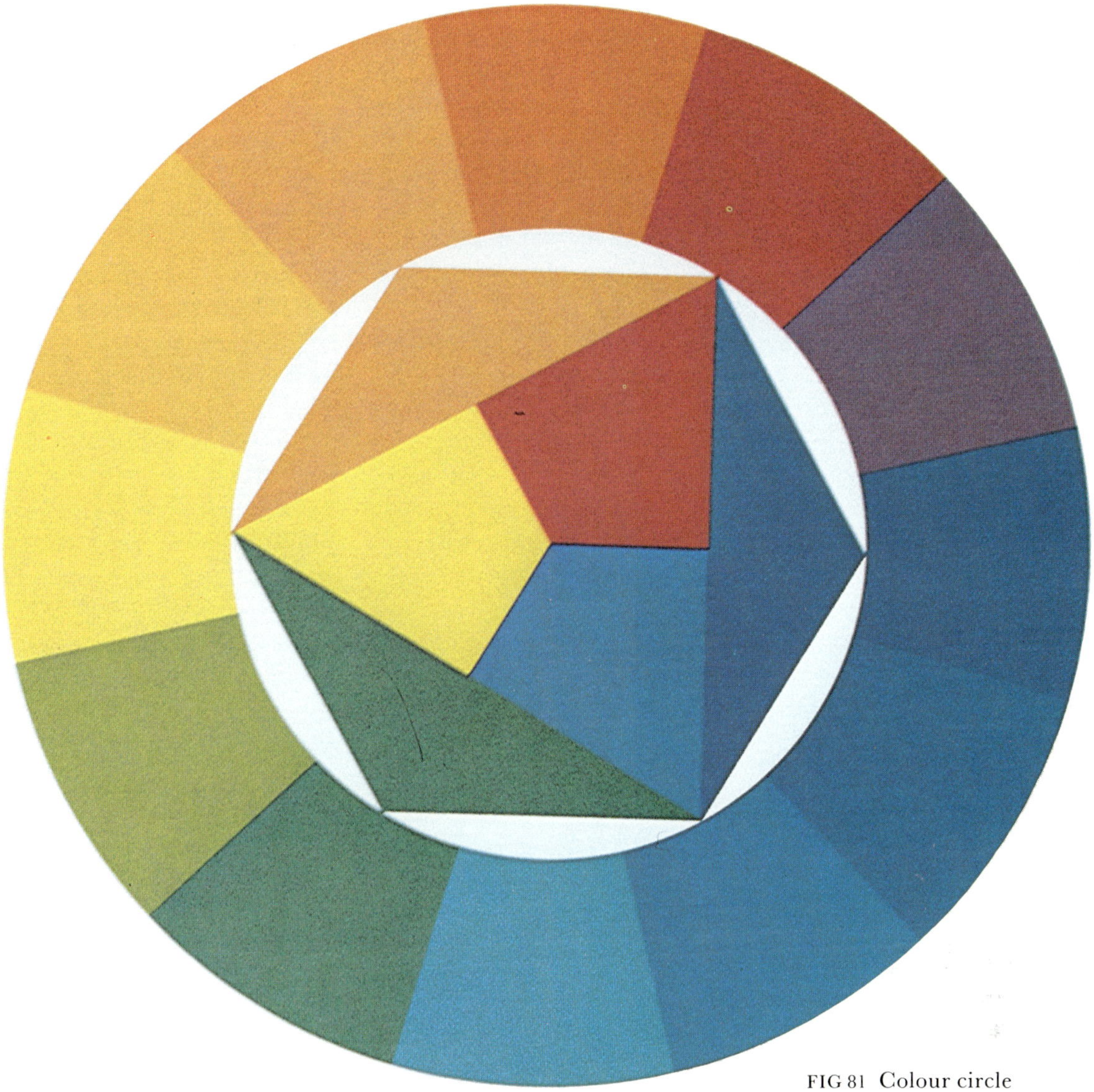

FIG 81 Colour circle

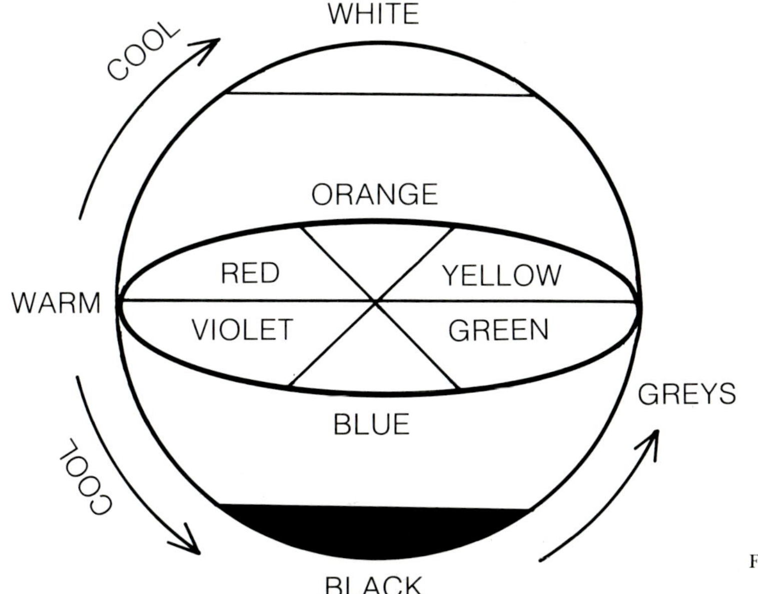

FIG 82 Tonal globe

in a three-dimensional form. If you examine the tonal globe (Fig 82) you will see that any pigment is at its warmest, i.e. has maximum chroma, in its pure state.

From this we may deduce in simple terms that the addition of black, white or any of the greys will cool the colour, in other words cause it to recede. You will ask, 'suppose that I require warm highlights and shadows: if I cannot use black or white, what then?' Remember that pigment is subtractive; by mixing red, yellow and blue a near black is obtained. If this dark mix is loaded towards the red primary, the dark will be warm; if it is loaded towards blue it will be cold. Warm colours advance and cold colours recede. Red is at the warm end of the tonal scale and blue at the cold end.

You now have two methods of tone control. There is one more (the most effective): the use of colour greys. Once again, remember that mixing of primary colours in equal chromatic parts will produce black. If you add white in varying amounts, the result will be greys. If you increase the amount of any primary colour, then the grey will be biased towards that colour; likewise, if you increase the amount of any two primary colours, then the grey will favour the secondary colour. There is a further use for colour greys: when they are placed adjacent to a primary or secondary colour, if the grey is biased towards that colour it will optically appear to reduce its brilliance. This effect is illustrated in Fig 83, which shows a range of colour greys and the comparative effect of brilliance reduction.

FIG 83 Colour greys

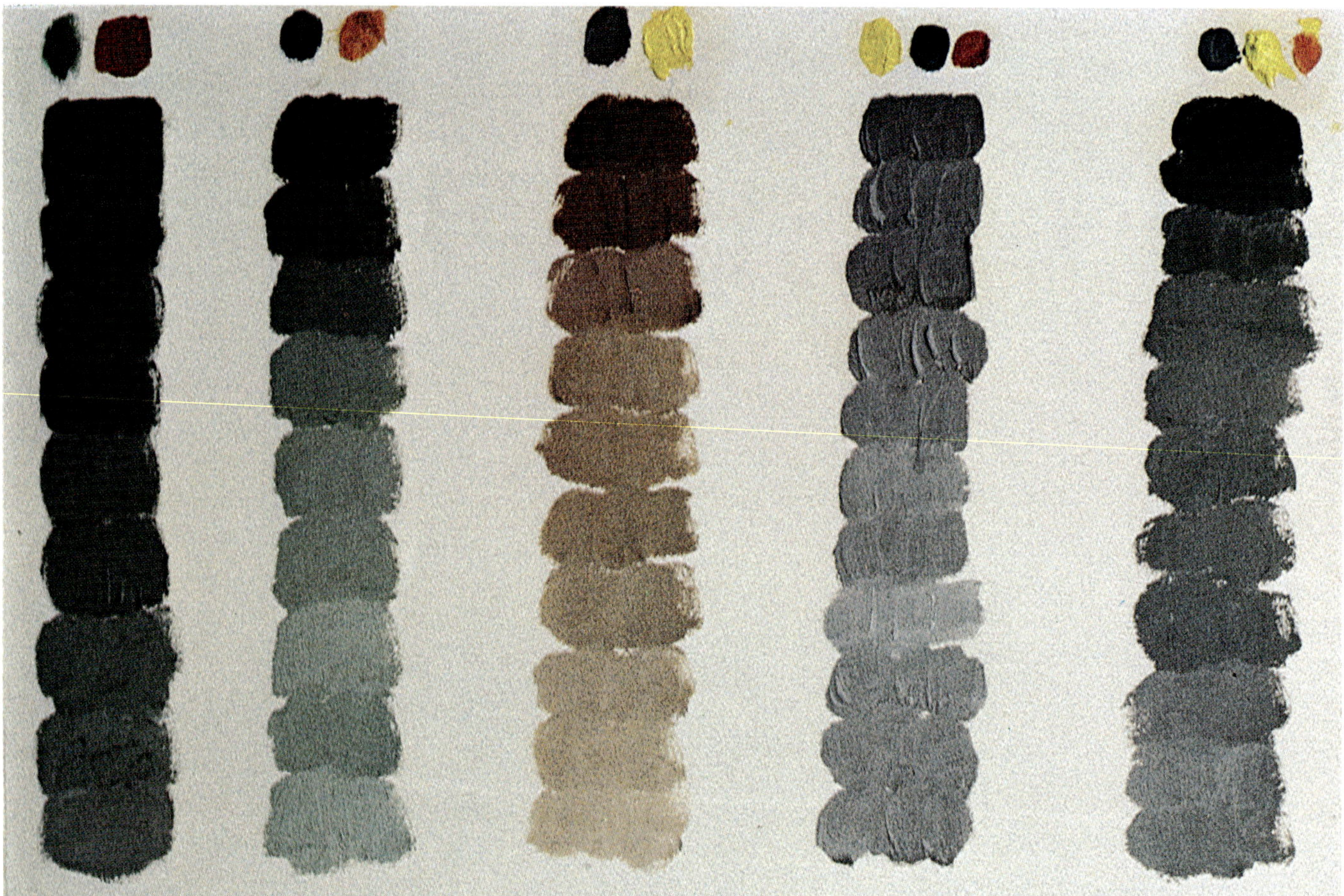

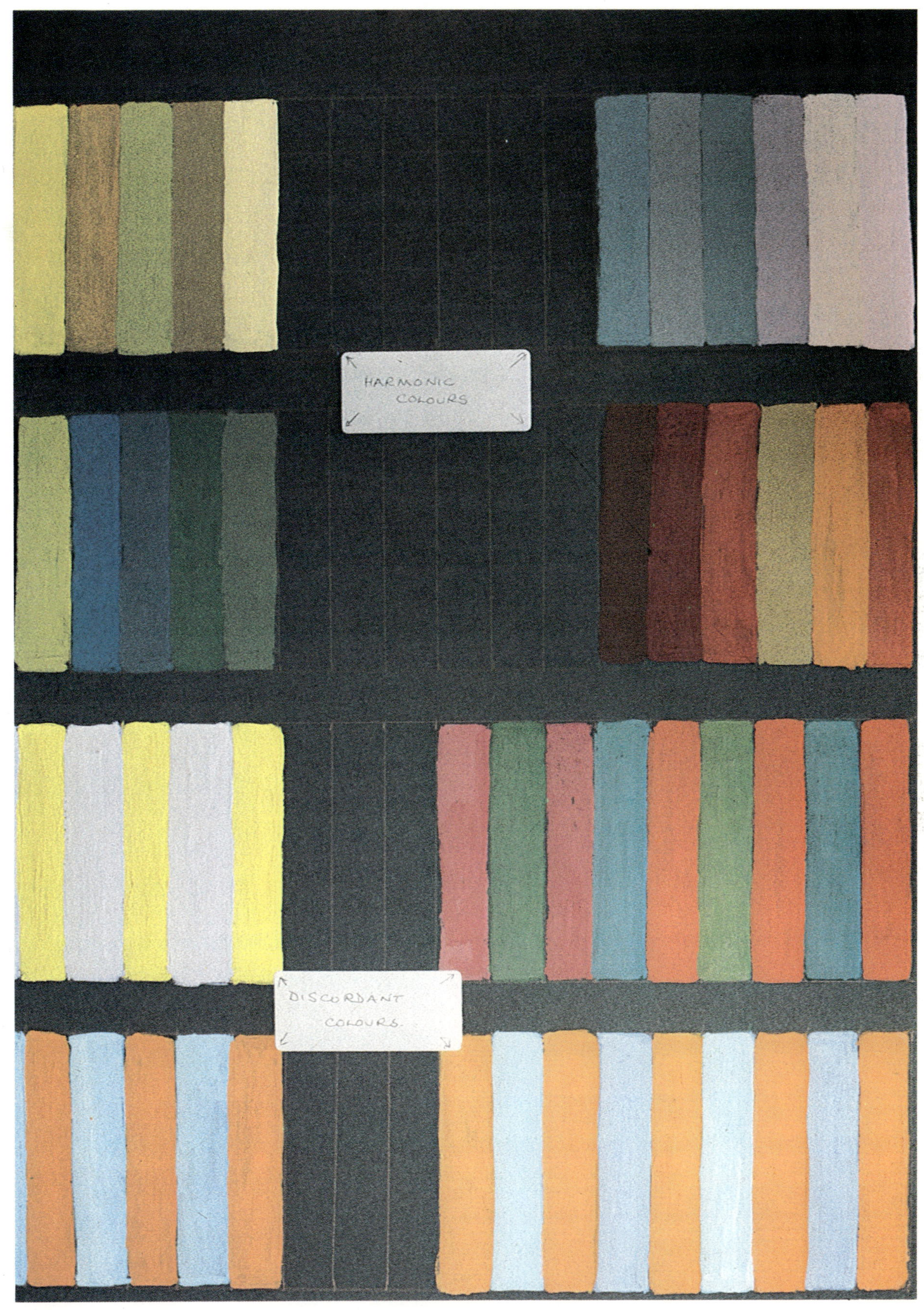

FIG 85 Optical fusing

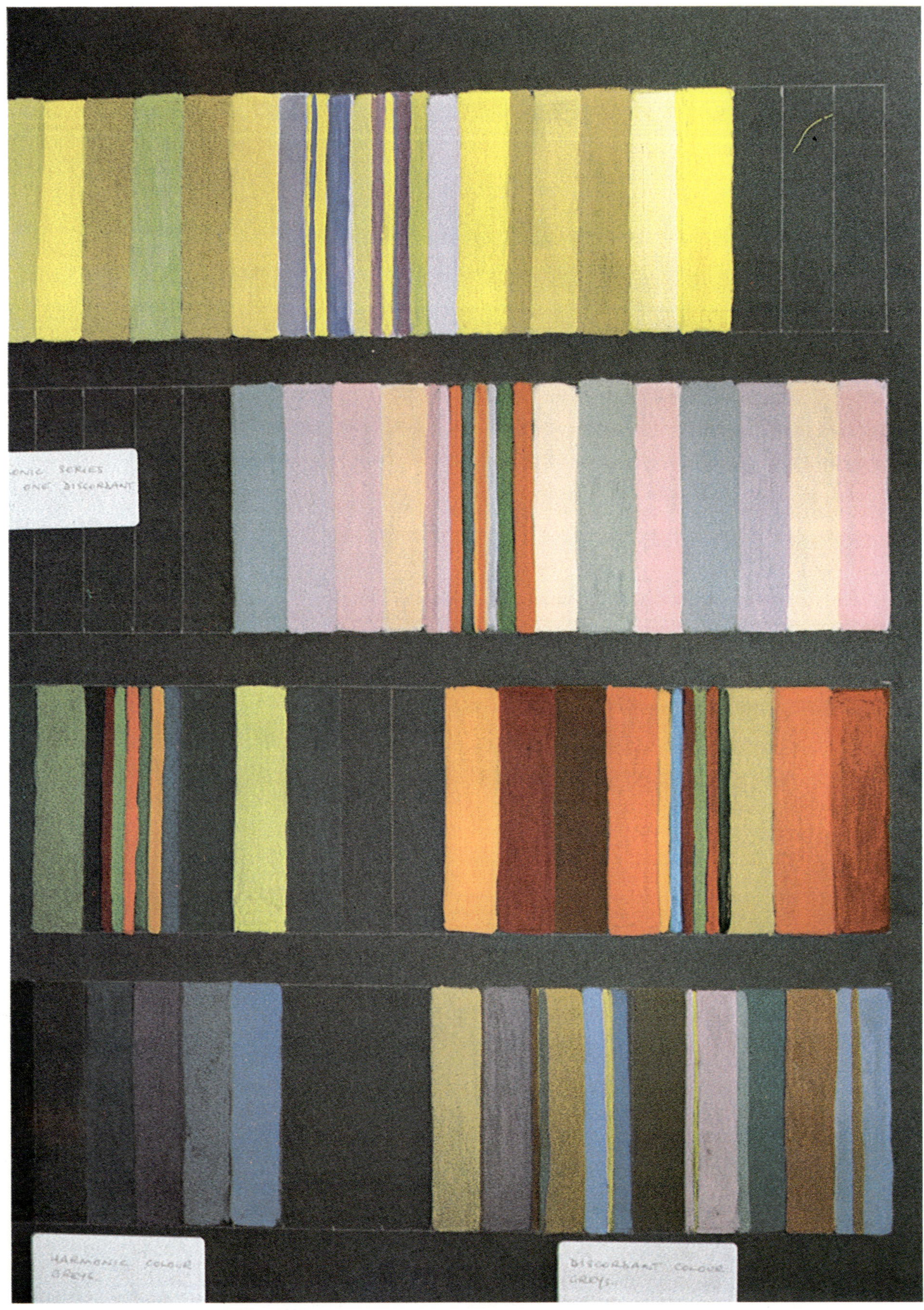
ONIC SERIES
ONE DISCORDANT
HARMONIC COLOUR GREYS
DISCORDANT COLOUR GREYS

FIG 86 Colour discords

therefore, the primary colour is red, the after-image colour is green/grey. This phenomenon occurs because the red sensor in the eye has become fatigued, allowing the blue/green sensors to take over for a short time. It is a useful exercise to try to make these colours with pigments.

The above exercise is useful because it leads into the area of optical mixing (which means the mixing of colours in the eye), of which it can be said that after-image plays an essential part. After-images are visual opposites, and the effects of optical mixing are similar to the mixing of coloured lights.

Optical mixing of pigments in an optically fusing method was used by the French artist Camille Pissaro, who employed a *divisionist* technique. *Divisionism* used complementary hue contrasts with short brush strokes placed in juxtaposition to each other, the choice of pigments being used to intensify and cancel. This technique of arranging colours in small areas attracted the attention of Georges Seurat and Paul Signac, who examined the principles of *divisionism* and developed a more exacting and scientific approach, which became known as *pointillism*. Fig 85 demonstrates the effect of optical fusing of colour and the colour vibration that occurs as a result. You will see that it uses pairs of complementary colours in narrow alternating strips. The same results can be obtained using a configuration of diametrically opposed dots, as in *pointillism*.

Finally, the use of discordant colours must be examined, as it is through these that the painting, through the interaction of these colours, becomes exciting. Not only must you select pigments which are discordant, you must consider configuration, size and shape, since these factors can assist or detract from the discordant values. Fig 86 demonstrates some colour discords in an orchestrated study – the colours are discordant, as is the orchestration.

In this section on colour theory and practice you have been introduced to primary, secondary and tertiary colour, colour harmony and contrast, colour relationships, tone control, diametrically opposed colour, colour blacks and whites, colour greys, broken colour, optical mixing and fusion, after-image and finally colour discord. All these play a major role in picture painting. This knowledge and awareness of colour may be applied to your knowledge of drawing, enabling you to fulfil and express your reaction to your surroundings.

Finally, colour can only be assessed in context. Never be afraid to experiment and try out new ideas. Painting is like music, except that it uses colour instead of sound, so, like the composer, establish a key for each composition – a colour key – and, as in music, use the overtones of that key to establish a colour theme, with its associated contrasts. Above all, use the harmonics and discords of colour to lift your work into a bravura painting, directing all your energy, perception and sensitivity to the subject.

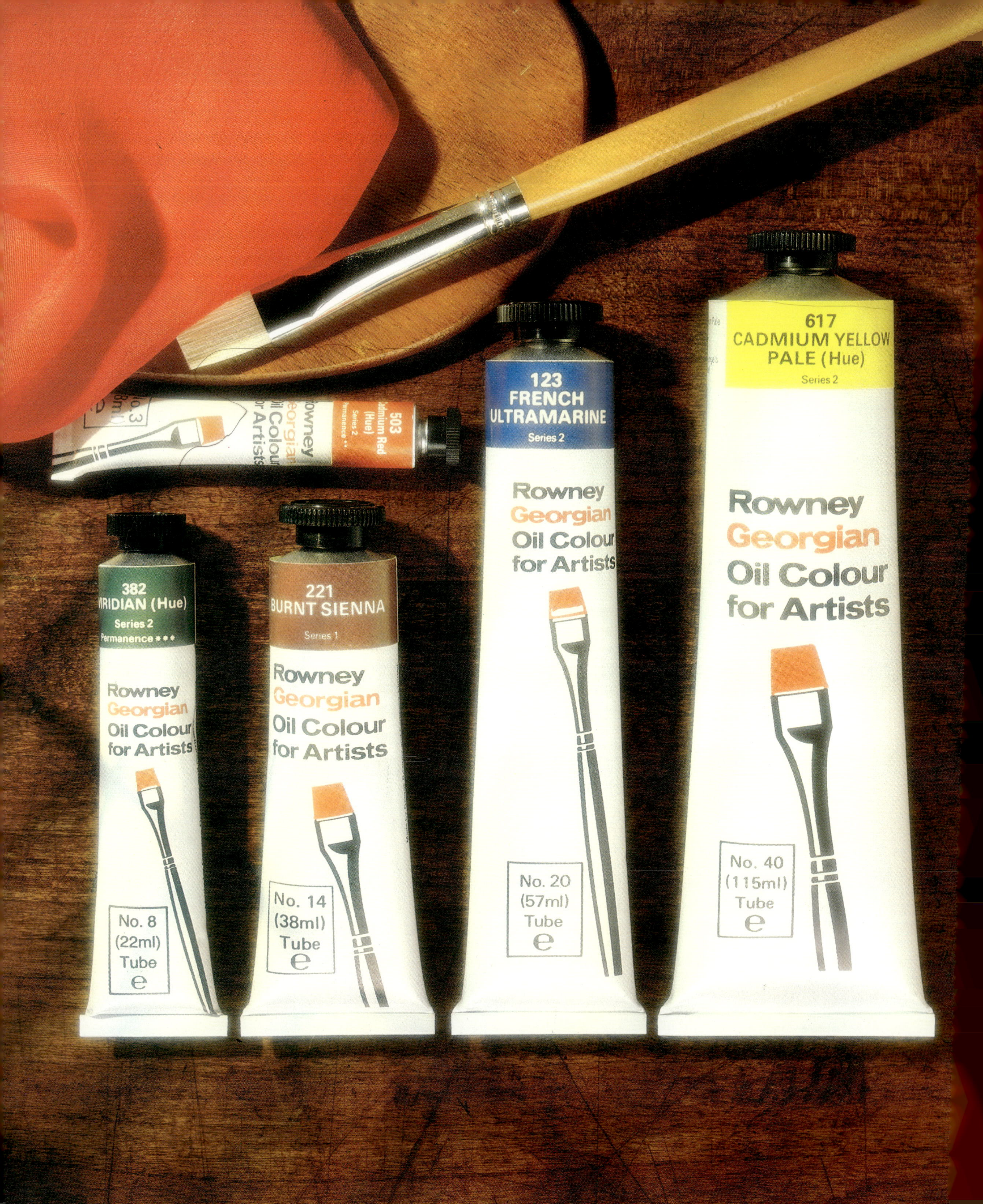
617
CADMIUM YELLOW
PALE (Hue)
Series 2

123
FRENCH
ULTRAMARINE
Series 2

503
Cadmium Red
(Hue)
Series 2

382
VIRIDIAN (Hue)
Series 2
Permanence ***

221
BURNT SIENNA
Series 1

Rowney
Georgian
Oil Colour
for Artists

No. 8
(22ml)
Tube
e

No. 14
(38ml)
Tube
e

No. 20
(57ml)
Tube
e

No. 40
(115ml)
Tube
e

5. PAINTING TECHNIQUES

Oil-painting

Oil-painting was first introduced in the early fifteenth century. Before this, the most widely-used method of painting was *egg tempera*. This required the powdered colours to be mixed with fresh egg yolk thinned with water. Sometimes the whole egg would be used. *Tempera*, which is still in use today, dries rapidly, which means that the painter who wishes to achieve three-dimensional modelling has to cross-hatch one colour over another. The development of oil-paints was the result of efforts to achieve slower and more accurate working, with richer colour quality through blending and glazing, but which at the same time, because of increased flexibility, encouraged alteration, correction and experiment. Over the years new painting surfaces and various new types of brush, as well as an increase in the number of pigments available to the artist, have been added to the repertoire. Nevertheless, the basic technique remains much the same.

Materials

You will find it more convenient to keep a permanent place to work in. Oil-painting seems to attract more clutter than drawing or water-colours, and in addition it is extremely annoying to have to pack everything away after each session. You will also need somewhere to keep wet paintings, which can take days or weeks to dry.

You will need an easel: the various types are described earlier. It needs to be rigid, as oil-painting can be quite vigorous. A paint table for brushes, media and palette is necessary – I use an old television trolley which has a storage cupboard underneath it for paints, media, etc. Two wide-based glass pickle jars are needed: one to contain turpentine and the other white spirit for cleaning purposes. If the floor coverings are not expendable, then a large sheet of plastic under the easel will protect them and prevent you from feeling inhibited. A further useful facility in the studio is a mirror, as looking at the reflection of your work allows you to see it as if it was a new study. It is easy, when working on a painting over long periods, to become too familiar with the work and to accept that all is as it should be. Seeing the painting from a different angle is as good as looking at it with a fresh eye. Finally, if space permits, a storage rack will allow you to store new canvasses and work in progress.

Oil paints

Lighting
A north light is without doubt the most constant light source there is. It has little variation in quality during the day and is therefore the best light to work in, but it is not essential. There are many ways of regulating the source and quality of light in the studio: blinds, curtains and even sheets of paper can be used to keep the light constant. Avoid working in direct sunlight, as this will be disastrous to your rendering of colour and tone.

When using artificial light, avoid using ordinary electric light bulbs on their own as they affect the yellows in painting. I use a photographer's flood-lamp, with a conventional 150 watt bulb, in conjunction with a striplight. The combination of the two gives a reasonable imitation of daylight. A spotlight can also be useful for creating harsh lighting effects.

Brushes and palette knives
A palette knife is a good tool for mixing paint. It can also be used for applying paint to the canvas or for scraping it off, although for applying paint and working it on the canvas I prefer to use a painting knife. This has a cranked handle and an extremely flexible blade. Fig 87 shows a selection of the various shapes of painting knives available. A painting knife can be very versatile in the hands of an experienced artist, but beware, as it can also produce very mannered and crude work.

Brushes can be very expensive, so choose only those you need to start with and add to them as need dictates. Sables are the most expensive: they are used to make precise detailed marks and for applying glazes to produce simple flat areas of paint. Because they are more resilient than other, similar brushes made from squirrel, ox-ear, etc, they last far longer if properly looked after. Today there is also a range of man-made fibre brushes. Among the best of these are the Daler-Rowney 'Dalon' series. These inexpensive brushes point well and have a very long life. The most commonly used brushes, especially for the large masses of a painting, are made from resilient hogs-hair. They come in four basic shapes: flat, bright, filbert and round. Fig 88 shows a selection of all those available. Decorator's brushes, plus some squirrel and camel-hair brushes in an assortment of sizes from ½ in to 2 inches, will be useful for painting the initial basic colours and masses. One or two larger decorator's brushes are essential for priming boards and canvas.

Brushes must always be thoroughly cleaned after use. Wash them in turpentine substitute or paraffin: never let paint dry on the brush. After cleaning in this manner, wash the brushes in soap and slightly warm water. Make a lather in the palm of the hand and press the hairs into it, then gently work the brush in the lather, making sure that the hairs are covered and that the soap reaches the ferrule in order to remove the spirit. Rinse in cold water and repeat two or three times. Remember it is important to keep the ferrule clean, as a collection of paint in it will rob the brush of its elasticity. Always store brushes in a drawer, or head upwards in a jar, and, where possible, protect the heads of expensive brushes with a plastic tube.

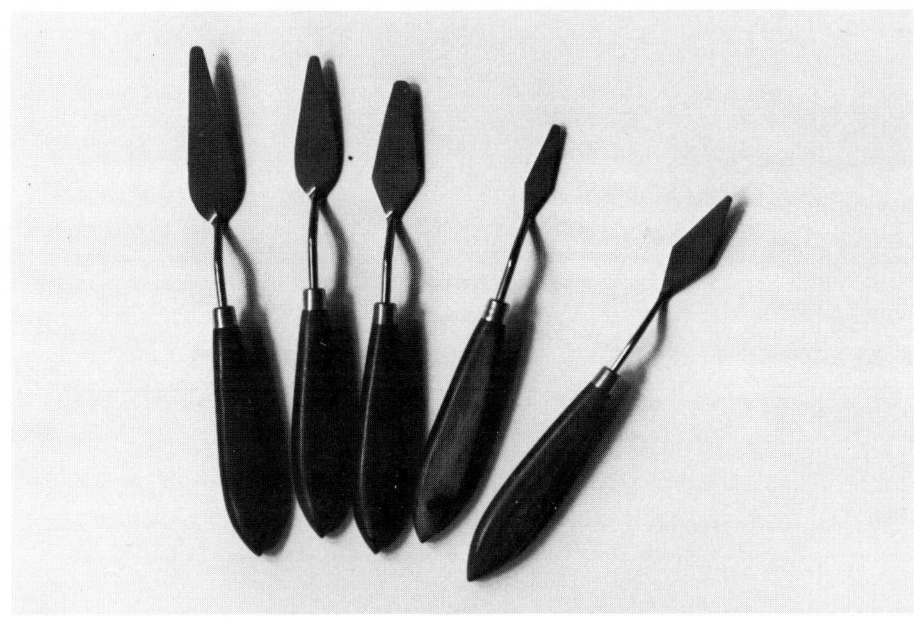

FIG 87 Painting knives

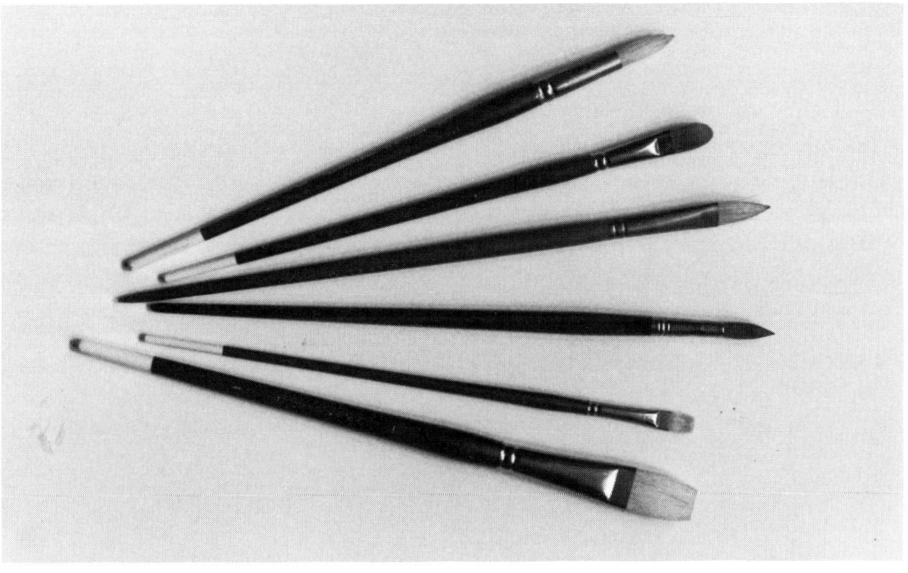

FIG 88 Oil-painting brushes

Painting surfaces

There are many manufactured surfaces on which to paint, from oil-sketching pads to the most expensive stretched canvas. As the exercises we are about to embark on are primarily concerned with finding out about the medium, it makes economic sense to make your own painting supports.

The following painting surfaces can all be produced at little cost and all provide an interesting surface on which to work. It is worth noting that the texture selected for a painting should be decided by the subject. With this in mind, when you prepare a surface for painting the ground you apply to it can be adjusted to suit the planned work.

Cardboard, strawboard, hardboard and plywood are inexpensive, particularly if you purchase off-cuts of the last two. If you wish to paint large works on these surfaces, it will be necessary to attach the panels to a batten framework. I have found that the largest panel that can be used without support does not exceed 36 inches x 30 inches. Hardboard must be sandpapered to roughen its shiny surface in order to allow the primer to key on the surface. A huge variety of materials can be used for ground on these panels, and each will provide a different texture. Old bed-sheets, pillow-cases, cotton shirts, hessian and old fragments of canvas can all be utilised for making exciting surfaces to paint on. Avoid all synthetic materials, as it is possible that the oil may dissolve their surface.

All these surfaces need priming before use and canvas needs to be properly prepared. Failure to take this precaution could eventually result in the oil rotting the material.

Priming canvas and boards

I use commercial primers, which are freely available and inexpensive. As acrylic paints are not suitable for use on an oil-primed surface, I have for some time now always used Daler-Rowney acrylic primer, which makes my supports suitable for either acrylic or oil paints. Before priming the surface, it is necessary to size the panel with glue size. This seals the surface to prevent sinkage of primer and, more importantly, the colours. Glue size is available from most hardware shops and comes in powder form, which is mixed with water and applied thinly with a decorating brush. Do not apply too thickly, as it will crack as it dries. Acrylic primer applied thinly will also act as a sealer for the surface. When the size is completely dry, apply the white acrylic primer as an undercoat. Do not attempt to smooth out the brush marks: these add to the 'tooth' of the surface. Should you wish to experiment with textures, add a little pumice powder to the final coat of primer, which will give a good tooth and texture. Daley-Romney acrylic *gesso* also provides an interesting surface, particularly if applied unevenly. You may also

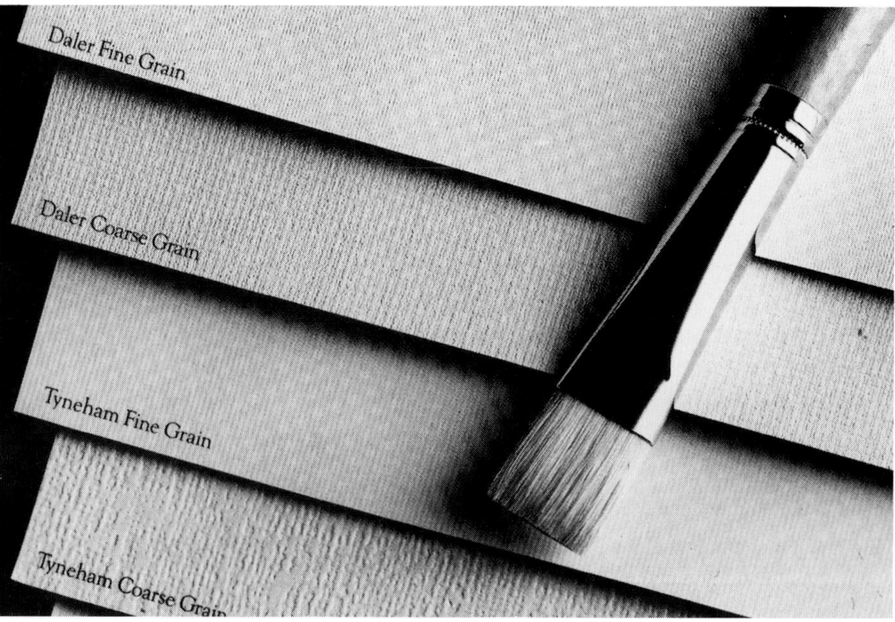

FIG 89 Various painting surfaces

FIG 90 Prepared canvas panels

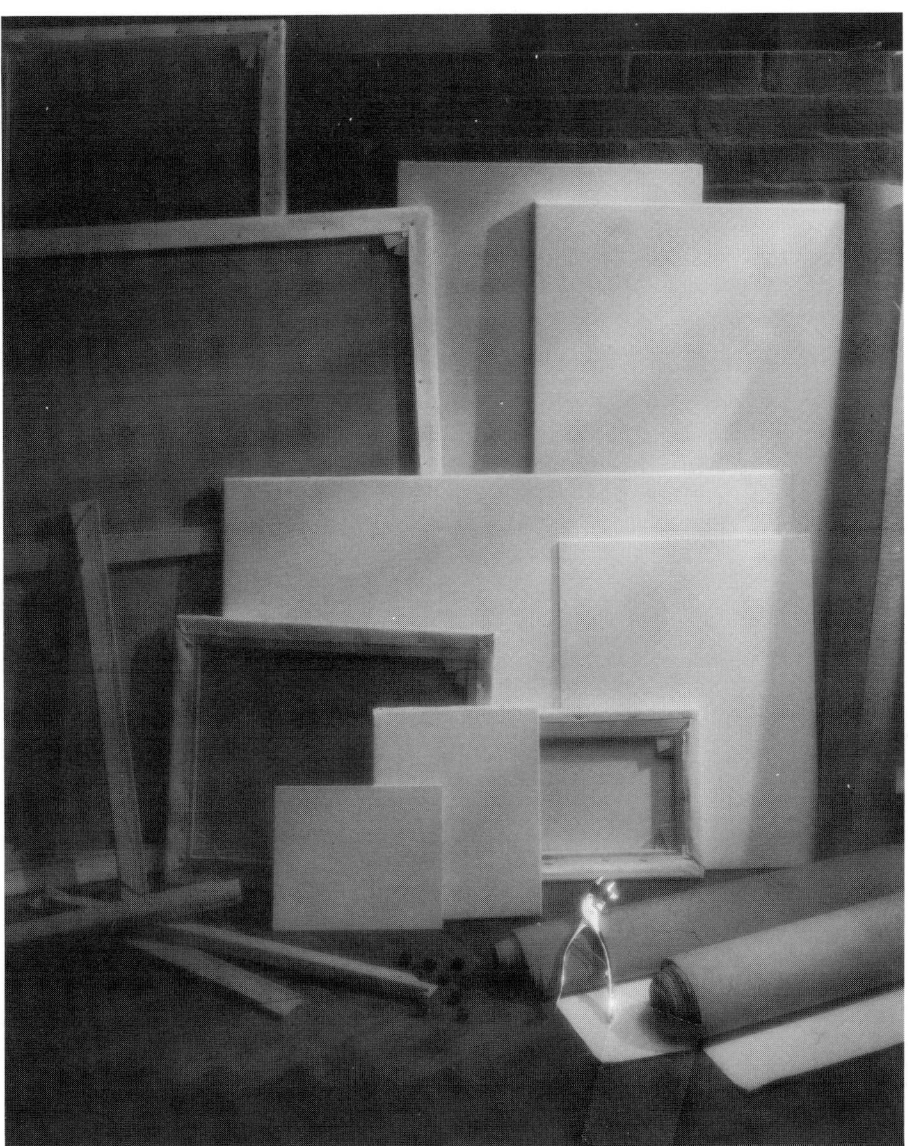

stretch some of the different fabrics mentioned earlier on hardboard or plywood, using the glue size as an adhesive. Leave a generous overlap to stick to the rear of the panel, and finally apply the primer. Fig 89 shows a variety of surfaces suitable for oil painting. Fig 90 shows a selection of prepared canvas panels that I use, each having a different characteristic.

Oil paints
The selection of pigments available today is overwhelming and, for the beginner, counter-productive. The similarity between colours with widely different names is confusing, but the very extent of the range tends to discourage mixing your own colours. You need only five tubes of paint: red, yellow, blue, white and black. These five tubes of colour will produce almost all the tones and secondary colours you need. Other colours can be added when you find you cannot mix the tint you require.

Oil paints are made in two types: artist's colours and student colours. Student colours are less finely ground and, in the case of expensive pigments, are usually chemical dyes with an extender. For the artist with a limited budget, the student range of colours is perfectly suitable, and they are just as stable. You can use artist's colours when you have acquired more experience. Oil-paints can either be thinned with turpentine and applied in thin washes, or they can be scumbled and rubbed over the canvas without thinning.

The most popularly used extender is a mixture of turpentine and linseed oil, mixed in the proportion two of turpentine to one of oil. Be careful not to over-use linseed oil, as it can, when used to excess, cause pigments to yellow and wrinkle on drying. It also slows down the drying process. There are many manufactured gels and media on the market, and although some affect the colour in the long term, they can be useful when time is limited, such as when working out of doors.

Technique
Oil-paint is a very versatile and flexible medium. The effect varies according to the surface to which it is applied – canvas, paper, cardboard, wood and many other surfaces have been used, each having a characteristic effect on the appearance and quality of the paint.

Two distinctly different techniques of oil-painting have developed. They are, in order of development, the 'layer' method and *alla prima*. The former, used for centuries, requires an underpainting of a single layer of opaque colour, which is allowed to dry. The modelling, contrast and tone are applied by a succession of transparent glazes, each of which must be dry before the next application is made. The thinnest paint is applied first and the thickest last. A simple way to remember the procedure is to think of the paint being applied from dark colours to light and from lean to fat. This will mean that the highlights have the heaviest impasto, as to paint in heavy impasto in the early stages of the work would produce cracking in the paint as it dries.

In *alla prima* painting wet paint is painted into wet paint, but still working from lean to fat, dark to light. *Alla prima* painting is freer and more spontaneous than the layer method. The paint is applied in a vigorous, fluid manner, making it adaptable to the experimental and innovative techniques that are necessary if you are to look for new ways of seeing and expressing what you see.

It is with *alla prima* that we are mainly concerned. The variety of approaches that can be explored are limitless. Learn to apply the pigment with impasto by using a painting knife; scrape it down so that you leave a little pigment trapped in the irregularities of the surface. Try adding a little varnish to the paint and mixing it with sawdust or plaster to increase body and texture. Keep these exercises on show where you can see them, as you will learn by looking at them.

There are many ways of starting an oil-painting, but drawing is common to them all – it is only the form of drawing that varies. Of course the basic disciplines of drawing discussed earlier form the basis of whatever method is chosen for painting. The most commonly used

FIG 91 *Still life* (Oil, 22" x 18")

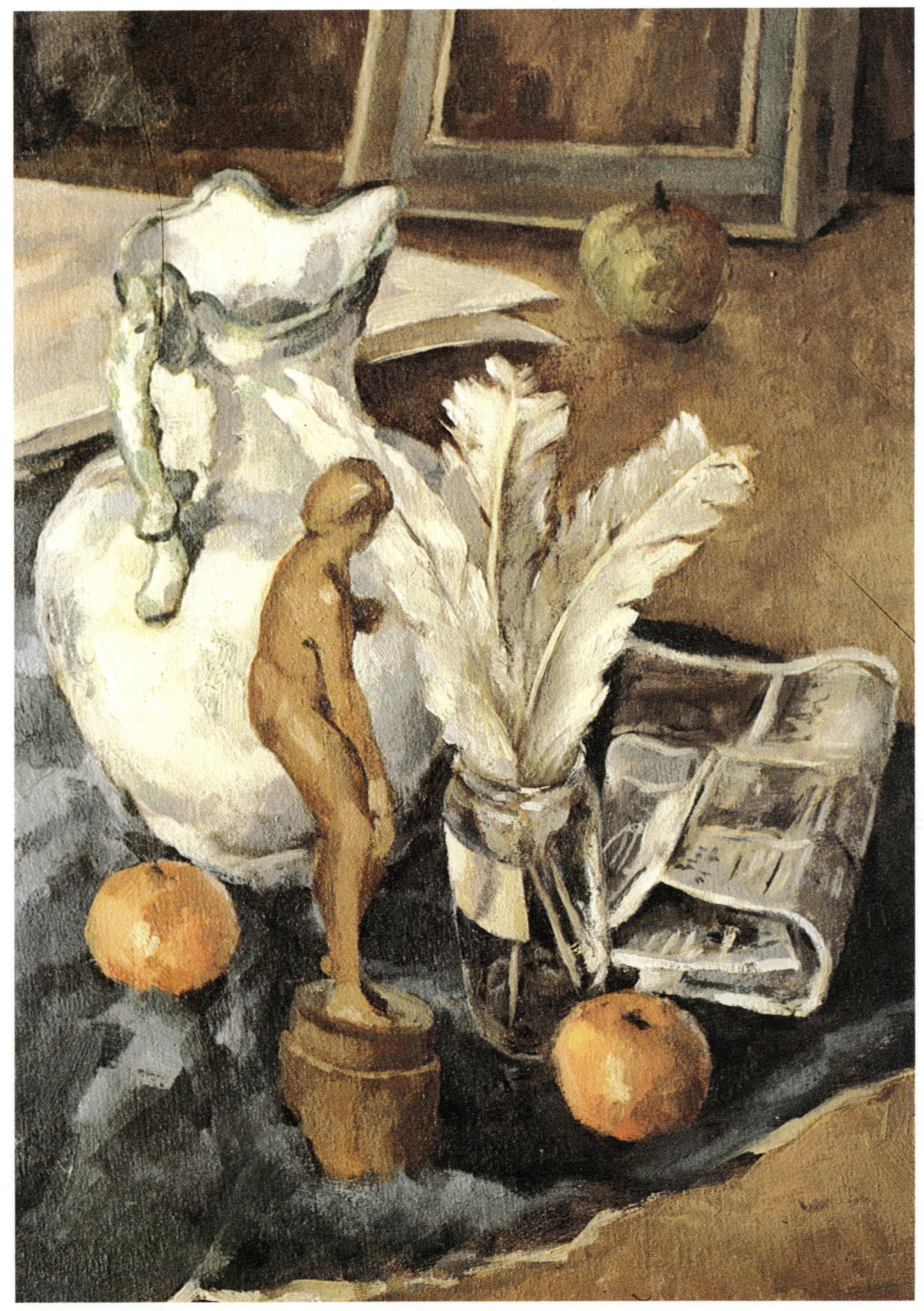

method is to draw directly on the canvas or board – this can be done in charcoal, pencil, ink, watercolour, acrylic or oil paint. Whichever method you adopt, it is usually useful to have done a sketch or two on paper before starting on the painting. Whatever medium I have selected for the drawing on the panel, I cover it with a fine drawing of thinned oil-colour applied with a small brush, as in Fig 91. For this exercise I have chosen a simple group of household objects. The drawing was lightly executed in charcoal, the surplus charcoal removed and the drawing laid in with a thin wash of French ultramarine paint. Using the five pigments selected – cadmium red, cadmium yellow, French ultramarine, titanium white and ivory black – mix the pigments that form the main colours of the subject. The mixture should be fairly thin, to help keep the brush strokes light and lively. The shapes can now be filled in using a No. 8 flat hogs-hair brush. Paint the shapes flat and as silhouettes, using a rag to make any corrections and a No. 2 hogs-hair brush to tidy and tighten the drawing where necessary. Try not to make the paint too smooth: brushes make marks that are individual to you: they are responsive to the hand and give a very personal look to everything you do. While working, stop from time to time and step back; examine the work and study the marks made by the brushes. Simplifying shapes does not mean they lose their identity: it helps to establish their identity and relationship with each other and the working surface. It also helps to suggest depth, even though the shapes are in silhouette.

Try varying methods of applying paint to different grounds of different colours, such as a small hardboard panel with just white primer, or a similar panel with a coloured ground of raw umber. Notice the difference in the paint characteristics and tone. Use the same subject for these exercises and try them on various types of surface, as suggested earlier. Keep them in your studio as a reference. These experiments in application will give each study a character of its own, help you to appreciate the qualities of different paint surfaces and encourage you to use your materials imaginatively.

In all these exercises remember how the subject was approached in the section on drawing. In all sound painting you will find the drawing underneath the painted surface: this is the foundation of painting. It is of special importance in oil-painting, which takes longer, allowing for greater in-depth understanding and reflection of the subject.

The use of colour allows perspective to be given an added emphasis. This is illustrated in Fig 92, a small oil-study of fruit. Notice how the planes of the surface of the apple are painted in lozenges of colour, each colour being representative of the apple but each making a contribution to the three-dimensional surface form by means of tone values and brush handling. A useful exercise is to make a one-colour study. For my study, Fig 93, I selected yellow. All the objects in this study are coloured yellow: the cloth, apple, book, flowers and the wall. Use a little black for darkening some of the colours, red to emphasise others, and add white to make highlights which need to be painted with impasto. Start the work by covering the panel with a middle tone of the

FIG 92 *Still life apples* (Oil, 12" x 10")

FIG 93 *Still life in yellow* (Oil, 10" x 8")

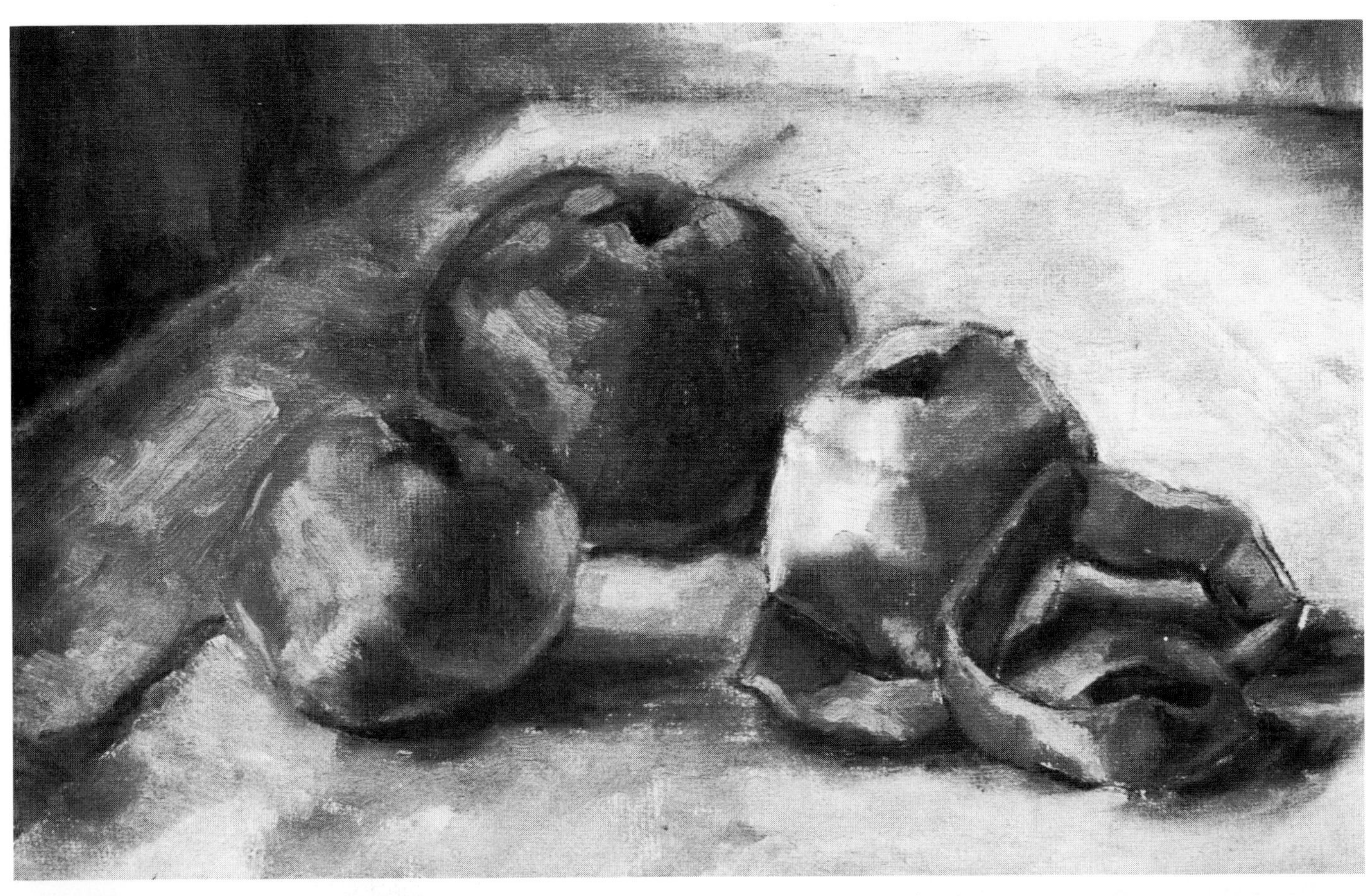

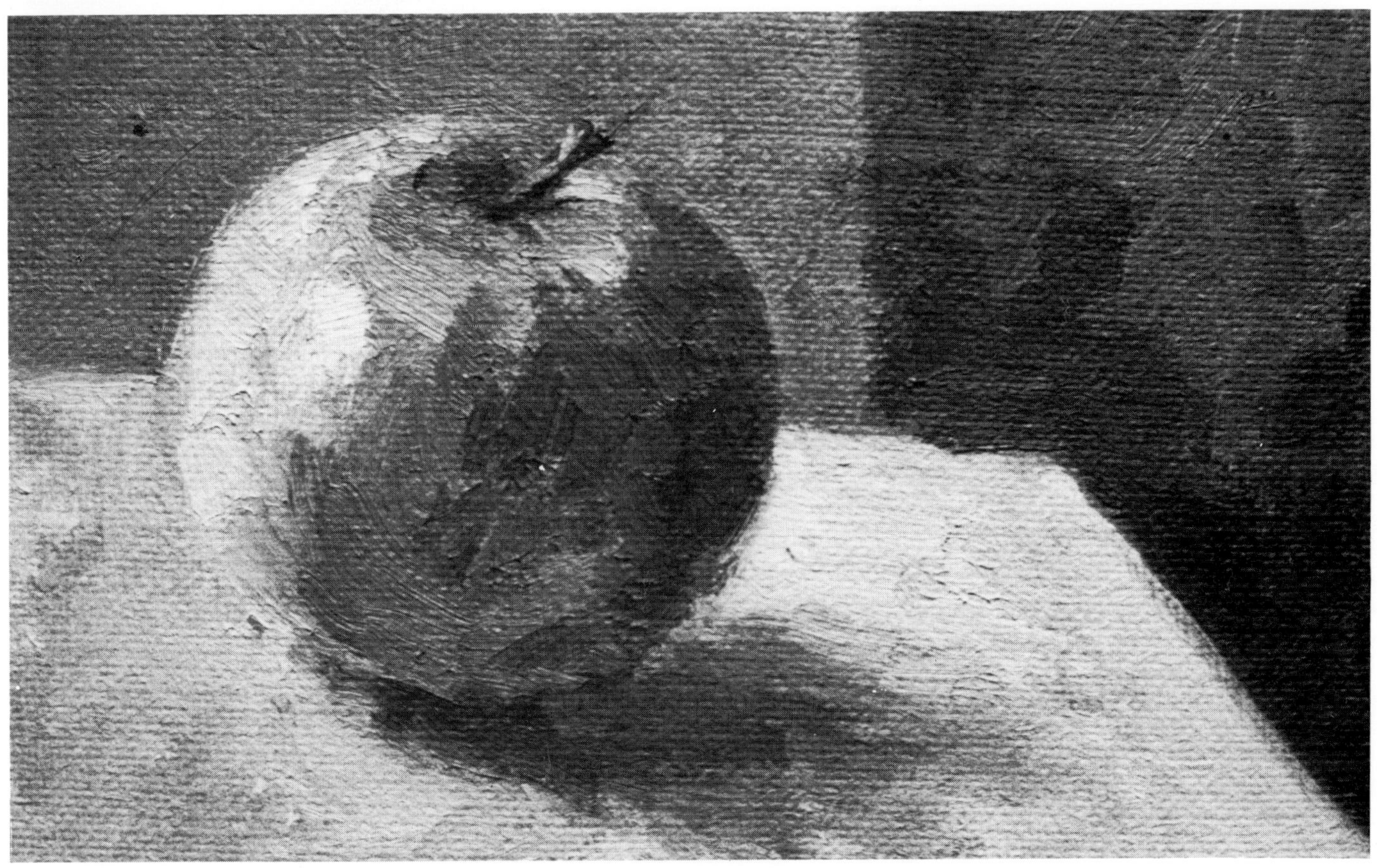

basic colour, then sketch in all the objects using a mix of yellows from your palette. Make a number of one-colour studies like this in a range of colours, from cool to warm – they need only be small – so that you can study them side by side. An understanding of one colour and all its tones will greatly enhance your understanding of what can be achieved in paint, and will give you mastery of the entire spectrum.

Acrylic paints using oil techniques

Acrylic paints are comparatively new and extremely versatile. They can be used effectively in transparent washes, glazes, or heavy impasto. Many thinning agents are available, but I find water just as effective.

The paints are completely waterproof, allowing one colour to be painted over another without risk of the underpainting being disturbed or bleeding through to the top colour – a decided advantage over other water-based paints. They dry very quickly, making them ideally suited for working out of doors, as you will not have to carry a wet painting home. I frequently use acrylics for preliminary sketches and studies for oil-paintings, and also as underpainting for oils. I would suggest that you use your oil-painting brushes for work with acrylics, but be sure that you do not let the paint dry on the brush. I always place brushes not in use in a jar of water and wash them thoroughly when I have finished.

FIG 94 *Acton Quarry, Dorset* (Acrylic paint, 42" x 28")

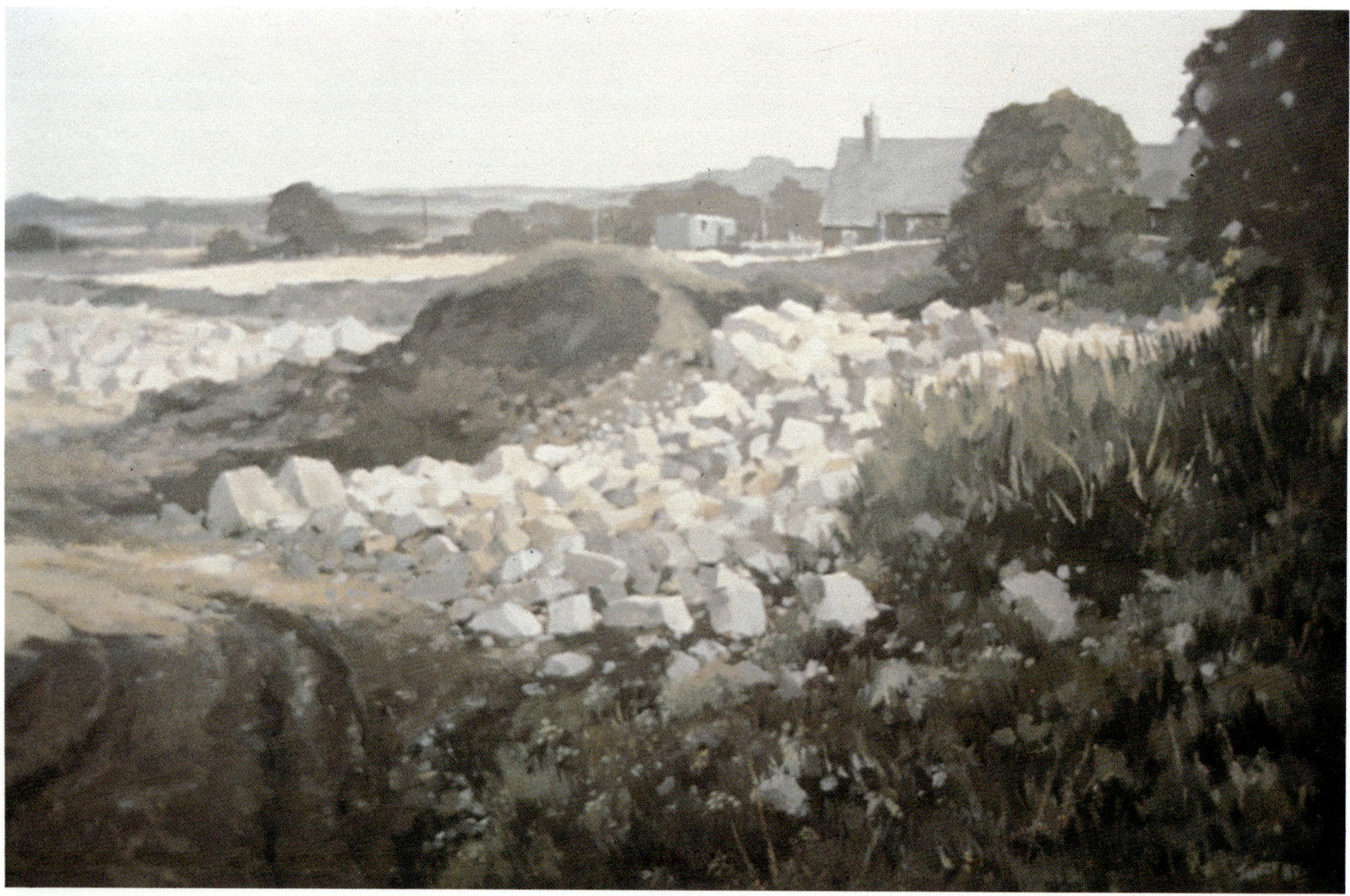

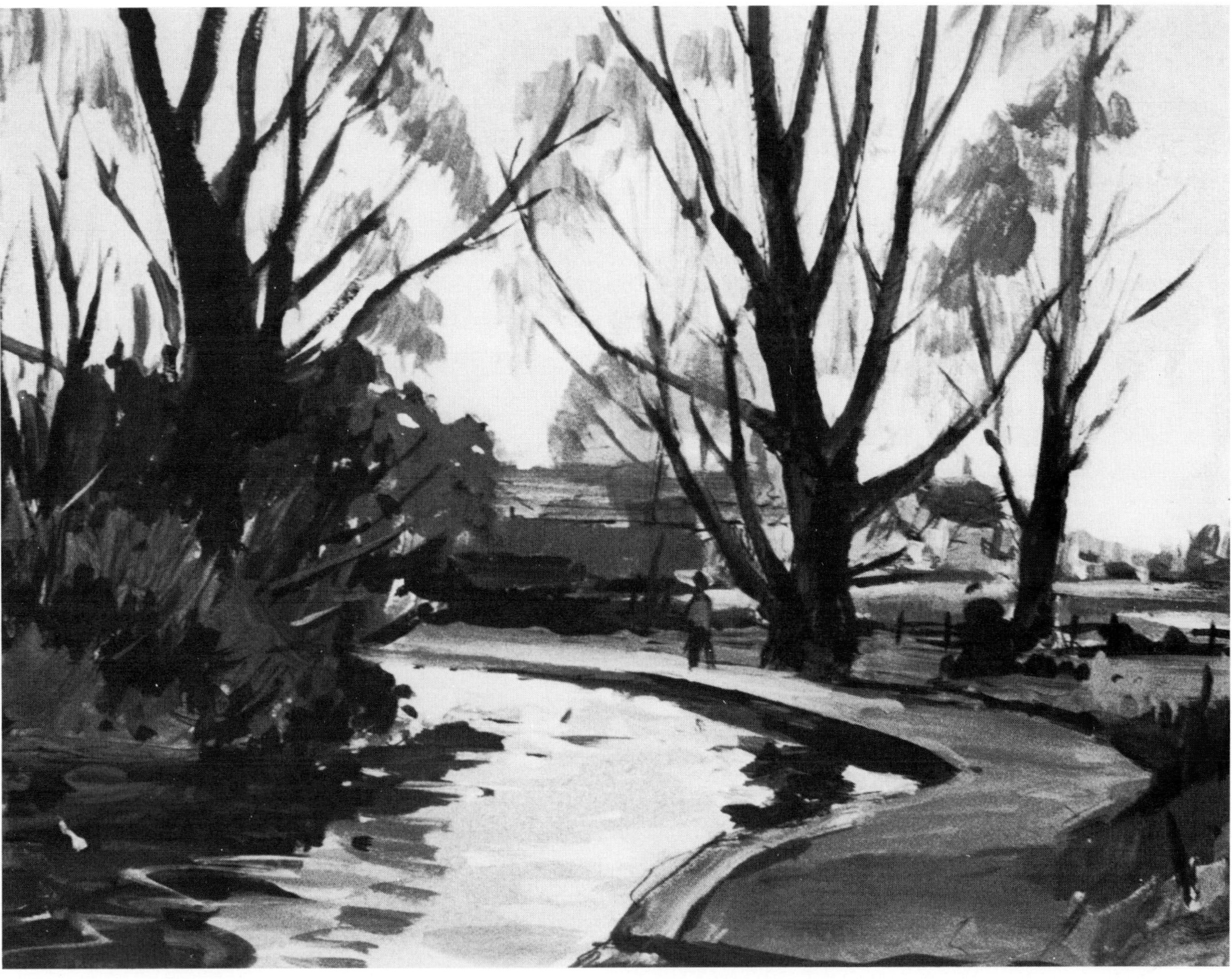

River walk, Dorchester (Acrylic, 18" x 14")

Acrylics can be painted on virtually any surface that is free from oil or grease. Fig 94 is an acrylic painting carried out on unprimed hardboard using cadmium red, cadmium yellow, ivory black and white. You will see that this work has been handled in exactly the same way as an oil-painting. As an exercise I would suggest that you start with an acrylic-primed panel and set up a simple still life of fruit. With the same range of colours used for oils, paint the subject in the same free manner, remembering that with acrylic, because of its versatility, you may paint in any way you like, but leave the heavy impasto until the final stages. Should you wish to adjust a tone, even at this stage, this is possible with acrylic because of its rapid drying. All you need do is glaze the area needing adjustment with a thin wash of modifying colour. Acrylics can also be applied with with a painting knife in exactly the same way as oil-paint. They can be varnished, using acrylic varnish, in either matt or gloss finish. For artists who find the smell of oil-paint offensive or upsetting to health, acrylics are ideal as they are virtually odourless.

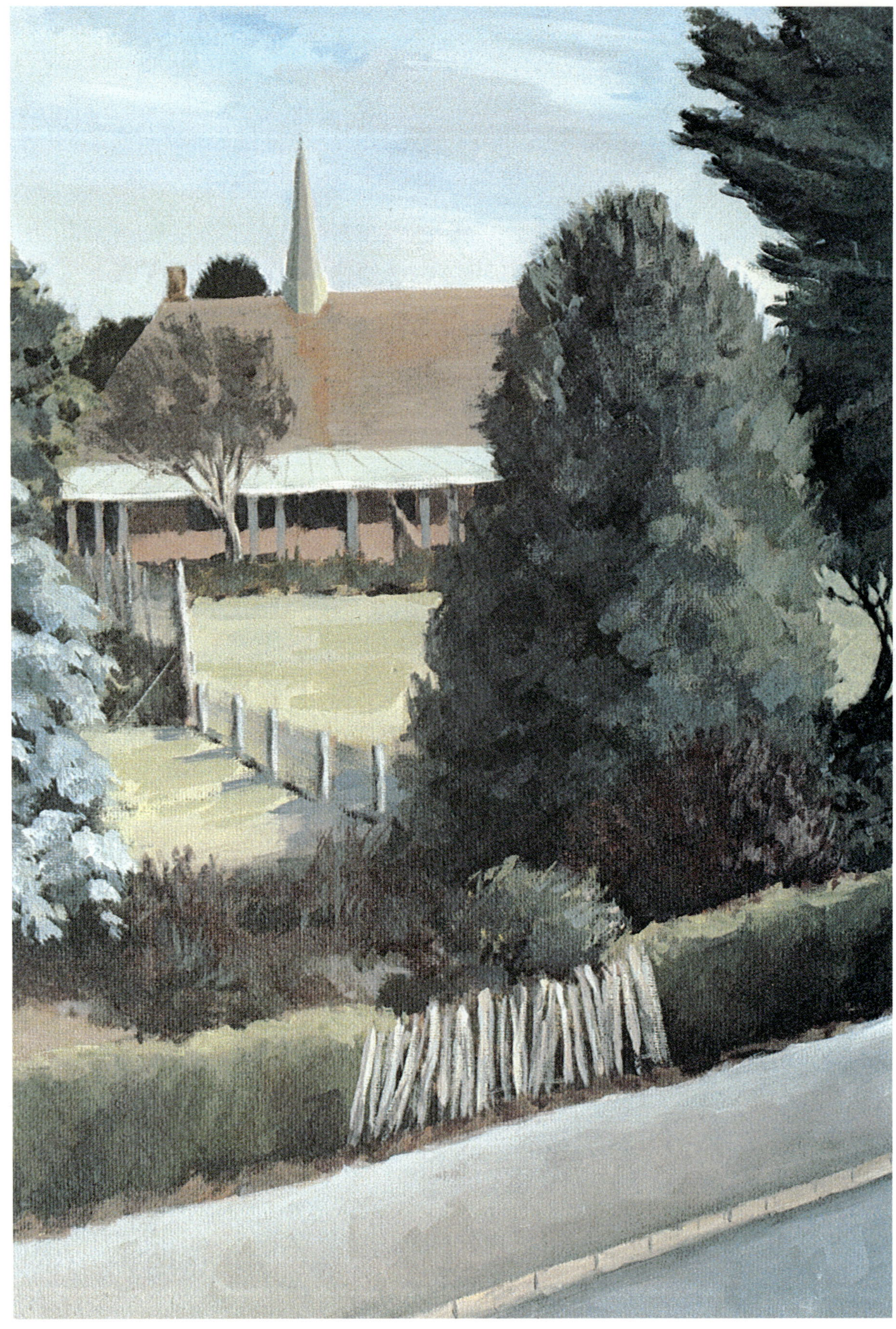

Water-colour painting

Most easels used for oil-painting can be used for water-colour painting. It is essential that the easel permit the working surface to be held in an almost horizontal position. For working out of doors, I prefer to work without an easel, keeping the board on my knee. If the subject requires a standing position, then a portable sketching easel will be necessary.

Paper for water-colour painting

Whilst it is possible to paint on any kind of paper, I would not recommend the beginner to use anything other than water-colour paper. This is made from rag and gives a sympathetic surface, which is amenable to a certain amount of correction, to paint on. There are many such papers to select from, offering a variety of textures and weights. The papers I find most useful are Bockingford, Saunders, R. W. S. Whatman and Arches. All water-colour papers are made in three surfaces: hot-pressed, not-pressed and rough. Generally speaking, I use not-pressed for the majority of my work, although occasionally, when subject demands, I use the other surfaces. The weight given to paper is determined by the weight per ream – the thinner the paper, the lower the weight. Before you can begin to use your paints, it is necessary to prepare and support the paper. You can just attach it to a drawing board, which is fine providing the paper is not too light in weight, as if the paper is thin it will cockle when wet. To avoid this, I always stretch water-colour paper of any size if the weight is below 140lb. To do this, it is necessary to soak the paper in water (I use the bath for this operation). The length of time for which the paper is soaked varies according to the type and weight, and I gauge this by the amount of movement left in the paper after it has been soaking for several minutes. I bend one corner slightly; if it springs back it has not soaked long enough, but if it stays in the bent position it has been soaking for too long. It should slowly return to the mid position. The paper should then be removed from the water, all surplus water removed from it by draining, and placed on the drawing board. Ensure that it is perfectly flat, attach it to the board all the way round with 2 inch gummed brown paper strips (not masking tape) and allow it to dry naturally. As it dries, it will shrink and tighten like a drum, providing a flat, non-cockling surface on which to work. Under no circumstances attempt to force-dry it, as the gummed strip will split and the paper be uneven as a result.

Water-colour paints

The colours used in water-colour painting are made of vegetable, mineral or animal pigments, mixed together with water and gum arabic. Glycerine is added to keep the colours moist. They are manufactured in tubes or pans of moist colour. Both types are of professional quality, and whilst there is a student range of water-colours, I recommend use of the professional quality because of their covering power and transparency.

Gouache or *tempera* colours are similar to water-colours and therefore deserve a discussion in this book. *Temperas* are diluted with water and

From the upstairs window, by Daphne Speight (Acrylic, 20" x 16")

require the same sort of brushes and papers as water-colours. The essential difference is that *tempera* colours have larger quantities of pigment and the lighter tones are obtained by the admixture of white pigment. Because of this difference we can observe the following: water-colours have a distinctive transparency; *temperas* are characterised by their opacity. This means that with *tempera* you can use light colours over dark in much the same way as with oil-paint, but if you dilute them with sufficient water the result is somewhat similar to water-colour. Because of the opacity of *temperas*, they may be painted on coloured surfaces, extending considerably the expressive capabilities of water-based colours.

Water-colour boxes and palettes
Most of the metallic and plastic boxes that water-colour paints are fitted in double as a palette for mixing colours. From experience, I have found that a small box to hold the tubes of my selected pigments plus two plastic meat trays (obtainable from freezer equipment shops) are quite sufficient for my needs. The trays need to be approximately 14 inches x 10 inches and 12 inches x 8 inches so that for transportation one will fit inside the other. The advantage of such trays is that they give plenty of mixing space for large washes, which so many of the more popular box/palettes fail to take into account. With this equipment you will need two substantial water pots. I have two collapsible pots that look remarkably like Chinese lanterns (Fig 95). The other piece of equipment I have found invaluable in the studio is a hairdryer for speeding up the drying process. I understand that battery operated models are available for outdoor working, although I have never found this necessary.

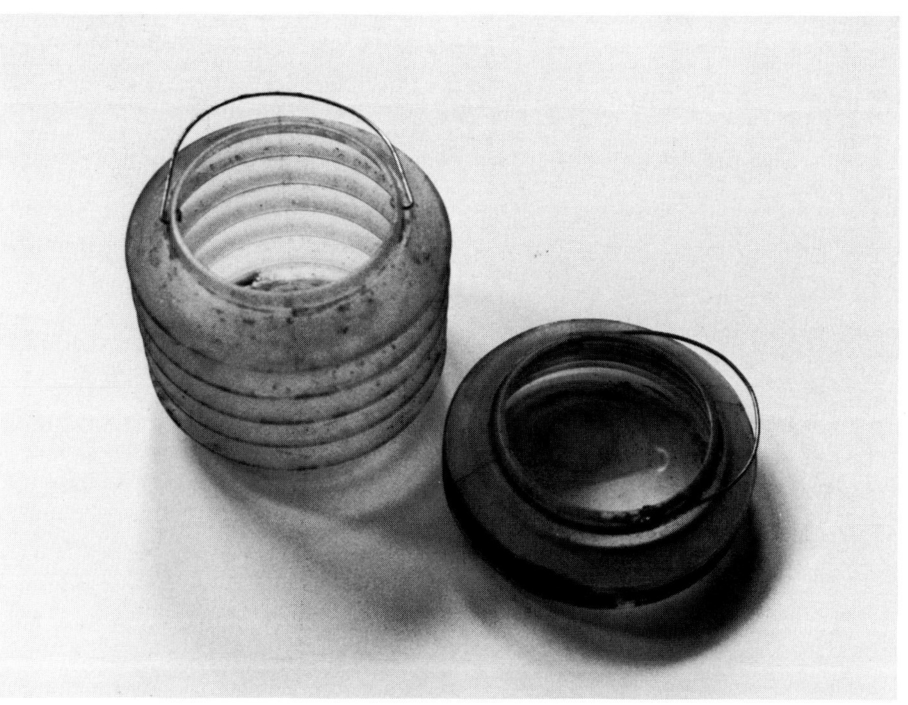

FIG 95 Water pots

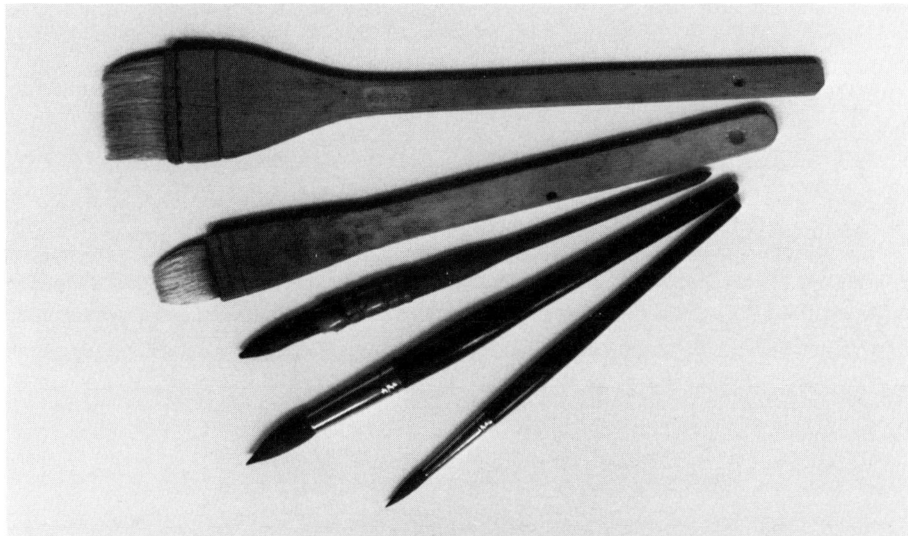

FIG 96a Water-colour brushes

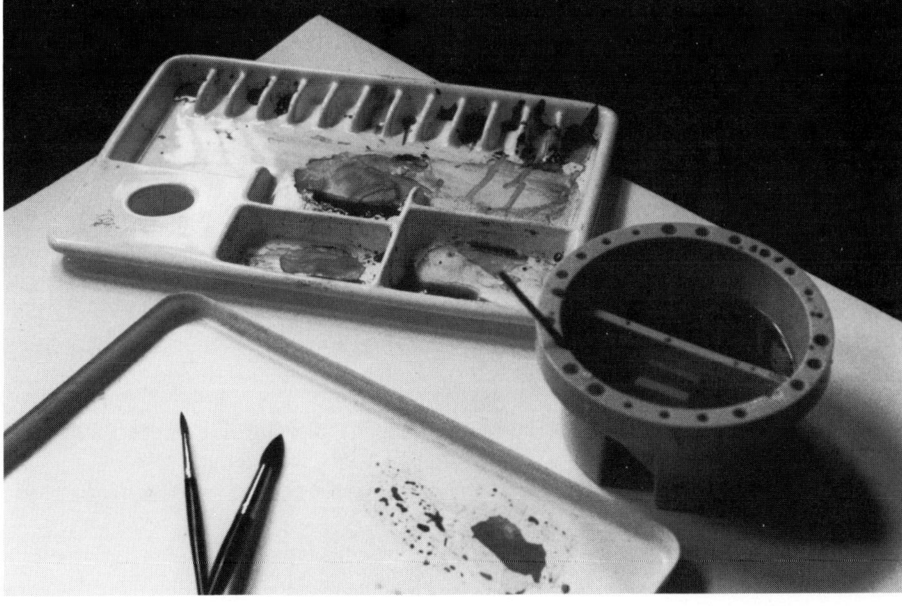

FIG 96b Water-colour equipment

Brushes

The best available brush for water-colour painting is made from sable hair, which is expensive, so for purely economic reasons, it makes good sense to limit the size of sable brushes. There are a number of first-class substitute brushes in the larger range (the Daler/Rowney Dalon series) which I have used successfully for some years now. In addition, french polisher's mops, which come in two or three sizes, are excellent as wash brushes and finally a 1½ inch Japanese *hake* or flat pastry brush is a firm favourite of mine. These, together with a sponge and some cotton wool, are my tool-kit for painting water-colour (see Fig 90). As you become more experienced, you will experiment with other types of brush and I commend to your attention flat and filbert-shaped ox-hair brushes in the larger sizes; also Chinese or Japanese brushes with pony and deer hair (these are particularly useful for fine line-work).

FIG 97 (overleaf) Types of water-colour washes

FIG 98 Tonal washes

Other useful materials
Masking fluid can be useful where you need to leave small or thin lines of white paper – window frames, masts of boats, or thin grasses in the foreground of a picture, for instance. A scalpel or modelmaker's knife is a useful tool for scraping out small areas of colour to achieve a specific effect. A candle to produce a resist to the water-colour is helpful, especially when painting the sparkle on water or the broken texture of a foreground. Lithographic masking tape can be useful when long straight edges are needed: I find this more sympathetic than masking tape, although in both cases it is important that they are used on good

quality paper, as with inferior paper they may pull away the surface. Finally, I use a large sponge for cleaning off washes that may have got away, a putty rubber for cleaning any small areas of drawing that can impinge on the final work, a small container of household salt (which can produce an interesting granulation effect, again most useful for foregrounds and textured surfaces) and a little pure turpentine spirit (which, when added to washes whilst still wet and allowed to dry with the wash, gives a marble-like texture to the paint).

Technique of water-colour painting
Learning to paint is hard enough, but painting in water-colour is even more difficult. It requires, as do all the visual arts, the ability to draw and draw well. This is a must if you are to master the craft of water-colour painting. To assist you in mastering the craft it is helpful to start with gouache, as this is a simpler medium to handle due to its opacity. As with oil-colour, keep the palette simple – cadmium red, cadmium yellow, French ultramarine, black and white. The first step towards handling the medium is learning to control a wash. Take a half imperial sheet of water-colour paper 140lbs weight: this will be approximately 16 inches x 12 inches. Divide this into four rectangles, 8 inches x 6 inches. Prepare a medium wash of French ultramarine and water in the palette; have a scrap of paper available to test the strength of the wash on, and a No. 8 and No. 12 sable or equivalent brush and a piece of towelling or a paper towel. Begin the first wash in the top left-hand rectangle on your prepared sheet of paper. Paint from side to side horizontally, using the No. 12 brush. Be careful with the amount of paint: the brush should be carefully loaded, so that it covers and spreads evenly without running or dripping. The second exercise is similar to the first. Using the square on the right side of the paper, paint vertically, keeping the brush loaded so that you are always painting wet in wet. In the bottom left-hand square, paint a dry gradated wash. Start by painting a band of intense colour from side to side on the upper part of the rectangle; now quickly wash the brush out, draining it slightly, and apply it to the bottom half of the blue band, dissolving and gradating the colour towards the bottom but painting from side to side at all times. Descend rapidly, pressing the brush to discharge more water; make sure the colour does not accumulate when you lift the brush. Finally, in the bottom right-hand rectangle, try a similar gradated wash, only this time on wet paper. To start, wet the paper evenly from top to bottom; drain off all excess water and, as before, paint a band of strong colour horizontally across the top. Now tilt the board so that the colour can drain down slowly; this is a wet gradated wash. Fig 97 shows all these exercises. Practise these until you feel confident that you can handle the washes at this scale, and then try even larger areas. As shown in Fig 98, also try dry washes in different tones, the tonal strengths being modified by weakening the colour by the addition of water. Try all these exercises using the three colours red, yellow and blue.

The Blackmore Vale (Water-colour,
15" x 12")

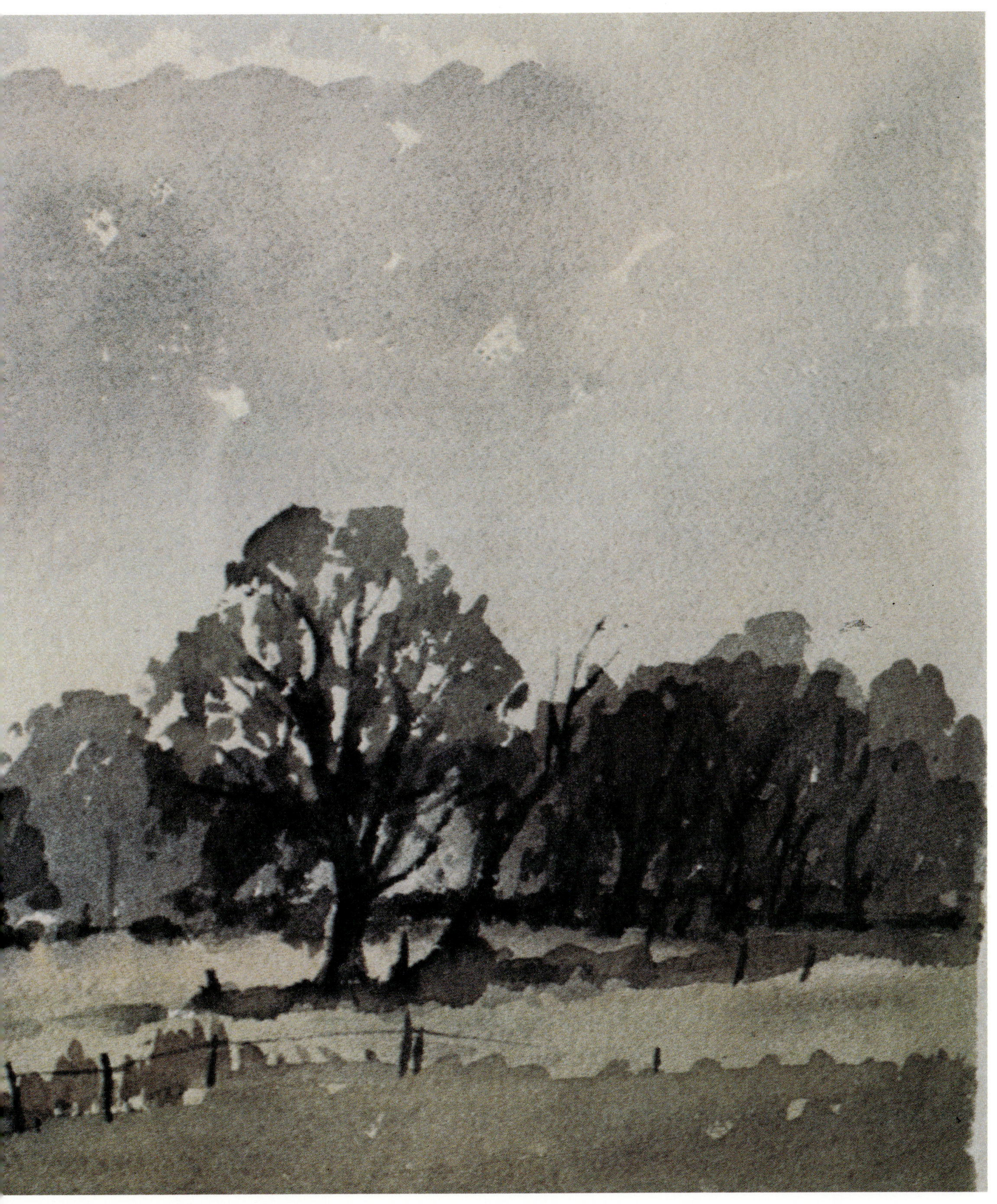

The following exercise can be done in gouache or pure water-colour, remembering that gouache may be applied opaquely and that the middle tones may have white in them, while the highlights most certainly will. Because of this, the method of application need not be so rigid. For this reason, the following description of technique is given with pure water-colour in mind, but can just as easily be used as a basis for painting in gouache. Pure water-colour is applied from light to dark, the first washes being quite ethereal; the really bright highlights are the white of the paper which has to be left unpainted, calling for strict control of the washes. It is possible, however, when the intense highlights are small, to use masking fluid as shown in Fig 99. The stronger, darker washes are then applied and finally the drawing is re-established by the use of the strong darks. For the subject illustrated in Fig 99 I used only two colours: cobalt blue and burnt umber. The drawing was done using a B grade pencil and was a simple line-drawing without shadows. The bright highlights on the glass were reserved with masking fluid. The second stage commenced with the paper being lightly sponged with clean water to remove any grease left by the hand when drawing. Whilst the paper was still moist, the background and the table were painted. When this was dry, I then painted the bottle and

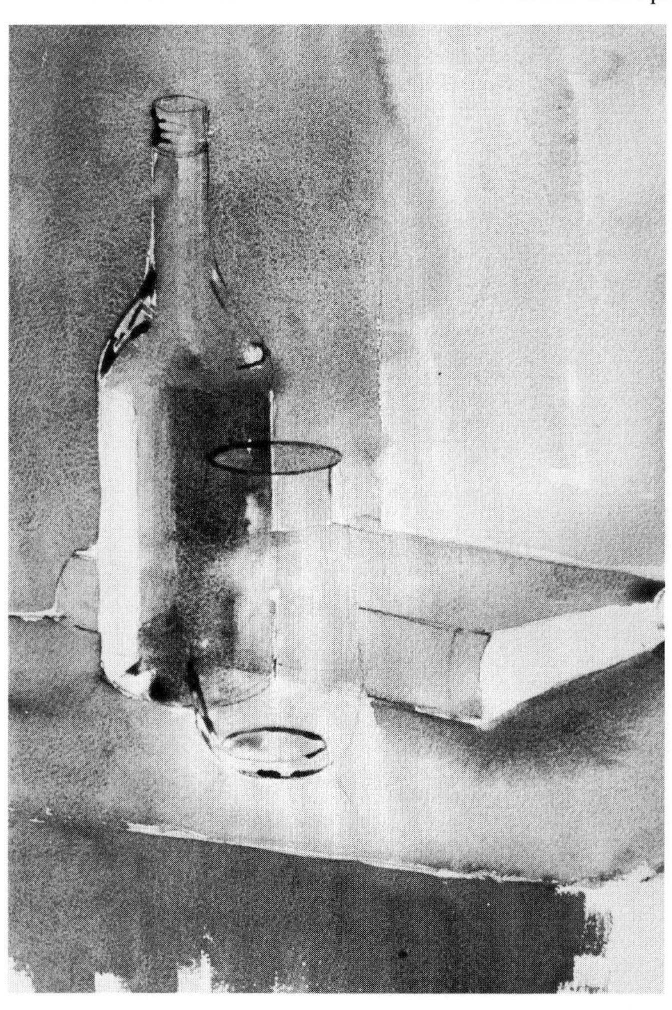
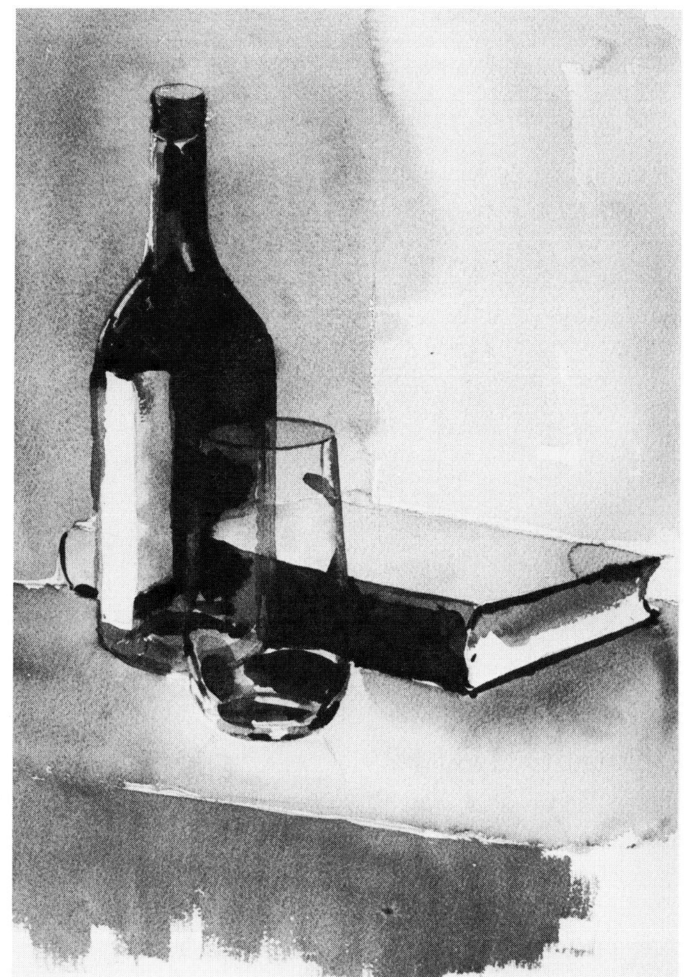

FIG 99(a-c) Progressive development of water-colour still-life.

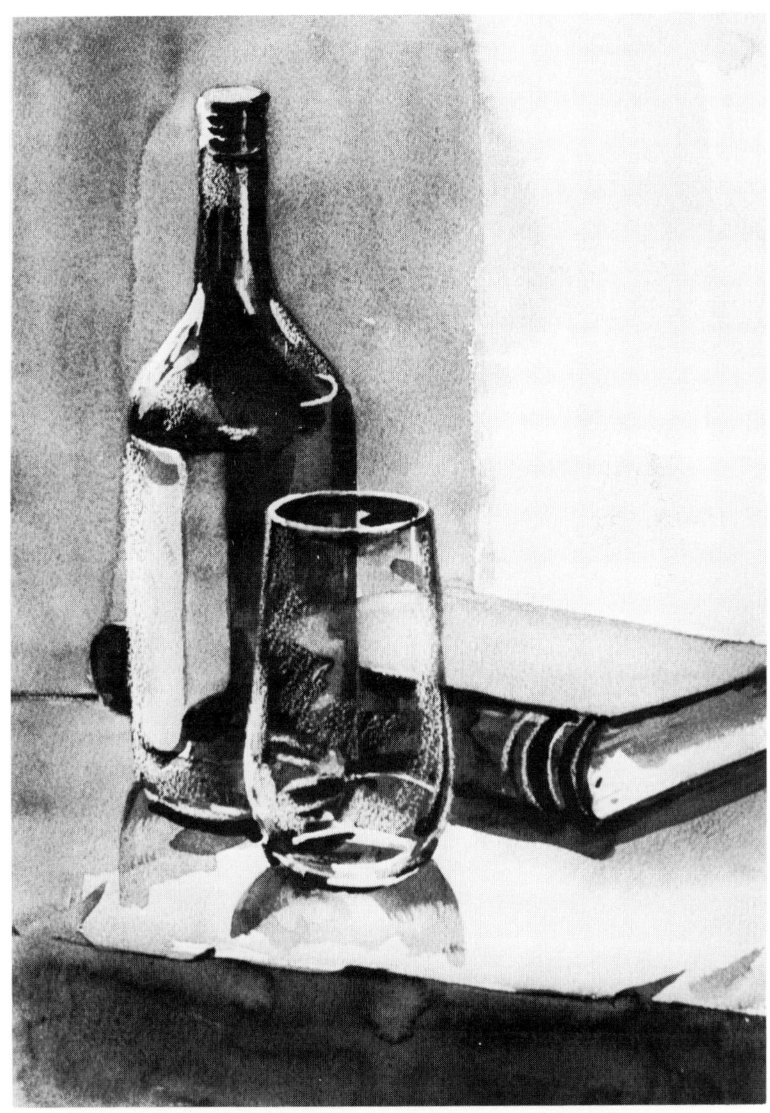

the book, starting with the lightest colours and working the dark middle
tones into the wet paint, reserving the highlights. The tumbler was
painted in conjunction with the bottle. As this was drying, I established
the cast shadows on the table and strengthened the background
slightly. The final stage consisted of painting in the crisp darks. These
required strong, dryish colour, as it was necessary to use this to
establish a little drawing that had got lost during the painting. All that
remained to be done was to remove the masking fluid, bringing the
highlights into play, which also helped to establish the tonal
relationships by bringing the glass forward of the bottle. Note how in
this exercise the light shines through the glass and illuminates the cast
shadow of the tumbler. This was achieved by painting the cast shadow
and whilst it was still wet, lifting the paint out with a dry brush, which
allowed the edges to fuse and merge.

This is the basic technique of painting in gouache or water-colour
and applies whatever the subject. A little later we will see how this basic
technique can be applied and broadened to cover the painting of a wide
range of subjects.

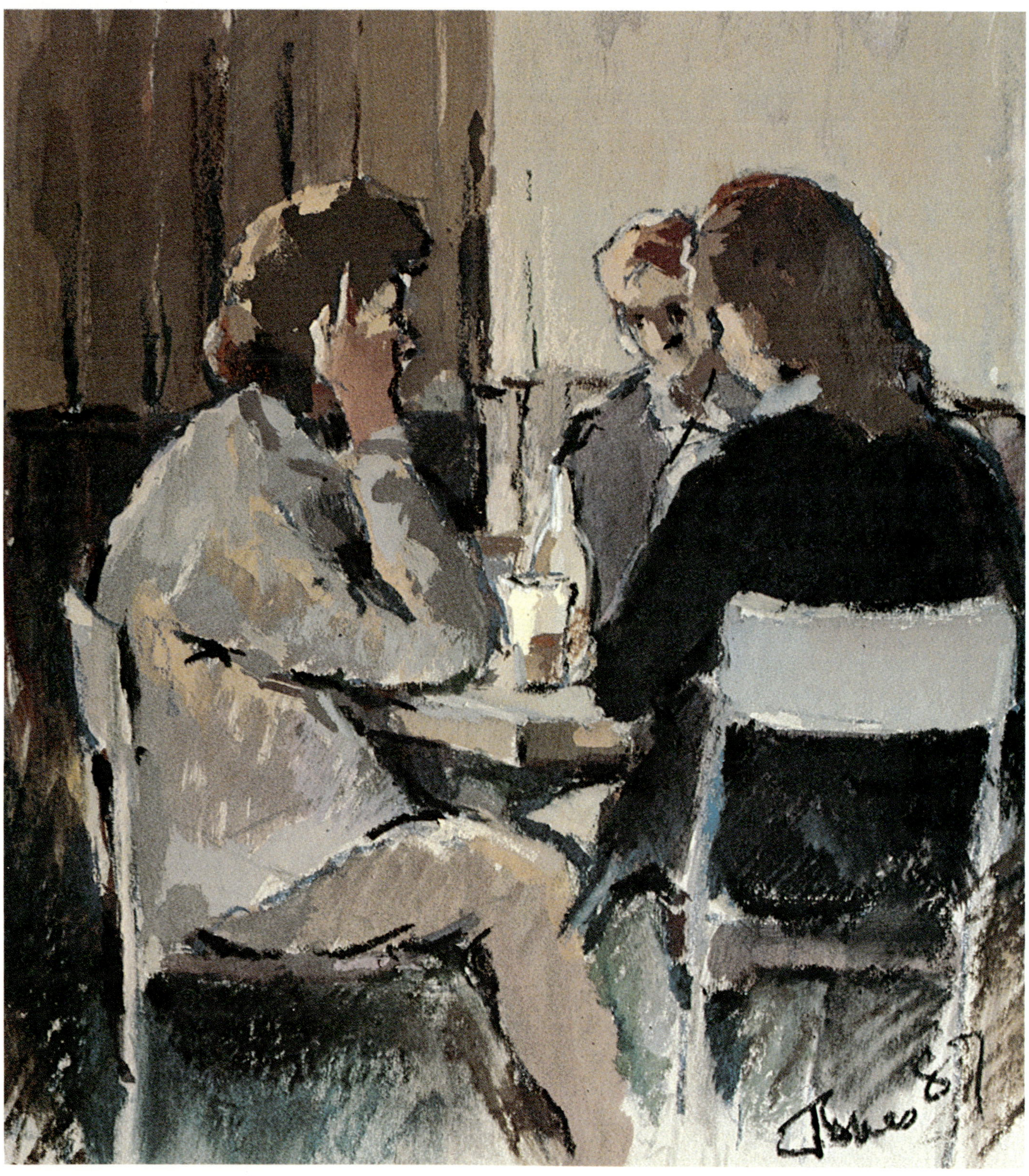

French café (Gouache, 18" x 15")
This work was painted on 140lb Bockingford water-colour paper which had been given a grey wash. After a number of preliminary sketches were made, the drawing was laid in with oil pastel. Following this the main shapes were established in water-colour, and a little ink added to give emphasis to the drawing. The contrast and modelling were then worked on, using gouache as I wished to introduce colour on to the grey ground and the opacity of gouache made this possible. Finally, emphasis to the shapes was introduced with oil pastel, which was also used selectively to enhance the contrast and modelling. The work was deliberately left vignetted at the bottom as I felt that to go any further would have been counter-productive design-wise

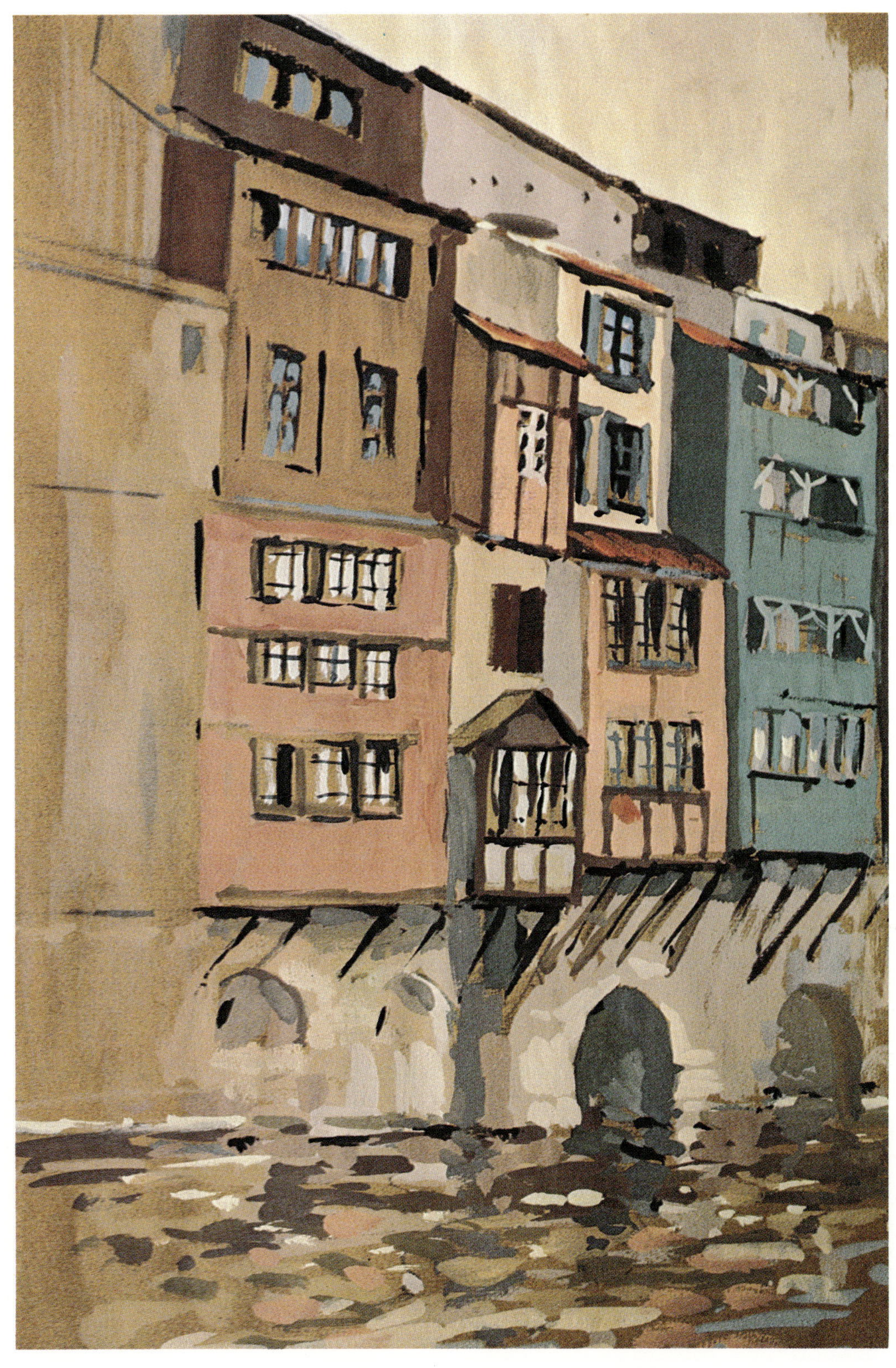

Buildings, Castres (Gouache, 12" x 10")

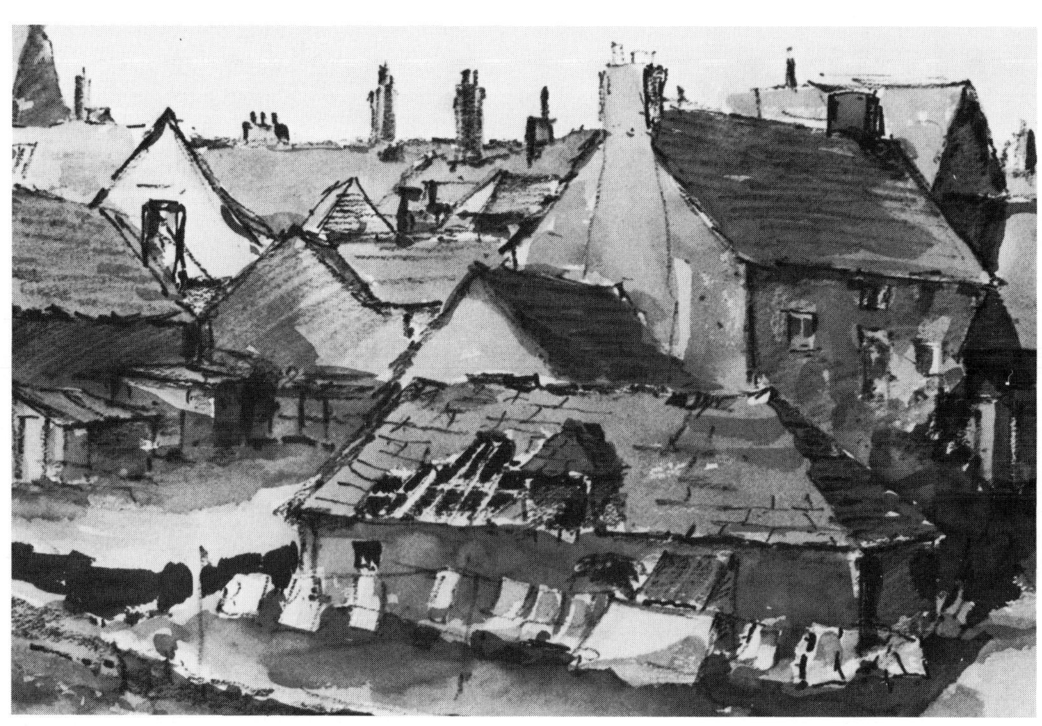

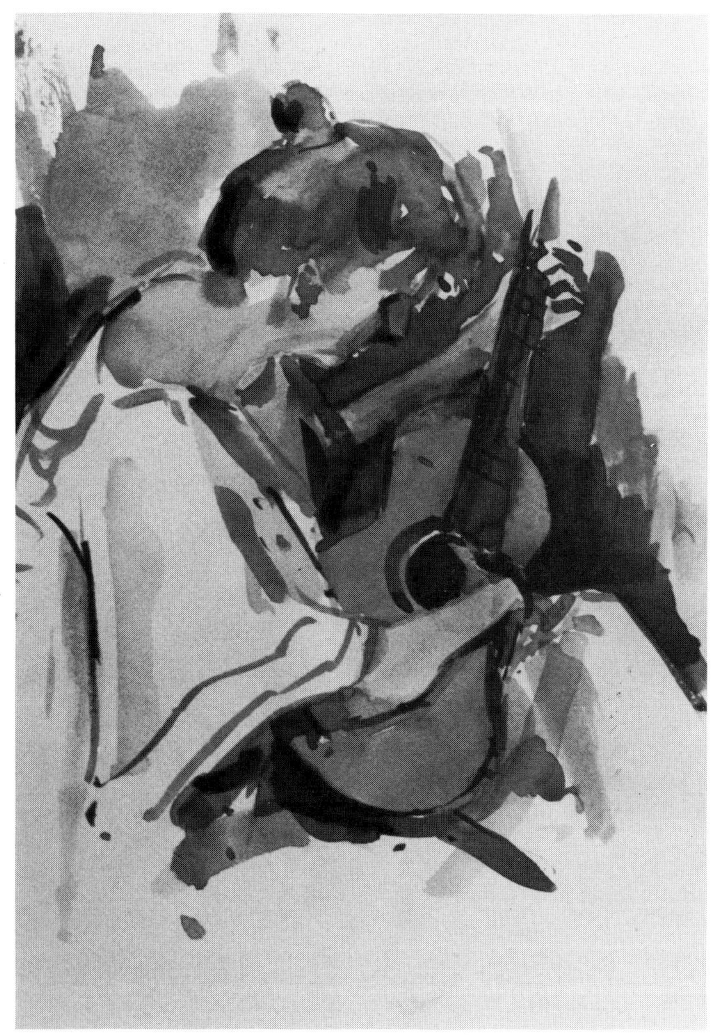

Corfe village, Dorset (Ink and wash, 15" x 11")

The guitarist (Water-colour, 10" x 8"). Painted directly from subject without drawing

Old Langworthy Farm (Water-colour, 15" x 11")

Lymington (Water-colour, 16" x 12").
Candle grease used to give texture in
foreground

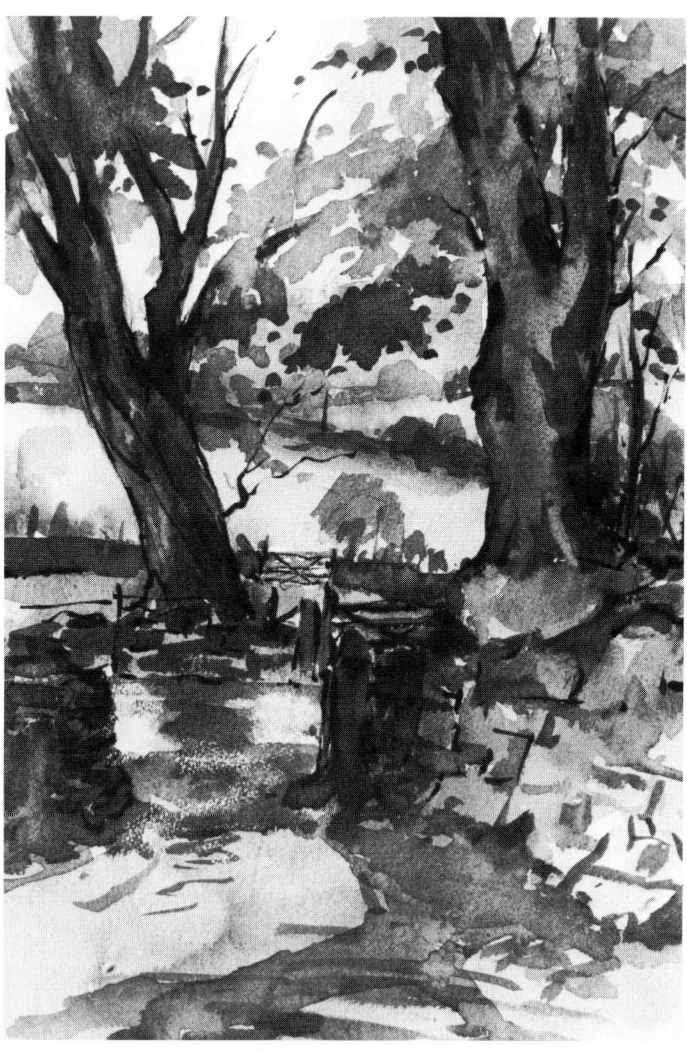

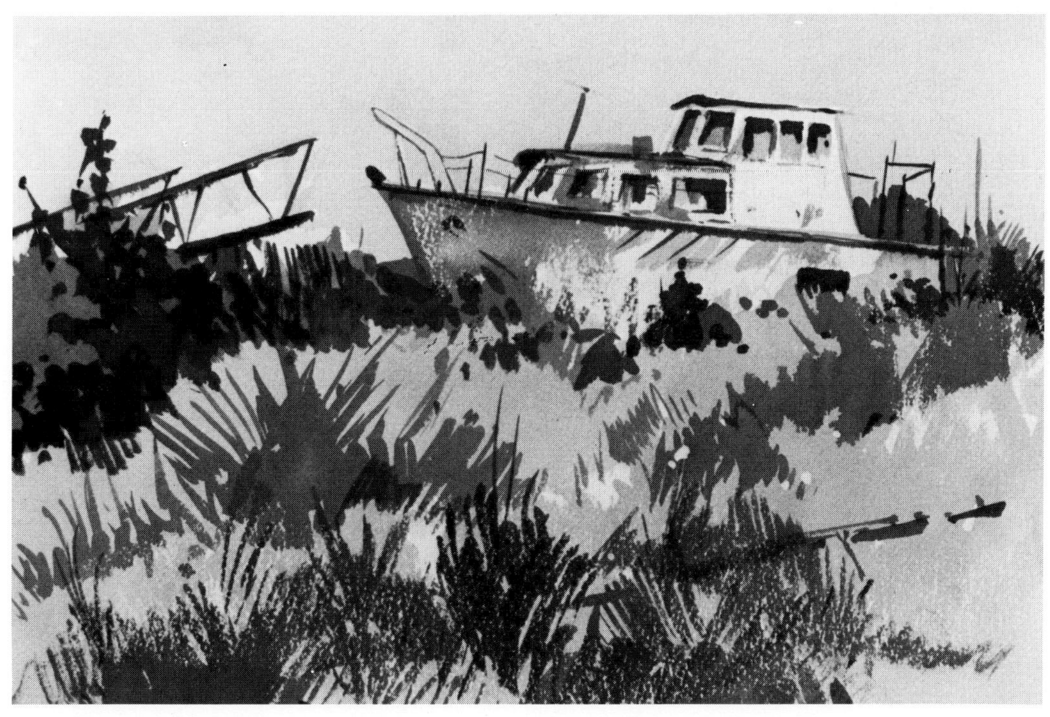

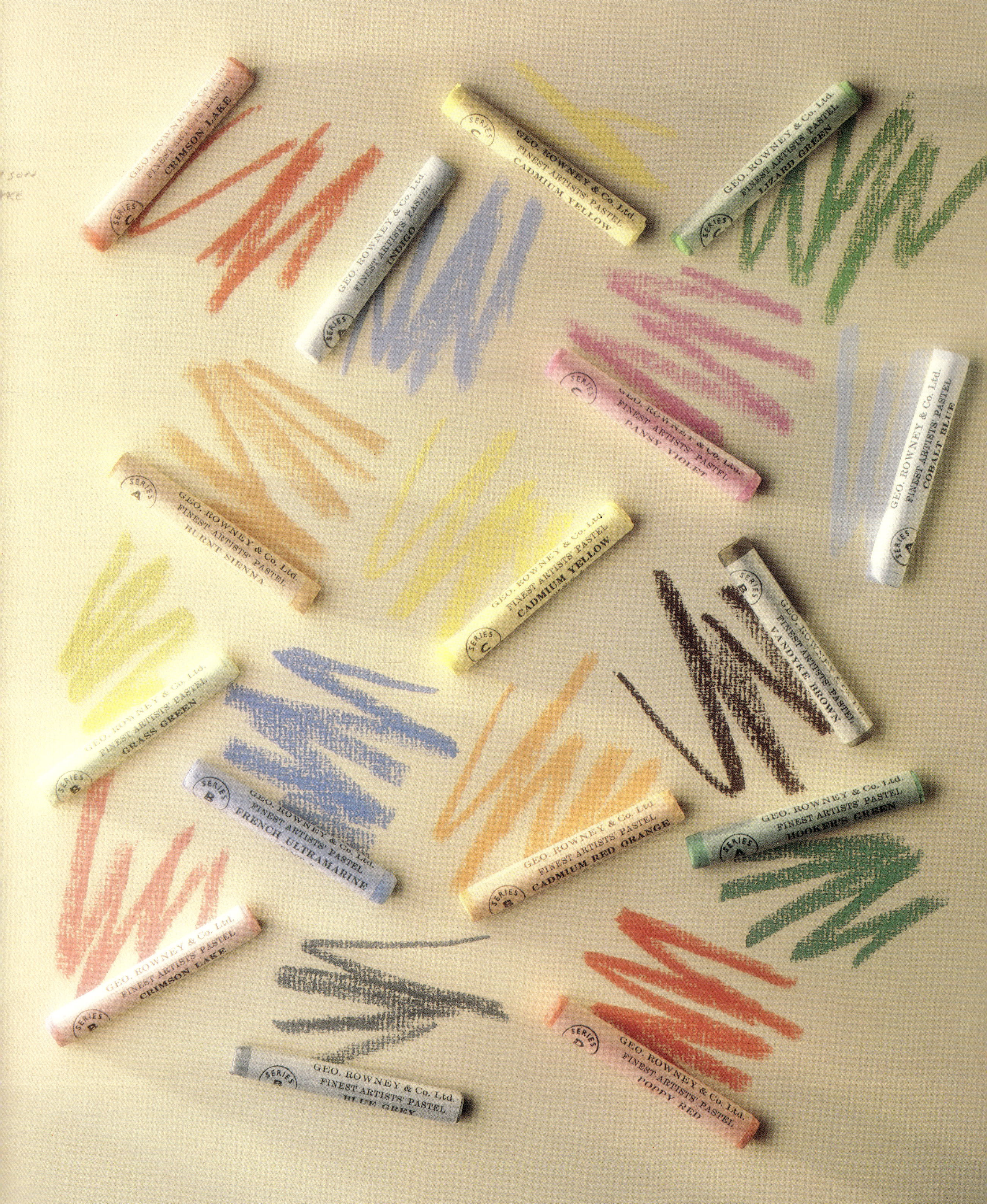

GEO. ROWNEY & Co. Ltd.
FINEST ARTISTS' PASTEL
CRIMSON LAKE
SERIES C
GEO. ROWNEY & Co. Ltd.
FINEST ARTISTS' PASTEL
CADMIUM YELLOW
SERIES C
GEO. ROWNEY & Co. Ltd.
FINEST ARTISTS' PASTEL
LIZARD GREEN
SERIES C
GEO. ROWNEY & Co. Ltd.
FINEST ARTISTS' PASTEL
INDIGO
SERIES A
GEO. ROWNEY & Co. Ltd.
FINEST ARTISTS' PASTEL
PANSY VIOLET
SERIES C
GEO. ROWNEY & Co. Ltd.
FINEST ARTISTS' PASTEL
COBALT BLUE
SERIES A
GEO. ROWNEY & Co. Ltd.
FINEST ARTISTS' PASTEL
BURNT SIENNA
SERIES A
GEO. ROWNEY & Co. Ltd.
FINEST ARTISTS' PASTEL
CADMIUM YELLOW
SERIES C
GEO. ROWNEY & Co. Ltd.
FINEST ARTISTS' PASTEL
VANDYKE BROWN
SERIES B
GEO. ROWNEY & Co. Ltd.
FINEST ARTISTS' PASTEL
GRASS GREEN
SERIES B
GEO. ROWNEY & Co. Ltd.
FINEST ARTISTS' PASTEL
FRENCH ULTRAMARINE
SERIES B
GEO. ROWNEY & Co. Ltd.
FINEST ARTISTS' PASTEL
CADMIUM RED ORANGE
SERIES B
GEO. ROWNEY & Co. Ltd.
FINEST ARTISTS' PASTEL
HOOKER'S GREEN
SERIES A
GEO. ROWNEY & Co. Ltd.
FINEST ARTISTS' PASTEL
CRIMSON LAKE
SERIES B
GEO. ROWNEY & Co. Ltd.
FINEST ARTISTS' PASTEL
BLUE GREY
SERIES B
GEO. ROWNEY & Co. Ltd.
FINEST ARTISTS' PASTEL
POPPY RED
SERIES B

Pastels

The use of pastels is a combination of drawing and painting. Pastels are available in two forms: soft pastels and oil pastels. They are held and used like charcoal, chalk or conté, and are made in many tints and colours. Because of the range, they can produce work of great strength and subtlety.

Soft pastels can be used on a variety of surfaces, the most commonly used being paper that is specifically manufactured for pastel. These papers are made in many colours, so the pastellist may select a ground which will be sympathetic to the subject. Many other surfaces are suitable for pastel, such as cartridge paper, water-colour paper, fine sandpaper, brown wrapping paper, cardboard, strawboard and, finally, canvas. Pastels are extremely delicate and can be easily smudged or blown off the surface. There are many ways of fixing pastels to give them durability. Use of spray fixers, or simply applying pressure to a piece of tracing paper placed over the pastel, will help to reduce the risk of damage. Applying steam from a hot kettle also helps to fix the pastel a little. Unfortunately, fixing of pastel drawings and paintings does kill the bloom – the minute particles of pastel dust that lie on the surface of the drawing and give the unique quality of brilliance and softness associated with the medium. To retain this quality I fix the early layers of the drawing, but never the final application. The only sure way of protecting pastel is to frame it under glass as soon as possible. This can create problems of storage and cost, so a cheaper alternative is to put them between sheets of newspaper and place a paperclip every inch or so right round the edge, ensuring that the pastel paper is trapped by the paperclip. The pastel can now be stored flat in a drawer. When framing a pastel it is necessary to ensure that there is a gap between the work and the glass. If these touch, a residue of pastel will adhere to the glass, spoiling the work. To achieve this gap, place the pastel behind a window mount cut from a ten or twelve-sheet mounting board (see Chapter 8).

Pastels are two-inch long sticks of powdered pigment mixed with gum arabic and precipitated chalk, with a wrapper giving the colour and the tint number. I use Daler-Rowney artists' soft pastels and, whilst the number of tints varies according to pigment, the low numbers indicate paleness and the high numbers the deepest tints. I have found that, in common with the other media, simplicity in the choice of colours is a good rule. I therefore tend to use as few colours as possible, but the full range of tints of each colour.

The methods of pastel painting are legion and all require a disciplined approach in the way you look after and keep your pastels ready for use. I have a segmented *Tupperware* plastic container in which I keep the colours separated into groups under the heading of pigments – all the reds are together with their tints, and so on. In each compartment I have some ground rice, which helps to keep the pastels clean, as they tend to rub against each other. The general rules for painting in pastel tend to follow the same principles that apply to other painting media. Boldness is a good habit. I break my pastels to enable me to paint with the side of the stick rather than with the point, as this removes a lot of niggling.

Pastels

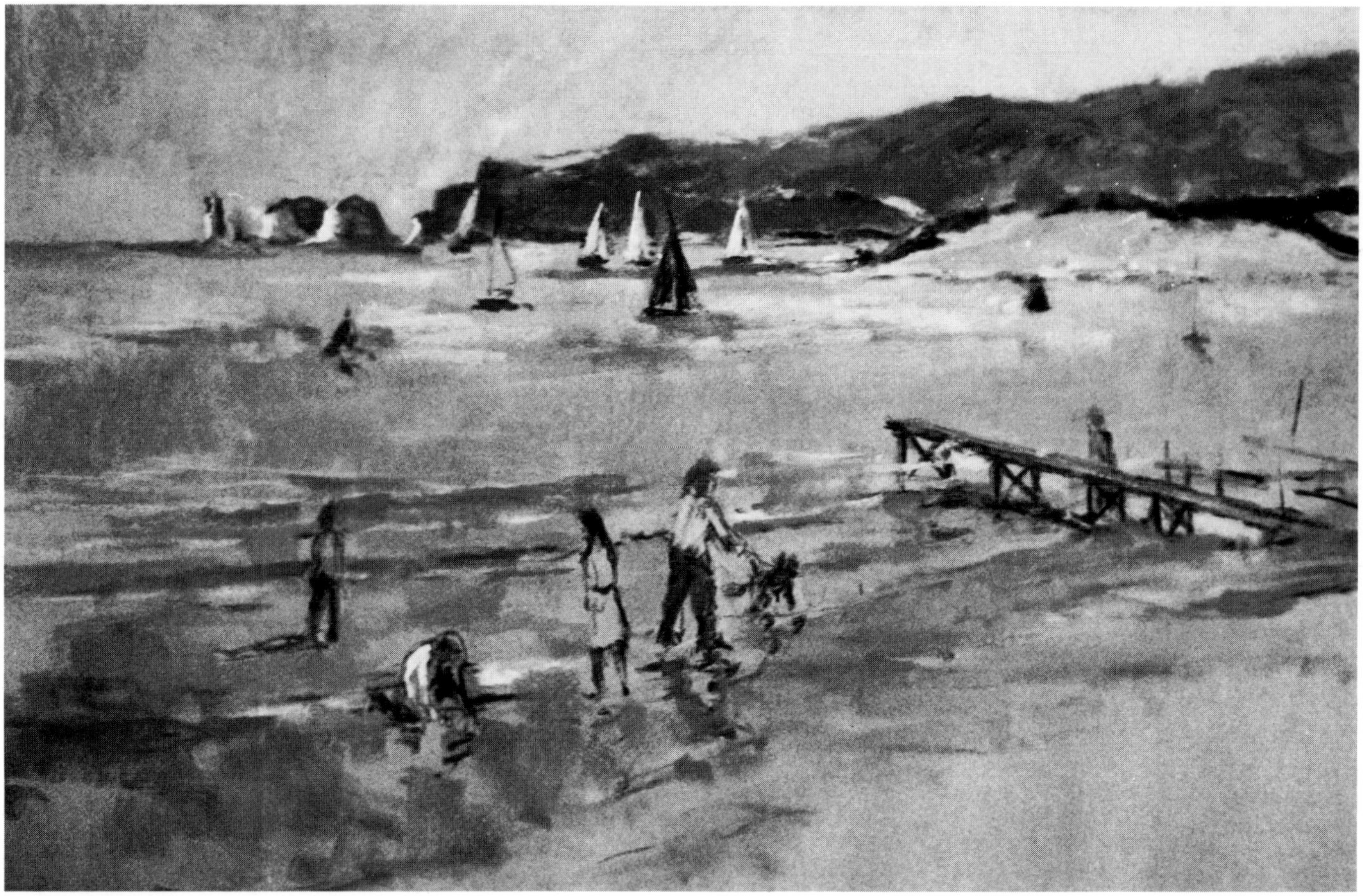

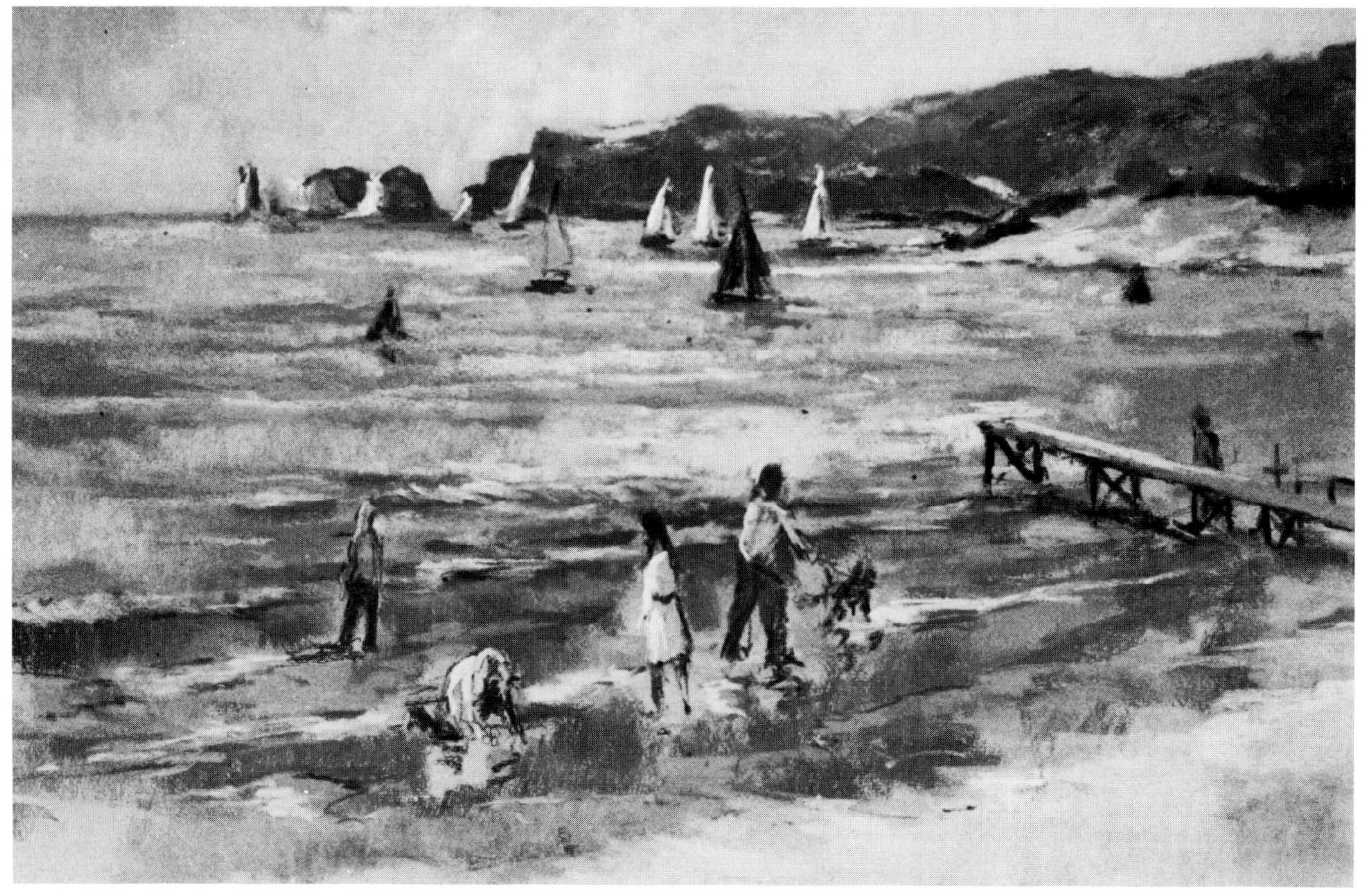

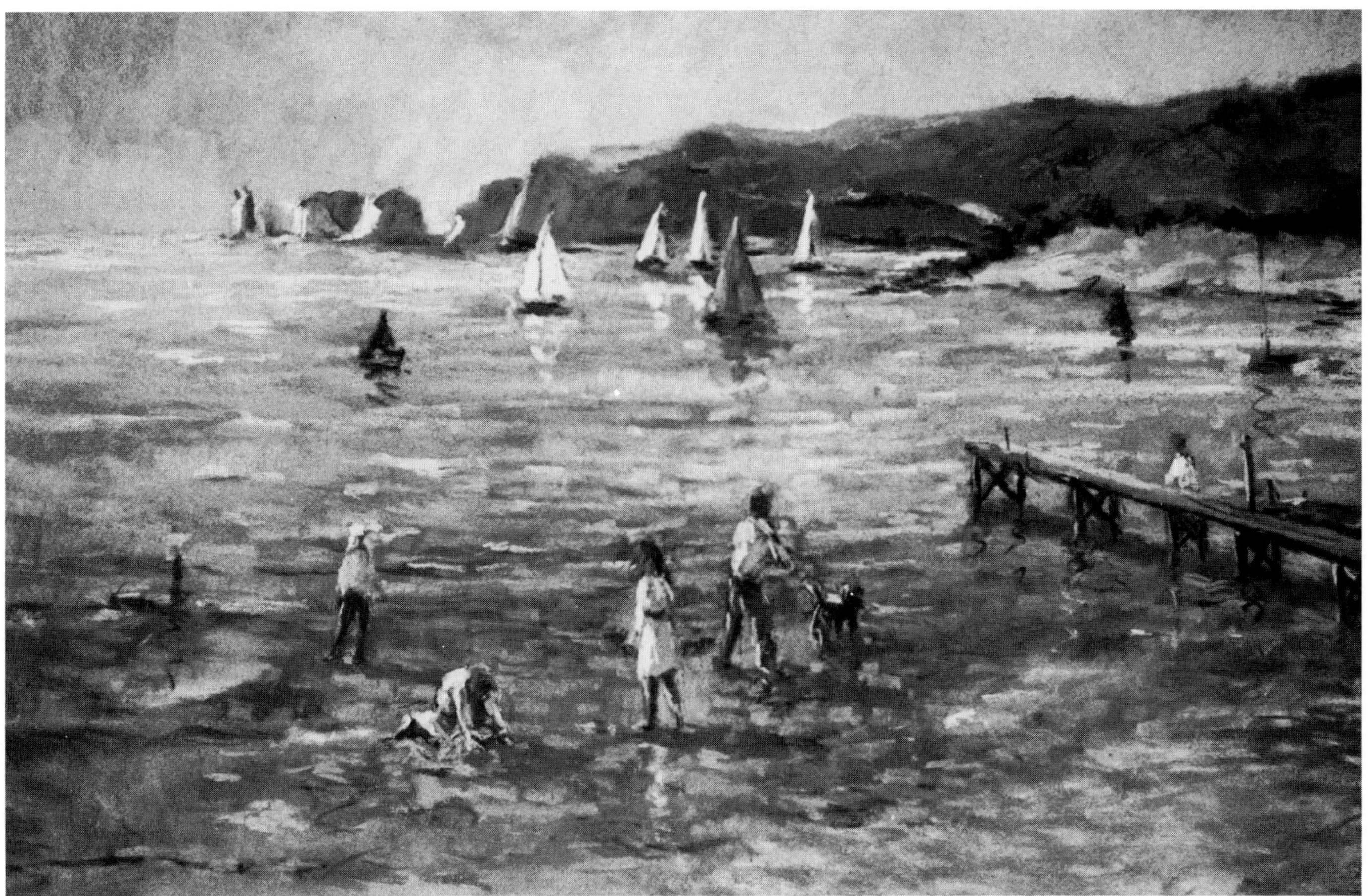

Fig 100 illustrates three stages in the development of a pastel painting. The subject, a seascape of the Dorset coast, was first drawn in charcoal. This was lightly fixed with a spray fixer, which has no harmful effect on the final work. When the fixer had evaporated, the shadows were lightly positioned using the pastels on their sides, applying them across the forms wherever possible. For this illustration I selected a heavy Fabriano Ingres paper tinted blue/grey, which I felt was sympathetic to the subject. Note how at this stage of the work the paper is allowed to show through the passages of colour. With pastel, no attempt is made at this point to indicate the details of the figures on the sands; all the effort is concentrated on the large masses. The second stage shows how the smaller shapes are made to relate to the surrounding environment, which usually means making some adjustment to the work done in the early stage. You will see that the highlights have been left out at all times in both stages. At this point I fix the work. This may sound like a contradiction, in view of my previous statements, but it will be covered by fresh pastel a little later. The next move is a very personal one. I rub the work lightly with fine sandpaper, remove the loose pastel dust and then fix again. The advantages of this are twofold: the rubbing removes the hard edges and at the same time it unifies the tonality. It is now possible to pick up and emphasise those areas that give sparkle to the work. In stage three you will see that the highlights have been added and that the whole work is pulled together. Note also that this stage is not fixed, so the bloom retains its freshness. The shadows have been invigorated by the cross-hatching of warm reflected lights. This technique is a favourite method with pastellists and is often used for optical mixing – for instance, yellow and blue lines cross-hatched produce green when mixed by the eye. This result is probably more easily achieved with pastel than with any other medium, and it has the added bonus that, should you find you are short of a particular colour, you can usually achieve your requirements using the optical mixing method.

Should it become necessary to make a small correction, the following practice will be helpful. Loosen the offending passage with a bristle brush, take the centre from a slice of new bread and then gently dab it on the loosened passage. The moisture in the bread will lift the pastel without smearing or leaving a grease mark.

Movement can be conveyed by drawing into the larger areas using the corner of the pastel as a drawing instrument. This has been done in the figures on the foreshore in the illustration. This is always useful for rejuvenating passages that have, for one reason or another, become lifeless. However, when drawing into these areas you must ensure that there is sufficient tooth still available on the paper, otherwise the pastel will slip and scratch the surface. The real pitfall the novice pastel painter will encounter is aiming for too high a degree of finish. Remember, once the drawing is established, lay in the dark areas, let the paper work in the middle tones and do not over-manipulate the pastel by excessive rubbing, unless it is going to make a contribution to texture.

Finally, pastels can be used on a variety of grounds. Sometimes they are effective on partly-coloured papers when using water-colours or inks. I have recently been using them on a ground coloured with acrylic paint. For this I prefer to use water-colour paper with a not-pressed surface. The advantages of this method are three-fold; the paper can be tinted with blocks of colour sympathetic to the subject; acrylic paint provides a firm feel to the paper without destroying its tooth; finally, because acrylics are polyester resins, the paper is given a thin coat of a polyvinyl-type film which makes the paper waterproof, preventing damp, one of the greatest hazards of pastel painting, from attacking the work from the rear.

The wheelbarrow (Pastel, 22" x 18")

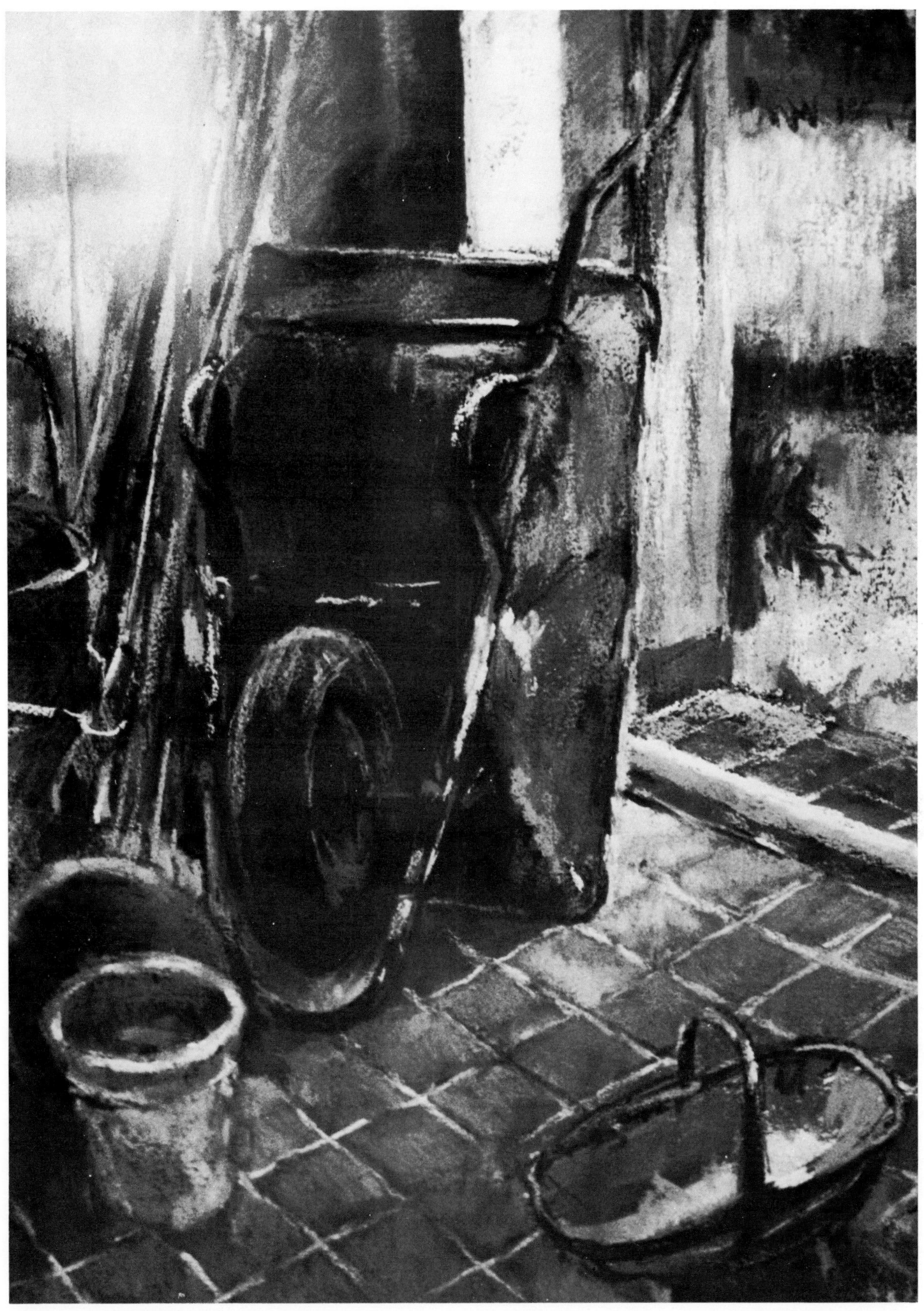

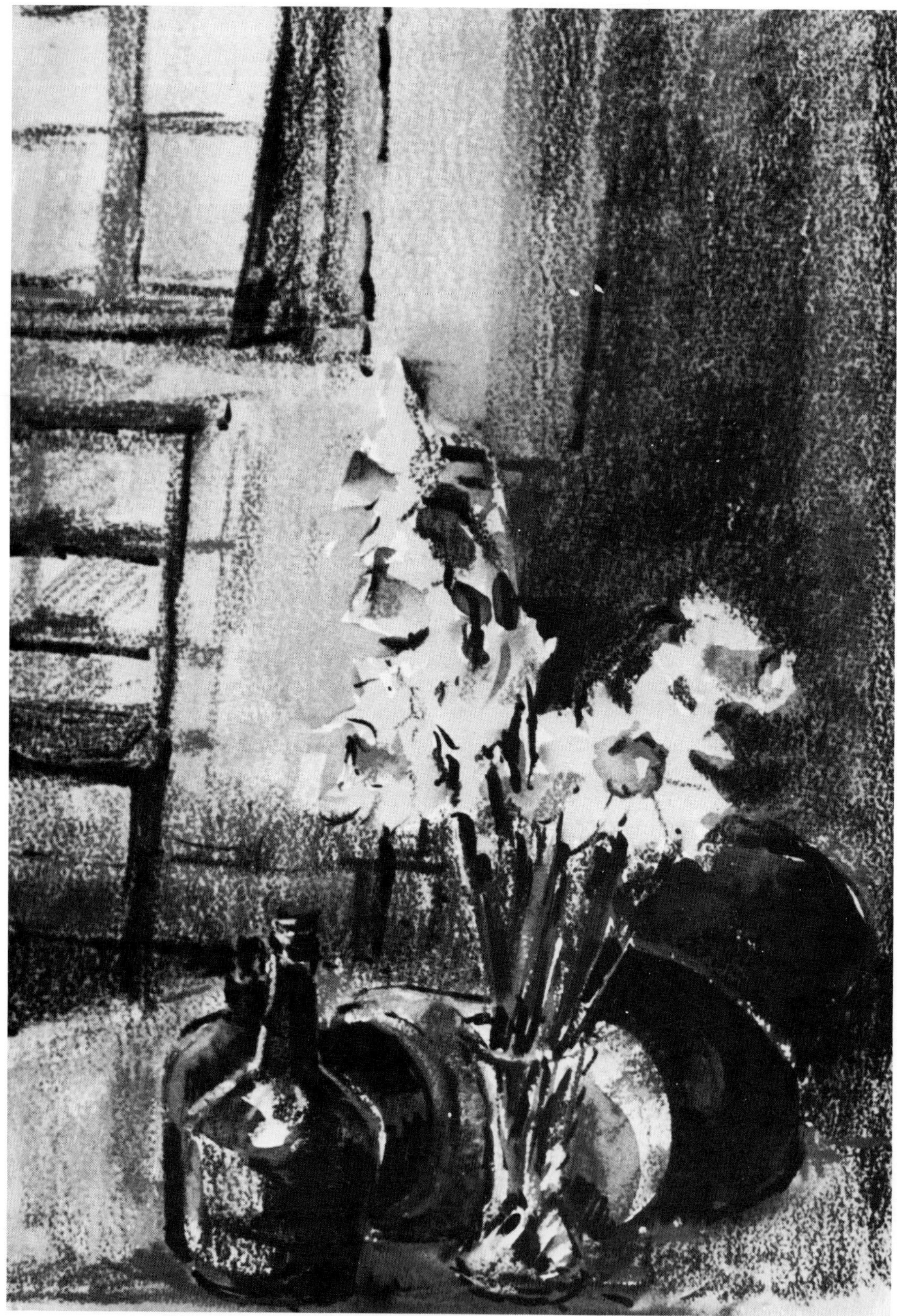

Daffodils and still life (Acrylic and pastel, 15" x 11"). The main shapes were laid in with acrylic paint and pastel applied to give emphasis to form and colour

PART TWO

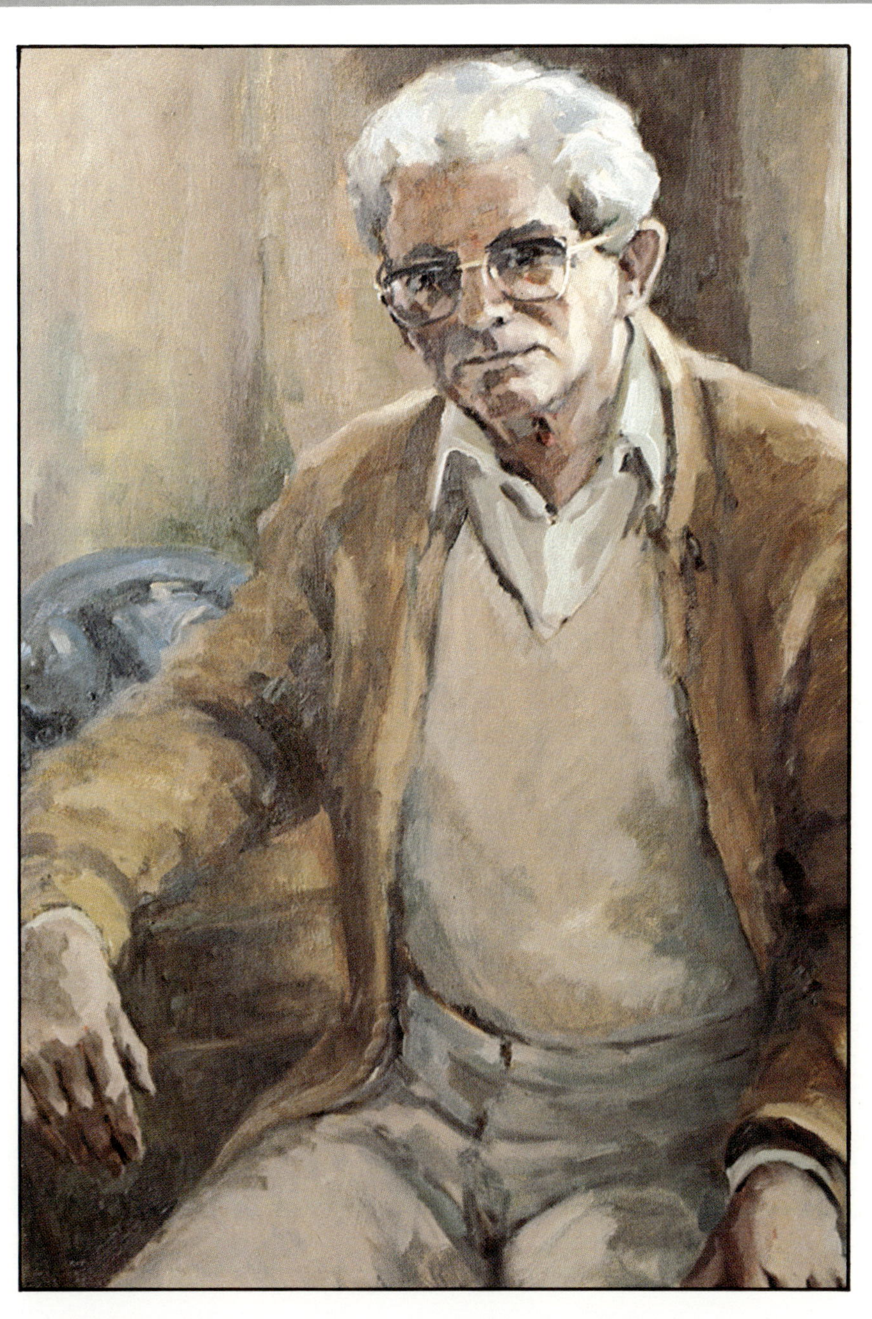

6. THEMES AND SUBJECTS

So far in this book we have dealt separately with drawing and the different drawing media – oil, water-colour, acrylic, gouache and pastel. To continue this separation is not only difficult, but unrealistic. The practice of painting will always require drawing – in fact, the very act of painting is drawing. To define the shape of an area of paint is quite simply drawing with paint. Although there are fundamental differences between the various media, the underlying principles that govern the selection and interpretation of what is seen within shapes and colours remains the same, whatever the medium.

In order to establish this philosophy, the remainder of this book will explore a range of themes and subjects, rather than specific media, so that they seem to be basically the same thing. Inevitably, some problems relevant to each technique will occur, and when this happens they will be isolated and studied in depth.

Still life has always intrigued artists. It is a group of objects arranged on a flat surface, and its content can vary immensely, both in shape and colour. Lighting, colour, variety of objects and position are all within the control of the artist. For your first attempt, select objects for their different shapes, forms and colours. Try setting subjects around a theme – kitchen utensils, the chairside table, garden produce or just some fruit. Explore the different shapes and textures. Fig 101 shows a solitary apple on a plate, painted in water-colour; Fig 102 shows the same subject painted in oil pastel. Note how the medium influences the treatment and reaction to the subject. Approach the subject from two or three different viewpoints and make a sketch from each position, selecting the most satisfying of your sketches for your work. Remember that a good composition does not automatically produce a good work. Finally, make sure that you have a comfortable position to work from. Drawing and painting is a memory exercise, even if the subject is right in front of you. You cannot look at the subject and work simultaneously; it becomes essential to develop a visual memory. Make sure that looking at the subject requires the minimum of physical effort, so that your energy can be expended on the subject.

Now set up a kitchen subject. Bear in mind all that you have learned about visual scanning, negative shapes and the use of shapes around the subject, such as curtains, the back of a chair or a corner of a table. Use these as references to draw outlines of the components accurately.

FIG 101 Still life of single apple on plate (Water-colour, 10" x 8")

FIG 102 Still life of single apple on plate (Oil pastel, 10" x 8")

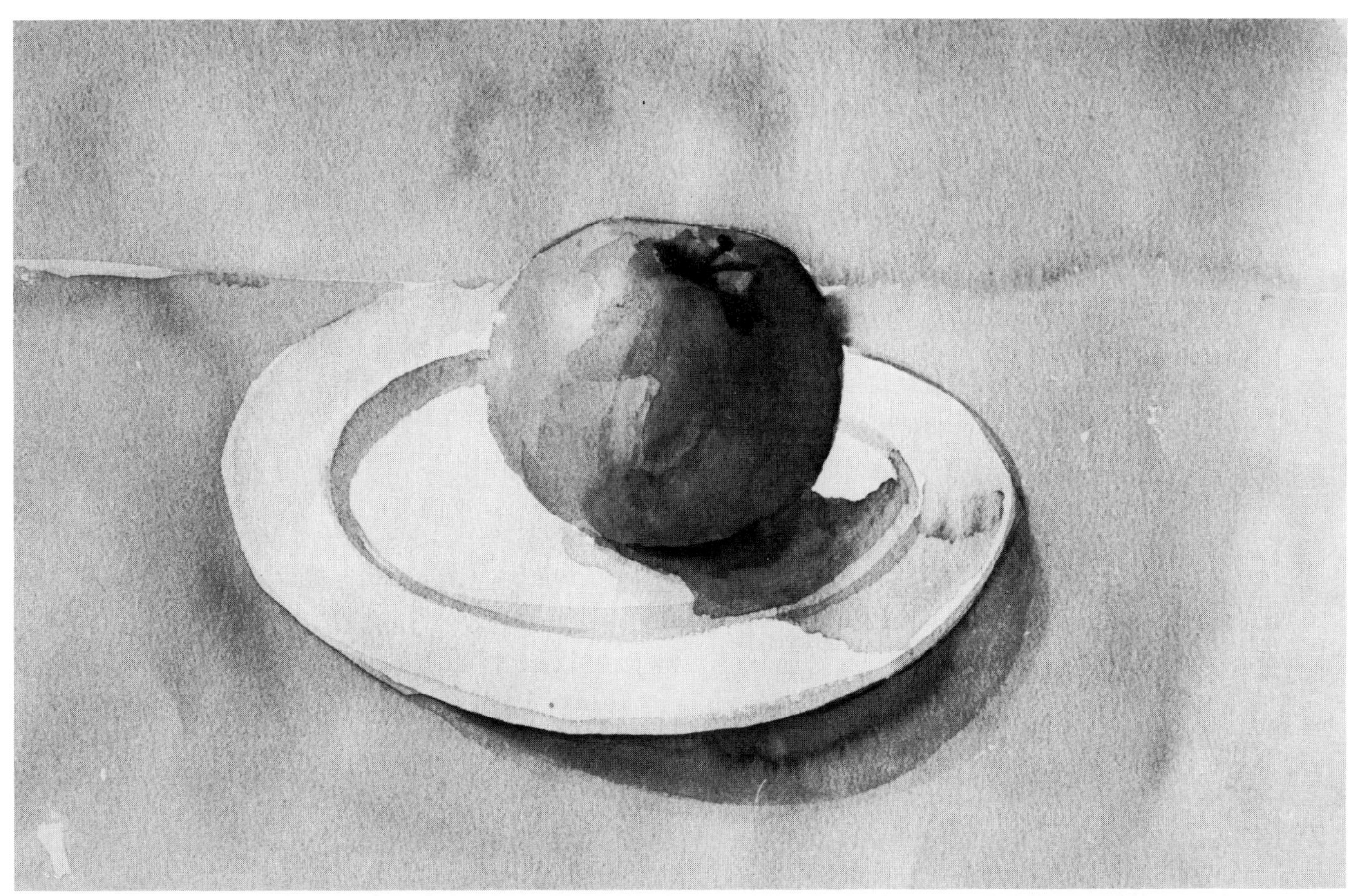

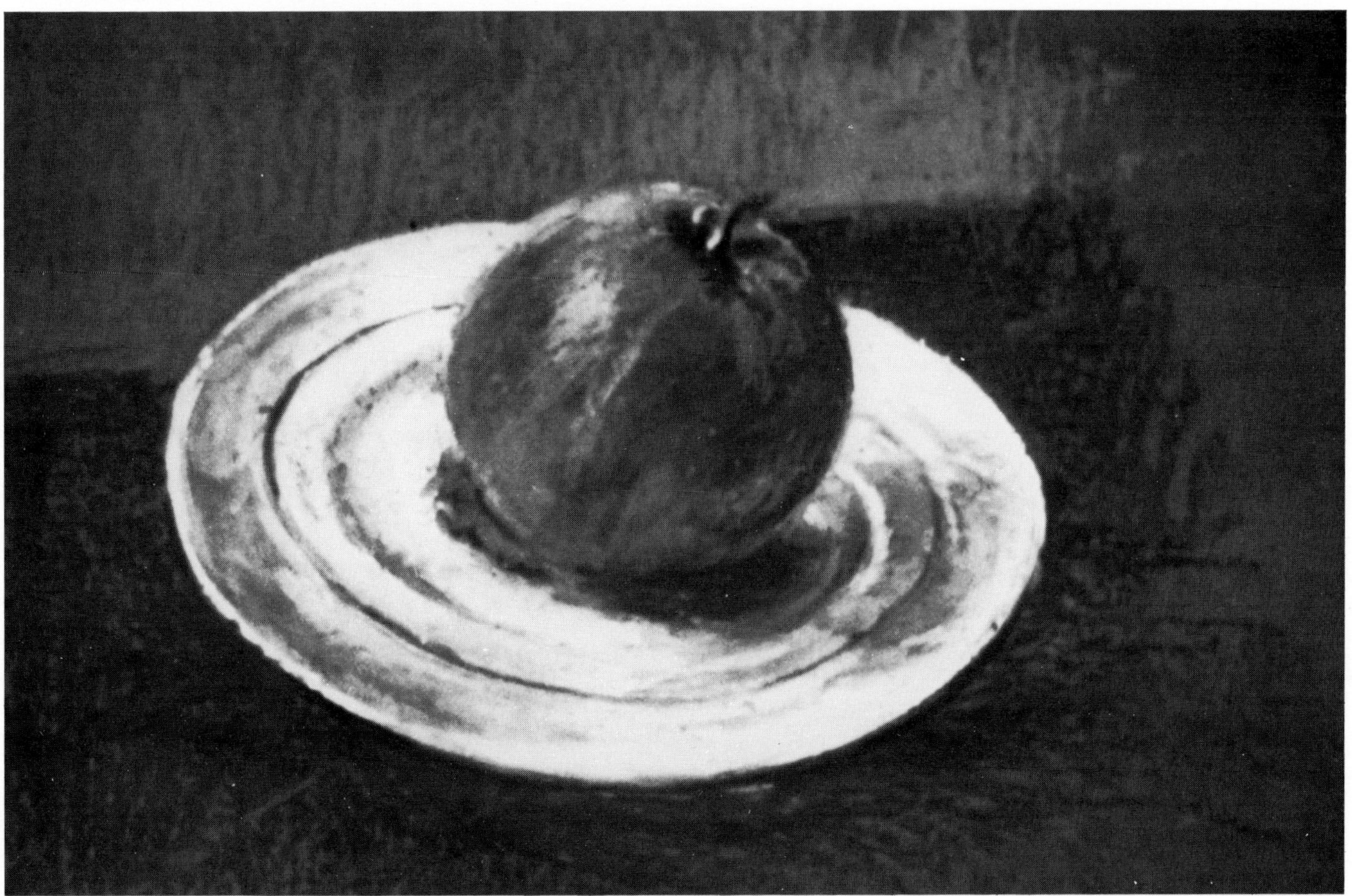

Refer to your earlier geometric studies, as these shapes will inevitably form the underlying structure of the subject matter. It is worth repeating that drawing is not just concerned with copying the light and dark areas; it involves analysing shapes and forms and understanding their solidity by the combination of line and tone.

Start the exercise by establishing the table using a pencil, and then lightly indicate the positions of the objects on the table. Make sure you examine carefully the shapes around and between the objects. This provides a good foundation on which to work. Apply a middle-tone wash to the table top and to the components, looking at the darkest areas first. Examine carefully the areas of light and shade, deepening the darkest tones where necessary. If you feel it helpful, re-emphasise the outlines with a pencil and check the relationship of each object to its surroundings. Finally, check that the spatial content and the tone values work, and that the construction of each part of the work has not got lost during execution. Finally, check that details such as handles actually look as if they fit and belong to the item they are attached to.

Now set up another still life: a green wine bottle, some fruit on a plate and a earthenware mug. Take a sheet of watercolour paper with a wet surface, and paint the silhouette shapes of each of the objects using a diluted wash of each local colour. In this exercise, do not draw on the paper to position the objects: paint them straight in. If you have made one or two preliminary sketches before painting, this should not prove too difficult. With the first washes dry, you may find that very little else needs to be done, except to include some washes to give value to the important colours and tones in the subject.

The shadows can now be analysed, distinguishing between the shadow and the local colour of the object. Check the comparative brightness of one light against the other. Similarly, decide on the darkest and lightest areas of shadow and lay the colours down in their correct tone values. At this stage of water-colour painting, I recommend that you allow each application of paint to dry before adding a further wash. As you become more experienced, you will be able to paint wet into wet with control. Now add the background and finally draw in stronger darks to bring out detail, such as where the fruit meets the plate. For this, you will need to use a smaller brush and be sure to be positive in placing the colour. To apply it in a laboured manner will almost certainly result in the colour underneath being disturbed. Finally, place the finished water-colour on an easel and study it.

Still life can consist of any objects: mechanical devices stretch the artist's capability to observe accurately and develop the ability to produce hard and mechanical drawing, whilst at the same time providing good practice for perspective and basic shapes.

Plants and flowers make fascinating subjects and of course, as with still life, are often part of much different paintings, such as portraits and landscapes. It is important to remember that the natural shapes of plants and flowers can be expressed in several ways, with free linear gestures that give an impression of the shape; as abstract blocks of

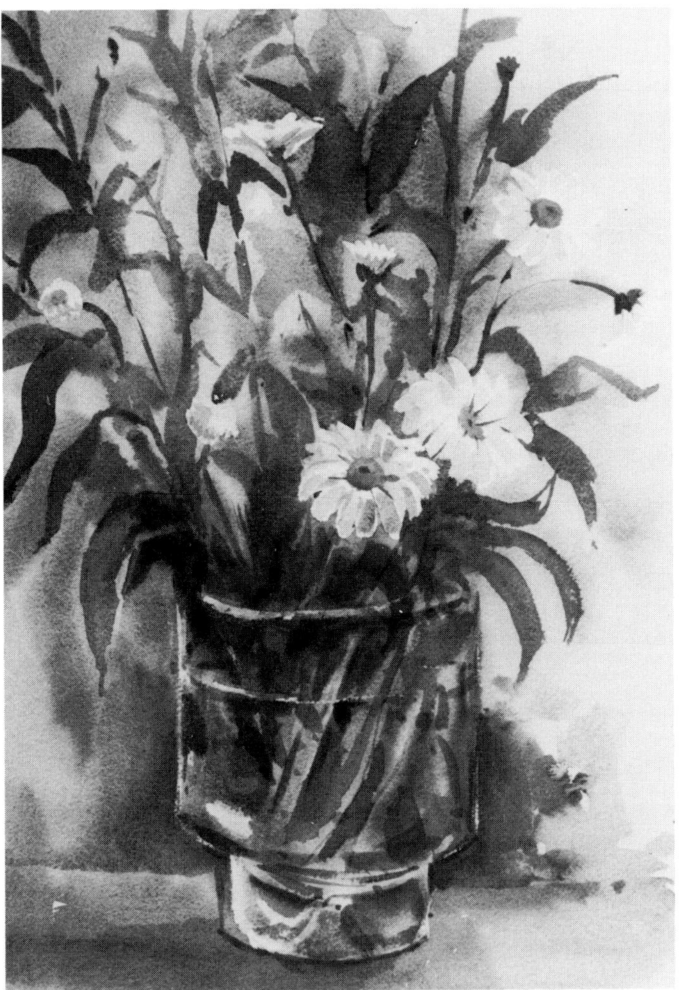

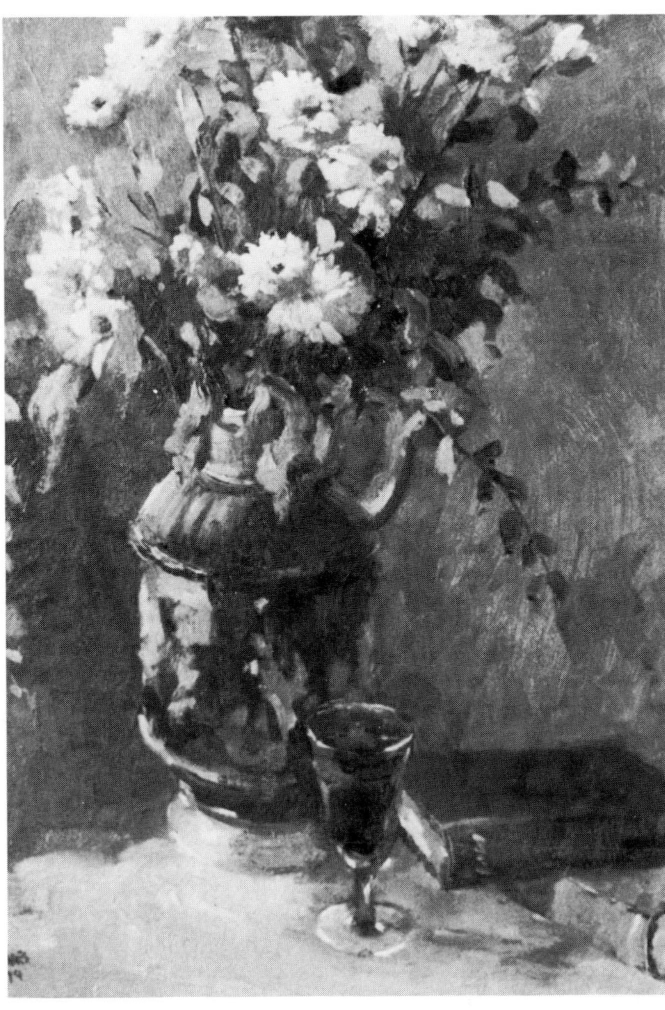

FIG 103 Study of daisies (Water-colours, 16" x 12")

FIG 104 Still life with flowers (Oil, 22" x 18")

colour suggestive of tone and hue; or as a detailed statement showing the exact construction of each part of the plant.

Fig 103 shows a study of *Daisies in a glass vase*, painted in water-colour. This study was painted rapidly. The petals of the blooms were masked with latex masking fluid to enable the background, stems and leaves to be painted freely. Latex masking fluid was also used to reserve the highlights on the glass. When the bulk of the painting was complete, the masking fluid was removed by gentle application of a putty rubber, exposing the white flower-heads. All that then remained was to indicate the modelling of the petals by painting the light and shade. When the painting was complete, I soaked it for two or three minutes in clean water to remove any hardness of edges that had crept in.

My painting *Still life with flowers* (Fig 104) is painted in oils and for this work I used a coloured ground, pre-staining the canvas with a coloured grey made using French ultramarine and burnt sienna. It was applied with turpentine and allowed to dry. The yellow blooms of the chrysanthemums were established immediately, and the rest of the painting developed around them, once again very freely. The tone of the Chinese vase was considered carefully, as I did not wish it to detract from the visual importance of the flowers; rather to complement them.

The ability to paint plant life will prove a boon when approaching landscape. Foregrounds are always a problem for artists, but become less of a headache if you have an understanding of plant growth. Indeed, many fine paintings, in all media, have been made using the foreground as the main subject. Setting up flower and plant subjects in the studio will provide you with an opportunity to study their movement, shapes, construction and the way the light plays on leaves changing their colour and tone under controlled circumstances. All of these will be helpful in the painting of landscape.

Landscape painting

Without doubt the most enjoyable form of landscape painting is painting out of doors. Making sketches and taking notes is the foundation of the landscape painter's work. All the media can be used in the making of sketches, and to solve the many problems encountered by the artist. Constant observation and making notes of the ever-changing scene will mean that you have to study skies, water, trees, light and movement.

Water-colour, because of its rapidity of handling, its freshness, and it ability to capture fleeting moments such as cloud movement, windblown trees and reflections in moving water, is a convenient medium to use for this subject. You will almost certainly exaggerate those moods of the subject which you find interesting – in fact, you will find it impossible to paint without this personal evaluation. It will result in minimising or totally ignoring some other aspects of the same subject. The final choice will depend on what you see and how you see it. You will of course be influenced by other artists' work.

You must decide on your reason for doing the piece of work. All forms of picture-making are valid, and with experience you will be able to let the subject decide which form the work should take. Always keep your preliminary sketches and studies, even when the painting is finished, as they are always interesting and form part of a library of information.

Landscape painting lends itself to such a variety of methods that it is important not to become too settled into one form or style of painting. I have found that the adaptability of landscape makes it most suitable for mixed media. Fig 105 is a mixed media study of a Dorset landscape. The foreground was of great interest to me and required special treatment. The drawing was made in a mixture of ink and pencil. When this was complete, I applied a light dressing of candle grease to the foreground area in order to provide a degree of resistance to the light colour wash I applied next. Whilst this was wet, I dropped a little salt into the wash. As the wash dried, the salt dissolved, so that the colour became mottled. This, coupled with the resist given by the candle grease, made a broken, irregular texture in the paint, making it most suitable for the foreground. The rest of the painting was established in water-colour and strengthened with gouache and ink where necessary. I then returned to the foreground where, with a brush, I indicated a little of the plant life and finally gave emphasis to some of the drawing

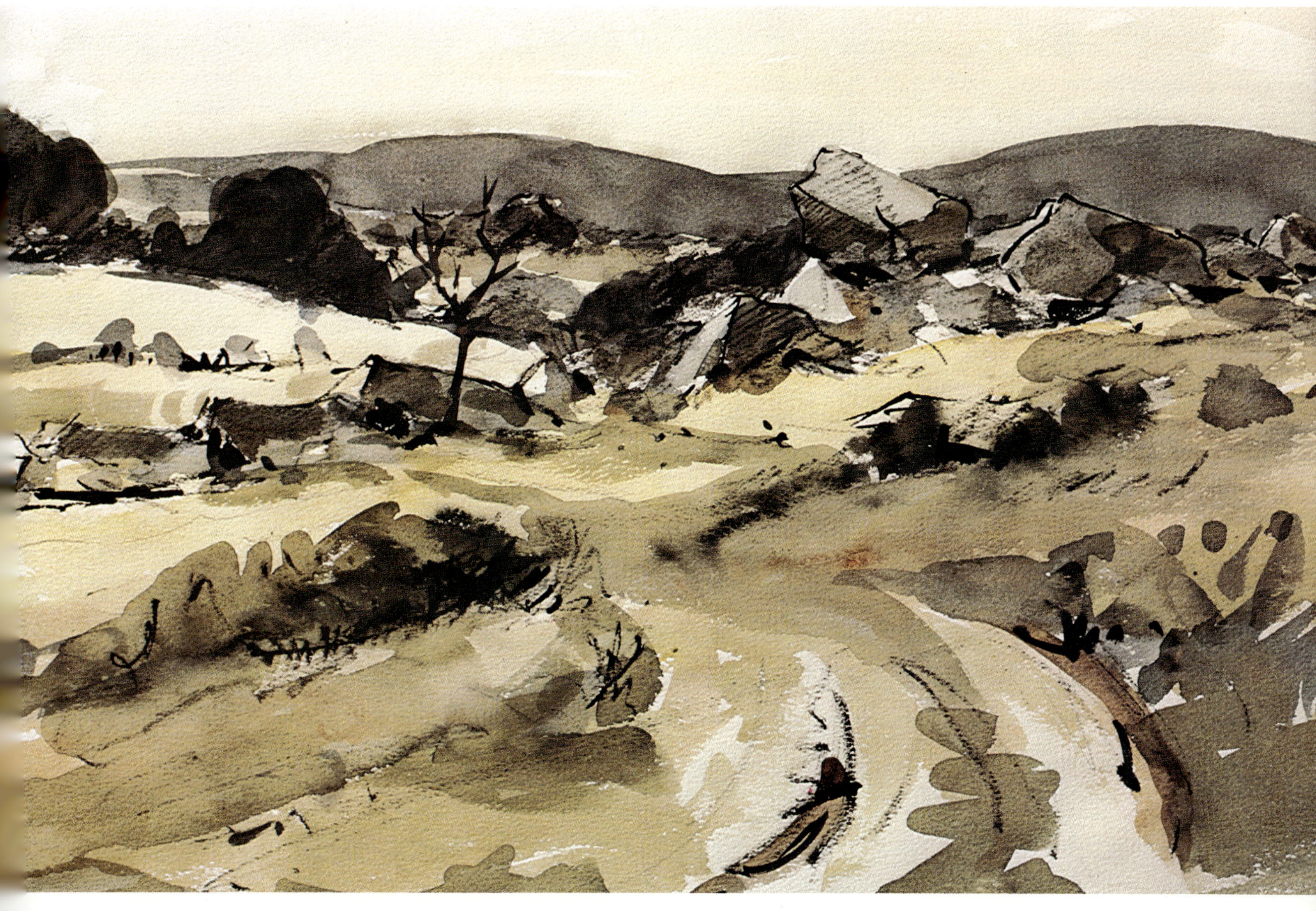

with a little oil pastel. Making this study gave me the opportunity to innovate with the various media, in what I considered the best interests of my interpretation of the subject.

For water-colour studies of the various aspects of landscape painting I recommend that you practise quick five-minute studies, aiming to capture the transitory effects, rather than the more detailed areas, of nature. Try capturing the effects of early morning mist with its ethereal light, or an approaching storm with the rolling storm clouds. Practise this technique indoors before attempting to apply it on site. Fig 106 shows a number of wet into wet five-minute water-colour studies of landscapes under different conditions.

FIG 105 Dorset landscapes (Mixed media, 15" x 11")

FIG 106 (overleaf) Series of wet into wet water-colour studies

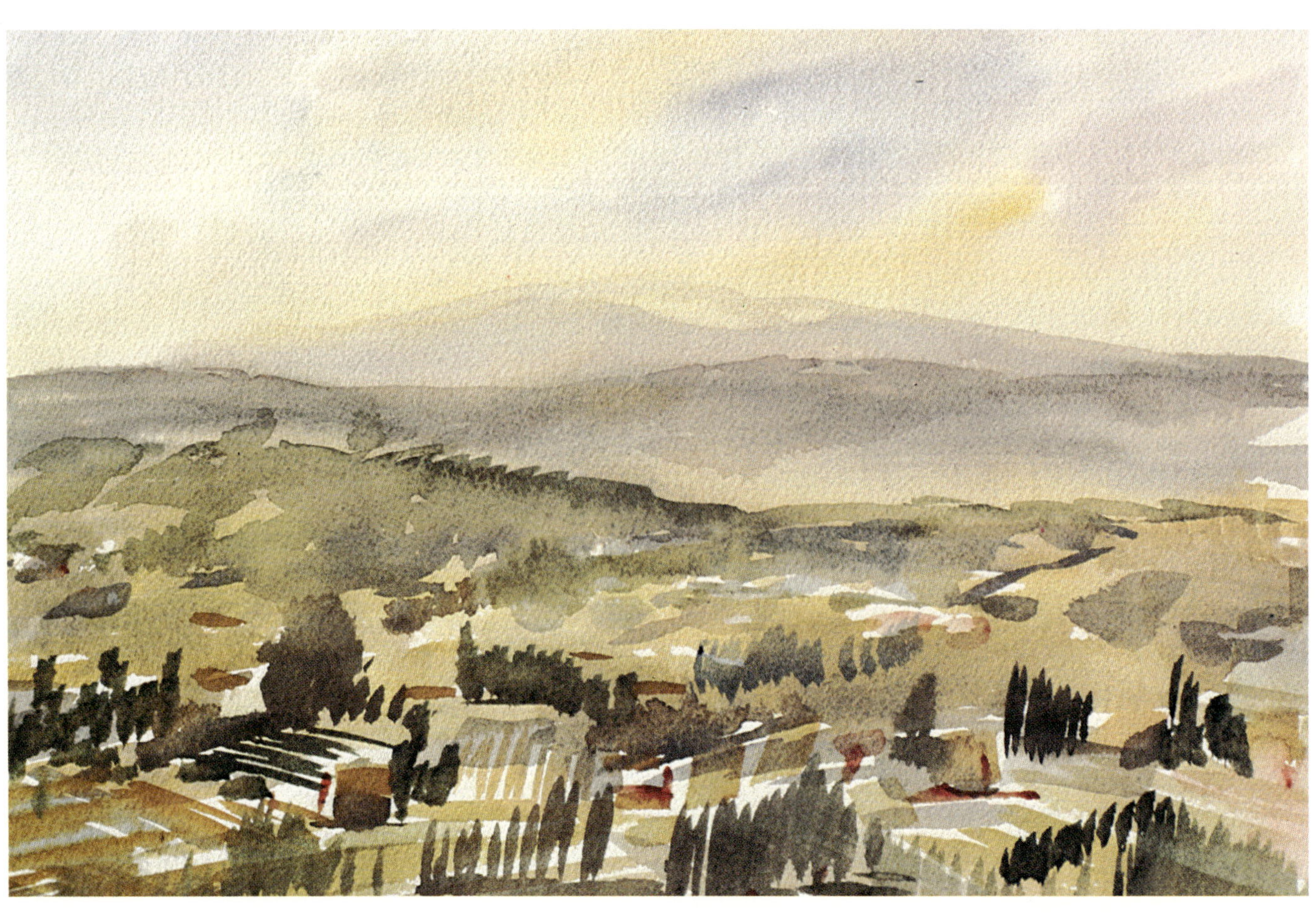

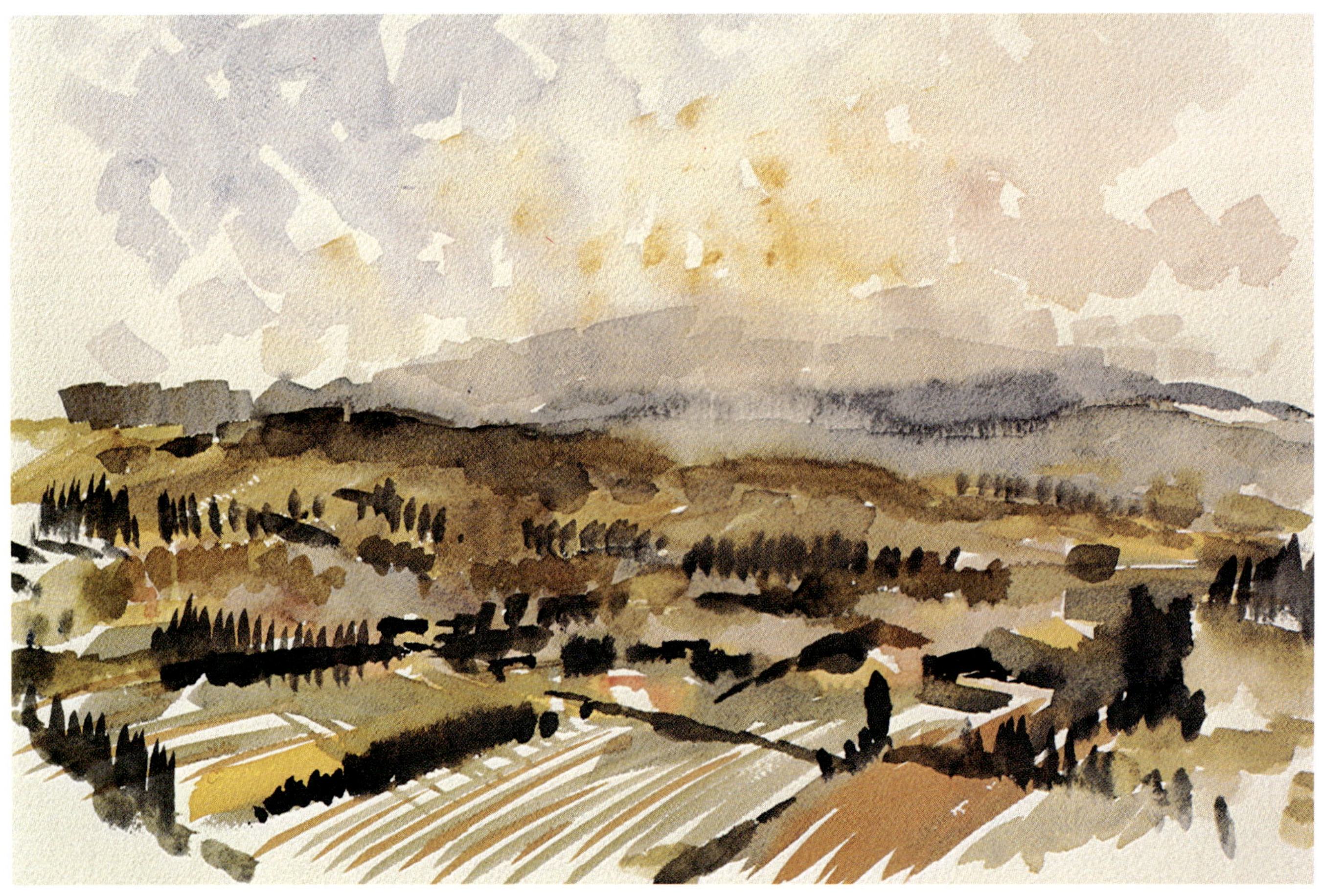

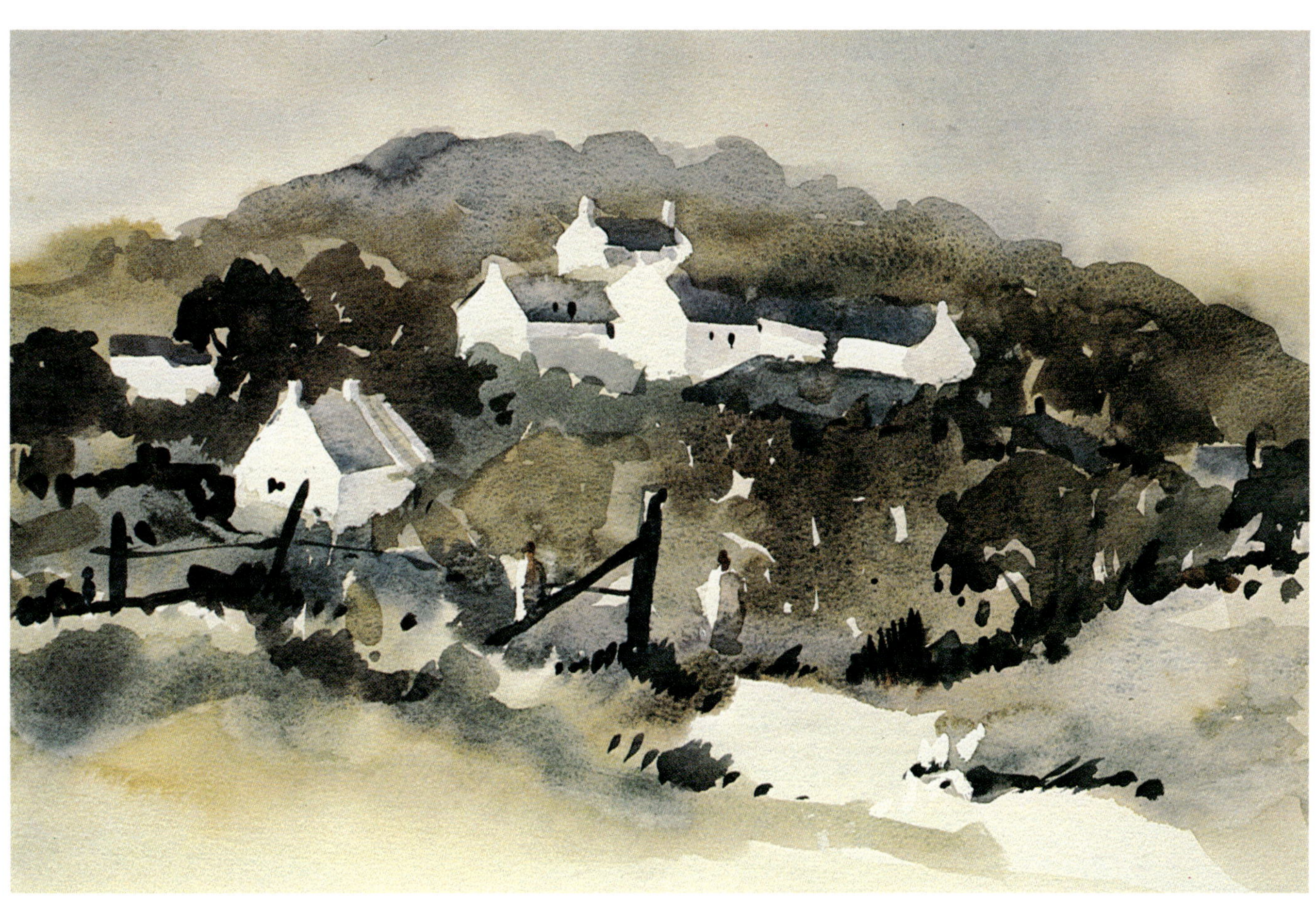

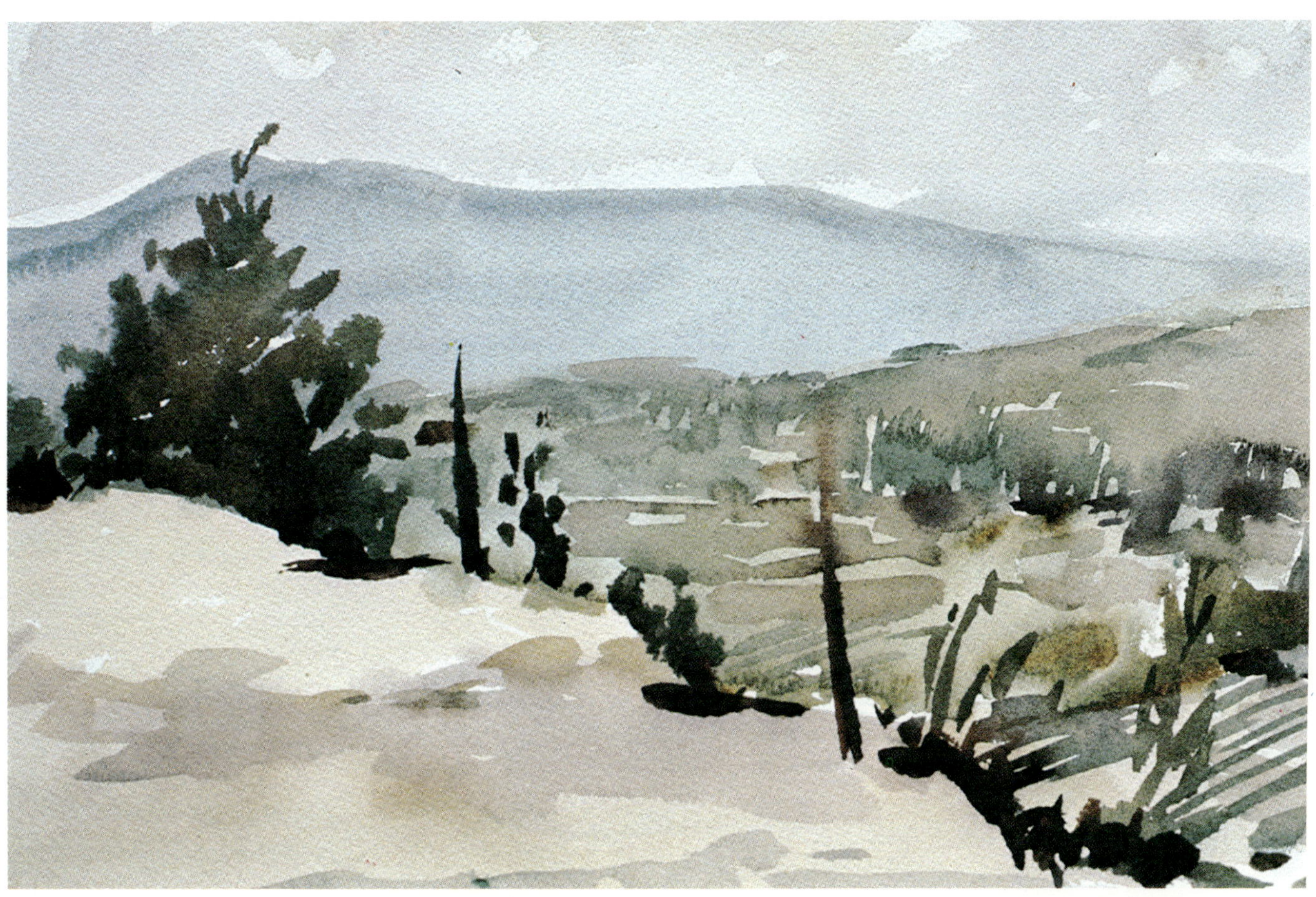

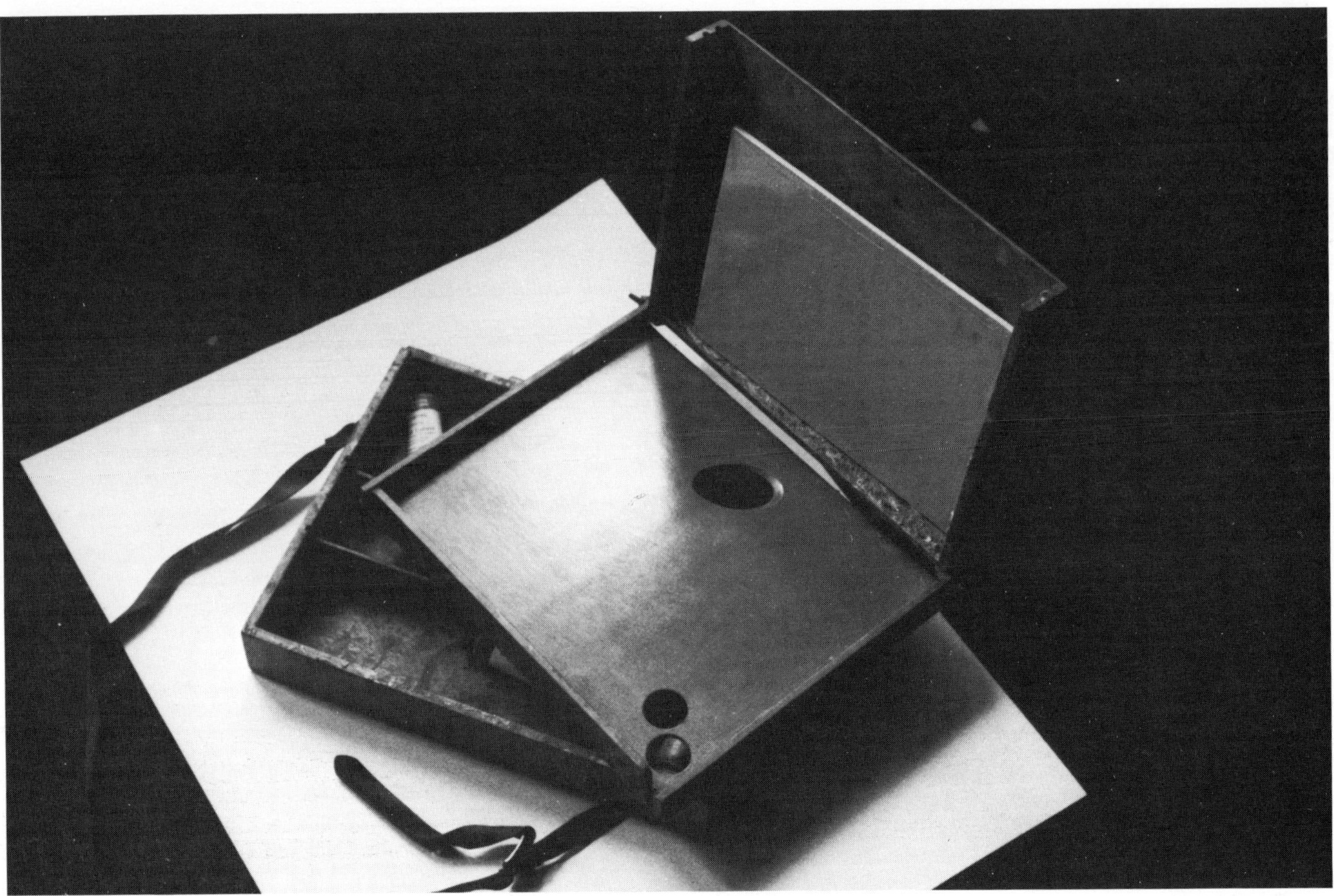

FIG 107 Pochade box

Oil-paint, acrylic colour and pastels are all suitable media for working out of doors, although I tend to restrict the size of the work, particularly in oils. Many of my oil sketches are executed using a pochade box (Fig 107). This is small and light and allows me to make small oil and acrylic sketches up to 12 inches x 10 inches in size. From small studies made on the spot using various media, larger works can be produced in the studio under controlled conditions. Fig 108, *Acton Quarry, Dorset*, is an example of such a work. The original sketches were made in oil-paint at the quarry and the large finished work, which measures 48 inches x 30 inches, is done in acrylic paint. Among the many advantages of working in the studio is that there are fewer things to divert attention from the original reason for making the sketch. The light is constant, the weather does not change and, of course, there will be no interruptions from interested spectators. It also provides an opportunity to re-evaluate the information in the sketch and adjust your thinking accordingly.

The same approach was used for the oil-painting *Across the gardens* (Fig 110). This was done in the studio from a water-colour sketch made on site (Fig 109). Many fine landscapes can, of course, be made direct from the subject, and certainly the visual experience of working direct encourages spontaneity and freshness. I do feel, however, that if sufficient time is taken in making decisions and those decisions are painted quickly, there will be little or no loss of sparkle or freshness in the studio work.

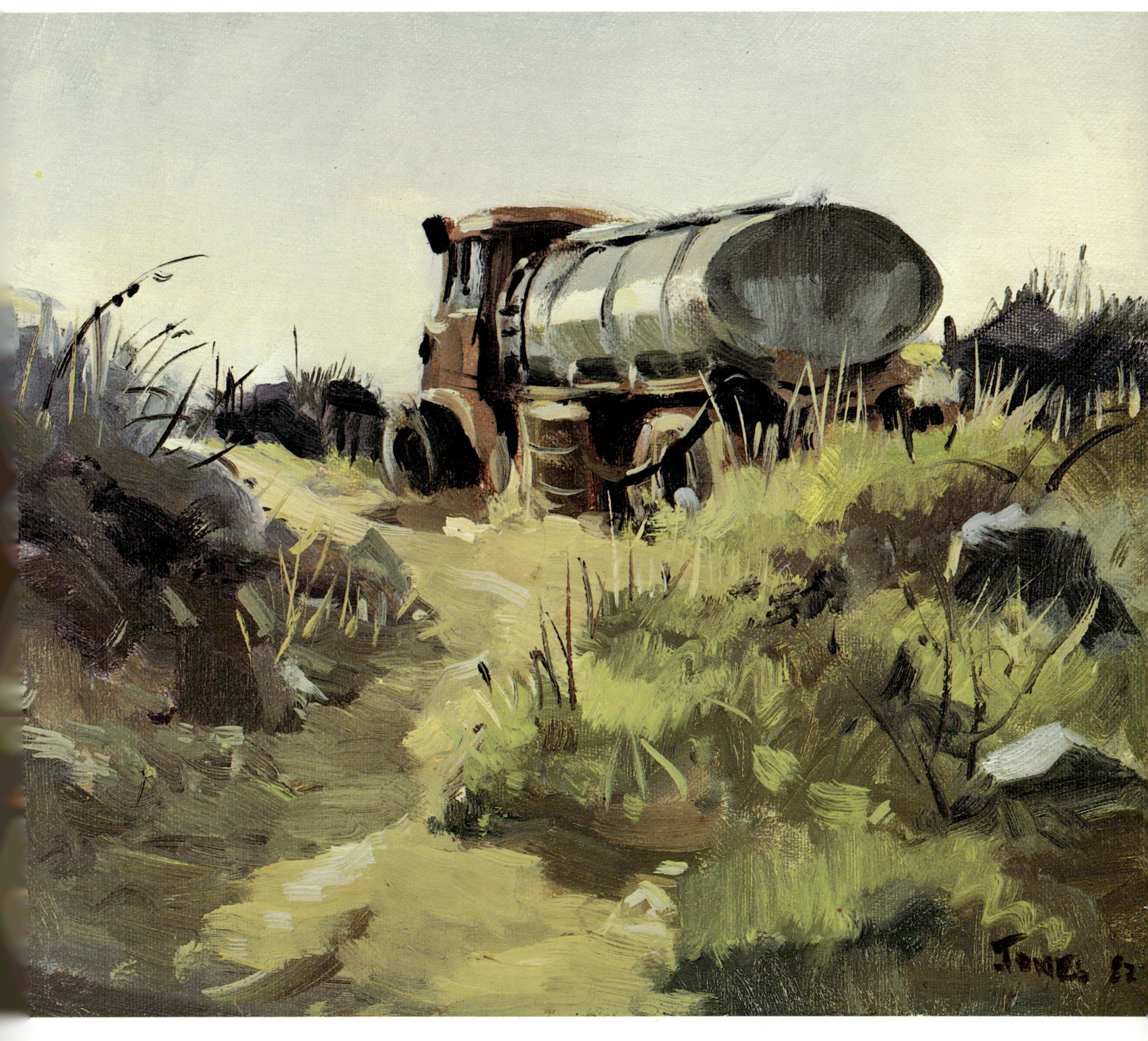

FIG 108 *Acton Quarry, Dorset* (Oil, 12" x 10")

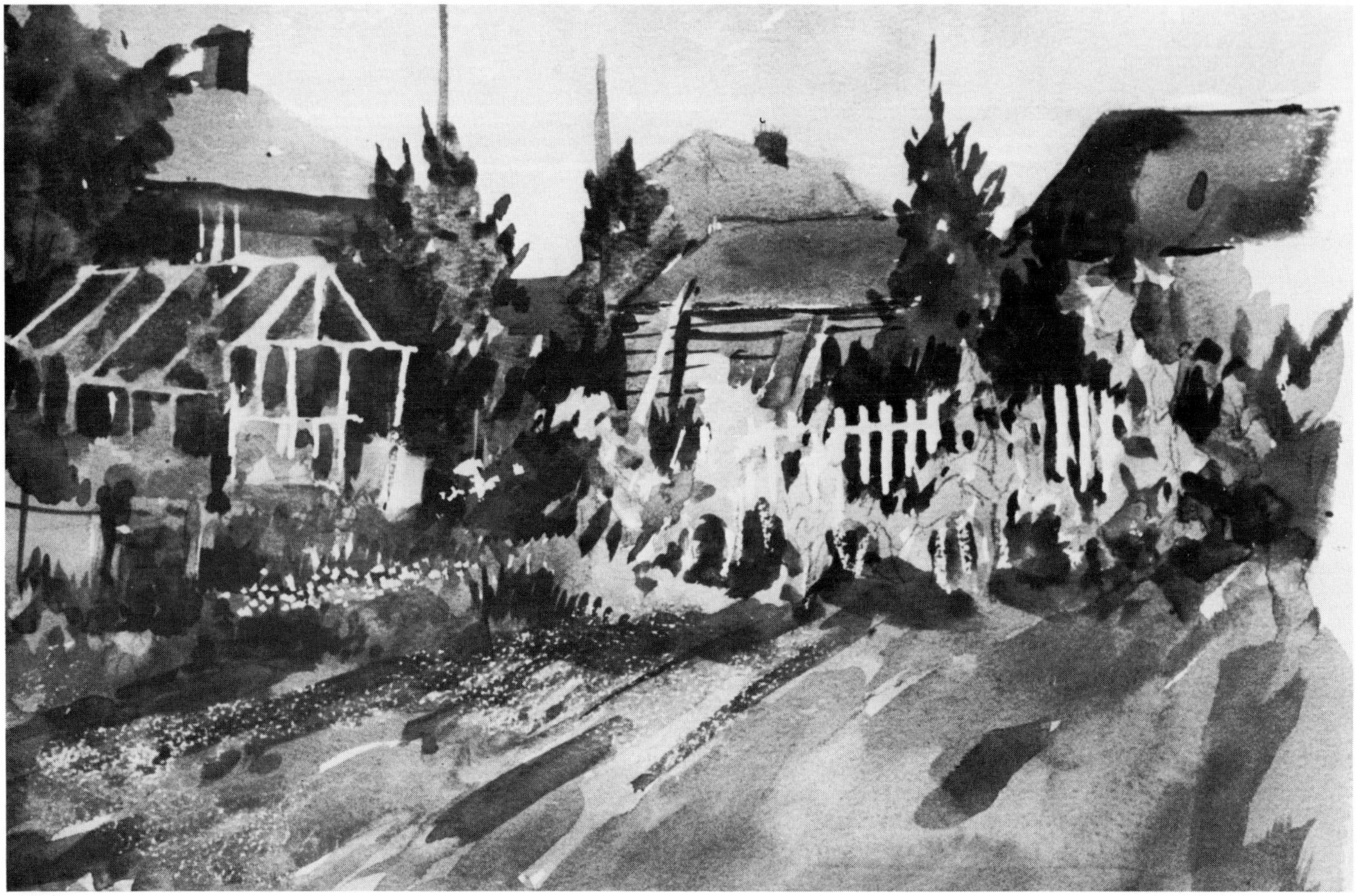

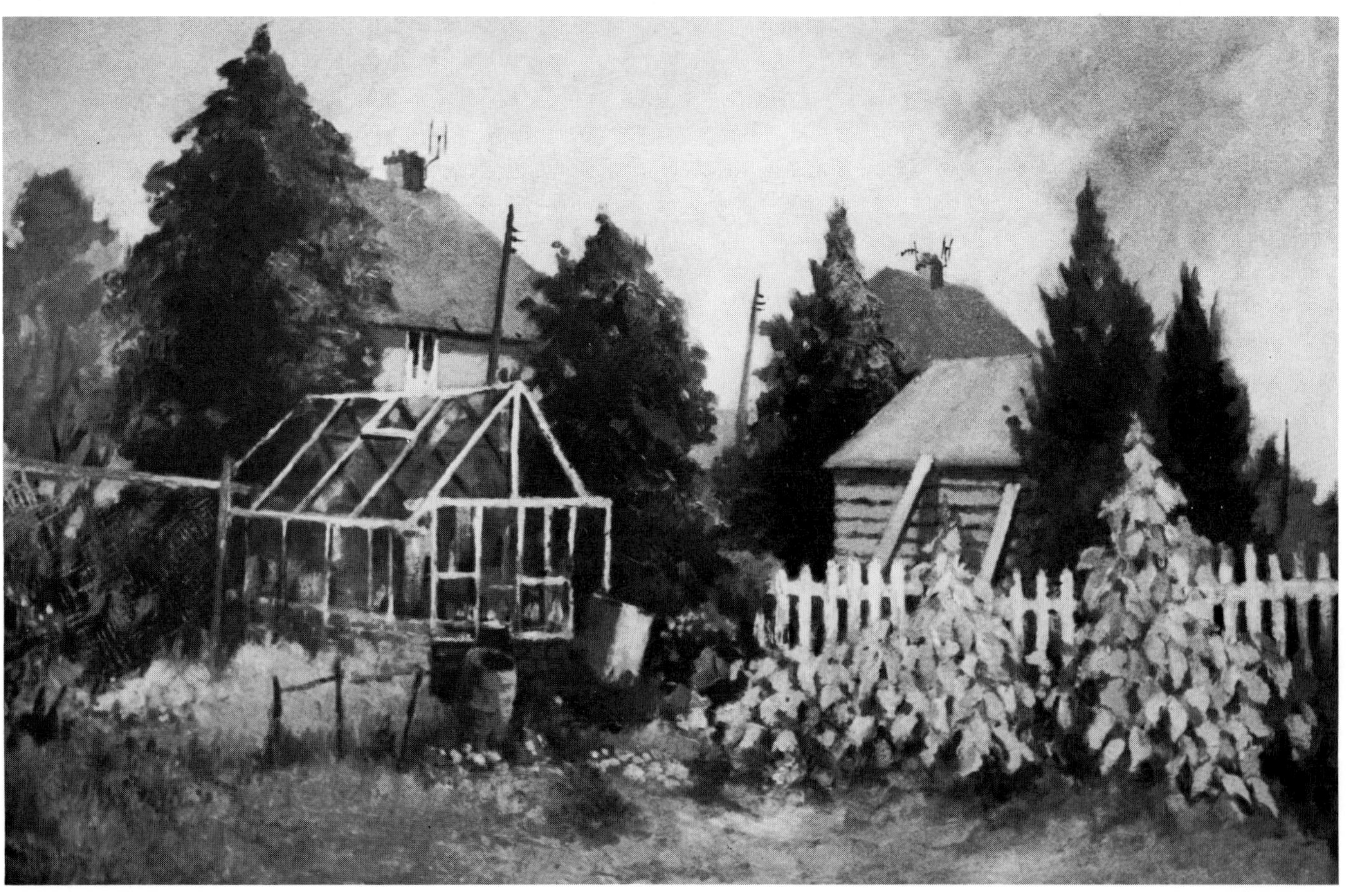

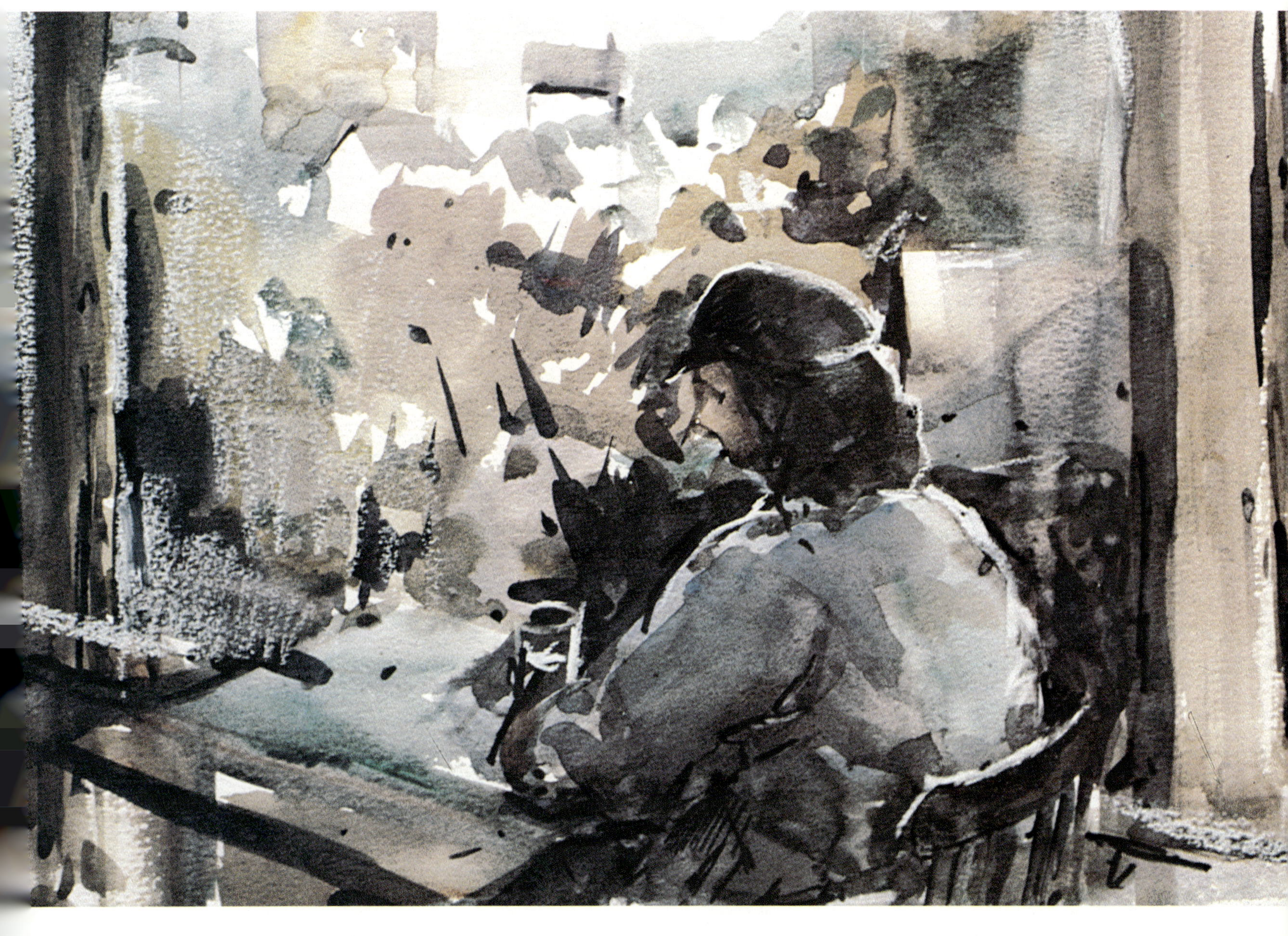

FIG 109 *Across the gardens* (Water-colour
sketch, 15" x 11")

FIG 110 *Across the gardens* (Oil, 36" x 25")

FIG 111 *The Breton café* (Water-colour, 16"
x 12")
This study was made in a Breton café
using water-colour, gouache, and litho
crayon. It was painted directly without
any pre-studies as time was of the essence,
because the girl could leave any time. I
was particularly interested in the feeling
of space and loneliness that the subject
suggested to me and I concentrated on
making as much of this as time permitted.
The initial painting was lightly carried
out in water-colour, and developed more
fully with gouache. The final accents
such as the light around the head were
put in with lithographic crayon.

Landscape can often be viewed through a window, and many fine paintings can be made from the inside looking out, once again allowing the work to be made from the subject, but under fairly controlled conditions. Very often the window frame or perhaps a plant on the window sill can be used to give a feeling of space and depth to such a picture. In my mixed media study of the *Breton café* (Fig 111) I have used a solitary figure for just this reason.

Landscape is not confined to the large panoramic scene. At the other end of the scale a small rockfall, such as *Landslide in the Luberon* (Fig 112) can make a most interesting subject with all the subtle nuances of shape, colour and tone. This was done in water-colour in the traditional manner.

Under the general heading of landscape it is important to subdivide landscape painting into townscape and marinescapes.

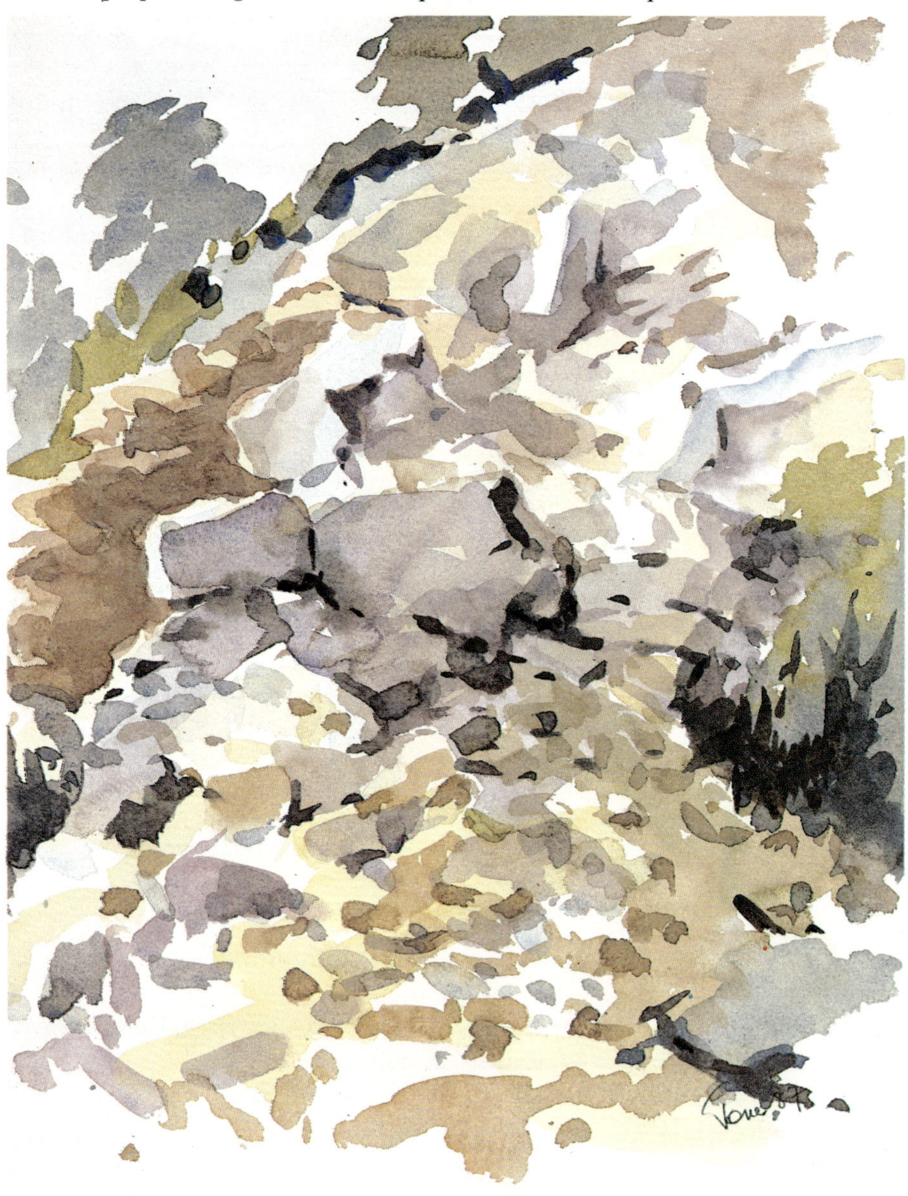

FIG 112 *Landslide in the Luberon*
(Water-colour, 16" x 12")

Townscapes

Artists have always been pre-occupied with portraying their surroundings, and cities and towns have been drawn and painted, often in great detail, since medieval times. These works give us an insight into the early life of European city dwellers. This desire to record towns and cities has continued, and today artists are just as concerned to express their reaction to their environment as they were in the past. They still find their own cities inspiring subjects, although they are probably concerned les with portraying them graphically, and more with capturing their atmosphere and emotional impact.

Cities have, of course, attracted painters for centuries, usually because of their architectural beauty which, when coupled with the light, can be instrumental in inspiring artists (such as Claude Monet's many pictures of Rouen cathedral). Industrial landscape can also provide the artist with a wealth of subject matter. The urban environment offers the widest range of subject matter, from objects within the landscape to the most involved panoramic views. Additionally, you may often select your viewpoint, working in one instance from ground level, or in the next from a high viewpoint, such as a multi-story car park.

As buildings are, by their very nature, geometric in shape and form, a great deal of understanding is necessary to make them appear convincing. It will be useful here to refer back to the section on basic drawing. Buildings give the opportunity to study shapes and surfaces, providing material to compose geometric shapes and patterns, and for interpreting the changes of tone and colour, often very subtle in their appearance. This array of visual stimulation opens the door to many different approaches in handling and interpretation.

Technological features, such as chimneys and gasometers, also provide the artist with a wealth of interesting shapes. Modern building constructions, with scaffolding and iron girders, make stark patterns against the the skyline. Television aerials, telegraph poles and wires all help to divide and contribute towards making linear patterns against buildings and roofs. Old buildings contrasted against new modern architecture also make for a response from the artist, asdo condemned or derelict buildings. Advertising hordings bearing remnants of torn and dilapidated posters can often be a feature of a cityscape.

Make many sketches and colour notes of your excursions into the city, building up a reference library of information. Treat your drawings and colour notes as an enquiry into the subject and use them as the basis for work to be completed in the studio. Paint the city on both fine and wet days: the reflections of colour and tone on a wet road can be the reason for the work, whilst the patterns of cast shadows made by the buildings could offer the inspiration for an abstract painting.

Perspective is important. Establish your eye-level at the outset of the drawing: without this being registered at the beginning of the sketch it may mean that it is valueless when you come to start your studio work. Most cityscapes will, because of the space required to paint on site, be painted in the studio. You will see how much easier sketching on site

FIG 113 *Avignon* (Coloured pencils, 10" x 8")

FIG 114 *St Saturnin D'Apt, Provence* (Water-colour, 16" x 12")

FIG 115 *The builders' yard* (Water-colour, 16" x 12")

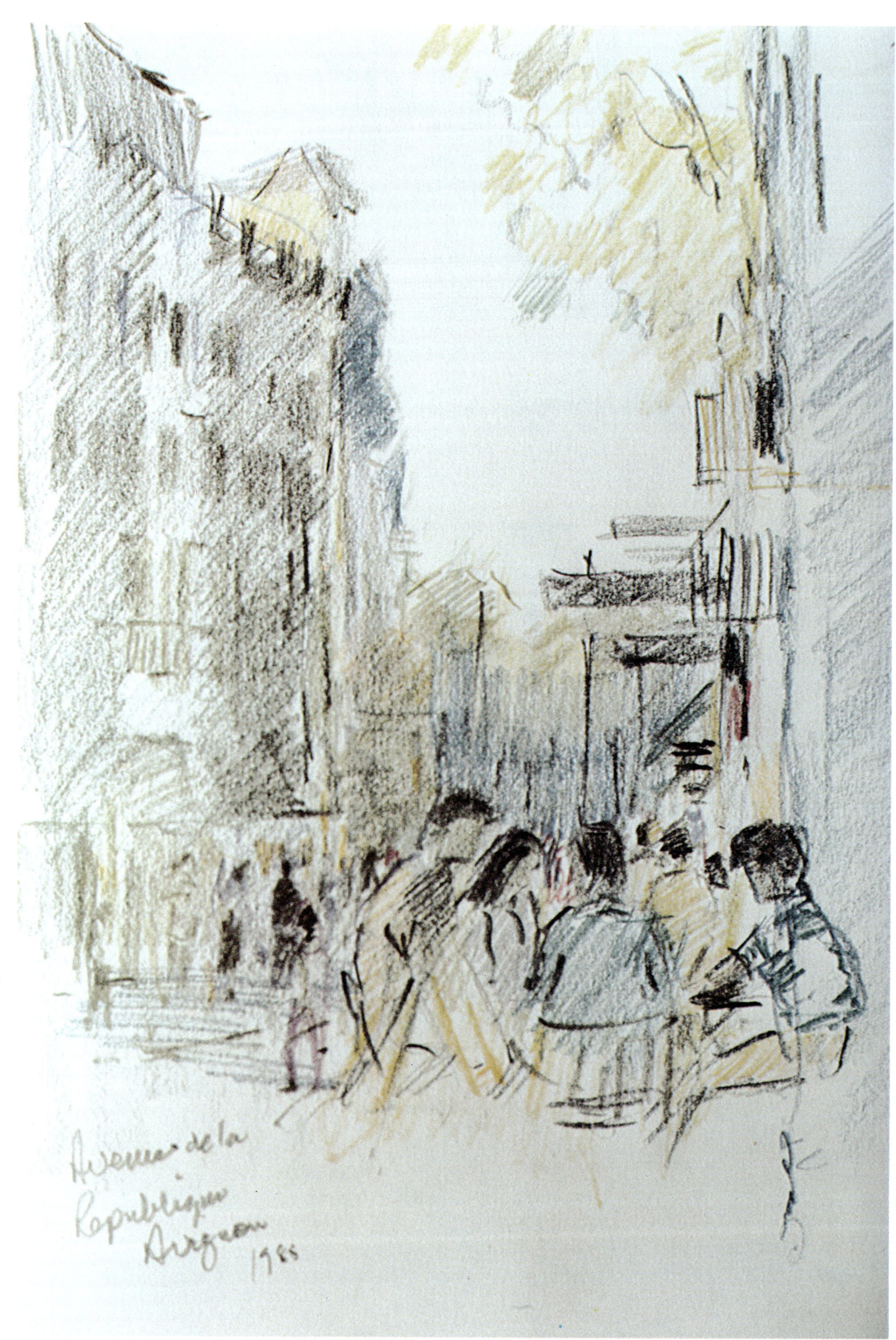

Avenue de la
Republique
Avignon
1988

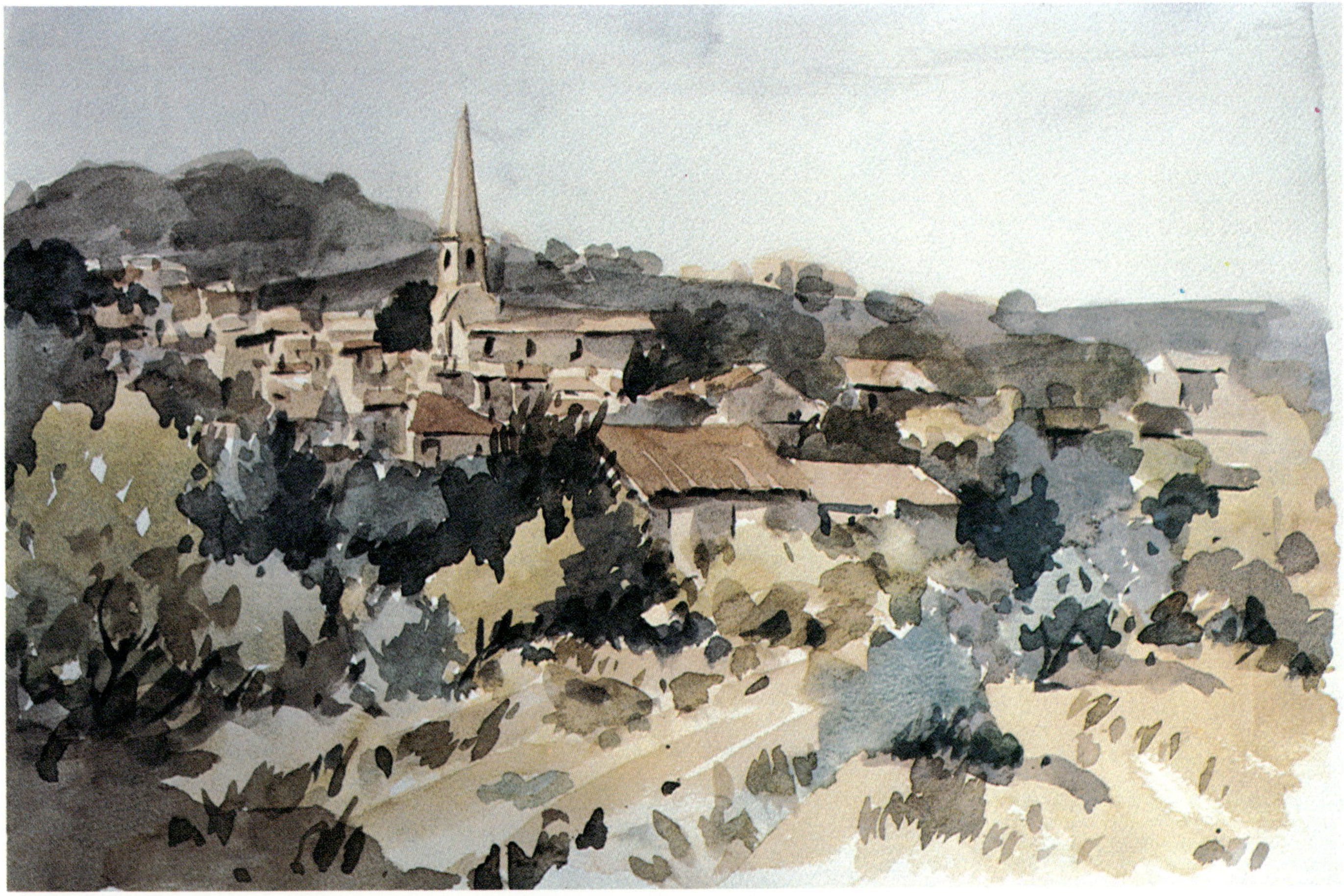

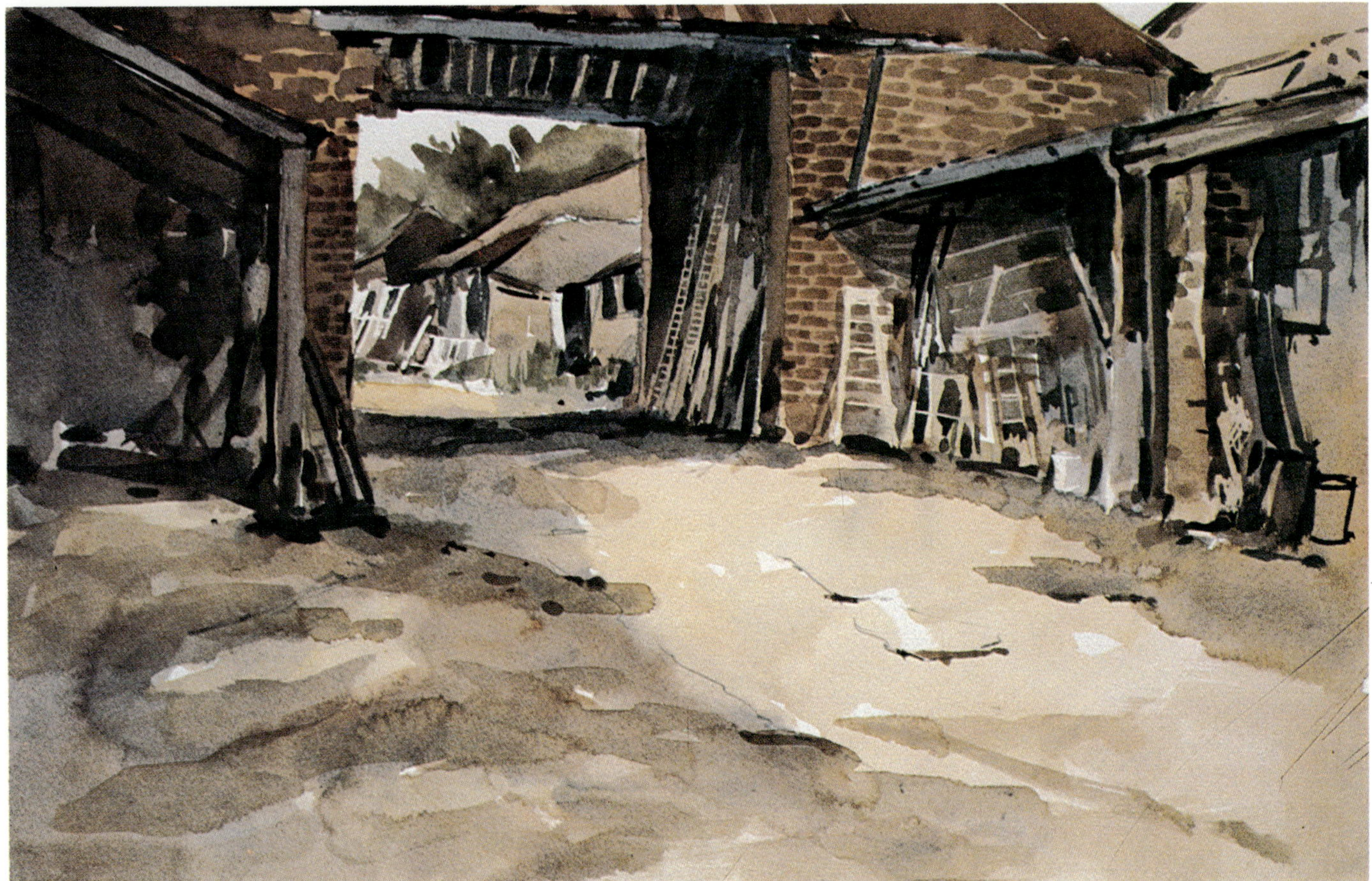

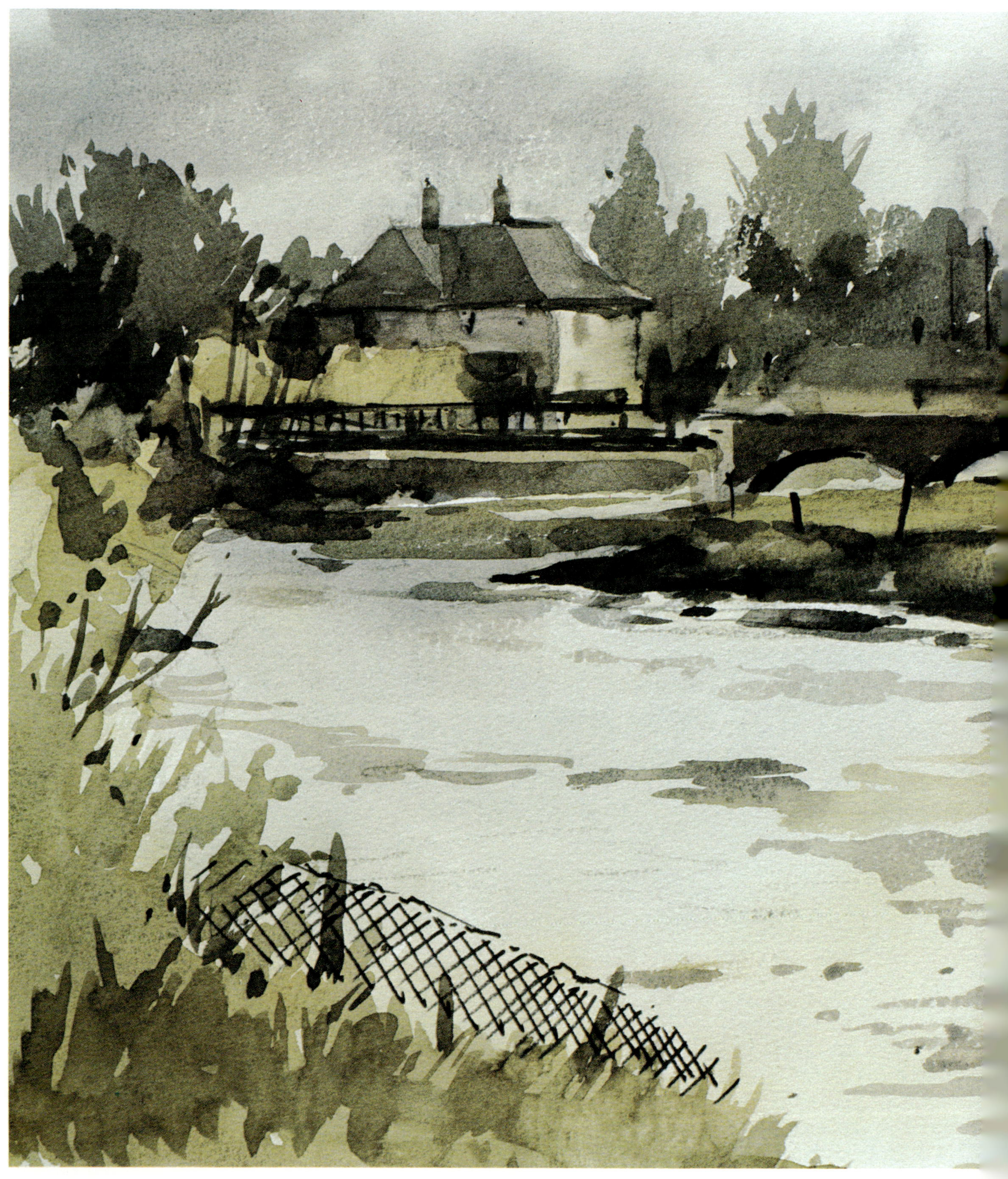

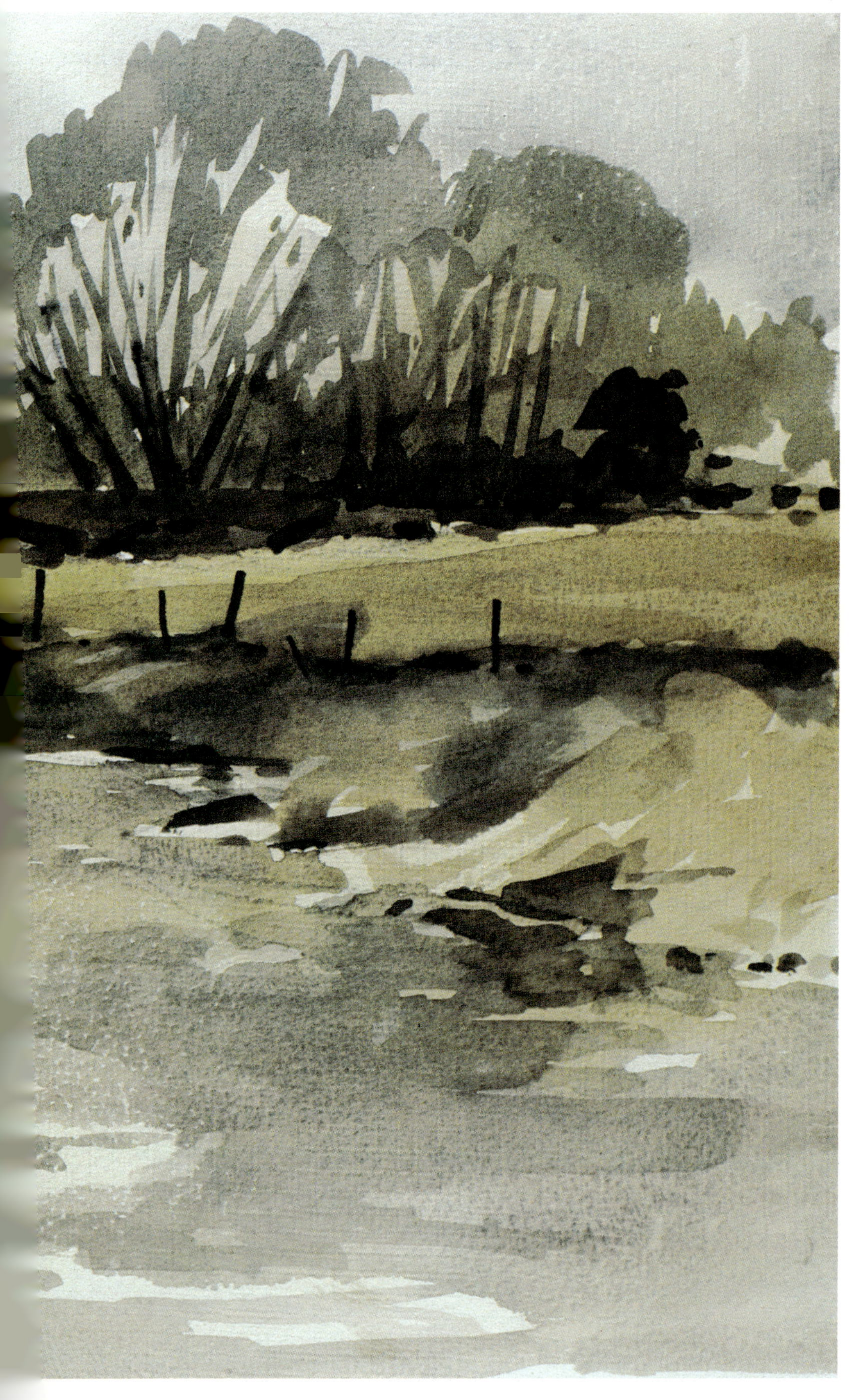

FIG 116 *The Dorset Stour* (Water-colour,
15" x 12")

becomes if you keep your equipment to a minimum: a small haversack with pencils, charcoal, sketching fountain pen and a small water-colour box – or, alternatively, a box of water-colour pencils and a small bottle of water and a No. 6 brush – plus a stiff-backed pad measuring 16 inches x 12 inches – will be all that you need to make colour sketches and notes.

Fig 113 is a typical example of a townscape sketch of Avignon, measuring 10 inches x 8 inches. It was drawn on the spot using a 2B graphite stick and water-colour pencils, and I aimed to capture the busy atmosphere. It was from a series of sketches such as this that the large (40 inches x 28 inches) acrylic painting of the Adelphi, London, was painted. This was worked on the smooth side of a hardboard panel which had been primed with acrylic primer. The acrylic primer was stained with a grey made from viridian and burnt sienna; the drawing was established in paint and the painting developed initially by establishing the large shapes of the buildings.

Fig 114 is a water-colour study of a French hillside town, St Saturnin D'Apt in Provence, and was painted on the spot. In this work my objective became capturing the light and timelessness of the place. Finally, Fig 115 is a mixed media study of the interior of a builder's yard, showing how there is within a townscape an almost infinite range of subjects which reflect contemporary urban life.

Marinescape
I have included under this heading all aspects of painting waterscapes, much of which has already been covered. It embraces all the aspects of rural landscape and townscape painting, and requires the artist to have the ability to record movement in shape, form, colour and tone. Atmosphere plays an important role in every aspect of painting subjects connected with water. Again the importance of building up a reference library of sketches, in line and colour, of all the artefacts connected with man's relationship with water cannot be over-emphasised. You will need to develop an understanding of the construction of boats and ships, marine buildings, slipways, ropes and of course the importance of reflections and light on water. Fig 116, a water-colour of a tranquil day on the Dorset Stour, contrasts quite strongly with the rushing water of the river Aven at Pont Aven in Brittany (Fig 117).

Boatyards always provide us with a feast of subject matter. They give us the opportunity to watch craftsmen at work and so to make studies of figures in action. I can easily fill a sketchbook with notes on a day spent in a boatyard. Fig 118 is a small oil-painting of one of my local boatyards, at Poole in Dorset. Shipyards are also good venues for marine still lifes. Every nook and cranny seems to have a subject tucked away. Then, of course, there are the bigger ports and the romanticism they can engender in us, arising from their promise of travel to exotic places and their large ocean-going vessels. Fig 119 is a drawing in mixed media of Southampton docks. The open sea and coastline also stimulate the artist, and encourage the development of large areas of colour in an attempt to capture the vastness of the sea and sky.

Finally, estuaries, especially tidal ones with their wet mud flats and boats heeling over causing shadows and reflections, require the artist to exercise all his skills and observation in the quest to solve the subtle changes of colour and tone that occur there. Using your sketchbook, make studies of these changes of light and tide. Observe the colour and tone of reflections under the hulls of boats at different times of day. Make use of buildings: cranes, etc, on the sky-line will all contribute towards the mood and ambience of the subject.

FIG 117 *Pont-Aven, Brittany* (Water-colour, 16" x 12")

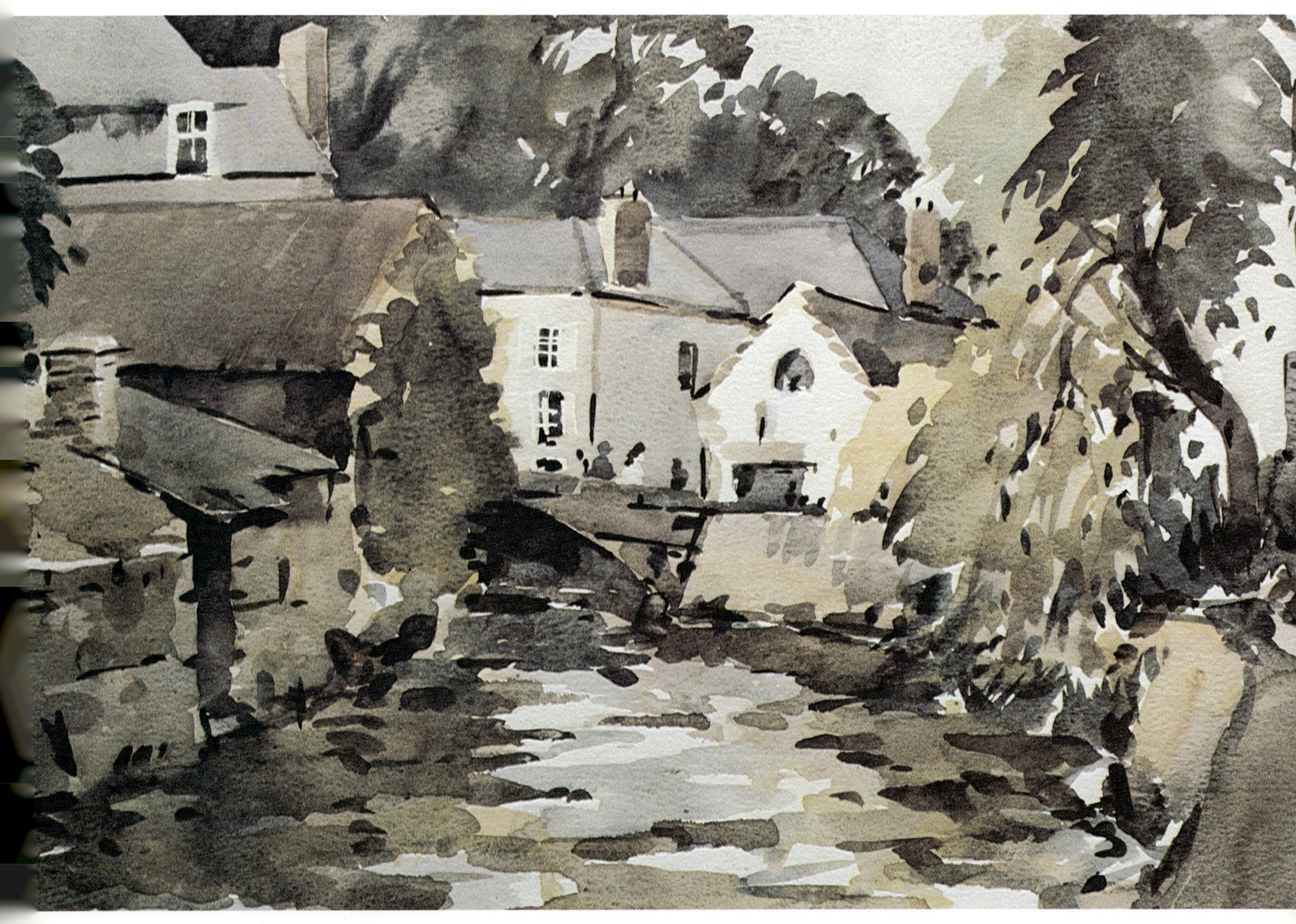

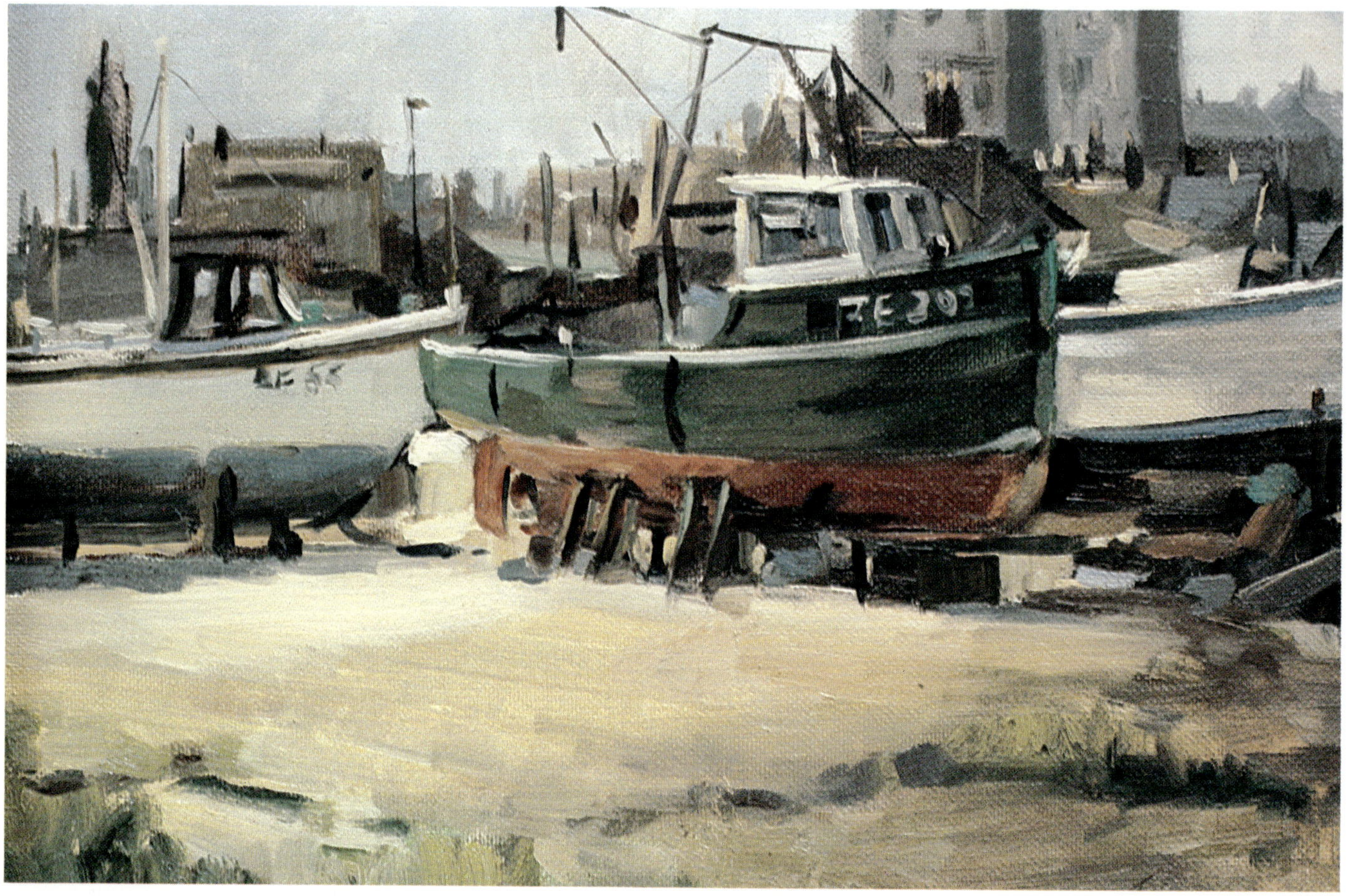

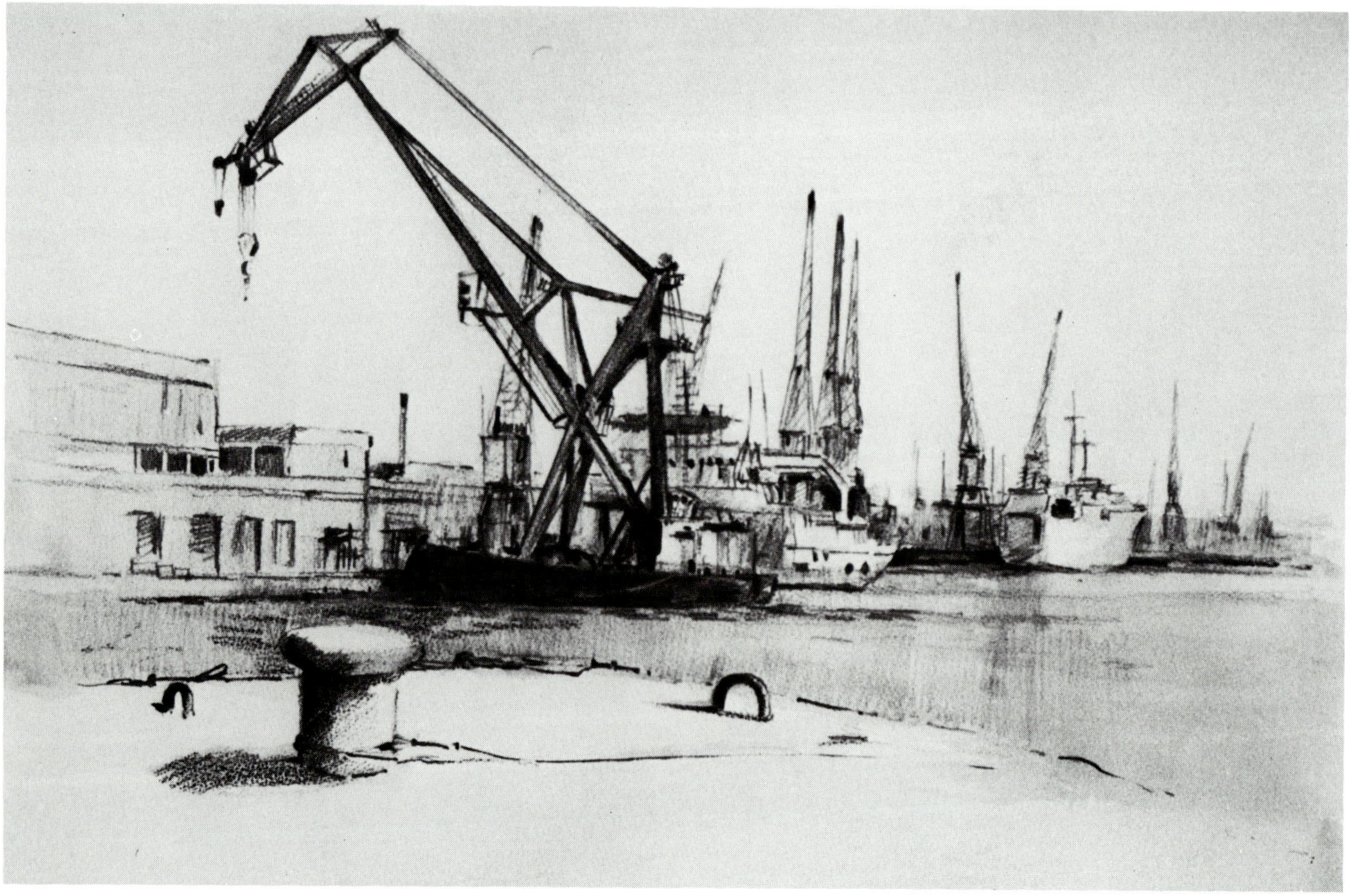

FIG 118 *Boatyard, Poole* (Oil, 12" x 10")

Figure and portrait painting

In this section, it will be necessary to refer to the earlier section on drawing the figure and portrait. For many centuries the artist has sought to depict mankind in all attitudes as a source of inspiration in his work. Drawing and painting the figure has long been a corner-stone in the education of art students, and remains so today.

As a first exercise, start with a self-portrait of just the head and shoulders. For this you will need a mirror. Place yourself near a window so that there is only one light source. Do not forget you will be painting yourself back to front. You will see that the head is positively lit from one side, with a shadowed darker side illuminated only by the reflected light. Pay great attention to reflected light in this exercise. The shadow area gains depth and solidity because of the reflected light and colour from its surroundings, just like the objects in the earlier still life exercises. It is a good thing to experiment by placing coloured drapes behind and to the side of yourself, and even by placing yourself between them and the light source. Remember that pale drapes throw back more light than dark ones, so select drapes that will reflect the atmosphere and mood that is synonymous with your own and get to work. Make sure that you are comfortable so that you can work for a sustained time and are able to return to your exact position after rest periods. Initially you should be concerned with understanding that the head is a solid object in space, lit as described. Indeed what you are about to paint should be seen as such, with distance between the viewer and the object and with space between it and its surroundings. It is important that you understand this. Note how the light and air move around the head, and how the strong contrasts of light and shade emphasise the solidity and form. Having given full consideration to the structure inside the painting, you must now determine what sort of arrangement you want – how you are going to interpret your portrait. To do this, you must decide on the best arrangement of shapes, colour and tone. It will require you to try a whole variety of poses and positions – try full face and three-quarter views, but always allow the head to adopt its natural posture. Ask these questions and only start work when you are convinced that you have selected an arrangement of shapes, colours and tones that satisfies your interpretative requirements.

The medium and approach will have to be decided on: you will have to consider whether your approach will be as objective as possible, or subjective. It is worth trying several approaches in different media, remembering that to work in different media can often be the catalyst for new ideas. Fig 120 is an example of self-portraiture where I set myself up in precisely the way suggested earlier. In this monochrome example, the penetration and determined concentration we all feel when working seems emerge in the painting.

Now to painting a portrait of someone else. This can be an intimidating prospect, and the attempt to achieve a likeness can become the main, almost obsessive, aim. This should not be your first consideration, however. Set about the painting in the same way as you did with the self-portrait, giving consideration to the arrangements of

FIG 119 *Southampton Docks* (Mixed media, 28" x 24")

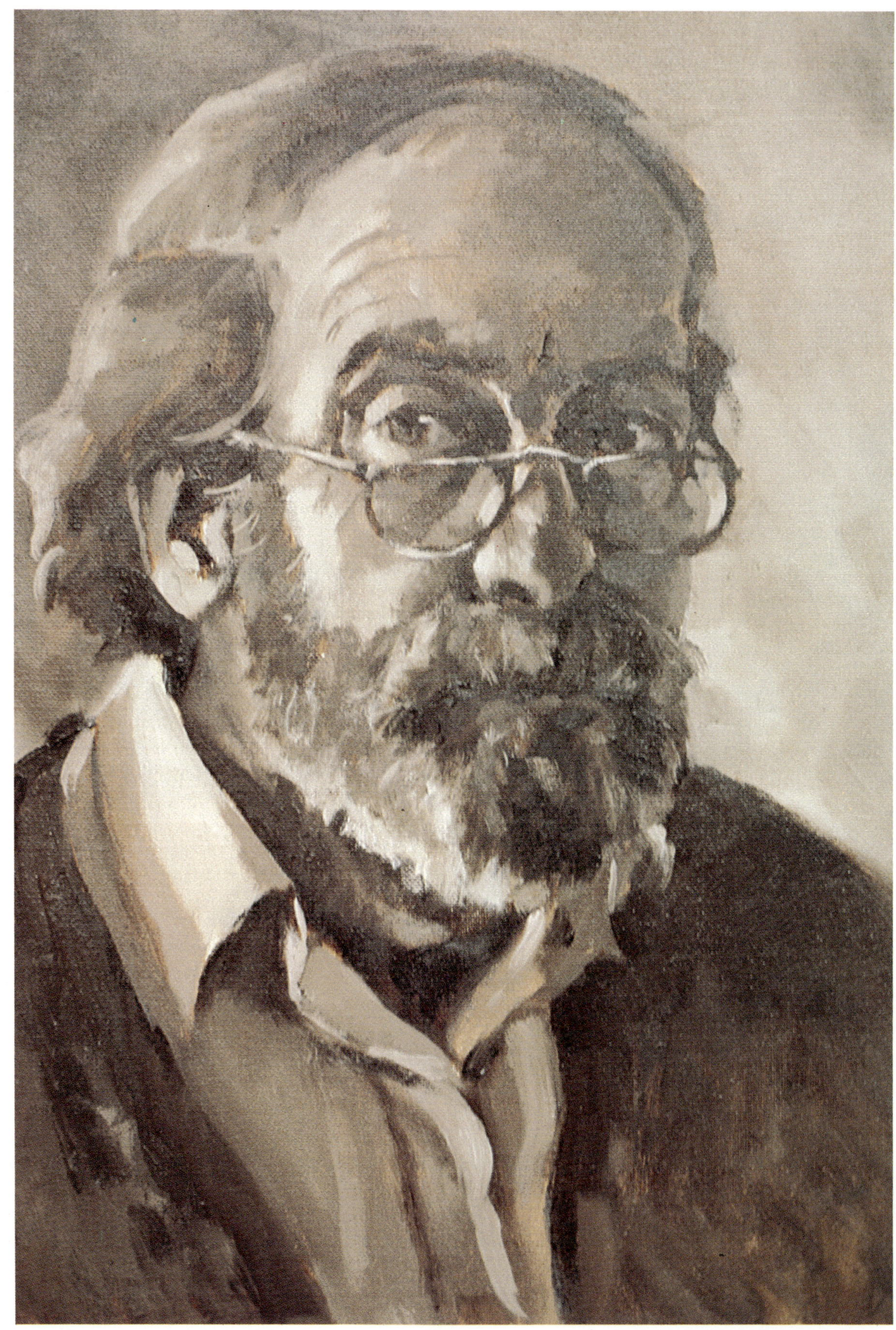

line, form, colour and tone. Providing you are methodical and your observation is accurate, you will in all probability achieve likeness within a well-composed, aesthetically pleasing picture.

Fig 121 is a portrait of an artist colleague, Avril Darby. This illustration shows the growth of the work from the preliminary drawing through the stages of development of the painting to completion. My aim in this work was to capture a moment of the artist in her environment, and to attempt to make a picture of a portrait. Painting people requires an ability to draw and to convey not only an understanding of the construction of the human form, but the skill to interpret and express reaction to the subject. This is certainly so in painting portraits: all too often, portraits are just a visual record of the sitter and tell us little or nothing about the person, his or her interests or profession. A pleasing portrait is one that will compel the viewer to look at it as a picture that has aesthetic appeal and yet leave him feeling he knows the sitter, even though they may never have met. I believe that with sound drawing and a firm understanding of the craft of painting, fine portraits can be painted which are not just portraits, but also pictures of high aesthetic content which will reveal much about the sitter and the artist who painted them.

So far the painting of people has been kept relatively simple. Arrangements have been uncomplicated, and have concentrated on the harmony of line, form, colour and tone. This aspect of picture-making will remain constant whatever the subject matter. The application of these principles, however, becomes more difficult when the entire human figure is introduced as the principal element within the picture.

The complexity of the human figure, with its infinitely changing form, is a problem that artists have wrestled with since earliest times. It is true to say that without some understanding and knowledge of anatomy it is difficult to understand the structure and movement of the figure, especially if the figure is clothed. To this end, I recommend that you take advantage of every opportunity to practise drawing from life, with the model either nude or clothed. This is not always easy for the leisure painter to do, but, if possible, join a further education art class or, alternatively, if you are a member of an art society or group, persuade a few of your friends to come in with you in hiring the services of a professional model. It is by drawing, and drawing alone, that we gain the understanding and experience to deal with the aforementioned complexities.

The painting of people at work, in an interior, or in any natural environment is often shied away from by artists, yet these situations provide a wealth of subjects that all can relate to and enjoy. I suggest you paint a figure in an interior as an exercise: my picture *Going to bed* (Fig 122) is an example of how an everyday event can become an aesthetically pleasing painting. This work, painted in oils, required a number of small pencil sketches in an attempt to resolve the problems mentioned earlier. You will find that painting a figure in an interior, at work or in any environmental situation makes you examine a known environment anew.

FIG 120 *Self-portrait* (Oil, 18" x 14")

FIG 121a Progressive development of portrait of Avril Darby.

FIG 121a Study of head and hands. In order to gain a greater understanding of the sitter, a number of studies were made of which these were but two. Drawings of the head included profile, three-quarter and full face. By drawing the head in such a comprehensive way I was able to gain a great deal of knowledge of the construction and, more importantly, the characteristic shapes that I felt worth developing. This drawing was executed in compressed charcoal and conté crayon on bronze coloured paper.

The hands were of tremendous importance in this work and, as with the head, a number of studies were tried. The one illustrated, showing the hands in operation, was, I felt, most in character with the sitter and this drawing was referred to for the final painting. As with the head, it was the construction that interested me most and this took a number of attempts before I felt confident enough to consider making an expressive study.

Pencil was used to make this drawing as I feel pencil is the most suitable medium for exploring the subject in the quest for knowledge.

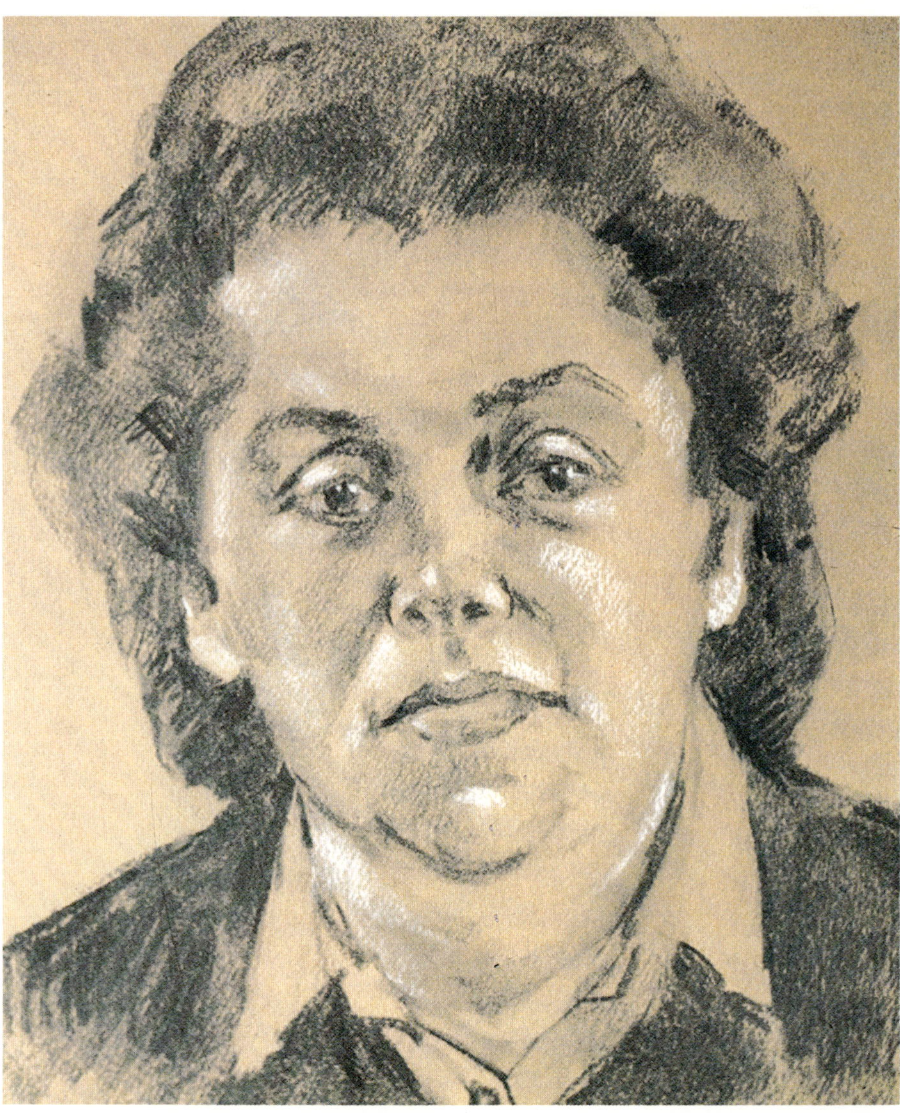

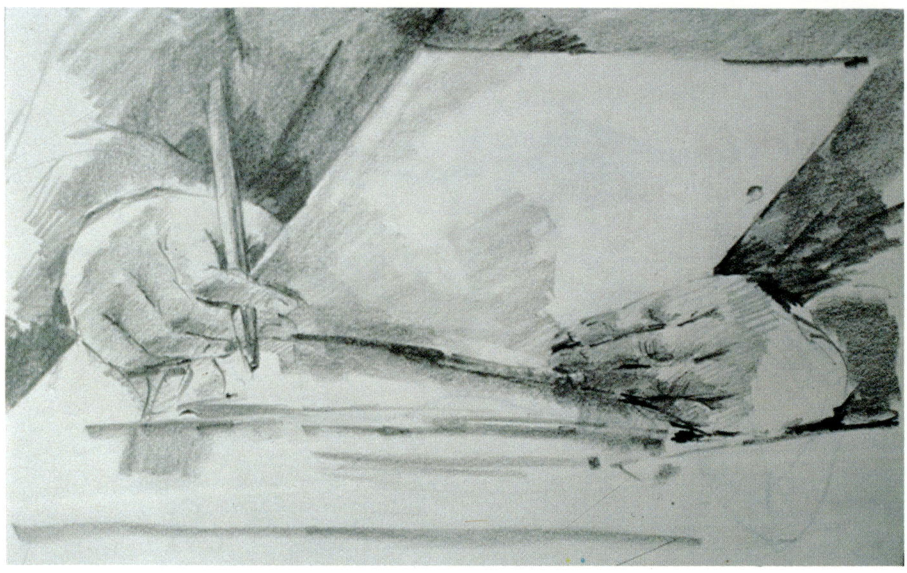

FIG 121b Composition and design. The composition of portraiture is where we can make pictures out of portraits. For this work a number of avenues were explored, all of which, I felt, led to nothing. I wanted to paint the person and her vocation. Consequently, I finally developed the drawing shown, which became the idea for the painting. It shows the artist, pencil in hand, looking at the subject. In the background, strategically placed for balance, are some brushes and the corner of a drawing board. Using charcoal and white chalk on grey paper I was able, when the linear design met my objectives, to indicate the lighting and some of the tone values. The drawing, although not in any way intended to be other than a working study, took less than half an hour and has in the main provided the basis of the painting.

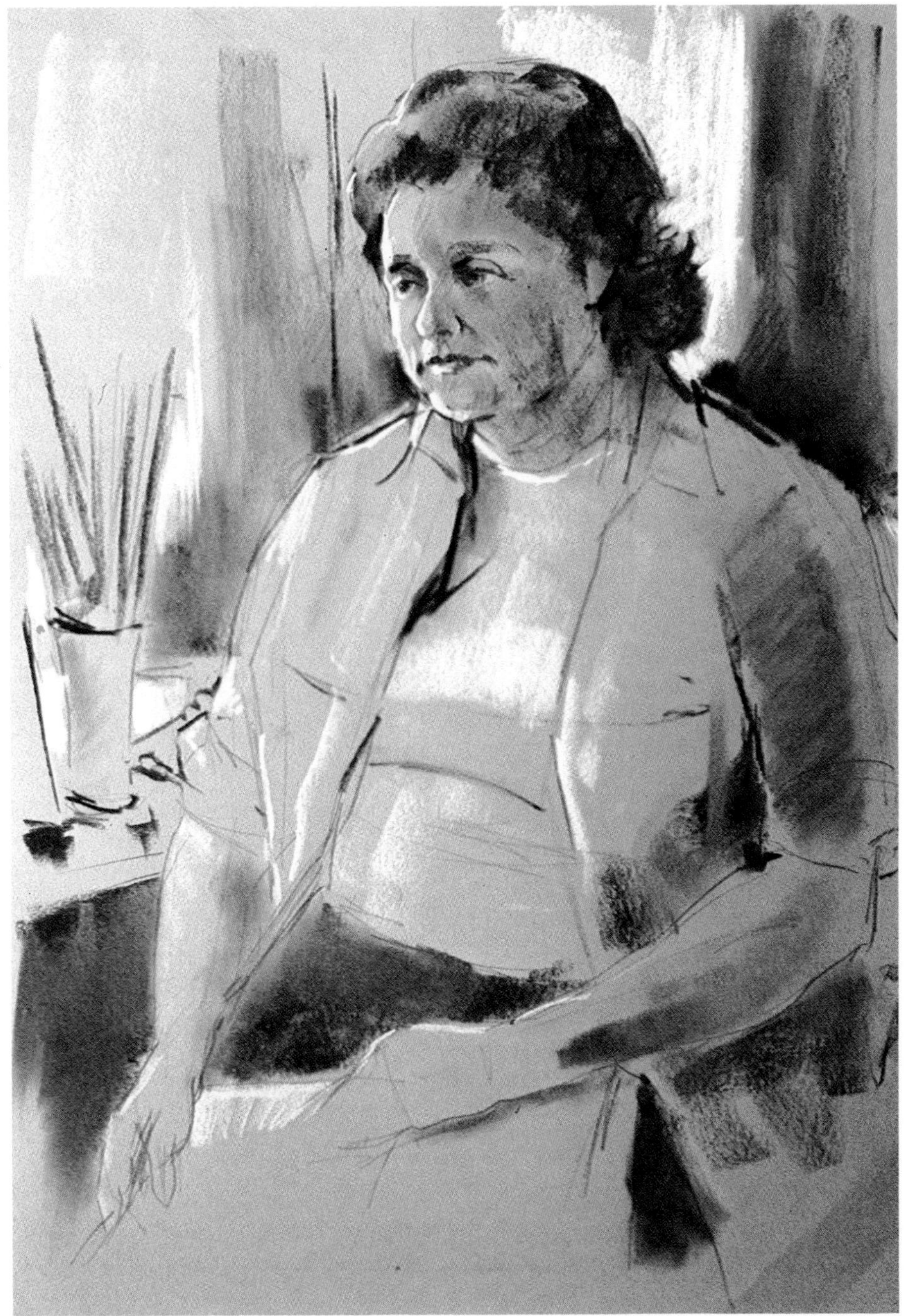

FIG 121c Establishing the design on the canvas. It is very necessary when transferring a design from a working drawing to a canvas to ensure that the scale of the work does not alter. The canvas size selected for this work was of proportionally the same format as the working drawing, so this did not present a problem, as I was able to increase the drawing on the canvas by a factor of two. The initial drawing was laid in using a mixture of cadmium red and viridian thinned with turpentine spirit, and at the same time the larger dark areas were indicated using the same mix. The work now has the appearance of a monochrome. The thinned paint, being substantially turpentine, will dry quite rapidly, allowing the main dark areas to be more firmly established.

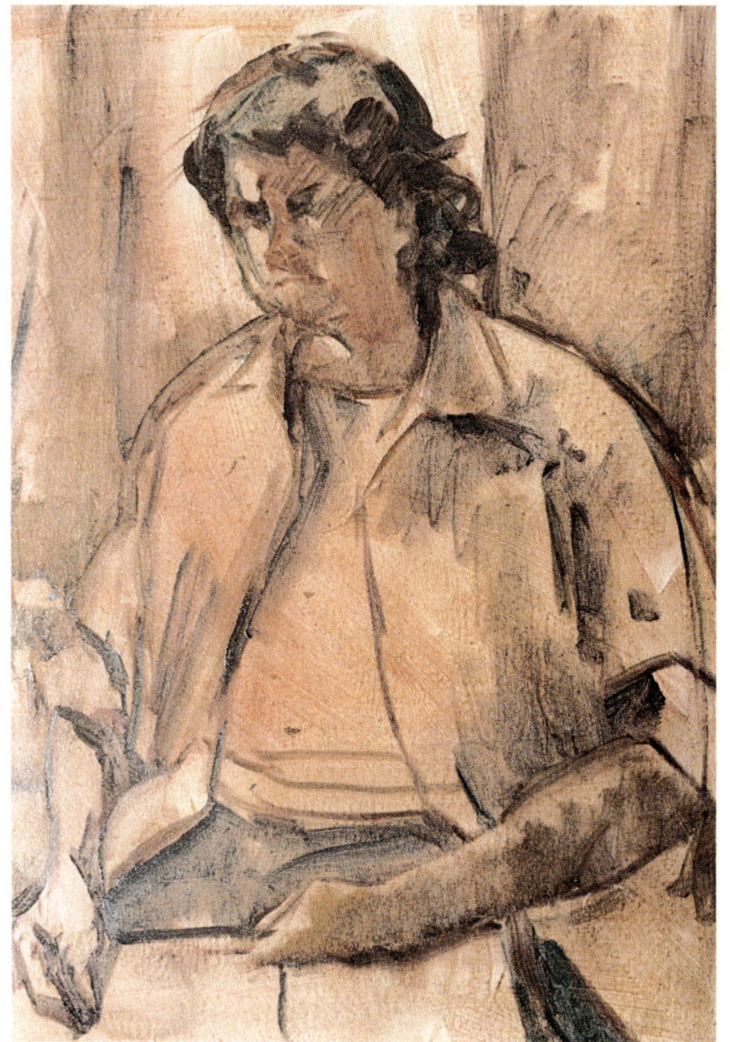

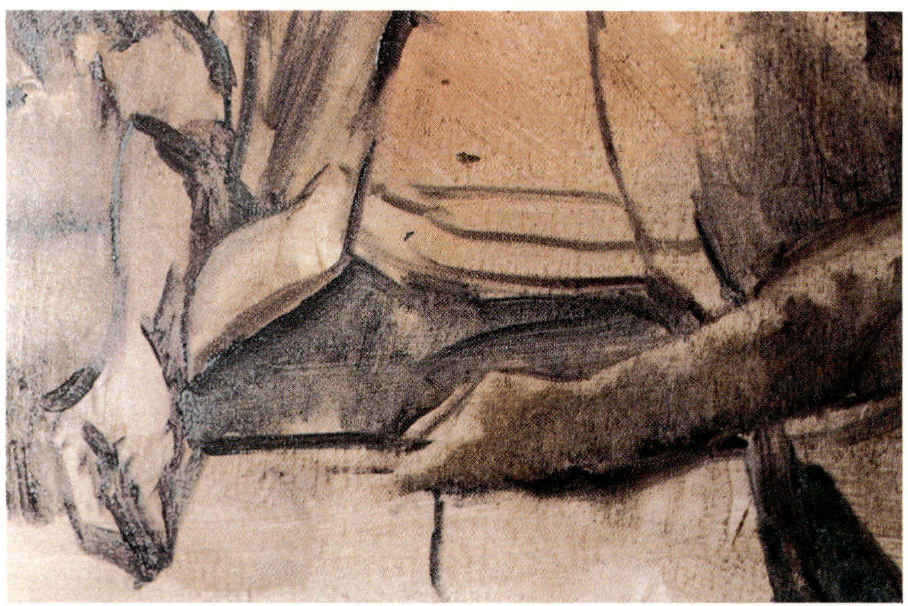

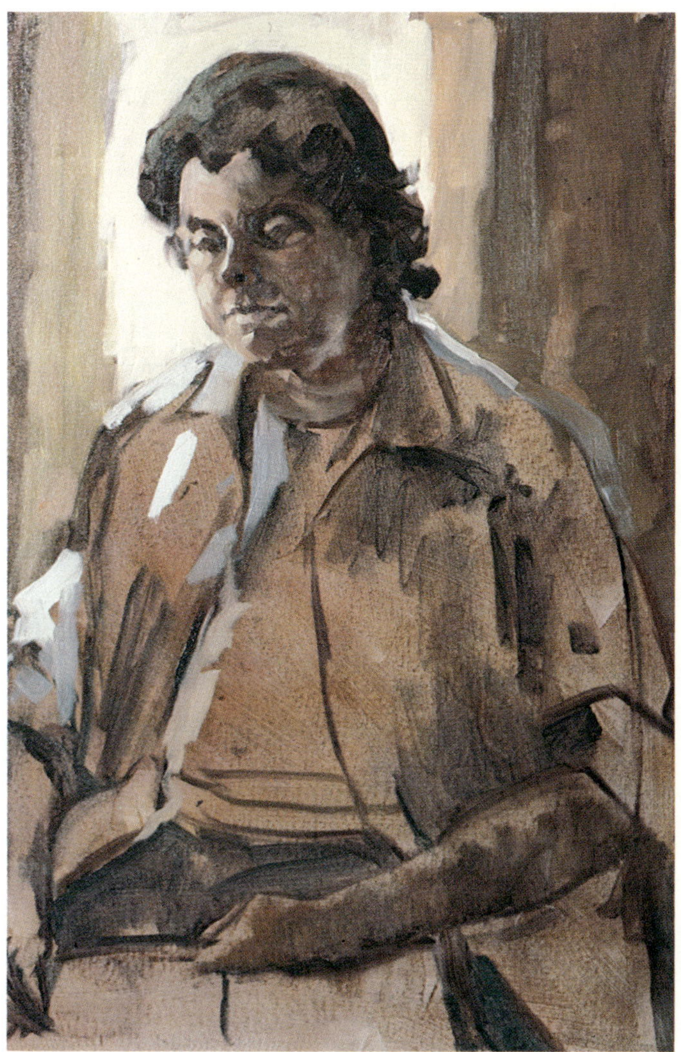

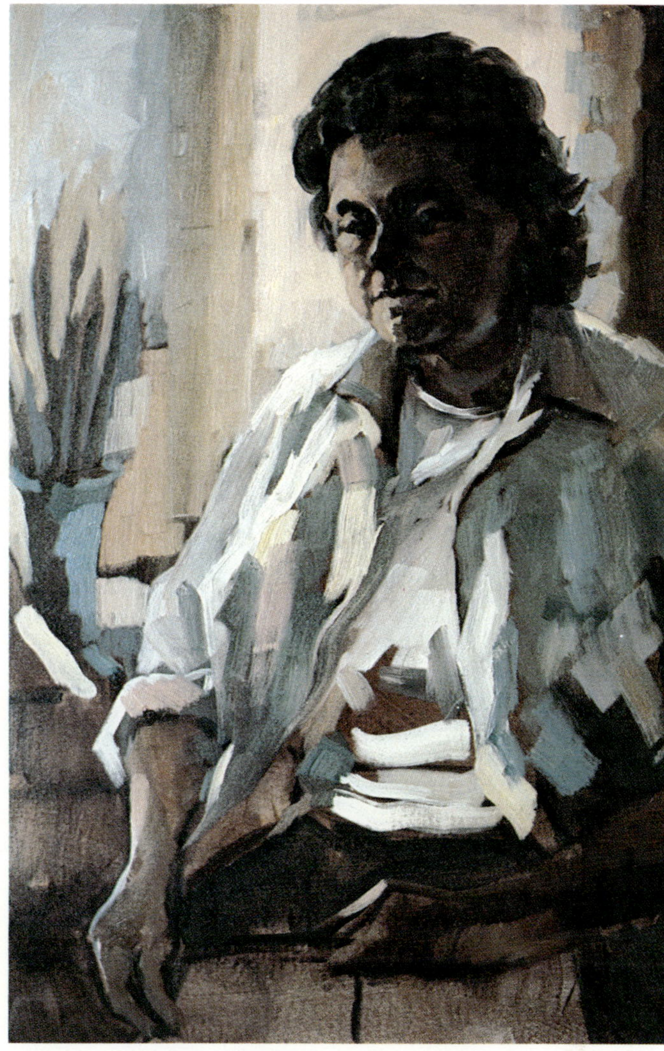

FIG 121d Establishing the main tonal and contrast parameters. At this stage the main areas of the work can be blocked in, starting with the shadows. These of course will be established in the local colour and of the correct tone value. This is important as it is at this stage that space and volume begin to emerge. These areas should be painted reasonably thin without losing the opacity of the medium.

I thin my pigments at this stage, and for the rest of the work, with turpentine and linseed oil, mixed in the ratio of two parts turpentine to one part linseed oil. It is a good tip to make the darks stronger at this point than they need to be, remembering that it is easier to make dark passages lighter than light passages darker. The middle tones can now be rubbed in, again acknowledging the tonal differences. Finally the highlights can be placed, giving a true feeling of space and volume. It is extremely important that the painting is handled in a free manner and that the whole canvas be worked on in order to relate the whole and that the brush handling will suggest the surface forms and textures.

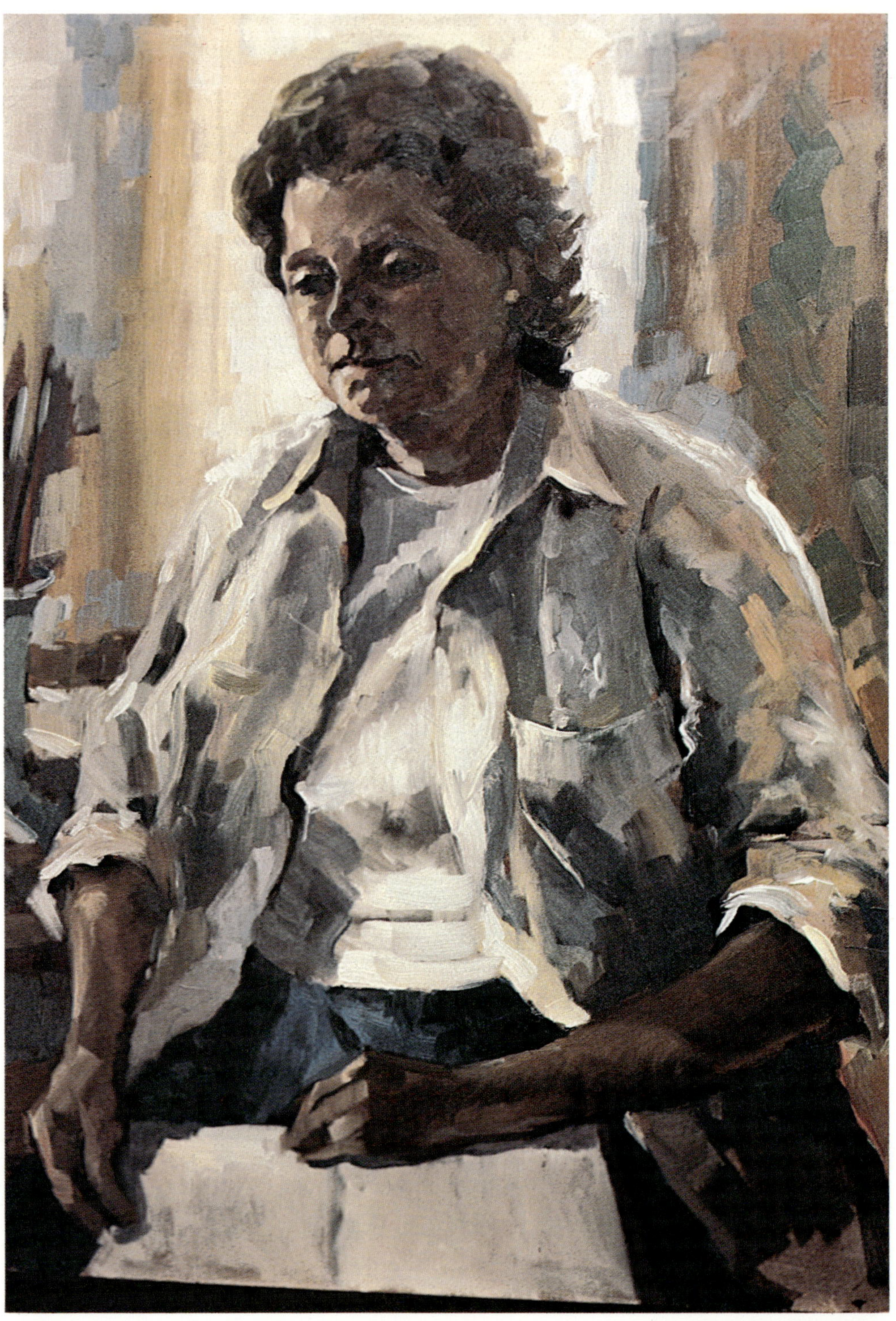

FIG 121e Developing the character of the sitter. It is now that the sitter's characteristics, already apparent in the earlier stages of the work, should be developed within the overall concept. In this painting, much of this was achieved by letting the highlights give emphasis to the shapes. The use of colour gives importance to the pleasurable concentration of the artist engrossed in her work. It also helps to convey the movement and light of what is obviously a very contented situation. The hands are also very much part of the portrait. They must be the sitter's and of the picture, yet not dominate the work. You will see this has been achieved by reducing the contrast range without forsaking the tonal relationship.

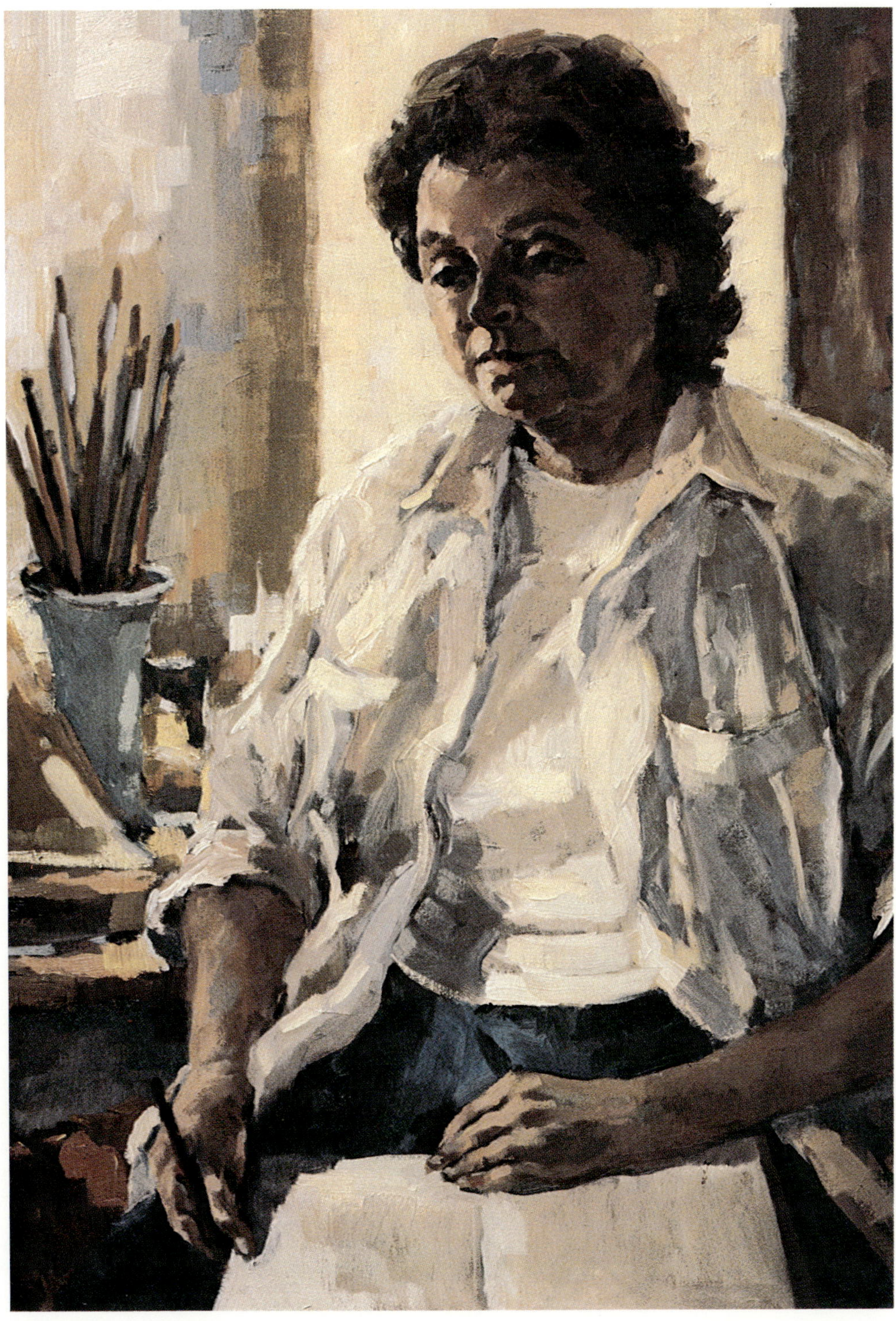

FIG 121f Pulling the work together.
In this, the finished work, much of the effort has been concentrated on ensuring that the figure and the background work together as a picture. This entailed ensuring that such areas as the worktop and brushpot complemented the portrait without intruding. The tone value of this entire passage is critically important; it is equally necessary to avoid over-detail. Again the controlled use of colour will play a major role in making a picture of a portrait. Finally the modelling and textures were checked and modified where I felt it to be beneficial, especially on the drapes. After a final period of looking I felt there was little more I wished to express.

FIG 122 *Going to bed* (Oil, 14" x 10")

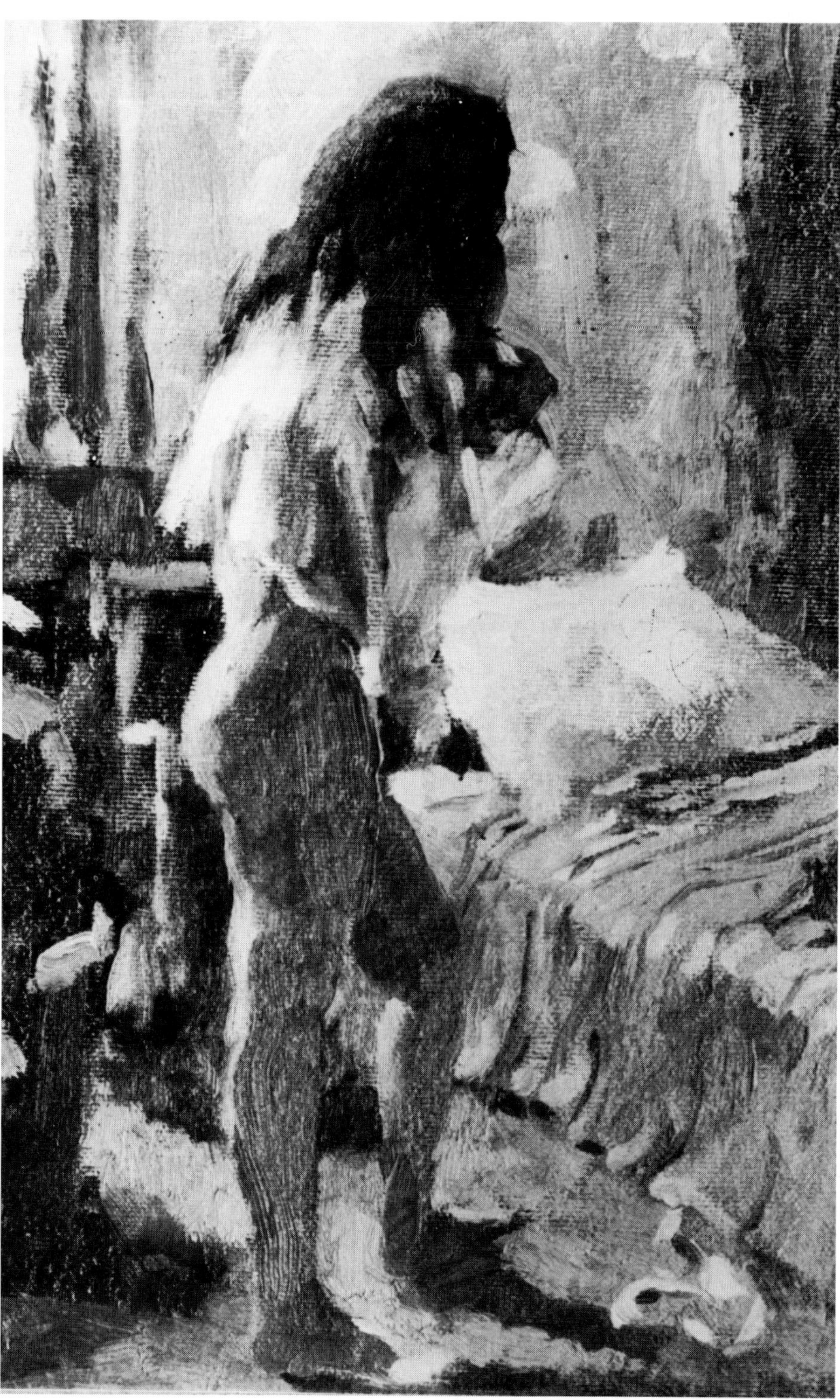

The decision as to whether the subject is clothed or unclothed will depend entirely on the theme of the work. With the clothed model, make sure that the choice of apparel is not entirely arbitrary. It must be considered as carefully as all the other ingredients of the painting, and particular attention paid to the colours and textures you intend to introduce. When positioning the figure remember to ensure it does not become dull and uninteresting: do not divide the space of the working surface equally. Place the figure slightly to one side and make it relate to the situation around it. Much can be achieved by colour relationships, which can be used to create total harmony, or you can use lighting to create tonal unity. The lighting of the subject largely establishes the mood of the painting, and it will require a certain amount of experiment to decide what suits you. Natural light of course varies, but can be controlled by the use of drapes or blinds; it can also be bounced off large sheets of white or coloured paper or cloth to create very interesting effects. This form of experiment with lighting can also be applied to still life and other subjects. Remember that objects only become visible because of the light shining on them. Some colours and textures absorb light almost totally, others almost totally reflect it, and there is a great deal of variation between the two extremes.

Human flesh, because of its light-reflective qualities, is a subject of interest and complexity. When deciding on a particular hue, it is not enough just to decide on the local colour; you must take note of the effect one colour has on another. You will see that light is reflected from one surface to another, thus causing a complicated interplay of colours which increases according to the variety of local colours in the setting selected for the painting. This play of colour exists more or less in every type of subject we tackle. Your task is to create the illusion of this play of colour in the simplest possible way, avoiding the temptation of seeing too much.

Painting, like drawing, requires the ability to see properly: that is, to be constantly aware of what you are looking for. You must think of painting as a language of shapes and colours which, when translated, will create the illusion of three dimensions on a two-dimensional surface. When composing the picture, think how you are going to suggest depth and space, analyse the colour of the atmosphere, and be prepared to make changes of scale, even to distort shapes in order to create an illusion of depth. Use doorways, windows and items of furniture as aids in your quest to achieve the most suitable setting. Remember that it is at all times entirely your decision how you compose the work and how you use colour and tone. These decisions must be made positively, as they are the basic ingredients from which you make your painting.

The next, and most natural, progression from painting a single figure is to paint two or more figures within a situation. In this sort of work it is the interaction between the figures that becomes the principal source of interest. My study *The patient* (Fig 123), an oil 14 inches x 10 inches, is an example of the interaction between two people. The work was commenced after a number of exploratory drawings were made and painted fairly quickly in the *alla prima* method. The most important technical problem in this work was to ensure that the spaces between the figures related to and assisted in my attempt to convey the concentrated interest of the doctor in the patient and the lethargic indifference, caused by sickness, of the patient to the doctor.

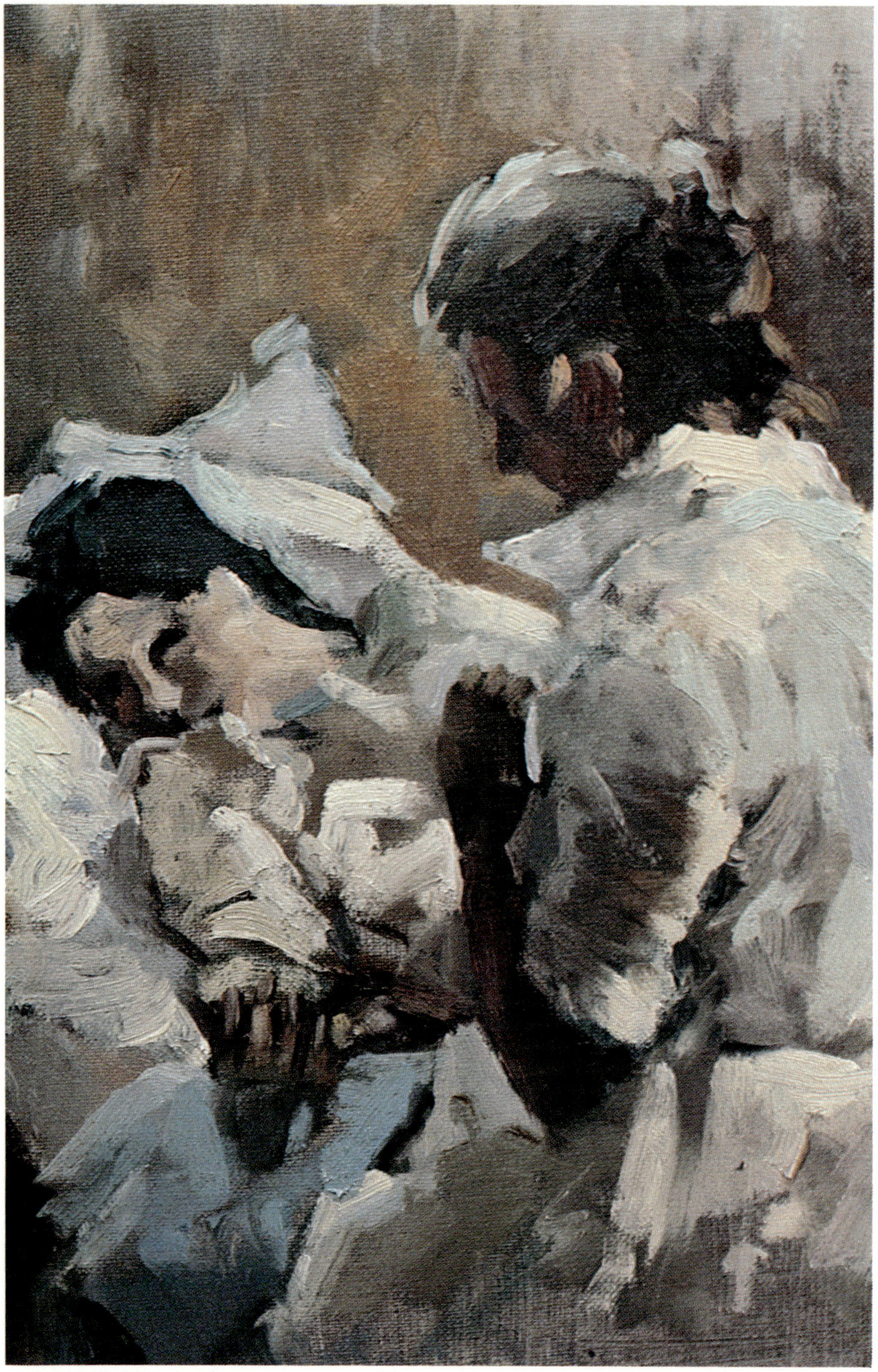

FIG 123 *The patient* (Oil, 14" x 10")

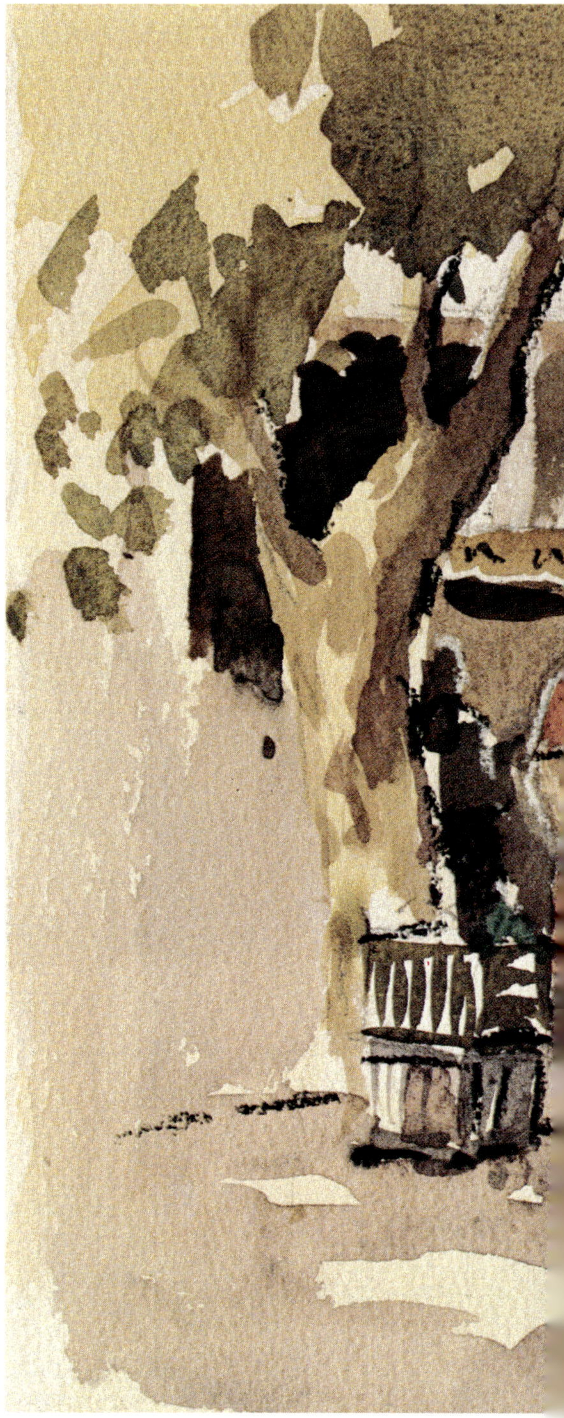

FIG 124 Sketch book study of a market place (Pencil 10" x 7")

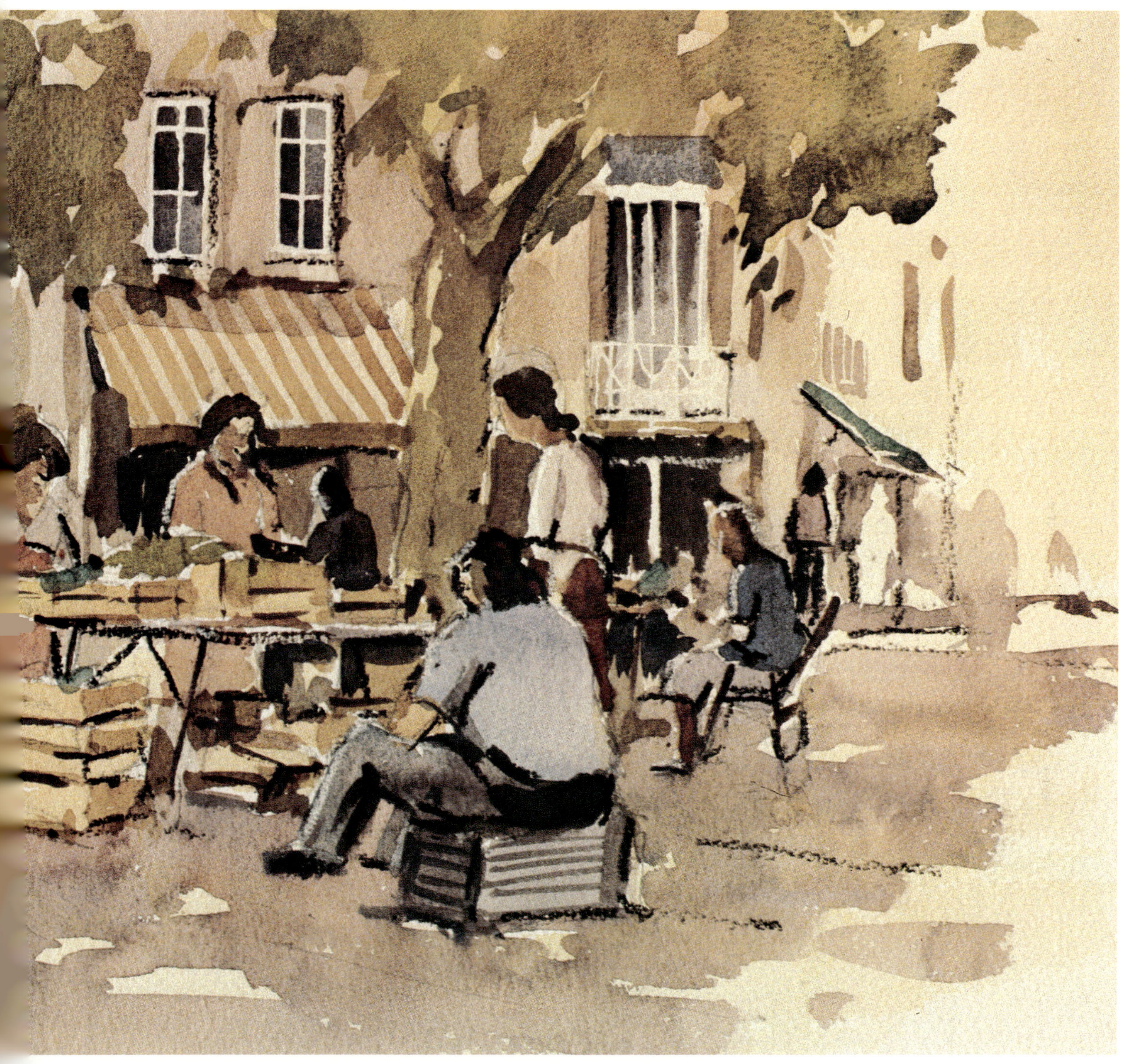

The eye-level plays a substantial role in the composition of groups of figures. Choose its position carefully; the entire mood of the work can be altered by raising or lowering the eye-level. To see this, try looking at the subject when standing on a chair, then look at the same scene while kneeling on the floor; note how the mood and emphasis change. If the figures are placed at different points in the picture plane, i.e. some further back than others, they stand on the same ground plane. Very often, space can be created by overstating a foreground figure and relating it to a figure in the background which has been drawn smaller and is understated.

Time must be spent in considering how the figures relate to one another within the picture. This is particularly important when painting people in an environment, and requires a great deal of thought as so many themes can be developed from it, and are provoked by human contact. By enclosing figures within the frame of the picture, you are suggesting that there is an involvement or connection between them. Like the writer of a novel or play, the artist has the chance to explore the way human beings become involved with each other, often for a fleeting moment, and the opportunity to freeze these moments for all time. The viewer of the work will be looking to see the inter-reaction between the various parts of the picture and whether the relationship between the various parts conveys the mood or reason for the work. Complex figure compositions are usually best worked on a larger scale. This type of picture demands a greater degree of flexibility in its handling, as the number of figures may be ten or more, for instance in a market scene, orchestra, football match, or a social gathering.

The collecting, by means of notes, drawings and photographs, of as much reference material as you can is an absolute must if the painting is going to carry conviction. Fig 124 is a page from my sketch book, showing notes made in a French market-place. Used with the photographs taken at the same time, these give much of the information needed to paint such a large subject. With such information, we are able to consider the composition. You will find that a lot of time needs to be spent in arranging and re-arranging the various elements, and you must be completely satisfied with the composition before beginning to paint. Look at some of the old masters' complex group paintings, not with a view to copying them, but rather to understanding the structure of a large number of inter-related elements. There are a number of loosely applied conventions of composition which have been developed over the years, and it is worthwhile finding out more about them. Using large complex groups of people as the prime element of the work will require consideration of the large schematic shapes which the figures are going to follow and where the main focal point or group is going to be placed. It will help if you are familiar with the Golden Section, as referred to in the section on basic drawing (p.57) and illustrated in Fig 37. Throughout the history of art certain traditions of composition that have been popular, for instance Renaissance artists inclined towards a symmetrical arrangement, but whatever the arrangement, the focal point was generally on or about the Golden Section.

When you are planning a large painting, you must be aware of the visual distortions that occur at the periphery of the picture, and which are due to the eye having to move to be able to see the entire canvas. The best way of overcoming this is to avoid putting in these areas any element which will attract the eye: in other words, use flat areas of tone in much the same way the Dutch master Vermeer did. Large pictures obviously take longer to paint, and will require you to work with consistency. You must select your palette and stick to it throughout; the addition of just one other colour will create a dissonance that will be harmful to the work. In any case, use of a limited palette will encourage harmony and unity in a situation where the number of elements can themselves create a certain dissonance. One final word on the practicalities of painting large works: set your easel so that you are able to walk well back from the work, otherwise you may find that the painting has become tight and laboured.

Many of these statements on the attitude to painting people are applicable to most other themes and subjects, and whilst many artists specialise and lean towards a specific field or area of painting, applying the basic principles outlined here and in other sections will enable you to tackle any aspect of painting and drawing.

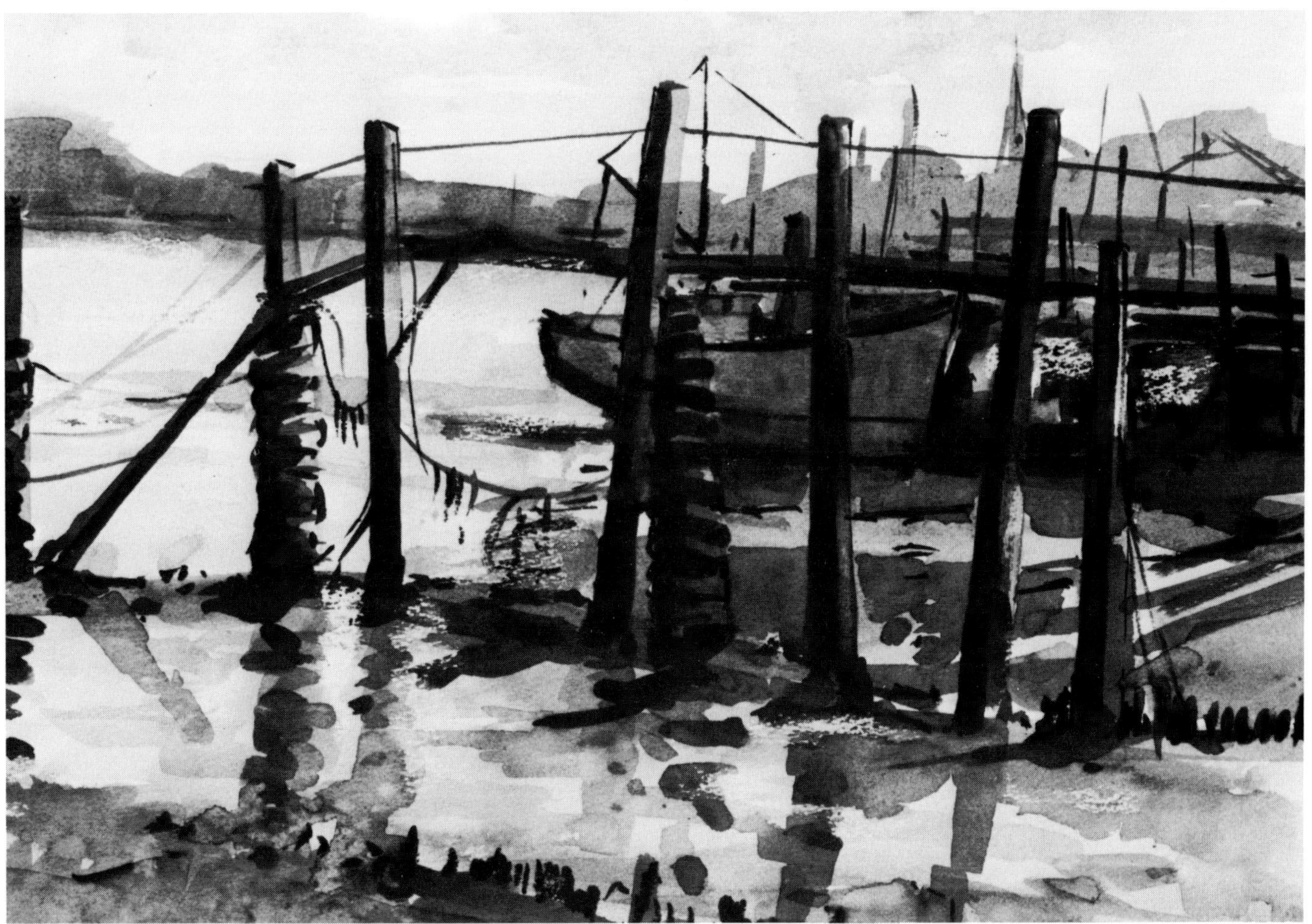

Hythe Jetty (Water-colour, 16" x 12"). Note bold treatment of reflections and shapes against the light

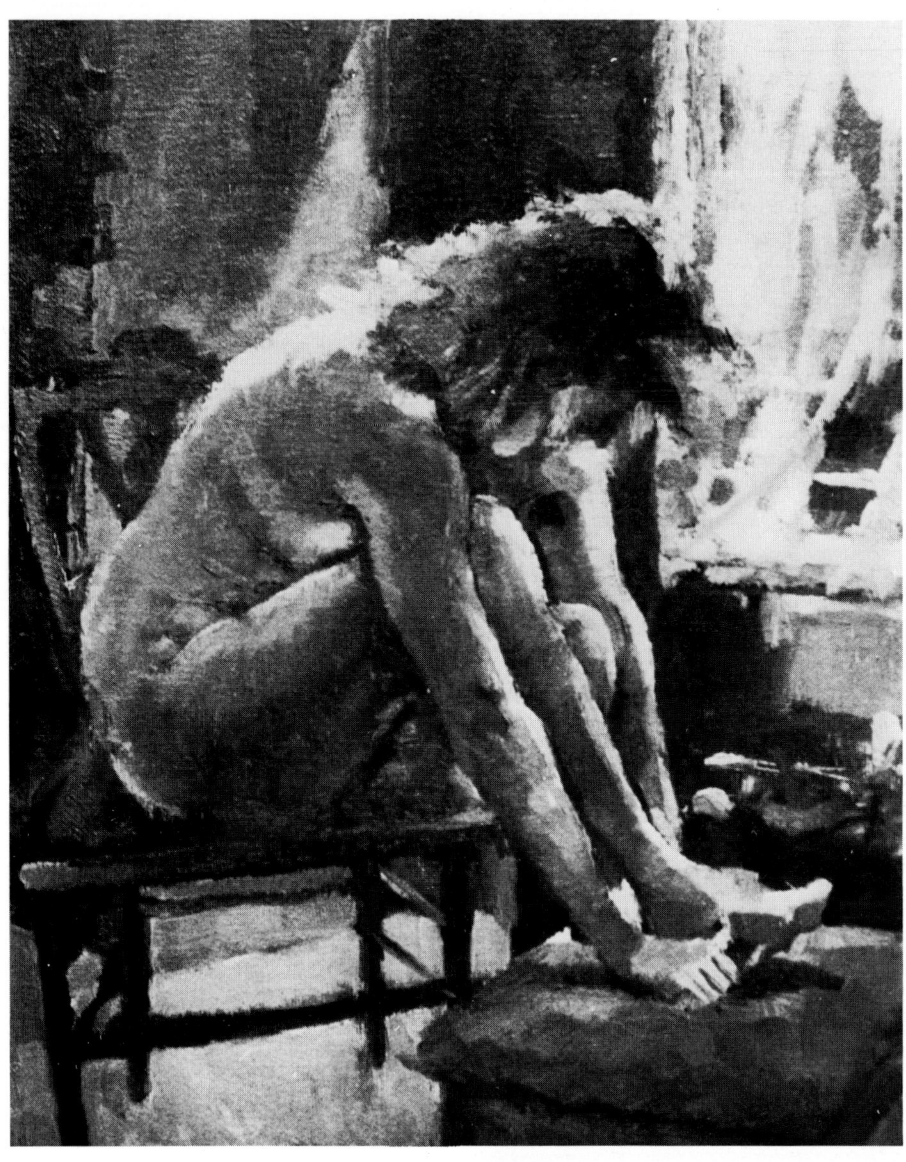

Getting dressed (left)(Oil, 16” x 12”)

Fest Noz (Below)(Oil, 20” x 16”)

Old Langworthy Farm (Right)(Pastel and
acrylic, 22” x 18”)

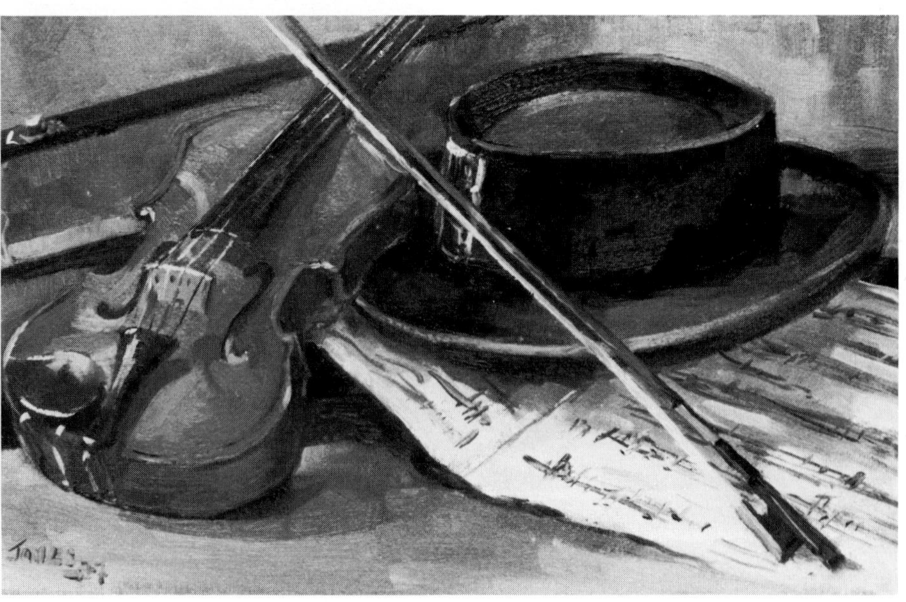

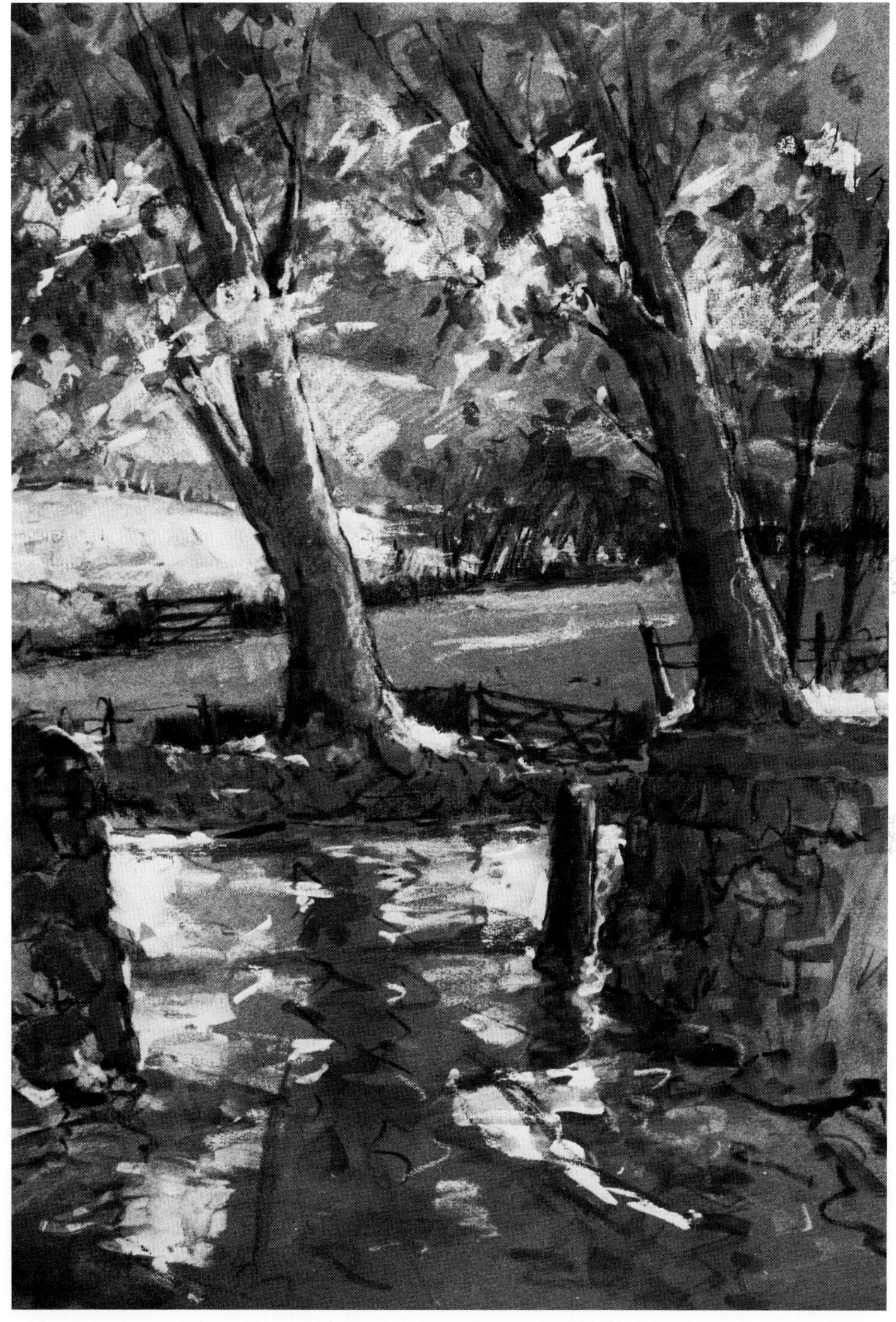

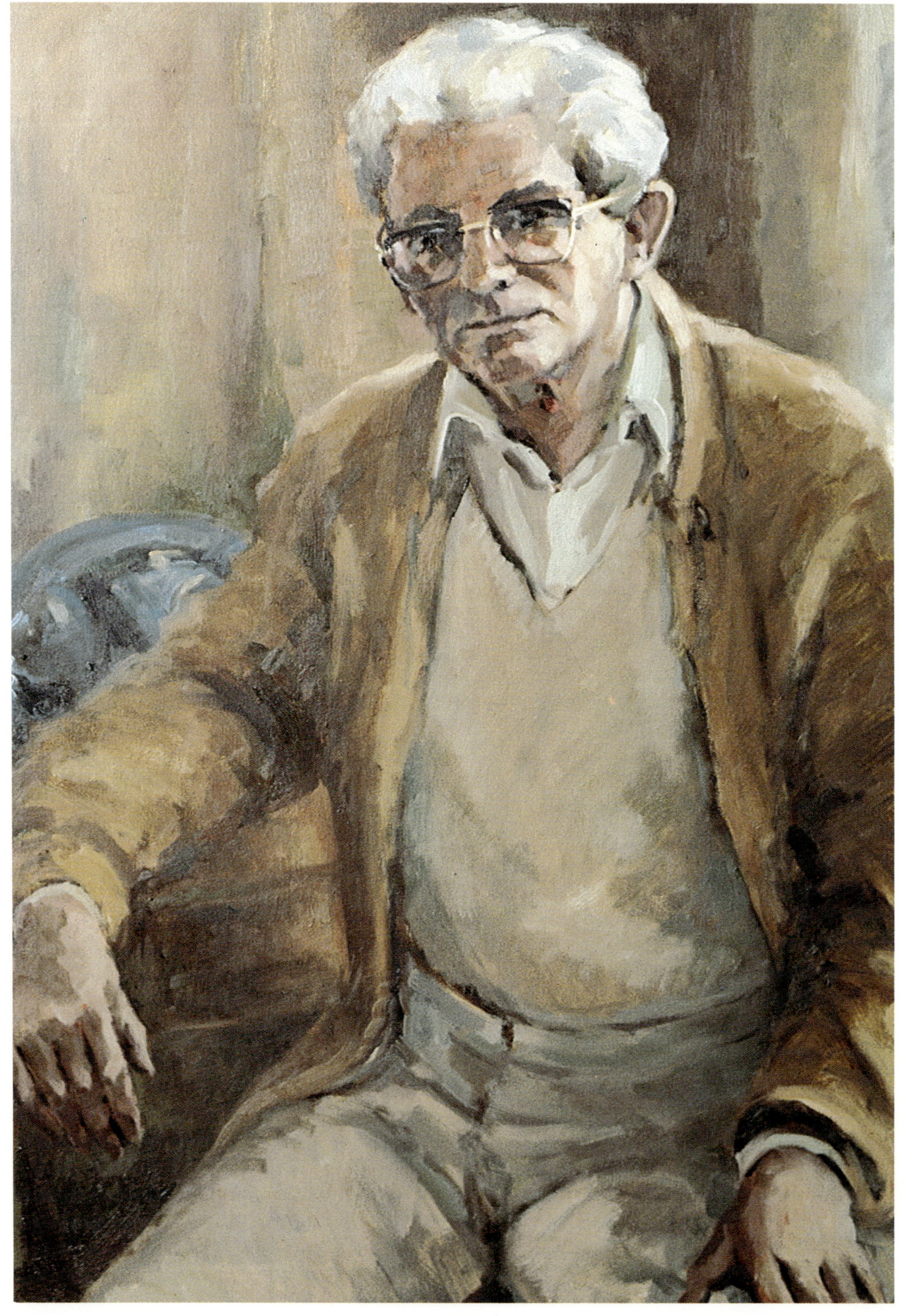

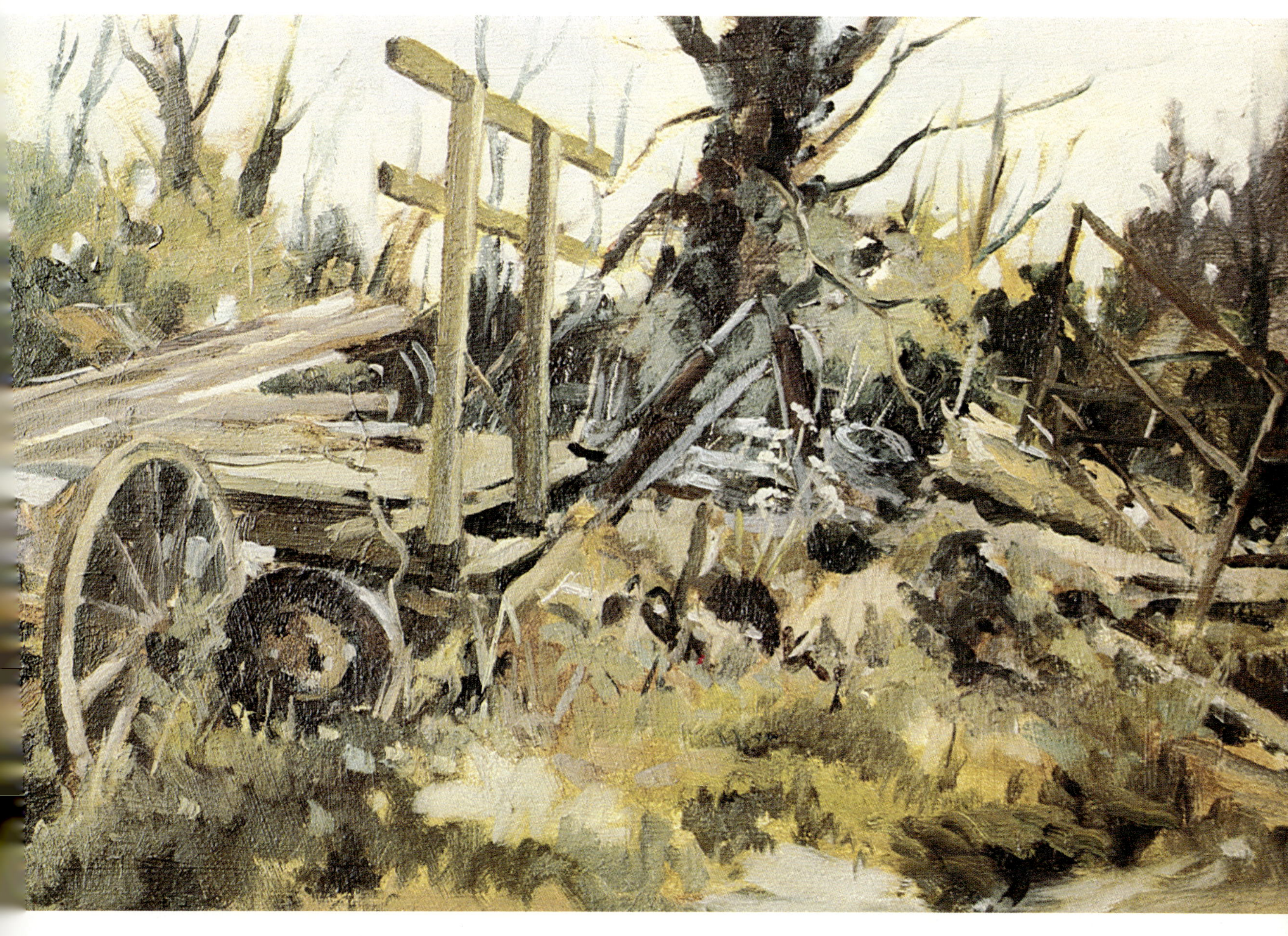

Farming equipment (Oil, 22" x 18")

Gordon White Esq. By kind permission of
Mr and Mrs White (Oil, 30" x 25")

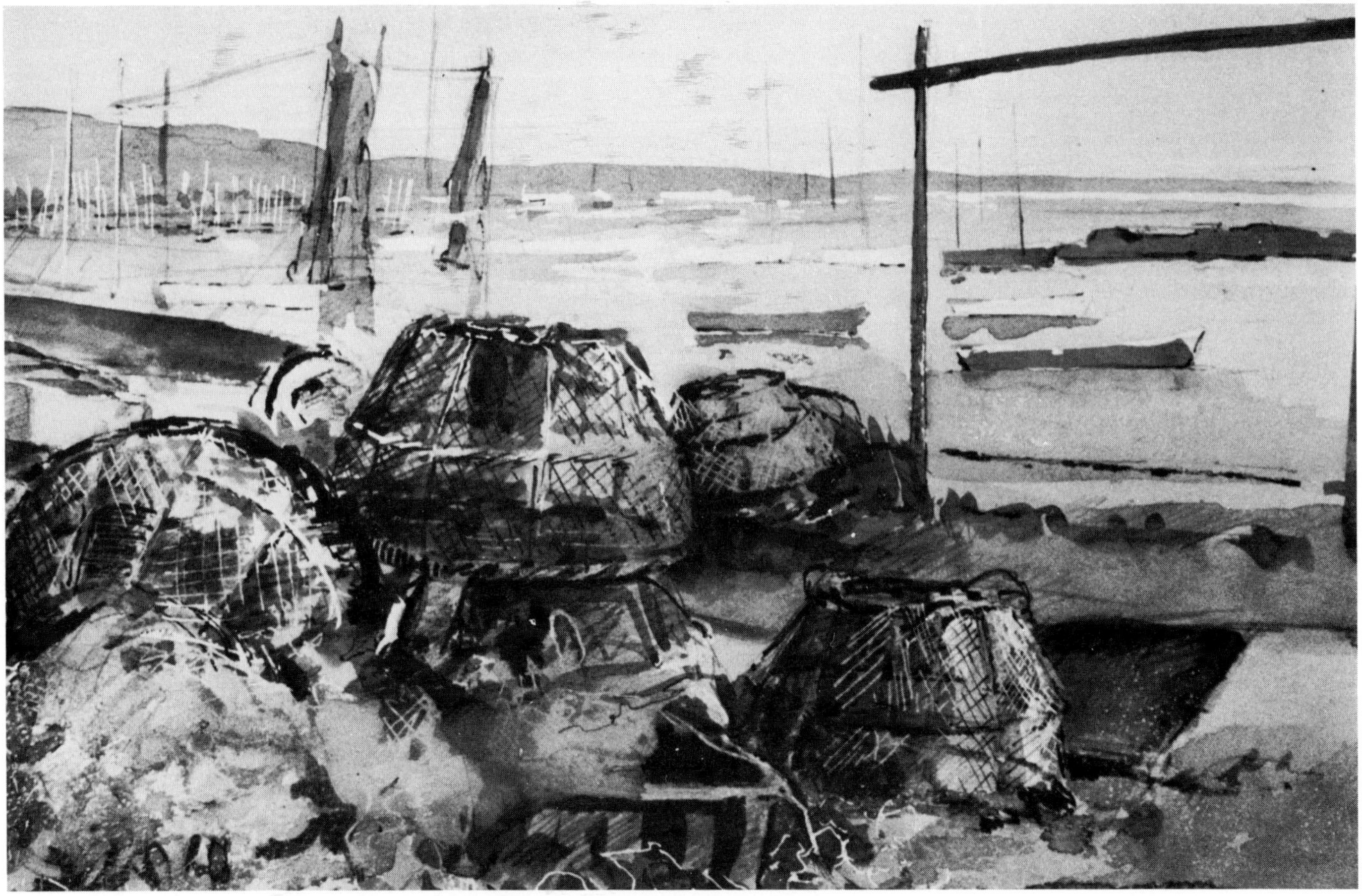

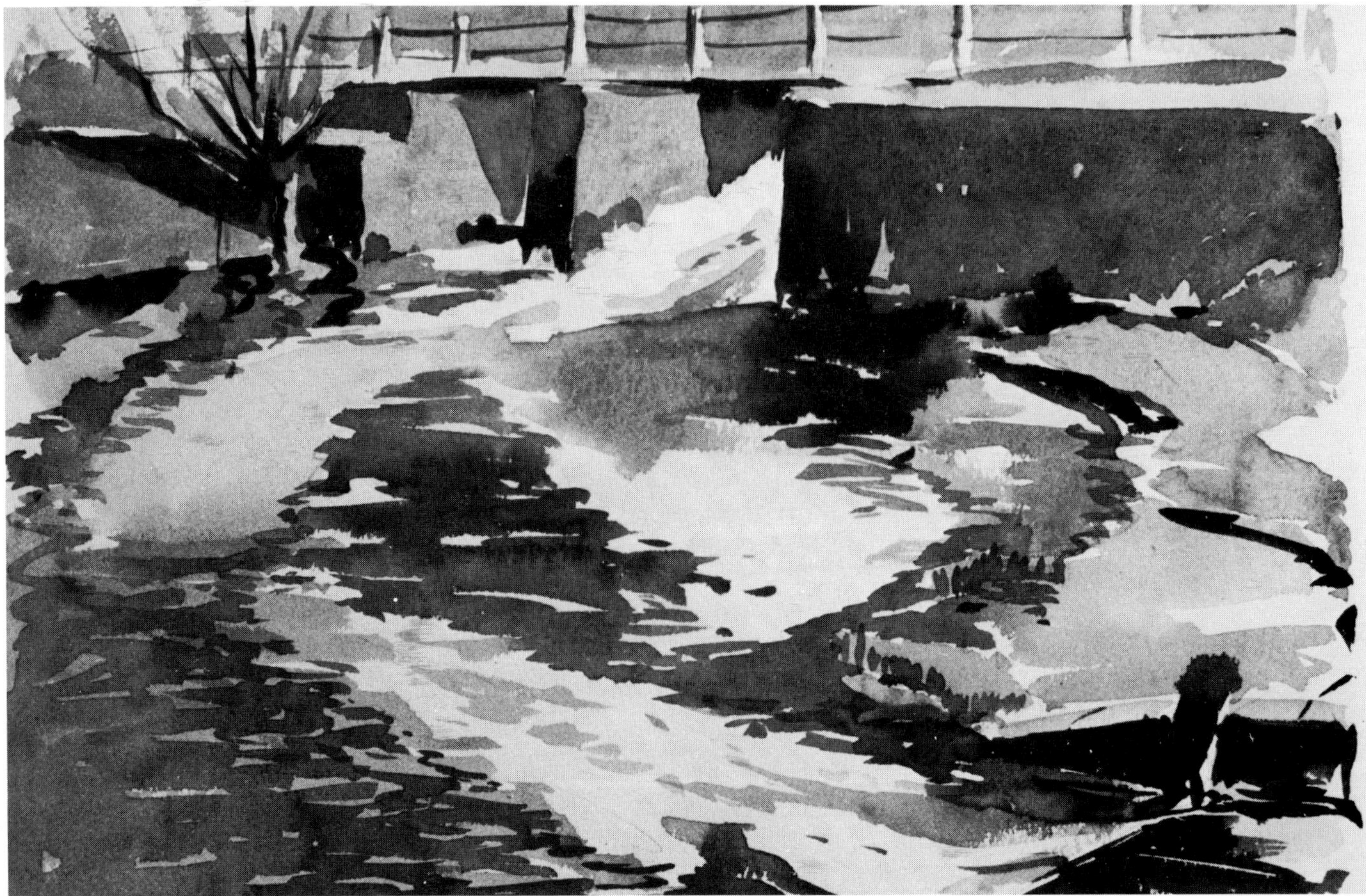

Lobster pots (Top left)(Water-colour, 16"
x 12"). Masking fluid was used in this
work to obtain the fine mesh on the pots
and to keep the paint handling free

Water movement (Bottom left)(Water-
colour, 15" x 11")

Corner of the studio (Top right)(Oil, 24" x
20")

Aperitifs (Bottom right)(Water-colour,
15" x 11")

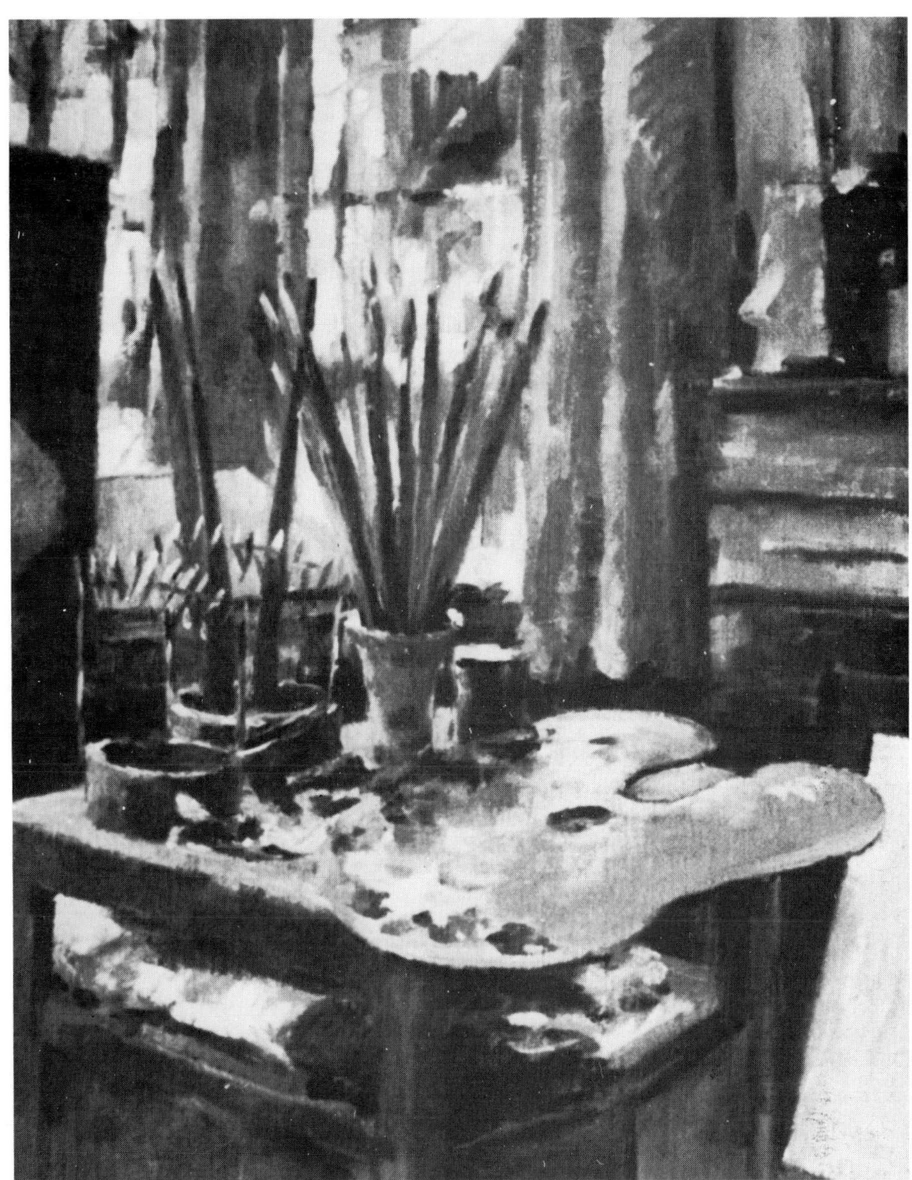

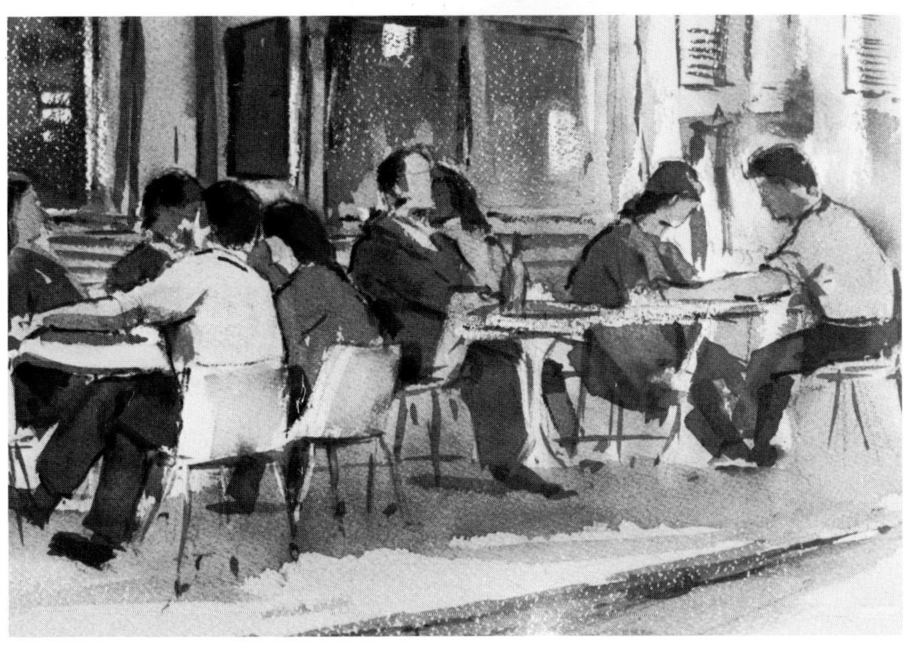

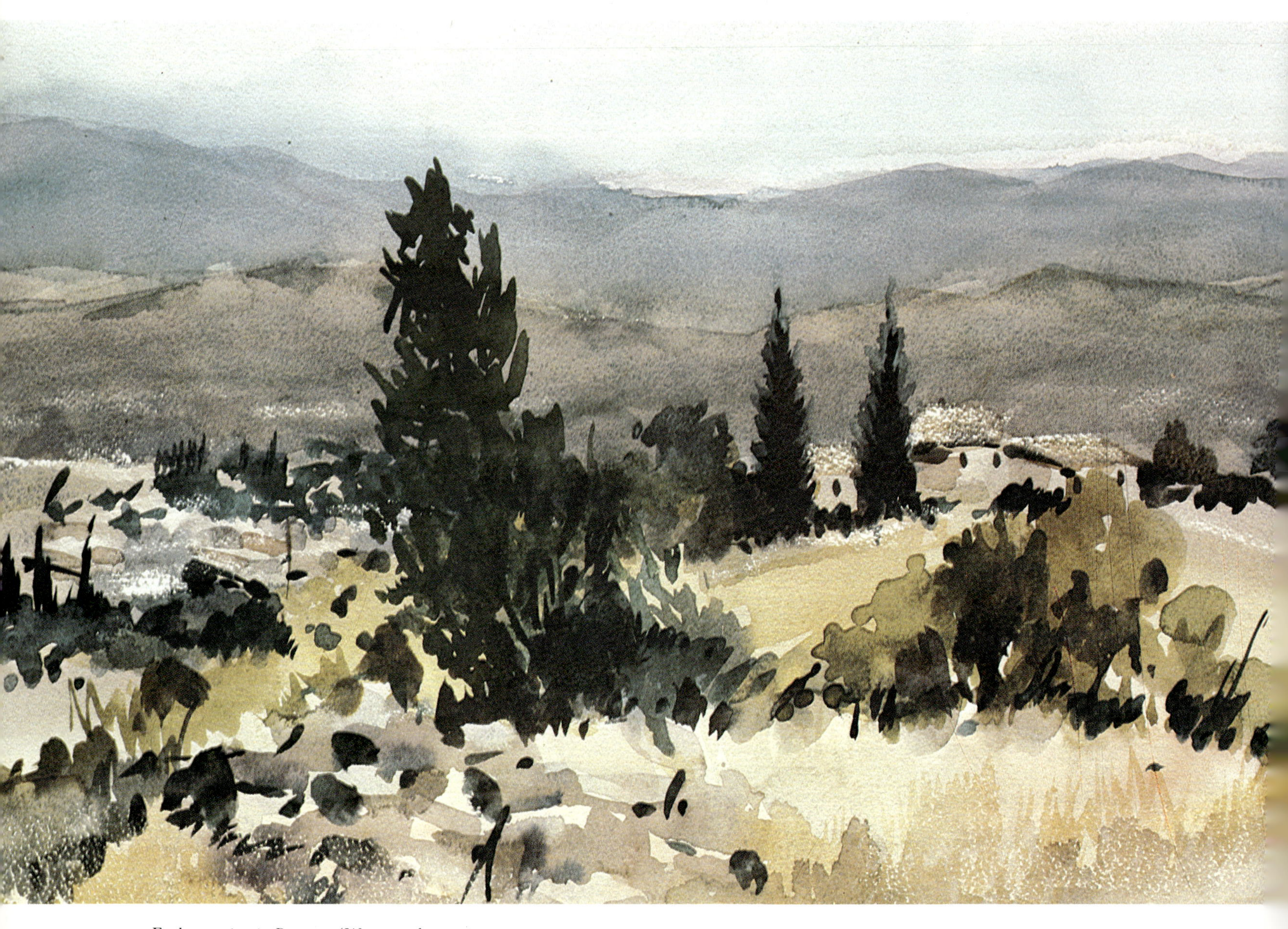

Early morning in Provence (Water-colour,
14" x 10")

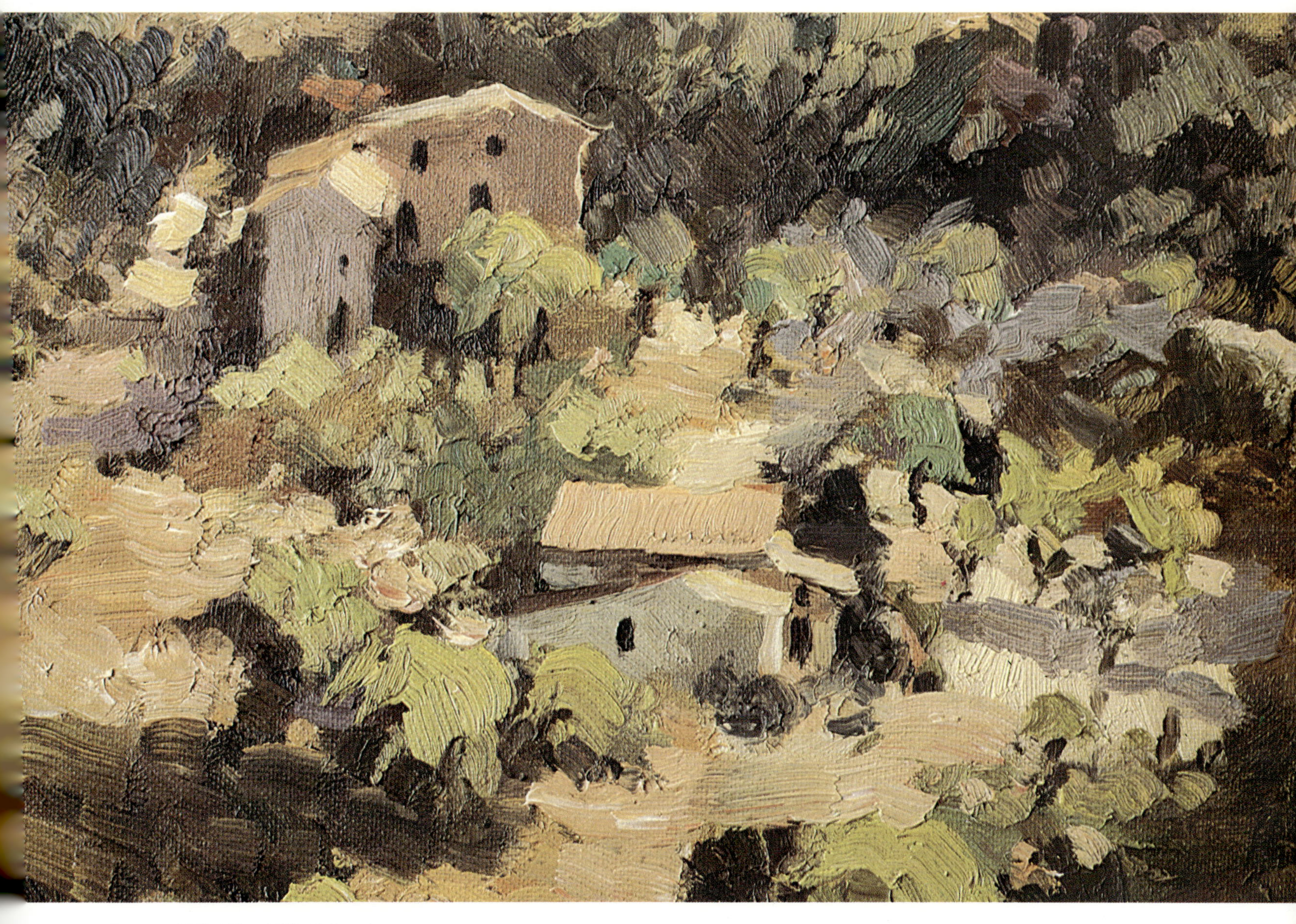

Provence (Oil, 12" x 10"). Painted on site
using the pochade box and three primary
colours only

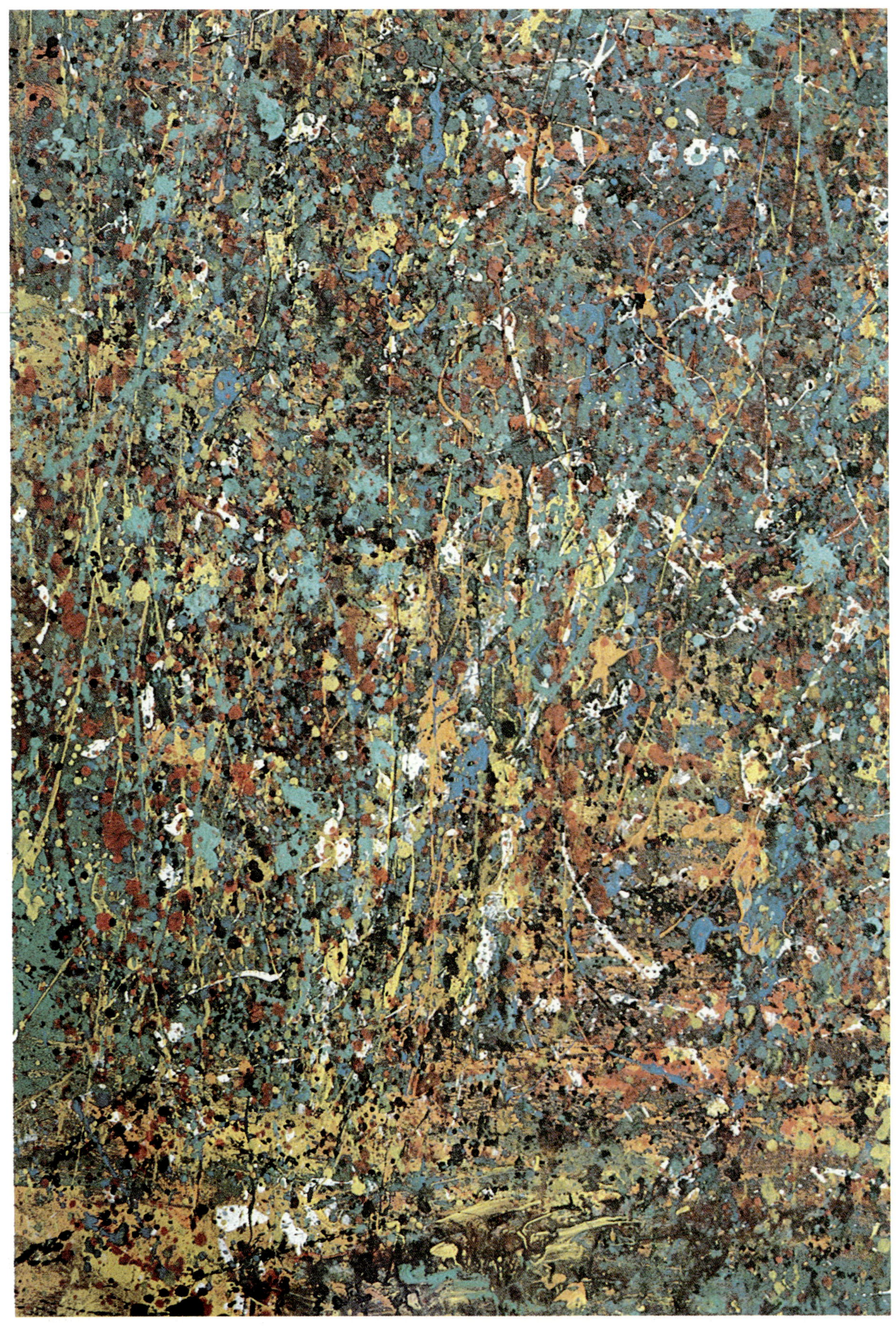

7. INNOVATION AND EXPERIMENT

I firmly believe that all artists should be prepared to experiment in order to continue the development of their creative powers. By this I mean experimentation with both media and interpretation. Throughout this book it will have been apparent that the subject is the only reason for painting and that the medium merely the vehicle for our ability to express a reaction to the subject. The nature of the experiment will, of course, depend on the subject and your reaction to it.

The structural aspects may suggest development, in which case you could look at the geometry of the forms. Fig 125, a work by a former student of mine, Pauleen Trim, is an example of an usual viewpoint coupled with an extremely individual interpretation of modern architecture. In my own work, *Toccata and fugue in D* (Fig 126), I have taken as the theme the musical composition of the same name by J.S. Bach, with its mathematical structure, and interpreted this in geometric forms and colours in much the same way as Pauleen Trim has interpreted the architecture. Alternatively, movement could be explored, in which instance rhythmical forms must be developed. The possibilities are limitless and ongoing, requiring you to be constantly looking and improving your awareness and perception, and this, coupled with the desire to experiment with technique, will allow you to paint in an entirely personal language. Fig 127 is a form of abstraction made on a social comment theme of unemployment benefit. This work, also by Pauleen Trim, shows a great deal of imagination and is a form of symbolism.

Painting may be termed experimental in many ways. From the moment we start to record the visual image, we have to experiment to find a language to interpret what we see in terms of realism. The word 'experiment', in the context of this chapter, has a different meaning. One definition is the evolution of new schemata for representing the world around us that will eventually become accepted as the public vision attunes to and establishes a rapport with that of the artist. A further, but paradoxical, meaning of 'experiment' is that it is something which must be carried out without any possibility of a successful conclusion. Or, to put it another way, it is a search which is self-justifying, without any objective criteria for success or failure. This is a complete departure in the role of the artist as we understand it, and involves a rejection of traditional values of picture-making.

Monet's garden (Acrylic, 40" x 30")

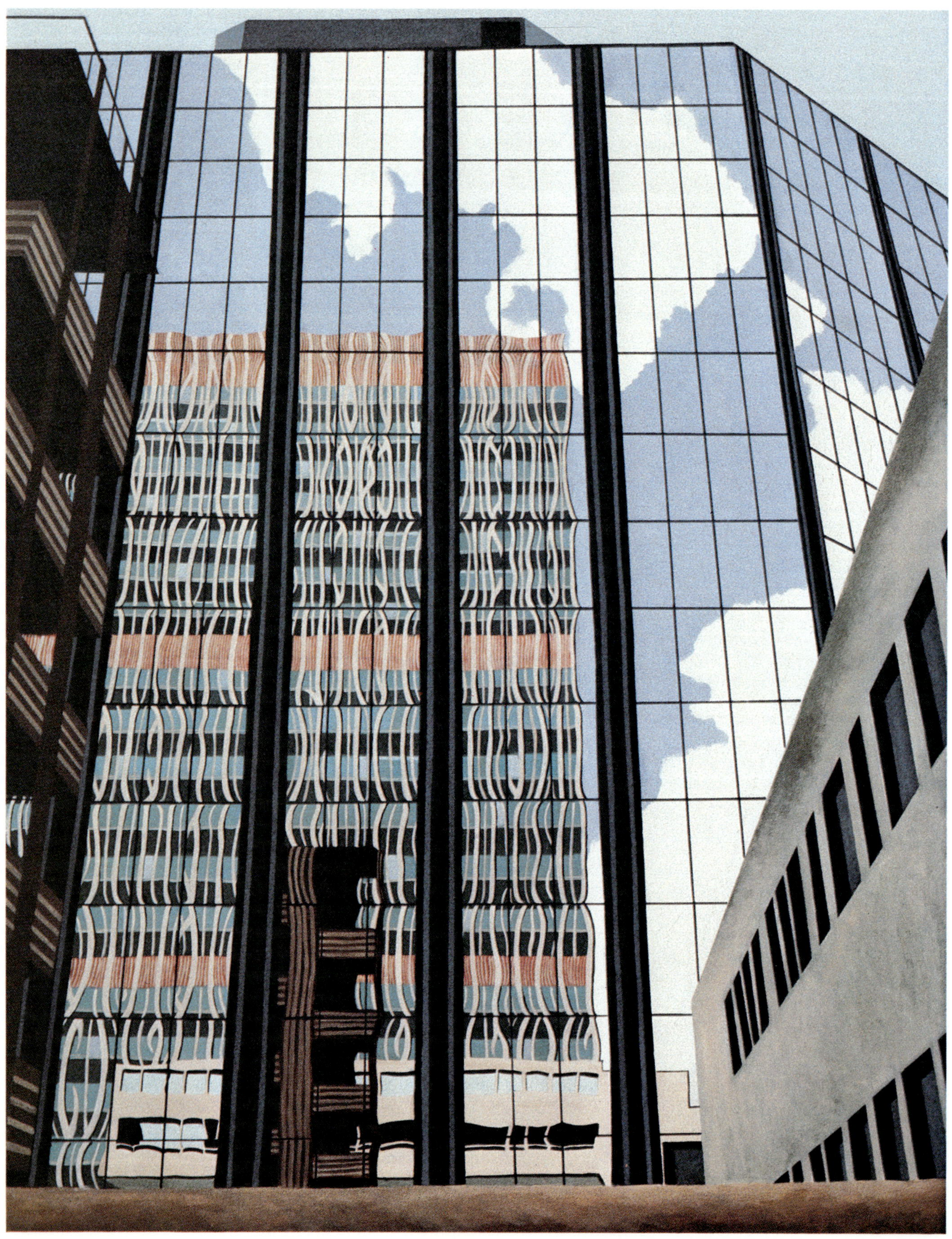

FIG 125 (left) Architectural study by
Pauleen Trim showing the abstract
qualities of reflections in the glass of the
building

FIG 126 (top right) *Toccata and fugue in D*
after J.S. Bach. Abstract design based on
the shapes of the music (Acrylic 48" x
32")

FIG 127 (bottom right) Symbolic painting
on the theme of unemployment benefit,
by Pauleen Trim

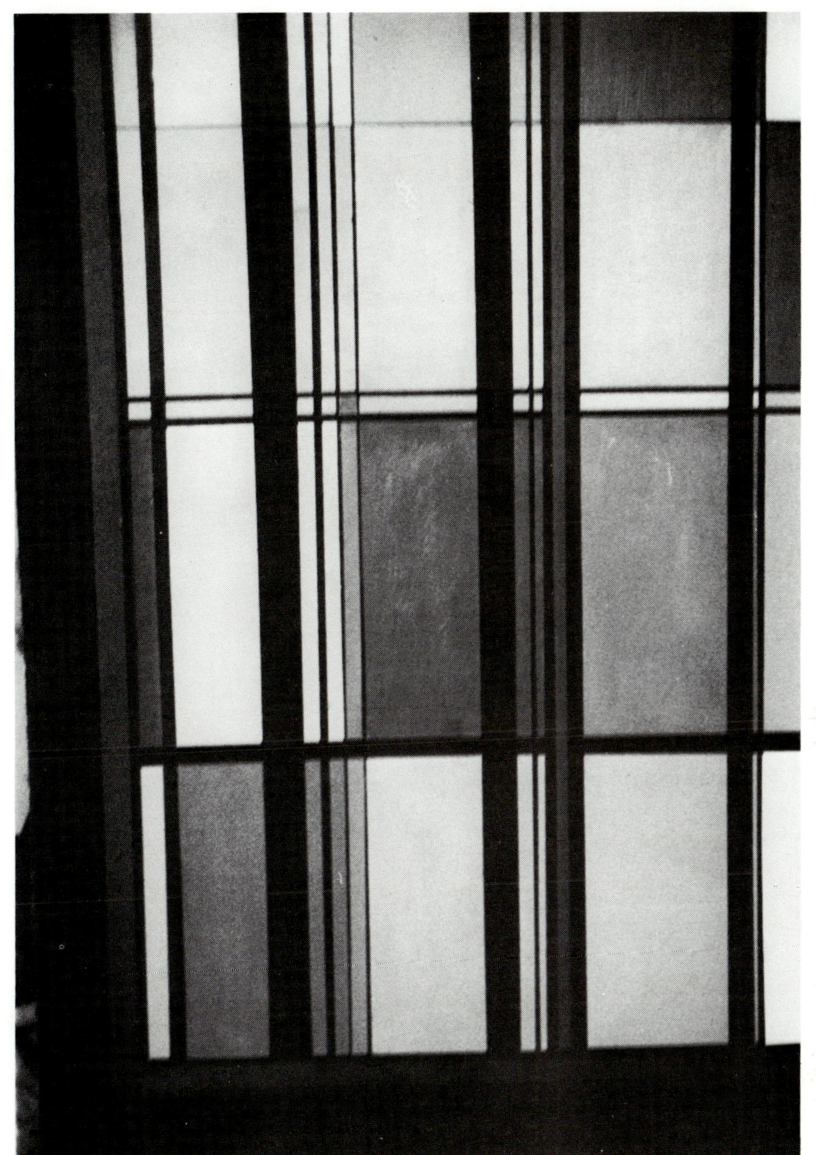

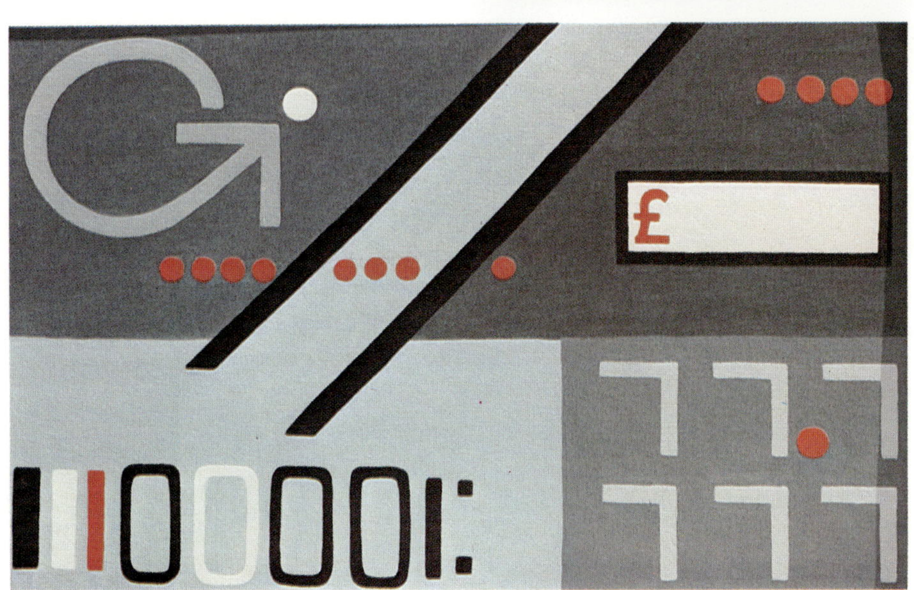

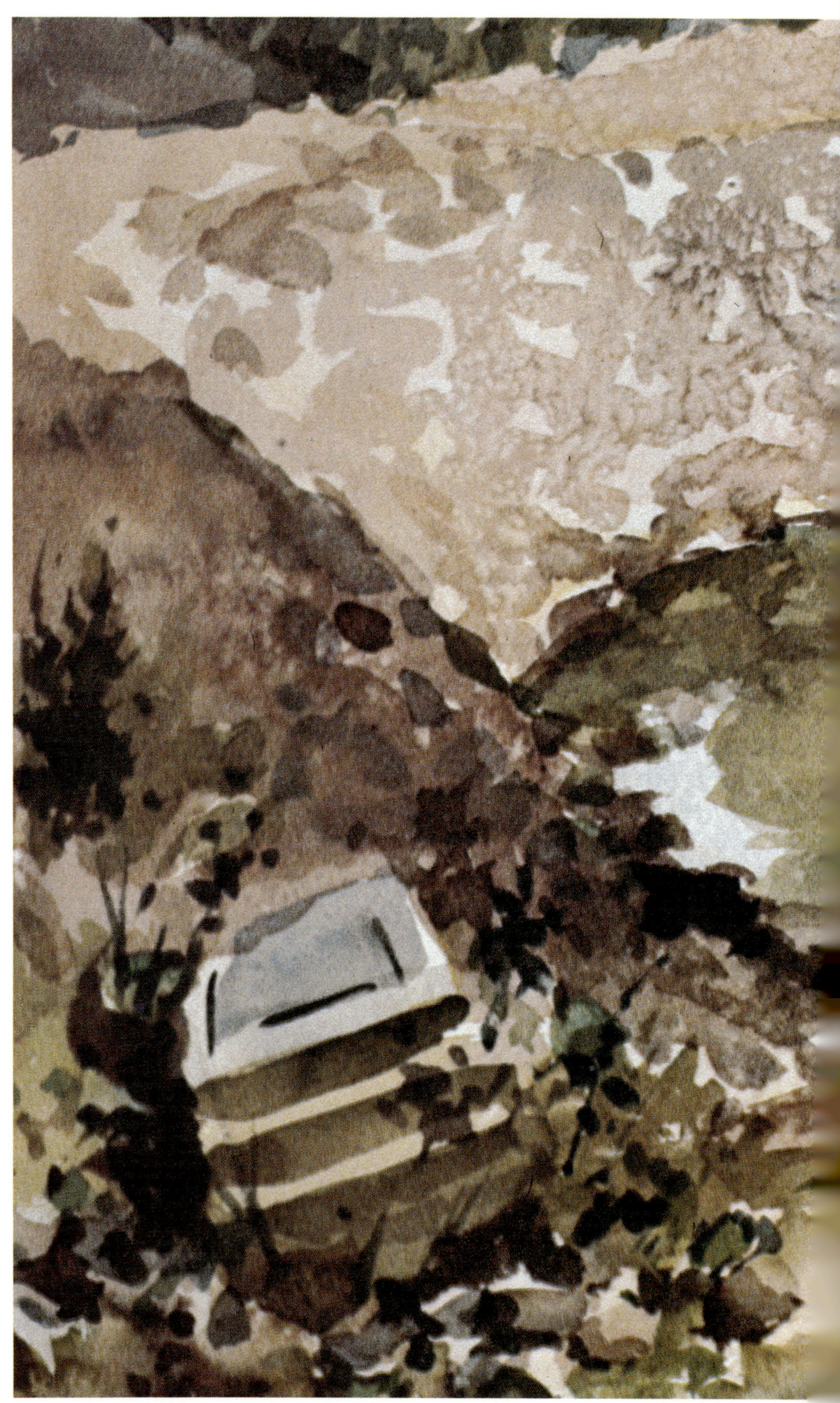

The Pit (Water-colour, 15" x 11"). To obtain the texture of the red stony ground I used salt. The first light wash of light red and crimson was allowed to dry completely. A second, much stronger wash was then applied and whilst this was still wet salt was sprinkled on to the work. This then dissolved and separated the colour, allowing the lighter colour underneath to show through, creating the illusion of stones

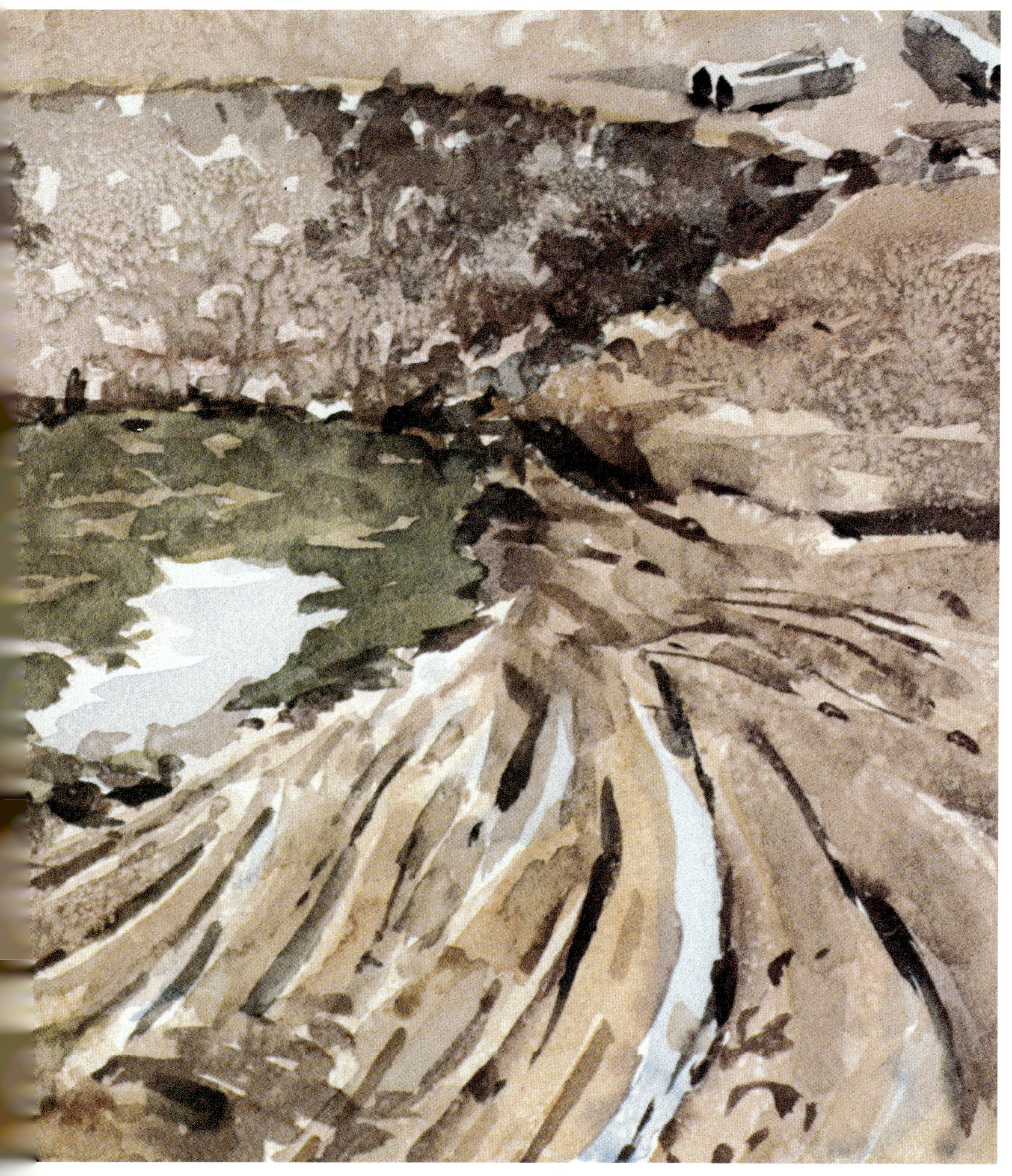

For the representational painter to embark on such a journey of exploration, I feel it is important to recommend a period of discovery, using the media discussed earlier, in a variety of ways, to express the subject in a graphic manner. It is hoped that this approach will stimulate awareness and sensitivity to the subject, and allow the perceptive powers of interpretation to develop. Remember that it is always the subject that will remain the springboard in any search for new frontiers of expression. Note also that the subject need not necessarily be a physical reality; it can come from the conscious or subconscious mind (the work of Surrealists is an example of this form of painting). The question is often asked, why do artists look for different and often unreal ways of expressing nature? An answer lies in that the invention of photography show artists that the realistic portrayal of objects was just one form of expression among many, with the result that the idea of penetrating reality became a reasonable aim, after many centuries of realism.

The first signs of conflict implicit in the notion of experimental painting emerged at the beginning of the nineteenth century and can be seen in the works of John Constable and J. M. W. Turner. Shortly before his death, Constable concluded a lecture at the Royal Institution with the question: ' Painting is a science and should be pursued as an enquiry into the laws of nature. Why then may not landscape painting be considered as a branch of natural philosophy, of which pictures are but the experiment?' This question can of course be applied to all branches of the arts. Later in the nineteenth century, the question was duly considered, and partly answered, by the Impressionists, with their scientific approach to the problem of painting light. At the same time, and partially because of this scientific approach, Paul Cézanne, using the Synthesists' doctrine, developed a vocabulary of forms that had their basis in the painter's distinctive methods, yet were adjusted to representing the external world. The two ideals are brought together in Cézanne's work: the interpretation of the natural world in terms of sphere, cube, and tone is not just a mannerism, but a way of penetrating the innermost structure of form. It is this understanding that leads us to the constructivist ideal. This is where we can perhaps adapt these ideals to our own work because, you will remember, it is on the basic understanding of the geometry of form that our drawing and painting are built. It was also partly from these precepts that the Cubist movement of Braque and Picasso was developed. By using geometric forms, the artist is able to explore spatial relationships and yet retain a link with natural realism.

For the more experienced painter, it can be a useful stimulus to further experimentation to translate a specific sketch into geometric shapes, giving emphasis to the spatial factors. Fig 128 is a geometric interpretation of a wooded landscape, using only primary and secondary colours. In this work an attempt has been made to break every important shape down to a geometric facet of a base colour, each colour being applied in full strength to give impact to the forms. The

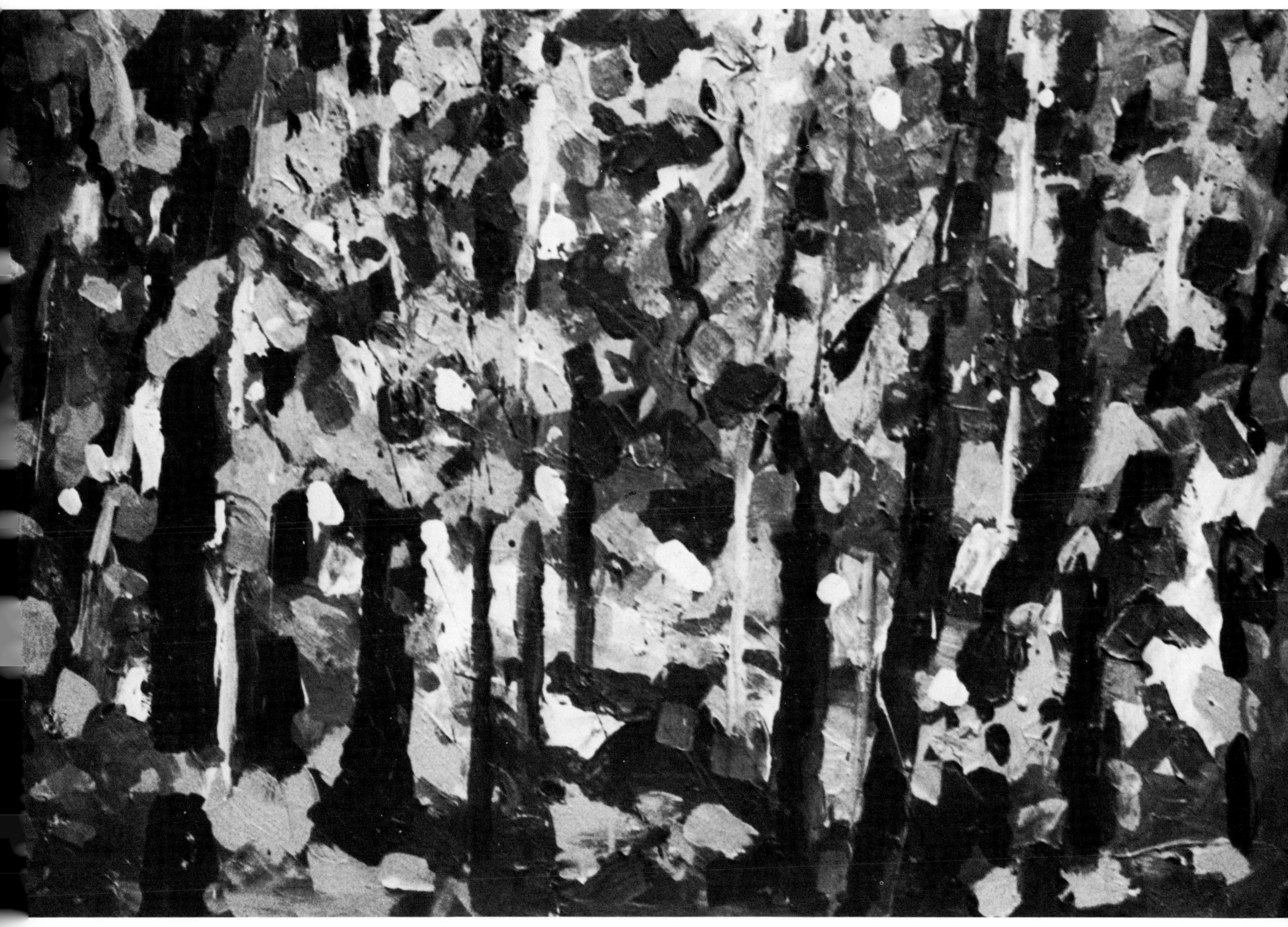

FIG 128 Landscape based on geometric
shapes to convey space and form (Acrylic,
28" x 24")

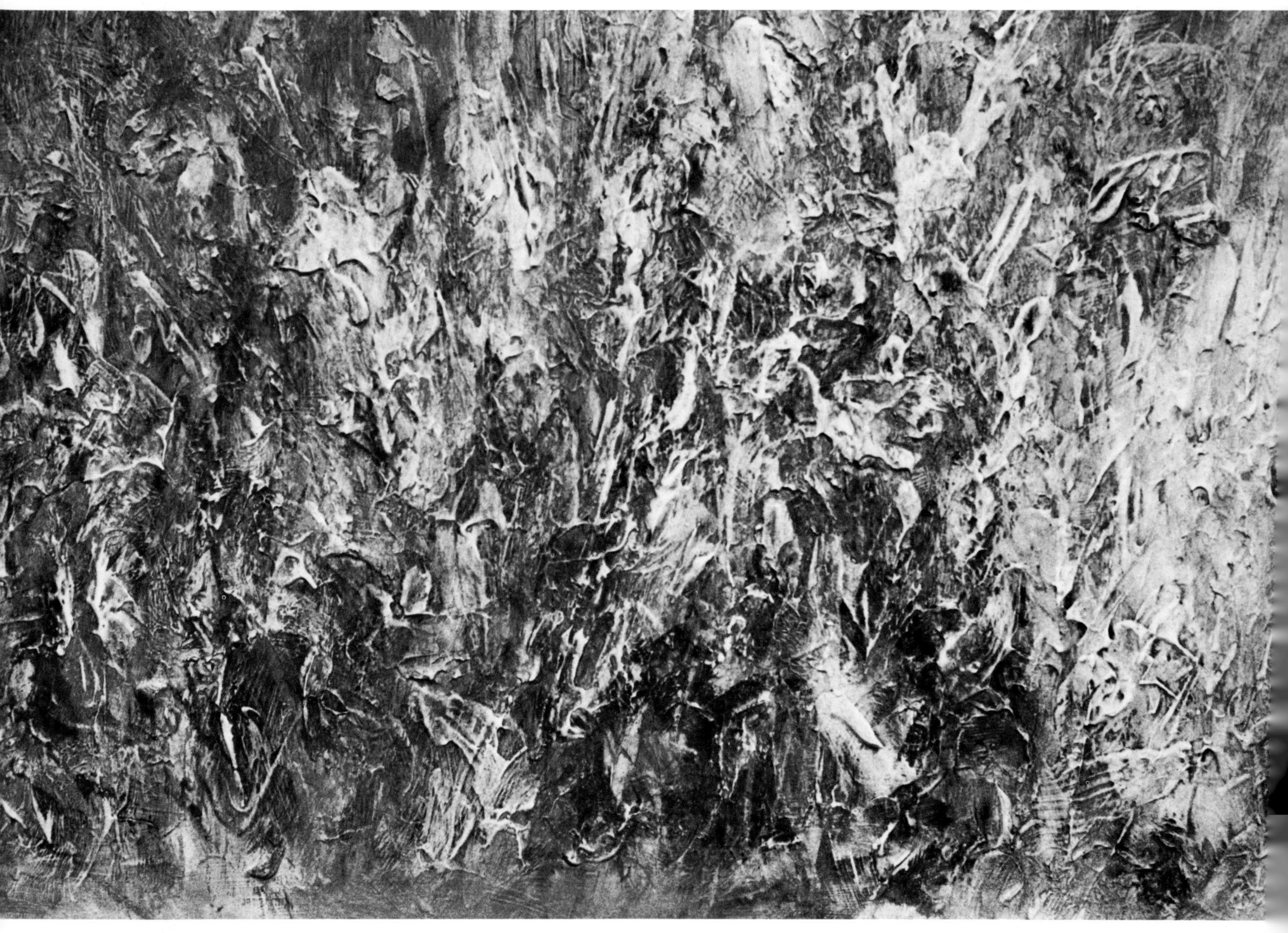

FIG 129 Textural painting to convey the
feel of grasses (Acrylic, 24" x 20")

tactile qualities of these shapes have also been developed, so that the work becomes a synthesis of geometry, texture, tone and colour in the quest to create the space between and around the picture's components.

Fig 129 illustrates textural painting more emphatically. I was concerned with exploring in part the abstract qualities of natural grasses and other flora found on the side of roads. To do this, it became necessary to apply the laws of reduction and destruction before any form of abstraction could be achieved. I therefore reduced to a small section the area of grass that I selected for the experiment, and mentally destroyed, in a figurative sense, what the subject was. Having proceeded thus far, I felt that the texture of my mental interpretation became the key to the abstraction. With this decision made, all that remained to be decided was how it was to be achieved. I prepared a panel with *gesso*, allowed it to dry and then applied a further uneven application of thick *gesso*. When this was dry I built up textures with texture paste where I felt them necessary. When they were dry, I floated washes of acrylic colour on them. The washes were applied several times, to emphasise the forms made by the texture paste and *gesso*, the density of the washes being greater when the colour became accumulated in the valleys of the irregular painting surface. Finally, as you continue to experiment, you will find that each idea becomes self-generating, in much the same way as a doodle can suggest ideas. My advice is to explore these: nothing is ever wasted, and who knows where these ideas will take us? Experiment with the media as well as with the subject. There are available many new materials which can be used in picture-making.

Collage, a form of picture-making using many varieties of materials from photographs, news cuttings and other kinds of objects arranged and glued to the painting ground, is often used in conjunction with painted passages. The cuttings and other materials used are sometimes selected for their subjectively related values, or alternatively for their formal and textural qualities. Fig 130 is an example of collage, and was part of an exercise in diploma studies by one of my students. As an aspect of experimental picture-making, collage was a technique begun by the Cubist painters and used by Matisse, Max Ernst and other surrealist painters in the 1920s. A further development of collage is *montage*, a pictorial technique in which cut-outs of illustrations are arranged together and mounted. Illustrations alone are used, and are selected purely for their subject and communication. Photomontage, which means using photographs only, is nowadays sometimes introduced into painting in much the same way as collage.

These are just some of the forms experiment can take and should, I feel, be examined by any serious student of the arts. To dismiss such art forms as frivolous is to deny the right to experiment in the quest for new ways of interpretation – surely the main function of any artist.

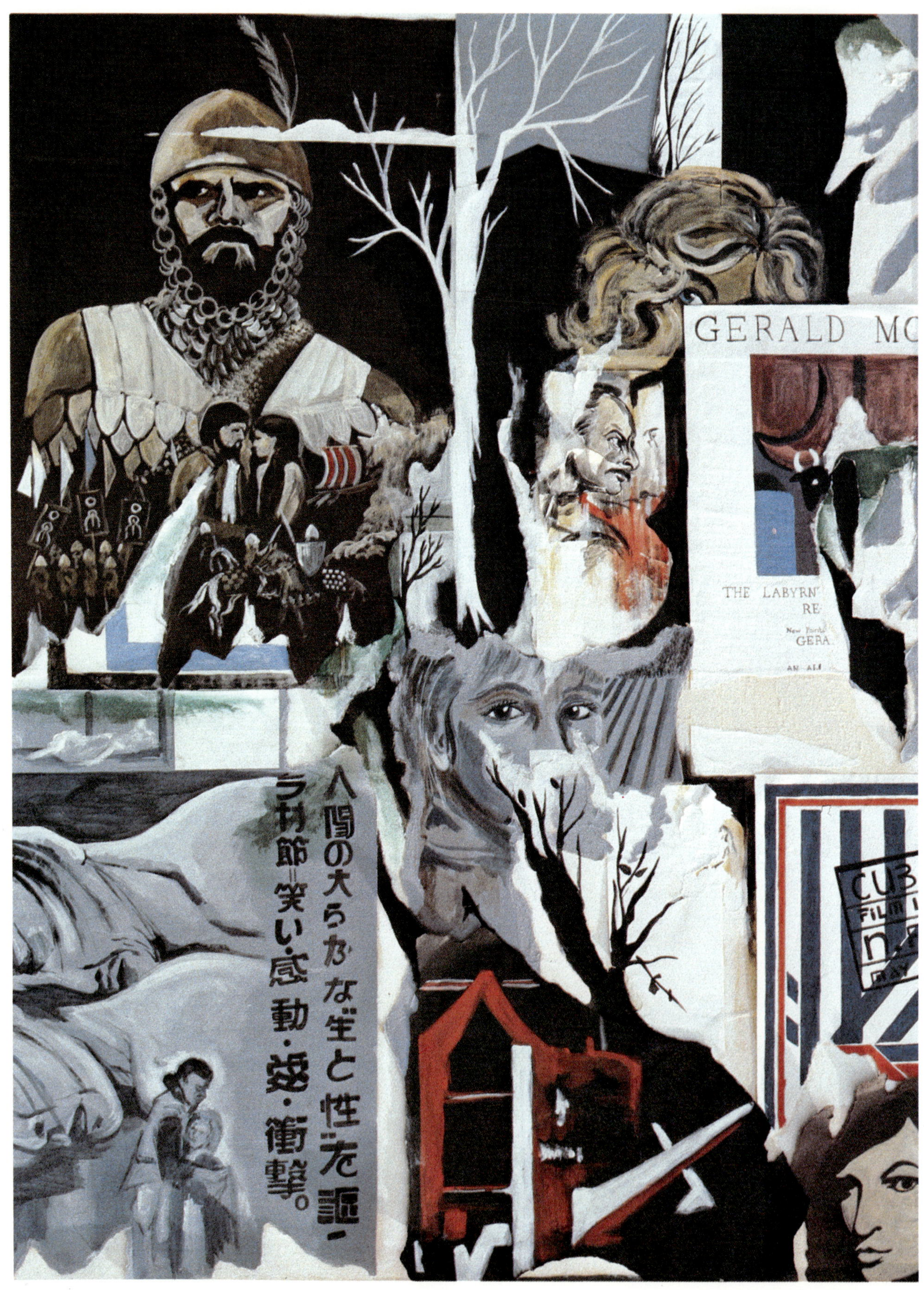
GERALD MO
THE LABYRN
RE
GERA
人間の大らかな生と性に左誕―
ラガ節＝笑い感動・愛・衝撃。
CUB
FILM

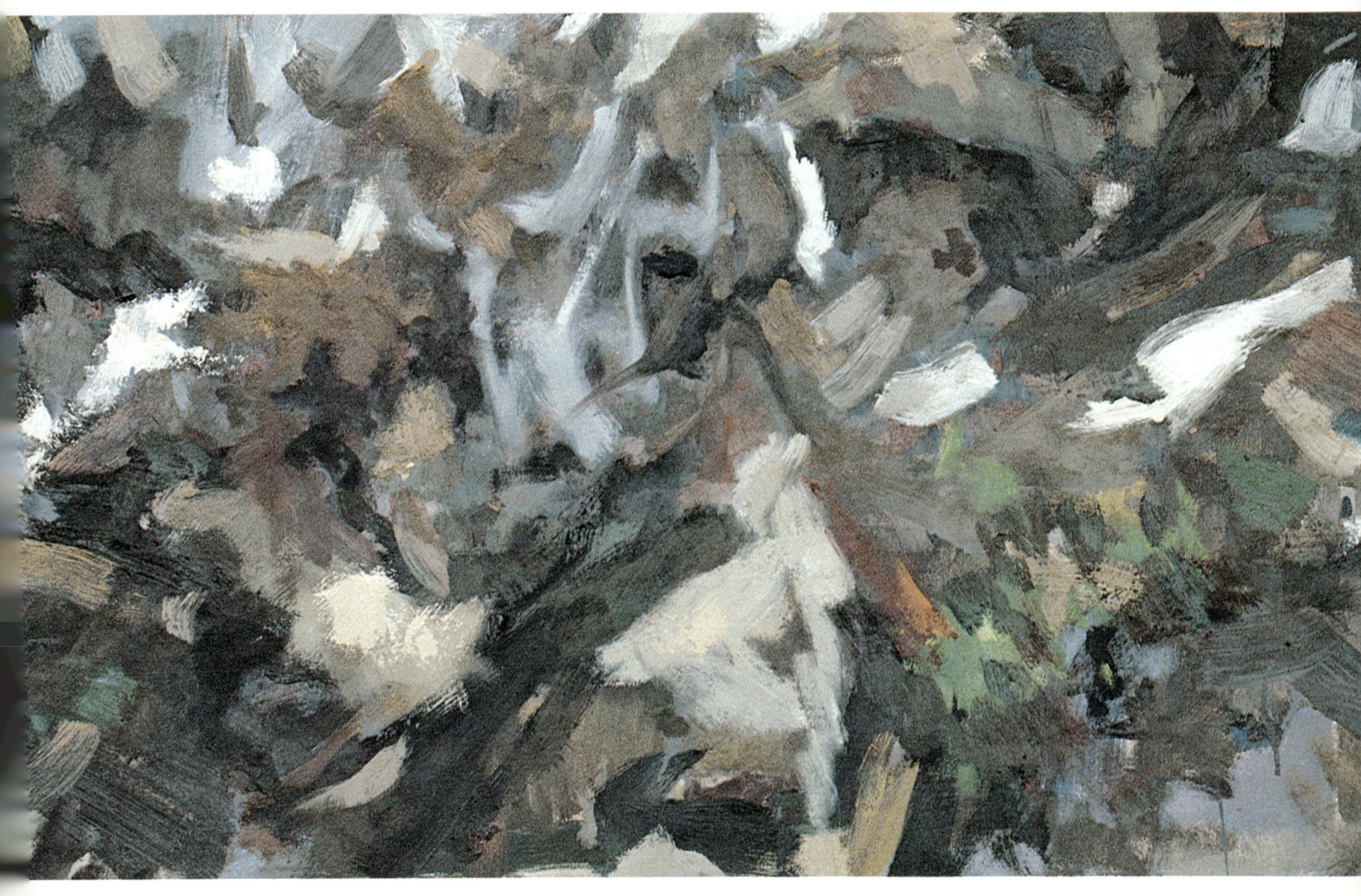

The aftermath (Oil, 40" x 30")

FIG 130 Collage by Pauleen Trim

8. PRESENTATION

The presentation of your work is always of great importance and requires a lot of thought. All too often the presentation is an afterthought, considered separately from the actual work. It is as important as painting the picture, and should therefore be considered as an integral part of the painting. It can mean the difference between selection or rejection in exhibitions, between selling or not selling, and affect the acquisition of commissions. Framing and mounting plays an important part in presentation, and we will consider these first.

In general, the frame and mount should complement the picture and not intrude on it. Many fine works are killed by their frames or mounts, or by both. The work must always be the final arbiter as to how it is framed and mounted. All too often one sees framed oil-paintings where the section or thickness of the moulding is too small for the painting. A boldly painted work, for instance, will look uncomfortable in a small or narrow moulding. Generally speaking, most oil-paintings and acrylic paintings painted in the manner of oils deserve a fairly substantial moulding. The only exceptions to this are large abstract or hard-edged pictures, which can often stand a small-sectioned metal moulding, or even just a thin batten round the edge of the canvas. It is not unusual to see very large modern works without any border at all.

Once the decision to frame a work has been made, the choice of shape and colour of the moulding becomes important and must relate to the work. A simple but effective rule to help in determining the colour of the moulding is to ensure that the dominant key of the painting is echoed in the moulding colour. The selection of the shape of the moulding is more difficult, and must come down to individual preference. However, if the work is highly decorative or ornate, then the moulding can be sympathetically decorative (not, however, to the extent that it will detract from the painting). With a simpler design and composition, uncomplicated mouldings will prove more suitable. The use of a frame which has two mouldings can sometimes be beneficial, particularly on very large works. The second moulding is used as an insert to the main moulding and will very often be canvas-covered. With the large selection of mouldings available today, it is possible to frame one's work attractively and at a reasonable price.

The framing of water-colours, drawings and pastels requires a different approach. Because of the delicacy of these works, it is

Window mount

FIG 131 Mount-cutter

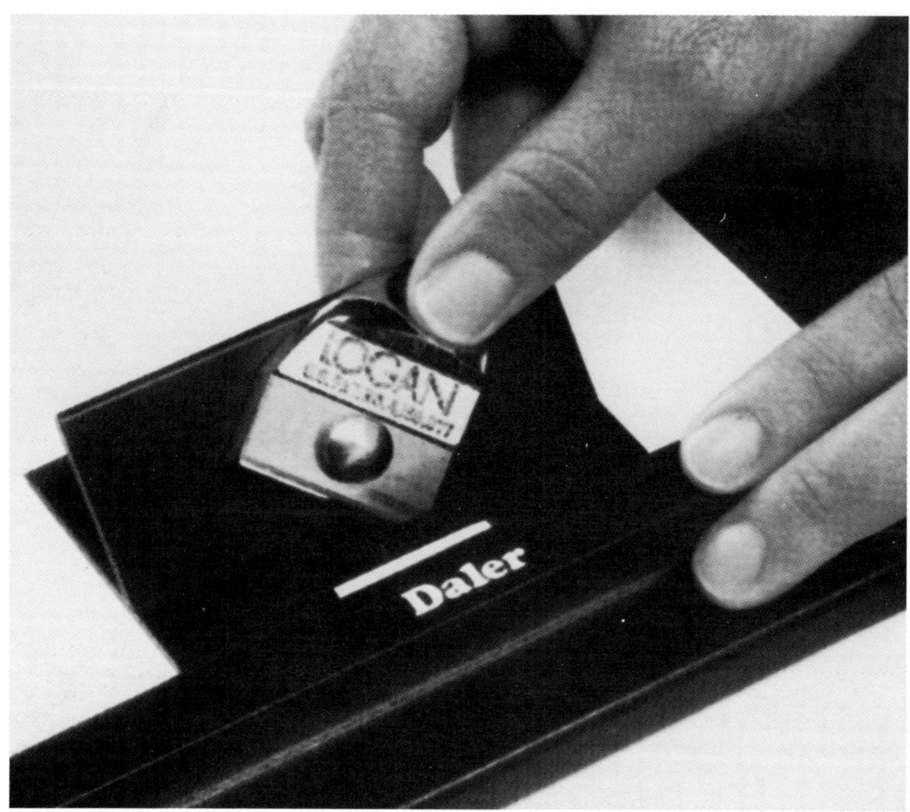

desirable to separate the frame from the picture. To do this, use a mount of the type often referred to as a 'window' mount. Mounts can be of any colour, to suit the work, and of varying thickness. Generally speaking, I prefer ivory mounts to plain white or coloured. White always appears too stark and coloured mounts, unless they are of the highest quality board, have a tendency to fade with prolonged exposure to light. If, however, the drawing is on tinted paper, it may be necessary to complement the work with a suitably coloured mount. There are a number of methods of mounting the work, from sticking it directly to the board, to cutting window mounts.

Window mounts are difficult to cut if you use just a straight edge and a modelling knife, in addition to which the window will not then have the bevelled edge which makes it more attractive. There are mount cutters on the market, one of which is illustrated in Fig 131. This cutter, which is distributed by the Daler-Rowney Company, will cut a bevelled mount from board of any thickness. If you intend cutting your own mounts, I would suggest that such a mount cutter is a necessity. It can sometimes be beneficial to the work to embellish the mount with a wash-line around the window. This is executed using sympathetically-coloured inks and water-colour. The colours used are determined by the work, but generally grey is sympathetic to the key of the picture. The wide range of mouldings now available for presenting glazed and mounted work makes choice quite difficult. The size of moulding will of course be determined by the size of the work, as the weight of the glass determines the size of moulding necessary to support the weight. When making a mount, it is a good idea to have a slightly bigger area of mount at the bottom, with equal top and side measurements.

You will see that presentation of work is of great importance, and this is never more so than when putting together a folio for presentation to a client or gallery. Water-colours, drawings and pastels all need to be mounted, and pastels, chalk and charcoal drawings should be protected with a transparent cover, such as data film. From experience, I have found that most clients will accept coloured photographs or transparencies of large works, especially oils and acrylics, in addition to one or two small originals, to give some idea of your handling capabilities. I also keep a photographic record of my work, including drawings, so that I have examples to hand should the need arise.

As I said at the beginning of this section, presentation of work plays an important part in the selection and rejection process at exhibitions. Exhibition committees do not like framing which is extreme or brash. Many London galleries will not accept work in black or white frames.

The time will come when you will feel ready to have an exhibition of your own. This is always an exciting experience, and calls for a great deal of planning. The first step is to find a gallery who will be interested in showing the work. They will want to see examples to ensure that it is of the standard and nature for which the gallery is known. You must also check that the gallery's wall space will be adequate for the size and number of works to be shown, and that the lighting will illuminate the works to your satisfaction. The financial arrangements have to be agreed and will usually be based on a rental plus commission basis, with the artist being financially responsible for publicity. These arrangements vary from one gallery to another, which makes it important to establish all the facts before committing yourself. Most art galleries have their own mailing list of interested picture lovers who wish to be kept up to date with exhibitions. It is important to add to this your own mailing list of people who are interested in your work, and to whom invitations to a private view should be sent.

The private view is always a pleasant social occasion and provides an opportunity to invite members of the press, local radio and television, who will probably wish to interview the artist, all of which gives the exhibition further publicity. Be certain that there is a good cross-section of work in the show, and that it is hung so that as far as possible the exhibits complement one another. Finally, try to visit the gallery during the exhibition, as would-be purchasers do enjoy meeting the artist, and this can make the difference between selling and not selling a work.

9. SOCIETIES AND ART EDUCATION

Artists have always found it necessary to exchange philosophies, finding that by exchanging their beliefs and views, a certain amount of mental cross-fertilisation takes place, and can add to and broaden their approach to their work. In most communities today there is an arts club or society, many of which are open to painters and non-painters alike. These groups play a very important role in the involvement of the community in our cultural life.

Art societies have differing criteria for membership, and offer a wide range of facilities. Apart from the more general type of club already mentioned, some have limited membership, often brought about by limitation of space or by a desire to achieve a reasonable level of attainment. Finally, there are those societies who, through selective membership, aim at the highest artistic qualities. For the potential new member it can be a harrowing experience to have to submit a number of works, usually six pieces, to a membership committee to achieve membership. For the newcomer, the first type of community arts club, where the only qualification for membership is enthusiasm, is without doubt the best. If the club has working sessions in drawing and painting, so much the better, for there is no better way of broadening your skills than by working with other painters. For the painter of greater experience who wishes to associate with artists of equal or greater attainment, then application to societies of the latter type is to be recommended.

A word of warning is necessary here. It is, I think, essential that the judging of work should be carried out by artists of unquestionable ability in their respective fields, and who will have the best interests and the artistic aims of the group they represent at heart. Many clubs today engage for their selection and membership committees the services of reputable artists who are not members of the club. This seems to make for greater harmony between the members, as the club committee is not involved in the decision-making other than in an overseeing capacity. This can substantially remove any discontent and at the same time contribute to the aim of achieving higher aesthetic standards. Visiting many art clubs in the course of a year as I do, I am constantly impressed by the genuine desire of the members to improve not only their own work, but that of the entire club.

Art education has developed substantially over the past few years, and now seems to cater for all levels of ability and a formidable range of specialist subject matter. For the serious student requiring more specialist and in-depth tuition, it is important to shop around to find a qualified tutor with whom you feel a rapport. Most art colleges, adult further education colleges and centres and private art classes will provide this sort of facility. As a student, it is important that you take full advantage of these establishments. The tutor is usually a professional with infinitely more experience than you. Most tutors I know want their students to succeed and will make every effort to help them, but they – and I speak from experience – find it very difficult to overcome preconceived ideas and closed minds, so empty your mind and give the tutor a chance to help you. Finally, it is quite pointless to undertake any form of art education unless you are prepared and able to practise the exercises done during the tutorial – without practice, the tutorial is wasted. There is no doubt that, with a structured approach to the teaching and a willingness on the part of the student to work and absorb the subject, anything is possible.

10. CONTEMPORARY WORK

In conclusion, let us take a look at current work in drawing and painting. Doing this objectively will help us to understand our own relationship to contemporary work. To do this, we need to examine it in relationship to similar work of previous periods, and with the role of the artist in these periods. It is not possible to do this in great depth in this book, although a good understanding can be gained from visits to national collections and from reference to the many fine books on art history. Certainly the changing demands of each period in the history of art are reflected in the works produced and in the training of artists.

Unlike the artists, the teaching disciplines are also subject to the influences of social, environmental and economic changes that occur throughout history. Thus, whilst many teaching disciplines have been added to and improved, many, alas, have disappeared altogether, to the detriment of art. There has, in my opinion, been far too much emphasis by art teachers, in the early periods of art education, on freedom of expression before the student has acquired sufficient craft skills to explore this for himself. The most affected area used to be drawing, but fortunately there are now conscious efforts to redress this weakness which once existed in many art education establishments in the 1950s and 1960s. In recent years, art education has been strongly influenced by technological progress and a re-awakening to a form of realism in painting, of which hard-edged painting is an example. The main contemporary trends include with this new realism a continuing development of abstract painting and a continuation of Expressionism and Impressionism.

With the advent of many new materials, including plastics and other man-made substances, the artist has been encouraged to experiment and innovate far more than previously, to produce new symbols of communication. Much of this work will seem strange and will of course take some time to acquire a real meaning for us. History has shown this to be quite usual, as it is inevitable that with any new work we have to come to terms with the language used. Much early experimental painting was ridiculed when first seen by the public, yet today is greatly revered and much sought after. History also tells us that art mirrors the society of which it is part, and this it will inevitably continue to do. The role of the artist in today's world of rapid change is difficult to predict. The lack of stability that rapid change engenders will encourage the artist to become an even greater social commentator than before, demanding a greater search for more emphatic means of communication, thus requiring further exploration and development of the painter's language.

This must result in a return to an in-depth study of drawing and painting, and of the painter's subjects. Failure in this will result in our contemporary painting having little aesthetic value, and even less spectator impact. Our role in this is clear: the drawing and painting of any subject requires that we understand that subject thoroughly, and communicate the reason for the work to the viewer. It has been said that if the reason cannot be seen in the work, it should not have been painted. This is true whatever language of expression we use.

I hope this book will have answered many technical and practical questions and at the same time have opened the door to the fascination of expressing your reaction to the world around you in drawing and painting. I hope also to have increased your awareness of and sensitivity to the subject, and your enjoyment of the visual arts. In closing, I would like to wish you all success in your endeavours in the endless quest towards expressing yourself in drawing and painting, and hope that you will find as much pleasure in your work as I do in mine.

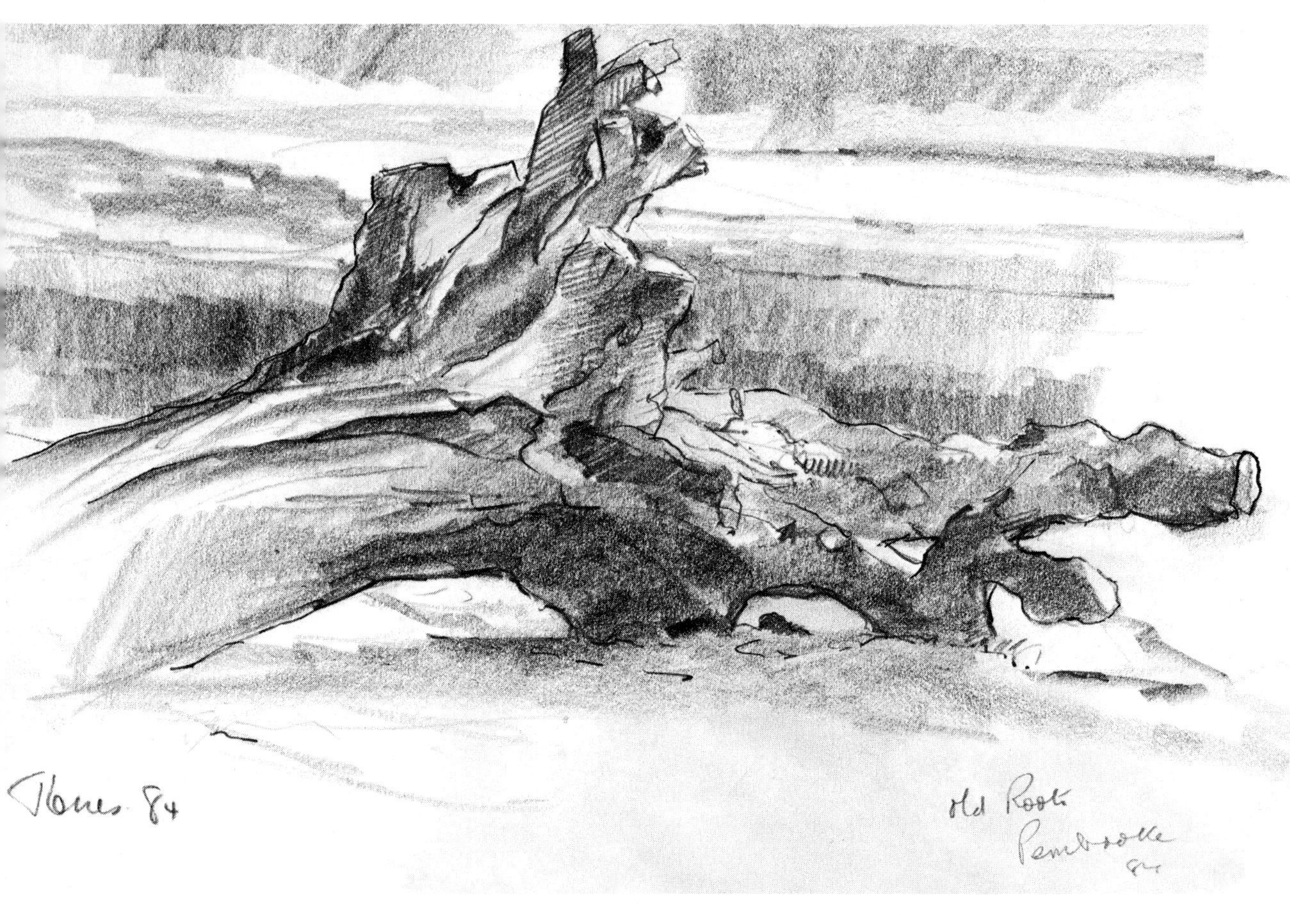

Sketch of dead tree. (Pencil, 10" x 7")

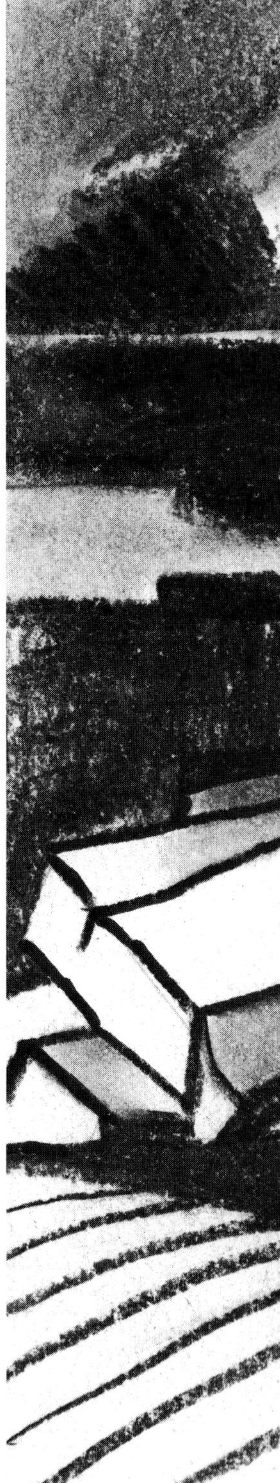

Abstraction of dead tree (Charcoal,
10" x 7")

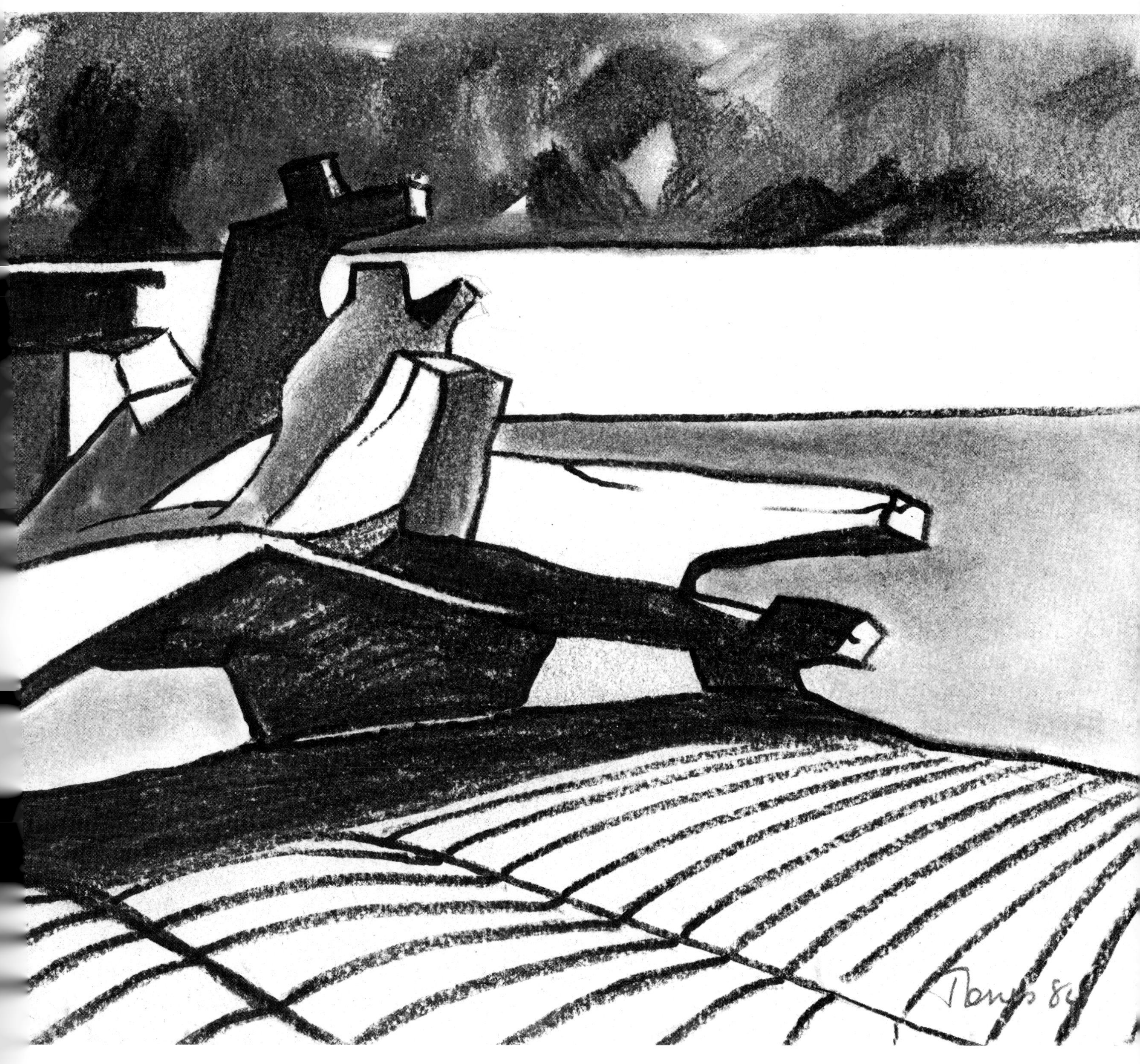

Major manufacturers and suppliers

Dryad/Reeves
PO Box 38
Northgates
Leicester

Daler Rowney
PO Box 10
Bracknell
Berks

A.W. Faber-Castell (UK) Ltd
Crompton Road
Stevenage
Herts SG1 2EF
Frank Herring & Sons
27 High Street West
Dorchester
Dorset DT1 1UP

Osmiroid International
Fareham Road
Gosport
Hants PO13 0AL

Rexel Ltd/Derwent
Gatehouse Road
Aylesbury
Bucks HP19 3DT

Winsor & Newton
51 Rathbone Place
London W1

Schwan – STABILO Ltd
74 Buckingham Avenue
Slough
Berks SL1 4PA

Conté
Park Farm Road
Folkestone
Kent CT19 5EY

Berol Ltd
Old Meadow Road
Kings Lynn
Norfolk PE30 4JR

FURTHER READING

CLIVE ASHWIN, *Encylopaedia of drawing*, B. T. Batsford Ltd
ARTHUR BAKER, *The calligraphy manual*, Dryad Press Ltd
WILFRED BALL, *Sketching for landscapes*, Dryad Press Ltd
WILFRED BALL, *Weather in watercolour*, B. T. Batsford Ltd
JOHN CRONEY, *Drawing figure movement*, B. T. Batsford Ltd
ALFRED DANIELS, *An introduction to painting with acrylics*, Apple Press
BETTY EDWARDS, *Drawing the artist within*, Fontana
SYLVIA FRATTINI, *Drawing detail*, Search Press
ALAN FURBER, *Layout and design for calligraphers*, Dryad Press Ltd
E. H. GOMBICH, *Art and illusion*, Phaidon Press
LOUISE GORDON, *Anatomy and figure drawing*, B. T. Batsford Ltd
LOUISE GORDON, *Drawing the human head*, B. T. Batsford Ltd
CHRISTOPHER JARMAN, *Illumination*, Dryad Press Ltd
EDWARD JONES, *Painting people*, B. T. Batsford Ltd
JOHN LANCASTER, *Basic penmanship*, Dryad Press Ltd
FELIX LORENZI, *Drawing made easy*, Angus & Robertston
JENNY MULHERIN, *Presentation techniques for the graphic artist*, Phaidon
FERENC PINTER & DONATELLA VOLPI, *A guide to drawing*, Dryad Press Ltd
MICHAEL WOODS, *Starting life drawing*, Dryad Press Ltd
MICHAEL WOODS, *Starting pencil drawing*, Dryad Press Ltd

INDEX

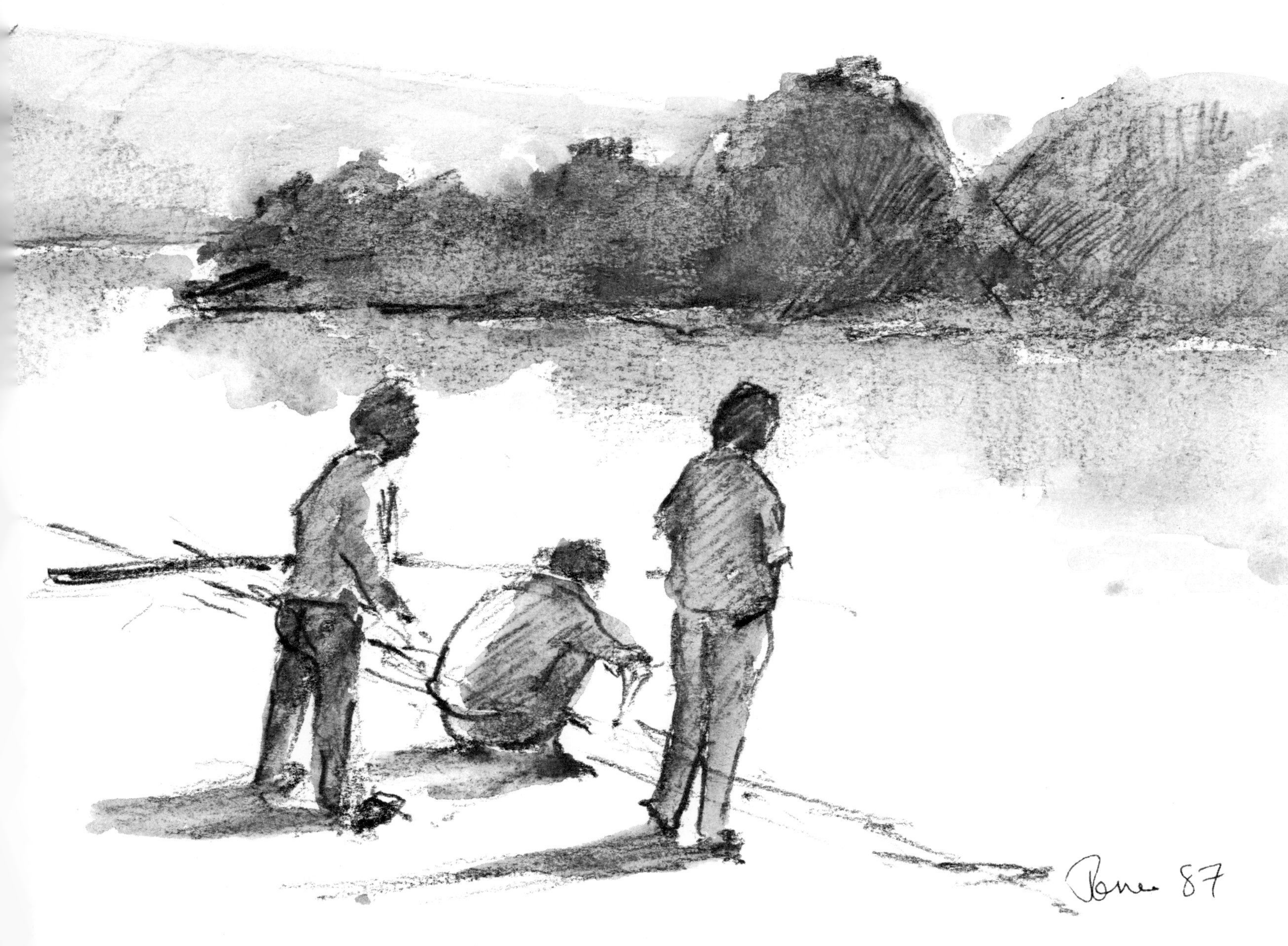